CW00730123

The Canadian Guide-Book

THE

CANADIAN GUIDE-BOOK

COMPLETE IN ONE VOLUME

A GUIDE TO

Eastern Canada and Newfoundland

INCLUDING FULL DESCRIPTIONS OF
ROUTES, CITIES, POINTS OF INTEREST, SUMMER RESORTS,
INFORMATION FOR SPORTSMEN, ETC.

REVISED AND CORRECTED TO DATE

By CHARLES G. D. ROBERTS

LATE PROFESSOR OF ENGLISH LITERATURE IN KING'S COLLEGE, WINDSOR, N. S.

AND

Western Canada to Vancouver's Island

INCLUDING THE CANADIAN ROCKY MOUNTAINS
AND NATIONAL PARK, AND
ROUTES TO THE YUKON GOLD FIELDS

WITH MAPS AND MANY ILLUSTRATIONS

NEW YORK
D. APPLETON AND COMPANY
1899

F
1009
.C23
1899

William J. Rucker

CONTENTS.

PROVINCE OF NEW BRUNSWICK.

PRINCE EDWARD ISLAND.

NOVA SCOTIA.

NEWFOUNDLAND.

WESTERN CANADA.

APPENDIX FOR SPORTSMEN.

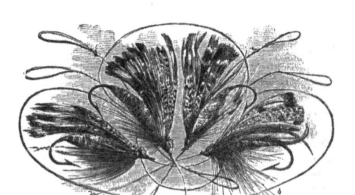

SALMON-FLIES.

LIST OF ILLUSTRATIONS.

MAPS.

SALMON.

INTRODUCTION.

The dear home of freemen brave and true,
And loving honor more than ease or gold.
AGNES MAULE MACHAR.

STRETCHING from the Atlantic to the Pacific, and from Lake Erie to
the Arctic Ocean, occupying a more spacious territory than the United
States and Alaska, lies the great dominion to which the name of Canada
now applies, a country whose people are engrossed in the work of na-
tion-making. Perhaps nowhere else in the world, at this present day,
are such mighty forces stirring to such gigantic and uncalculated issues.
Within a decade there has come about such a change in the spirit of
the Canadian people that outside observers, judging from data of ten
or fifteen years ago, find themselves pathetically astray in their conclu-
sions; for the name of Canada, almost in a day, has become a name to
conjure with, from corner to corner of this confederation which we
have molded out of the once scattered and half-antagonistic provinces
of British North America. To the tourist whose interest centers chiefly
in men, in institutions, in ethnological and political problems, this country with a future and not without a significant past offers the strongest
possible attractions. To those who look for magnificence or charm of
landscape, for an invigorating climate, for the wholesome relish of rod
and gun and paddle, this region of the North makes no less active appeal. Its deficiencies, of course, are those of all new countries—its
fields have not been sown thick with blood and tears, its cities lack the
magic of inexhaustible memories, the treasures of a long-established
civilization. One city, Quebec, seems old to us, and has gathered about
its diadem of ramparts much of "the light that never was on sea or
land"; but, compared with Old World cities, it is a growth of yesterday.

The section of Canada which is here designated as Eastern Canada
is in the main coextensive with old Canada and Acadia. The rich and
populous section of Ontario which lies between Lakes Erie and Huron is
avoided, as belonging rather to the Western than the Eastern tour.
Toronto forms the most convenient center from which to start west or

1

east. The term Eastern Canada includes a large section of Ontario, with the provinces of Quebec, New Brunswick, Nova Scotia, and Prince Edward Island. Newfoundland, and that part of Labrador belonging to Newfoundland, though not attached to Canada, are touched upon in the following pages, for the convenience of tourists who may wish to visit them. The territory to be described may most conveniently be covered in a round trip, offering abundant choice of routes, and opportunity for attractive side-trips from the most important towns along the way. It is a small territory compared with the rest of the Dominion, but it contains the bulk of the population, much of the finest scenery, many of the best hunting and fishing resorts, and nearly all the history, tradition, and romance which combine to clothe the name of Canada with something like a savor of antiquity. Here was the center of French power in the New World, and here was fought to an end the contest between France and England. About Quebec and Louisburg, Annapolis and Beauséjour, battled the Leopards and the˙ Lilies for the dominion of half a continent. Quebec is still mighty, the gateway to Canada; but at Louisburg the sheep pasture now where stood but yesterday a great stronghold, the "Dunkirk of America." There broods a spell of mystery and romance about the site of this obliterated city. The magnitude and the heroism of the struggle for New France have been perpetuated for us by Parkman, and the pathos of its termination, as represented in a single episode, by Longfellow.

The climate of the St. Lawrence region and the Maritime Provinces is in general not unlike that of New England. The climate of Nova Scotia, in particular, is neither so hot in summer nor so cold in winter as that of the neighboring New England States. Summer tourists will need to make such provision against cool evenings and occasional fog as they would make if visiting the seaside resorts of Maine. In northeastern Quebec the summers are often chilly, and down the giant funnel of the Saguenay there blows at times, in mid-summer, a wind which makes the snuggest wraps desirable. As for the fogs that sometimes roll in on the Atlantic coast, one may escape them by a jaunt of a mile or two into the interior, or face them and experience the miracle which they will work on dull or faded complexions. It is to the benign ministrations of the fog that the women of the Atlantic seaboard owe the bloom and freshness of their faces.

The traveler who is well supplied with American bank-notes will find no difficulty with the currency. American bills are good all over

Canada. American silver, except in the border communities, is sometimes liable to a discount, and in some places may possibly be refused.
The silver coinage of Canada is uniform for the whole Dominion, and
with this the tourist should keep himself well supplied.

Concerning the opportunities for making purchases, a Canadian
writer says:

"If the tourist be desirous of economizing ingeniously, he will purchase himself a suit of clothes in Toronto, Montreal, or Halifax, getting
a strong, English-looking material of Australian wool, woven in Canada; and he will save fifty per cent over a similar article purchased in
Boston or New York. It is, of course, not ready-made goods that we
refer to, but suits made to order. In Halifax, a suit of best Canadian
tweed, durable and stylish, may be got from a first-rate tailor for $16
to $20; and a faultless dress-suit of best material for $35. In some
of the smaller towns, such as Truro and Windsor, in Nova Scotia, skil-
ful tailors who have learned their trade abroad, and keep themselves
abreast of the fashion, are able, on account of low rents and small
taxes, to furnish thoroughly satisfactory suits of fine Canadian tweed,
of quiet and correct pattern, for $15. The lover of furs will of course
make his (or her) purchases in Toronto or in Quebec city, where the
great fur-shops supply these goods in variety and of best quality, at
prices quite unheard-of in American cities. Indian work—moccasins,
bark- and quill-work, etc.—are usually to be purchased at counters in
the chief hotels and on the Saguenay steamers, and at so-called 'Indian
bazaars' in Montreal, Halifax, and St. John. In Quebec such things
are sold in the quaint old house wherein the body of Montgomery was
laid out."

All the baggage of travelers is subjected to an examination on
passing the borders; but the customs officials, as a rule, are courteous,
and the search is not severe if the traveler shows a disposition to
facilitate it.

On the round trip from New York or Boston and back, by way of
Niagara, Toronto, Montreal, Ottawa, Quebec, Halifax, and St. John, the
tourist will find the best of traveling facilities and accommodations.
The various railroad and steamboat lines by which he may make the
journey are equipped with all modern conveniences; and the hotels in
the cities above named, as well as at many other places along the route,
are first class in every respect. This applies equally well to some
of the side-trips which will be mentioned in the following pages; but
on others wilder regions will be traversed, where a similar degree of
comfort and luxury is not to be expected.

In the summer season round-trip tickets are issued from New York and Boston and other centers; and detailed information may be obtained at the railroad and steamboat agencies. At a rough estimate it may be said that the round trip from Boston or New York by way of Niagara, Toronto, Montreal, Quebec, Saguenay, Halifax, and St. John, will cost from \$40 to \$55 in fares, according to choice of routes.

The plan of the book, its arrangement and classification of matter, and the system of treatment, are based on the famous Baedeker Handbooks, which are conceded to possess in a pre-eminent degree the grand desiderata of compactness, portability, and facility of consultation. As much aid as possible is afforded to the eye by printing the names of places and objects either in *italics*, or, where they are of sufficient importance, in **large-faced type**.

The very rapid growth of Western Canada since the completion of the Canadian Pacific Railway has led to a demand for information concerning that section of the Dominion. The traveler or tourist who comes from abroad must now cross the continent. He desires to see the North Shore of Lake Superior and visit the famous fishing-grounds of Lake Nepigon and the beautiful Lake of the Woods region. The new province of Manitoba and its handsome capital of Winnipeg claim attention. Then, after seeing the broad buffalo plains, the great glaciers and snowy peaks of the Rockies are full of interest to those who are seeking for the beauties of Nature. The sportsman will desire to pause at some convenient spot, such as the Rocky Mountain Park, and indulge his taste with gun or rod. Finally, there are British Columbia, and Vancouver's Island, one of the beautiful inlands off the North Pacific Coast. As a guide or handbook of these and other equally attractive places, a description of Western Canada has been added to this edition of APPLETONS' CANADIAN GUIDE-BOOK.

Niagara Falls from Prospect Park.

APPLETONS'
CANADIAN GUIDE-BOOK.

PROVINCE OF ONTARIO.

Niagara Falls.

Shall not Niagara's mighty voice
Inspire to action high ?
'Twere easy such a land to love,
Or for her glory die.

E. G. NELSON.

THE tourist who proposes to visit the **St. Lawrence** region and **Maritime Provinces** of Canada will do well to travel with the sun, beginning with Ontario and ending with New Brunswick or Nova Scotia. Traveling in this direction, the descent of the St. Lawrence by boat is open to him, with its charm of historic landscapes, and its exciting experiences at the rapids of Long Sault and Lachine.

A little north of west from New York or Boston, on the isthmus between Lakes Ontario and Erie lies **Niagara**, whither all roads lead. Here we reach the frontier of the Maple-Leaf Land, and here our trip may be properly said to begin.

Countless pens have striven to depict the sublimities of Niagara, and have only succeeded in proving the hopelessness of the effort. I will not add another to the list of failures. Not only are words inadequate to convey any just impression of the stupendous cataract, but the eye itself, on first beholding it, quite fails to grasp its magnificence. No one can be said to have seen the Falls who has taken but one look and then passed on. To rightly apprehend them one should halt for some days at Niagara till his eye adjusts itself to the new proportions, and, like the boy that mocked the owls on Windermere, he feels that

" the visible scene
Has entered unawares into his mind,
With all its solemn imagery."

Not many years ago the Falls were so hedged about with extortionate charges that the tourist, unless a millionaire, was constrained to grasp his purse-strings and flee from the spot with the smallest possible delay. Now, however, all that is changed, and on the Canadian and American side alike the view of the falls is free. One pays only for such unessential extras as crossing the ferry or visiting The Cave of the Winds behind the cataract. The whole may be done on foot or with the aid of the street-cars which run between the *Whirlpool* and the Falls, and Niagara need be costly to none but those who desire to make it so. By means of the Niagara Falls Park and River Railway (electric), running for a distance of 13¼ miles from Queenston to Chippewa on the Canadian side, and by the Niagara Falls and Lewiston Railway (electric) on the American side, running from Lewiston to Niagara Falls, a distance of 7 miles, a very satisfactory view of the Falls and the river may be obtained. Cab charges are regulated by law, and hotel rates * are much as elsewhere, varying from $1 to $4 a day.

The Falls are situated on the Niagara River, about 22 miles from Lake Erie and 14 miles from Ontario. This river is the channel by which all the waters of the four great upper lakes flow toward the Gulf of St. Lawrence, and has a total descent of 333 ft., leaving Lake Ontario still 231 ft. above the sea. From the N. E. extremity of Lake Erie the Niagara flows in a N. direction with a swift current for the first 2 miles, and then more gently with a widening current, which divides as a portion passes on each side of Grand Island. As these unite below the island, the stream spreads out to 2 or 3 miles in width, and appears like a quiet lake studded with small, low islands. About 16 miles from Lake Erie the current becomes narrow and begins to descend with great velocity. This is the beginning of **The Rapids**, which continue for about a mile, the waters accomplishing in this distance a fall of 52 ft. The Rapids terminate below in a great cataract, the descent of which is 164 ft. on the American side and 158 ft. on the Canadian. At this point the river, making a curve from W. to N., spreads out to an extreme width of 4,750 ft., embracing Goat and the Three Sister Islands. **Goat Island**, which extends down to the brink of the cataract, occupies about one fourth of this space, leaving the river on the American side about 1,100 ft. wide, and on the Canadian

---

* The best hotels are—on the American side, the *Cataract House, International Hotel, Kaltenbach's, Prospect House, Spencer House*, and *Tower House;* on the Canadian side, the *Clifton House.* The legal tariff for carriages is $2 per hour, but it is usually easy to arrange special terms. All tolls are paid by the traveler.

side about double this width. The line along the verge of the Canadian Fall is much longer than the breadth of this portion of the river, by reason of its horseshoe form, the curve extending up the central part of the current. The waters sweeping down the Rapids form a grand curve as they fall clear of the rocky wall into the deep pool at the base.

Niagara Falls and Vicinity.

In the profound chasm below the fall, the current, contracted in width to less than 1,000 ft., is tossed tumultuously about, and forms great whirlpools and eddies as it is borne along its rapidly descending bed. Dangerous as it appears, the river is here crossed by small row-boats,

which are reached from the banks above by an inclined railroad, and
the Maid of the Mist, a small steamer, makes frequent trips to the edge
of the Falls.   For 7 miles below the Falls the narrow gorge continues,
varying in width from 200 to 400 yards.   The river then emerges at
Lewiston into a lower district, having descended 104 ft. from the foot
of the cataract.

Here at Lewiston, where ends the gorge, was once the site of the
cataract.   Instead of plunging into a deep chasm and hiding its grandeur from all but those who would search it out, the gigantic torrent
rolled, in full view of the world, over the lofty line of Queenston Heights, the escarpment of the high plateau of the upper lakes.
The recession of the Falls to their present point is thus discussed
by the Duke of Argyll :

FORMER POSITION OF THE FALLS.

" A very curious question, and one of great scientific interest, arises
out of the great difference between the course of the Niagara River
above and below the Falls.   It has, in my opinion, been much too
readily assumed by geologists that rivers have excavated the valleys in
which they run.   The cutting power of water is very great, but it varies
in proportion to the liability of floods, and the wearing power of stones
that may be carried along; much also depends on the position of the
rocks over which a river runs.   If the stratification present edges
which are easily attacked or undermined, even a gentle stream may cut
rapidly for itself a deeper bed.   On the other hand, when the rocks do
not expose any surfaces which are easily assailable, a very large body
of water may run over them for ages without being able to scoop out
more than a few feet or even a few inches.   Accordingly, such is actually the case with the Niagara River in the upper part of its course from
Lake Erie to the Falls.   In all the ages during which it has run into
that course for 15 miles it has not been able to remove more than a
few feet of soil or rock.   The country is level and the banks are very
low, so low that in looking up the bed of the stream the more distant
trees on either bank seem to rise out of the water.   But suddenly in
the middle of the comparatively level country the river encounters a
precipice, and thenceforward for 7 miles runs through a profound cleft
or ravine the bottom of which is not less than 300 ft. below the general
level of the country.   How came that precipice to be there?   This
would be no puzzle at all if the precipice were joined with a sudden
change in the general level of the country on either side of the river—
and there is such a change—but it is not at the Falls.   It is 7 miles
farther on.   At the Falls there is no depression in the general level
of the banks.   Indeed, on the Canadian shore, the land rises very considerably just above the Falls.   On the American shore it continues at
the same elevation.   The whole country here, however, is a table-land,

The American Falls.

and that table-land has a termination—an edge—over which the river must fall before it can reach Lake Ontario. But that edge does not run across the country at Niagara Falls, but along a line much nearer to Lake Ontario, where it is a conspicuous feature in the landscape, and is called Queenston Heights. The natural place, therefore, so to speak, for the Falls would have been where the river came to that edge, and from that point the river has all the appearance of having cut its way backward in the course of time. Sir Charles Lyell, the eminent geologist, came to the conclusion, from comparison of the rate at which the cutting back had been observable within the memory of man, that this cutting back is about one foot in each year. At this rate the river would have taken 35,000 years to effect its retreat from Queenston to the present position of the Falls."

The following brief account, condensed from Appletons' General Guide, of the various points of interest at the Falls, will indicate the wealth of material on which local guide-books exercise their powers of description and imagination:

Goat Island is the point usually visited first. It is reached by a bridge 360 ft. long, the approach to which is just in rear of the Cataract House. The bridge itself is an object of interest, from its apparently dangerous position. It is, however, perfectly safe, and is crossed constantly by heavily laden carriages. The view of the rapids from the bridge is one of the most impressive features of the Niagara scenery. Below the bridge, a short distance from the verge of the American Falls, is Chapin's Island, so named in memory of a work man who fell into the stream while at work on the bridge. He lodged on this islet and was rescued by a Mr. Robinson, who gallantly went to his rescue in a skiff. About midway of the stream the road crosses Bath Island. A short walk brings us to the foot-bridge leading to Luna Island, a huge rock-mass of some three quarters of an acre, lying between the Center Falls and the American Falls. The exquisite lunar rainbows seen at this point, when the moon is full, have given it the name it bears. Just beyond Luna Island a spiral stairway (called "Biddle's Stairs," after Nicholas Biddle, of United States Bank fame, by whose order they were built) leads to the foot of the cliff. From the foot of the stairs, which are secured to the rocks by strong iron fastenings, there are two diverging paths. That to the right leads to the **Cave of the Winds**, a spacious recess back of the Center Falls. Guides and water-proof suits for visiting the cave may be obtained at the stairs (fee, $1.00), and the excursion is well worth making. You can pass safely into the recess behind the water to a platform beyond,

Magical rainbow pictures are found at this spot; sometimes bows of
entire circles and two or three at once are seen. A plank-walk has
been carried out to a cluster of rocks near the foot of the fall, and
from it one of the best views of the American Falls may be obtained.
The up-river way, along the base of the cliff toward the Horseshoe
Falls, is difficult and much obstructed by fallen rocks. It was from a
point near Biddle's Stairs that the renowned jumper, Sam Patch, made
two successful leaps into the water below, in 1829, saying to the
throng of spectators, as he went off, that " one thing might be done as
well as another." Reascending the stairs, a few minutes' walk along
the summit of the cliff brings us to a bridge leading to the islet on
which stood the famous Terrapin Tower, which having become dangerous was blown up with gunpowder in 1873. The view of the Horseshoe Falls from this point is surpassingly grand. It was estimated by
Lyell that 1,500,000,000 cubic feet of water pass over the ledges every
hour. One of the condemned lake-ships (the Detroit) was sent over
this fall in 1829 ; and, though she drew 18 ft. of water, she did not
touch the rocks in passing over the brink of the precipice, showing
that the water is at least 20 ft. deep above the ledge.

At the other end of Goat Island (reached by a road from the Horseshoe Falls), a series of graceful bridges leads to the Three Sisters, as
three small islets lying in the Rapids are called. On Goat Island, near
the Three Sisters, is the Hermit's Bathing-place, so called after Francis
Abbott, " The Hermit of Niagara," who used to bathe here, and who
finally drowned while doing so. At the foot of Grand Island, near the
Canada shore, is Navy Island, which was the scene of some interesting
incidents in the Canadian Rebellion of 1837-'38, known as the Mackenzie War. It was near Schlosser Landing, about 2 miles above the Falls,
on the American side, that during the war the American steamer Caroline, which had been perverted to the use of the insurgents, was set
on fire and sent over the Falls by the order of Sir Allan McNab, a
Canadian officer.

The State of New York purchased, in 1885, the property bordering
the Falls, and laid out Niagara Park, to be controlled by a State Commission, empowered to remove all obstructions to the view, and to im-
prove the grounds. No charge is made for admission to Niagara Park.
A " vertical railway," running on a steep incline, leads from the park
to the base of the cliff ; and from its foot the river may be crossed in
the steamboat the Maid of the Mist. The passage across the river is

perfectly safe, and is worth making for the very fine view of the Falls obtained in mid-stream. A winding road along the cliff-side leads from the landing on the Canadian side to the top of the bluff, near the Clifton House. By climbing over the rocks at the base of the cliff on the American side (turn to the left after descending the railway), the tourist may penetrate to a point within the spray of the American Fall, and get what is perhaps, on the whole, the finest view of it to be had.

The Canadian side of the river may be reached by the steamer Maid of the Mist, or by the new bridge, which crosses the river at the place formerly spanned by the structure originally known as the " New Suspension Bridge." This bridge, like its elder prototype (the Grand Trunk Suspension Bridge), is now giving place to a new one in a similar style of construction, a steel arch, and the views of the Falls afforded in crossing it are among the best. A road to the left from the bridge terminus leads along the cliff, affording good views of the American and Center Falls. A short distance above the terrace near the Falls is the spot still called Table Rock, though the immense overhanging platform originally known by that name has long since fallen over the precipice. From this point the best front view of the Falls is obtained, and that of the Horseshoe Fall is incomparably grand. The concussion of the falling waters with those in the depths below produces a spray that veils the cataract two thirds up its height. Above this impenetrable foam to the height of 50 ft. above the Fall, a cloud of lighter spray rises, which, when the sun shines upon it in the proper direction, displays magnificent solar rainbows. The appropriateness of the name Niagara ("Thunder of Waters") is very evident here. At Table Rock may be procured guides and water-proof suits for **the passage under the Horseshoe Falls** (fee, 50c.). This passage (which no nervous person should attempt) is described as follows by a writer in Picturesque America: " The wooden stairways are narrow and steep, but perfectly safe ; and a couple of minutes brings us to the bottom. Here we are in spray-land indeed ; for we have hardly begun to traverse the pathway of broken bits of shale when, with a mischievous sweep, the wind sends a baby cataract in our direction, and fairly inundates us. The mysterious gloom, with the thundering noises of the falling waters, impresses every one ; but, as the pathway is broad, and the walking easy, new-comers are apt to think there is nothing in it. The tall, stalwart negro, who acts as guide, listens with amusement to such comments, and confidently awaits a change in the tone of the scoffers. More and more arched do the rocks become as we proceed. The top part is of hard limestone, and the lower of shale, which has been so battered away by the fury of the waters that there is an arched passage behind the entire Horseshoe Fall, which could easily be traversed if the currents of air would let us pass. But, as we proceed, we begin to notice that it blows a trifle, and from every one of the 32 points of the compass. At first, however, we get them separately. A gust at a time inundates us with spray; but the farther we march the more unruly is the Prince of Air. First, like single spies, come his winds; but soon they advance like skirmishers; and, at last, where a thin column of water falls across the path, they oppose a solid phalanx to our efforts. It is a point of honor to see who can go farthest through these corridors of Æolus. It is on record that a man, with an herculean effort, once burst through the column of water, but was immediately thrown to the ground, and only rejoined his comrades by crawling face downward, and digging his hands into the loose shale of the pathway. Prof. Tyndall has gone as far as mortal man, and he describes the buffeting of the air as indescribable, the effect being like actual blows with the fist."

Termination Rock is a short distance beyond Table Rock, at the verge of the fall. The spray here is blinding, and the roar of waters deafening.

Below the Falls are several points of interest, which are best visited on the American side. The first of these is the steel arch bridge finished in 1897. The span between the piers of this bridge is 550 ft., and a trussed span at each end 115 ft. long connects the arch with the bluff. The total length of the bridge with the approaches is 1,100 ft. It has two decks or floors, the upper one 30 ft. wide, occupied by the double track of the Grand Trunk Railway, the lower comprising a broad carriageway in the center, with trolley tracks each side and footwalks outside of all, making a total width of 57 ft. The fee for crossing the bridge is 25c. for pedestrians, which confers the right to return free on the same day. From one side of this bridge a fine distant view of the Falls is had, and from the other a bird's-eye view of the seething, tumultuous **Whirlpool Rapids.** Three hundred feet above may be seen the new Michigan Central R. R. Cantilever Bridge. By descending the elevator, which leads from the top to the base of the cliff near the site of the old Monteagle House, a nearer view is obtained of these wonderful rapids, in which the waters rush along with such velocity that the middle of the current is 30 ft. higher than the sides. Three miles below

Luna Falls and Rock of Ages.

the Falls is the **Whirlpool**, occasioned by a sharp bend in the river, which is here contracted to a width of 220 ft.

From Niagara to Toronto.

From Niagara Falls one has a choice of routes to Toronto. One may go by the Grand Trunk or Canadian Pacific around the head of the lake, or by rail to the river bank below the Rapids, and thence by steamer straight across Lake Ontario from the mouth of Niagara River. The land route (fare, single, $2.65; return, $4.45), which is the longer, affords an opportunity of seeing that magnificent engineering work the Welland Canal, and of visiting the cities of St. Catharines and Hamilton. If one goes by the river route (fare, single, $1.50; return, $2.30), one sees the beauties of the Niagara district, the gardens of Canada, the storied Queenston Heights, and the delightful summer resort of Niagara-on-the-Lake, besides enjoying a cool sail of 40 miles across the waters of Lake Ontario.

THE WATER ROUTE.

By this river route the tourist finds yet further latitude allowed him. The journey from the Falls may be made on the Canadian side either by the Grand Trunk Railway to Port Dalhousie and thence across Lake Ontario, or by the Michigan Central to Niagara-on-the-Lake or along the American shore by the New York Central to the wharf at Lewiston, 7 miles from the mouth, where one meets the fine Clyde-built steamers of the "Niagara River Line," making connections across the lake four times each day. A very popular route is by steamer from Toronto to Queenston on the Niagara River, where connection is made with the Niagara Falls Park and River Electric Railway. This road follows the line of the river to the cataract and the village of Chippewa, three miles beyond. This line is so laid out as to take in all the best views of this interesting trip—the changing scenery along the river, the varying phases of the river itself, the whirlpool foaming in anger and succeeded by the stretch of quiet water beyond, the view of Queenston Heights, surmounted by Brock's historical monument, the steel arch bridge, the approach to the Falls, showing the American Falls, Goat Island, and the Horseshoe Falls, and then the near view of the roaring cataract itself. The cars on this road are so constructed that every passenger has a clear and unobstructed view of the scenery on either side.

The New York Central runs through **The Gorge** itself, along a ledge which has been carved out of the face of the cliff, beneath which is the Great Gorge Route of the Niagara Falls and Lewiston R. R., which runs close to the water's edge. Above towers the beetling front of rock, and far below thunders the tremendous torrent. In the gorge of Niagara the water does not flow, or rush, or dart, but it bounds and bursts as if belched forth from some hidden volcano. Presently the mad flood is caught and enchained for a time in the sullen vortex of the Whirlpool. Of this unmythical Maelstrom one catches a thrilling glimpse from the car window. Then the gorge narrows again; and plunging through short tunnels, swerving dizzily on its airy shelf, round jutting peaks, the road threads the windings of the abyss, gradually descending, till it comes out upon the lower level at Lewiston. Here is the head of navigation, and at the dock, to the side of which the railway has now been extended, the tourist steps on board the steamers. The river rests here in a great, slow-reeling eddy. In this eddy the steamer turns, and is grateful for the service of the revolving current.

Opposite Lewiston rise **Queenston Heights**, the most famous battle-field of the War of 1812. Here, for an autumn day, three quarters of a century ago, raged a bitter struggle between the American and Canadian forces, resulting at length in victory for the Canadians, who paid too dear for their triumph, however, with the death of their heroic leader, General Sir Isaac Brock. May it prove an augury of perpetual peace and good-will along these frontiers that when, two days after the battle, General Brock was being buried in one of the bastions of Fort George, minute-guns were fired from the American Fort Niagara across the river, as a tribute of respect to their illustrious adversary!

On the summit of the Heights stands the monument which has been erected in memory of the favorite hero of Canadians. This is the second monument erected on the spot, the earlier and smaller one, built by a grant from the Provincial Parliament in 1824, having been blown up in 1840 by a scoundrel named Lett. The new monument was erected by the voluntary contributions of the militia and Indian warriors of Canada. It is a massive stone structure 190 ft. in height, 19 ft. higher than Nelson's Column in Trafalgar Square. At the top, beneath a colossal statue of Brock, is a gallery reached by 235 steps. Standing on this gallery one sees unroll before him a matchless panorama, of battle-field and vineyard, of cataract and quiet stream, of dark wood and steepled villages and breadths of peach-orchard, and fortresses no longer hostile; and far across the blue waters of Ontario the smoke of the great city toward which our feet are set.

From Lewiston to Niagara-on-the-Lake the river flows for 7 miles rapidly between high, wooded banks, studded with gardens and comfortable homes. If the tourist has started on the Canadian side, the Michigan Central R. R. takes him direct to Niagara-on-the-Lake. This route, as it winds down the side of the Niagara escarpment, gives a wide range over the fertile Niagara plains with all their glory of peach gardens and vineyards, and also a distant view of Queenston Heights and Brock's monument. But it must be acknowledged that it is as much less picturesque as it is more convenient than that by crossing to the American side.

Niagara-on-the-Lake, where of old the fortunes of peoples were wont to be decided by the sword, where Indians, French, and British, Americans and Canadians have contended for the supremacy of the Lake regions, where the first Parliament of the old province of Upper Canada was held in 1792 in ancestral fashion in the shade of a spreading oak, is now but a merry watering-place. In the neighborhood is the battle-field of **Lundy's Lane,** the scene of a hard-fought struggle between Canadian and American forces. The chief episodes that now stir the surface of Niagara's summer calm are the Saturday evening hops at the Queen's Royal Hotel, which are attended by the American officers from Fort Niagara opposite, and by gay yachting parties from Toronto. The country round about is a garden; there is capital bass-fishing to be had, and the facilities for boating and bathing are not to be excelled. In the days of its political and military importance the town bore the more business-like name of Newark. Chief hotels: *Hotel Chautauqua, Queens Royal Hotel,* and *The Oban.*

The run across from Niagara to Toronto occupies about two hours, and in the tourist season the lake is usually unruffled. As Lake Ontario, however, is 180 miles long and about 70 in extreme breadth, it possesses every facility for an occasional storm of genuine Atlantic proportions. The Chippewa, Corona, and Chicora, of the "Niagara River Line," however, are Clyde-built ocean-going craft of steel, and maintain regular service in all weathers, leaving Lewiston every week-day at 8 A. M., 10.30 A. M., 12 noon, and 5.40 P. M., and Niagara-on-the-Lake half an hour later. There are officers of the American and Canadian customs on the boat to examine baggage during the trip across; and the Niagara River Navigation Company issues through tickets and checks through baggage in connection with the main railroad and steamboat lines of Canada and America. Returning steamers leave Toronto 7 A. M., 11 A. M., 2 P. M., and 4.45 P. M.

THE JOURNEY BY RAIL.

If one chooses to go by land around the head of the lake his way lies through a fine country. The Grand Trunk and Canadian Pacific Rys. run from the Falls to Hamilton, whence the traveler is carried eastward to Toronto over the same tracks. A few miles west of Niagara by the former route is Merritton, where the railway plunges into a tunnel which leads it under the Welland Canal. Merritton is otherwise known as Thorold Station, as it is there that passengers leave the train for the little town of Thorold on the canal. In this neighborhood is the bat- tle-field of **Beaver Dams**, which Canadians regard with pardonable pride. During the War of 1812, when the Americans were in posses- sion of Fort George and Niagara and the British troops had fallen back on Burlington (now Hamilton), the British general advised the Canadian volunteers to disband and return to their homes, as he was contemplating the possibility of abandoning all that section of the province to the foe and retiring to Kingston. In this crisis, being thrown entirely upon their own resources, the Canadians proved themselves equal to the emergency. What followed has been thus described by Miss Louisa Murray: " Merritt's militia regiment of light horse, with some other militiamen and volunteers, established themselves at a building known as ' De Cew's stone house,' converting it into a little fortress, whence they harassed the Americans, driving off their foraging parties, and intercepting their supplies, with such success and impunity as only an intimate knowledge of the country could have given them. Colonel Boerstler was sent from Niagara with two field-pieces and 600 men to break up this little stronghold, and one or two other outposts of the British, who, since the decisive battle of Stony Creek, were moving back toward Fort George, and he might have succeeded but for the patriotic spirit and bravery of a woman. Laura Secord, the young wife of James Secord, a militiaman lying wounded at Queens- ton, saw the American troops moving from Niagara, and, learning their destination, set out at night, and walked twenty miles through the woods to warn the little band at the stone house of Boerstler's ap- proach. At any time it would have been a difficult journey, but in war time, with the risk of meeting some savage Indian or other lawless marauder in the lonely woods, only a woman of singular energy and courage would have undertaken it. Mrs. Secord, however, accomplished it in safety, and when Colonel Boerstler arrived at Beaver Dams at 6 o'clock in the morning, he found his march impeded by a small number of militiamen, hastily collected, and a party of Indians led by their chief, young Brant. This number, altogether about 200, seemed trebled when seen through the thick foliage of the trees, from among which they poured volley after volley from their muskets on the surprised and bewildered Americans, every volley accompanied by the fierce yells of the Indians. While Boerstler was still uncertain whether to advance or retreat, Ensign Fitzgibbon, with 40 soldiers, the only British troops in the neighborhood, arrived at the spot and took in the situation at once. With admirable courage and coolness, he tied a white handkerchief on a musket, and, holding it up, advanced alone, calling on the enemy to lay down their arms and surrender; upon which Colonel Boerstler, believing that the whole British army was in front, surrendered his force of 600 infantry, 50 cavalry, 2 field guns, and a stand of colors, to the young ensign and his 240 men." The victory is commemorated by a small granite monument, with the inscription "Beaver Dams, June 24, 1813." The heroic achievement of Laura Secord has been made the subject of a historical drama by Mrs. S. A. Curyon, and of a stirring ballad by Charles Mair.

The city of **St. Catharines** is on the Welland Canal, about 3 miles from its Lake Ontario outlet. The trade center of this inexhaustibly fertile Niagara region, and supplied with unlimited water-power by means of the canal, St. Catharines has become an important commercial city. It is purely a product of the canal, and owes its existence as a city to the indomitable energy of William Hamilton Merritt, who conceived the idea of the great engineering work and finally pushed it to completion. St. Catharines has important ship-yards, mills, and machine-works; handsome public buildings, first-class hotels, and one of the best collegiate institutes in the province. It is also a very popular health resort, much visited by Southerners. The waters of its mineral springs rank high among the medicinal waters of the world. There is fishing in the neighborhood for black bass, perch, and pickerel. Chief hotel the *Welland House* ($2).

The **Welland Canal**, connecting the waters of Lakes Erie and Ontario, is a work of tremendous importance, giving as it does an outlet to the sea for the vast trade of the Great Lakes. The canal is 27 miles in length from Port Colborne on Lake Erie to Port Dalhousie on Lake Ontario. The difference in level between the lakes is about 327 ft., which is overcome by a system of 25 lift-locks. All the masonry of the work is of splendid and massive proportions, and is built of an enduring gray limestone.   At Welland the canal is led over the Chippewa River by a costly aqueduct.   The original feeder of the canal was the Chippewa River, which proving at times inadequate, a branch canal was cut to the Grand River.   Of late, however, arrangements have been made by which the canal is always adequately supplied from Lake Erie itself.   Along the line of the canal are strung a number of prosperous villages.   The first sod of the original canal was turned in 1824.   Mr. Merritt's modest conception was a canal " 4 ft. deep, 7 ft. wide at bottom, 19 ft. wide at the water surface, and to accommodate vessels not exceeding 40 tons burden."   The present structure has a width at the bottom of 100 ft., and accommodates vessels of 1,500 tons.

Leaving St. Catharines our train passes the villages of Jordan and Beamsville, and 27 miles from Niagara we find ourselves at the busy village of Grimsby.   Here is the summer resort of **Grimsby Park**, with its famous Methodist camp-meeting ground in a grove of oaks and pines beside the lake.   The region about Grimsby is literally one great peach-orchard.   It is estimated that there are something like 400,000 peach-trees in the Niagara district, which ships annually over a million baskets of this delicious fruit.   The beauty of the peach-orchards, whether in bloom or when bending under their wealth of luscious pink and white and golden spheres, is something that beggars description. The peach harvest begins about the end of July and continues until the middle of October.   The peaches are shipped all over Canada in baskets covered with pink gauze.   In this favored region flourish also apples, pears, plums, cherries, all kinds of small fruits, melons, quinces, grapes, walnuts, chestnuts, and even figs.   Beyond Grimsby we have only the stations of Winona and Stoney Creek to pass before we come to Hamilton.

Hamilton.

The chief hotel of Hamilton is the *Royal* ($2.50 to $4 a day), which is first class in every respect; but there are many other good hotels, such as the *St. Nicholas* ($1.50 to $2) and the *Dominion* ($1 to $1.50), where the tourist may be accommodated more cheaply.   The city is well supplied with restaurants, called coffee-rooms.   The chief club is the Hamilton Club.   Theatres, the Grand Opera-House, Association Hall, Alexandra Arcade.   The city is traversed by street-cars, and hacks are to be obtained at the station and the cab-stands as well as at the chief hotels,

The city of Hamilton is beautifully and fortunately situated at the head of navigation on Lake Ontario. Across the upper end of the lake, where the northern and southern shores stand but 5 miles apart, the east winds of centuries have heaped together a long bar of sand nearly a thousand feet in width. This is known as **Burlington Beach**, and it cuts off from the stormy lake the quiet waters of Burlington Bay, the harbor of Hamilton. A short canal through the Beach connects the inner and the outer waters. The Beach is a favorite summer resort for the citizens of Hamilton.

Hamilton lies at the foot of a steep hill called the "Mountain," and occupies one of those "benches" which surround the lake, and probably mark a former level of its surface. The site of Hamilton was chosen originally by a loyalist refugee, one Robert Land, on account of its splendid landscape. The "**Mountain**" is a portion of the Niagara escarpment, which here curves grandly back from the lake to form the amphitheatre which the city occupies. Down a great sloping strath, dividing the heights in this neighborhood like a gigantic gutter, at the foot of which now lies the town of Dundas, geologists tell us that, in remotest ages, the waters of Lake Erie discharged themselves, instead of at Niagara.

Hamilton may be said to have had its birth in the War of 1812, when Burlington Heights became a center of military operations, and one George Hamilton cut up his farm into town lots. In 1824 the cutting of a canal through Burlington Beach began the prosperity of Hamilton, which, however, was sadly interfered with by the cholera plague and great fire in 1832. Hamilton was not disheartened, and went to work again with the pluck and spirit which have earned her the title of "the Ambitious City." Her ambition bids fair to be gratified in all save one particular—and in that she has by this time relinquished all hope. Of old, she thought to outstrip Toronto; but when, in 1888, with a population less than 45,000, she saw Toronto with 170,000, she probably changed the tenor of her ambition to something more within the range of possibility. Her ancient rivals, Ancaster and Dundas, she has long ago left utterly behind, reducing them to the rank of suburban villages. Her own population is now 50,000.

Hamilton is a wealthy and tirelessly energetic city, with manufacturing interests out of all proportion to its size. It is the cathedral city of two dioceses, the Anglican bishopric of Niagara and the Roman Catholic bishopric of Hamilton. The city has handsome public buildings, and stately private residences on the Mountain.   Cresting the height are the spacious buildings of the Lunatic Asylum.   A stately thoroughfare, dividing the city from the Mountain to the bay, is McNab St., named for Hamilton's hero, the politician, patriot, and soldier, Sir Allan McNab.   It was he who, during the rebellion in 1837, shattered the power of the rebels at Toronto, and organized the flotilla on the Niagara which cut out the steamer Caroline and sent her over the Falls.   On the heights stands Dundurn Castle, where Sir Allan used to live, looking out over the city whose prosperity he had done so much to promote.   One of the most delightful features of Hamilton is what is known as "**The Gore.**"   This is a spacious and beautiful public garden in the heart of the city, with the busiest thoroughfares all about it.   The open space, which is cool and musical with fountains and brilliant with flowers, is triangular in shape, and formed by the converging of York, James, and King Sts.   Overlooking "The Gore" are the thoroughly artistic buildings of the Hamilton Provident and Loan Society, the Canada Life Assurance Company, and the Court-House. But 6 miles from Hamilton, and connected with it by a steam tramway, is Dundas.   In one thing Dundas can never be outrivaled by Hamilton, and that is in her magnificent landscape, which opens like a dream before the traveler's eyes as he sweeps around the mountain.   At the foot of the lovely Dundas Valley lies a wide marsh which goes by the nickname of "Coote's Paradise," after an English officer, Captain Coote, who was deeply enamored of the fine duck, snipe, and "coot" shooting there to be obtained.   The marsh still maintains its reputation ; and in Burlington Bay are good black bass, silver bass, perch, and pike fishing.   The pike take the trolling-spoon freely during the latter part of August, but at other times rise better to the live minnow.

From Hamilton to Toronto, if wearied of the rail, one may go by the steamers of the Hamilton Steamboat Co., four times daily (fare, 75c.), a trip of 33 miles along a pleasant coast.   The boats are fast and comfortable, and call each way at Burlington Beach and at the vast strawberry-gardens of Oakville.   The tourist desirous of visiting the Northern Lakes, or what is perhaps more widely known as the Muskoka region, may branch off by the Hamilton and Allandale Line from Hamilton via Beeton and Barrie, and leave Toronto till his return, but the fastest train services center in Toronto.   **Beeton** is of interest as the center of the great honey industry of Ontario.   The

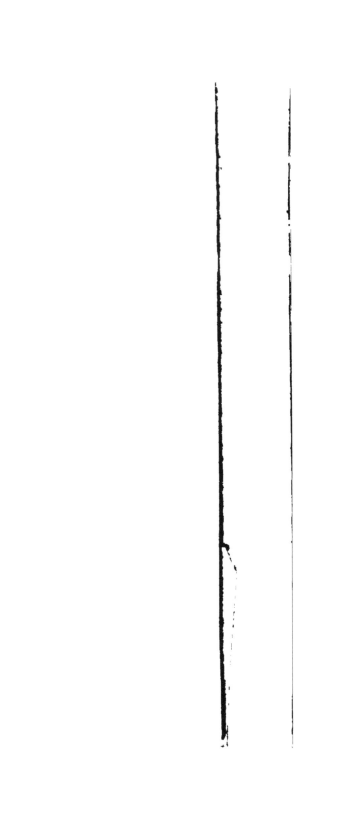

whole surrounding country is full of bee farms, and sweet the summer through with the scent of honey-bearing blossoms. The pedigrees of the swarms are watched with the same care that breeders of thorough-bred cattle give to their stock, and solitary islands in Georgian Bay, to the north, are made use of as bee nurseries to preserve the purity of the favorite strains. The science of apiculture at Beeton has been brought to a high degree of perfection. At Barrie, on Lake Simcoe, we meet the line from Toronto *via* Bradford.

Toronto.

The approach to Toronto is more effective by water than by land. As the steamer passes Gibraltar Point, she rounds into a safe and spacious harbor crowded with the traffic of the lakes. This harbor is formed by what is known as The Island, which is the great summer pleasure-ground for the inhabitants of the city. **The Island** is to Toronto what Coney Island and Manhattan Beach are to New York. It is really nothing more than a great sand-bank formed by the drift and offscourings from Scarboro' Heights, and its shape is continually changing. The lighthouse on Gibraltar Point, built within a few feet of the water, stands now some distance inland. A few years ago the Island was connected with the mainland by a strip of beach to the east, but storms having breached the isthmus at Ashbridge's Bay, a narrow channel was formed which has since been widening. The Island is fringed with lightly-built summer cottages whose thresholds are ceaselessly invaded by the sand-drift. All summer the white beaches swarm with merry life and the shallow pools with bathers. High over the cottages and the willow thickets tower the gables of a great summer hotel, originally built by Hanlan, the ex-champion oarsman of the world. It has since been much improved. Adjoining it is a fine bicycle track, with a grand stand. There are various entertainments on summer evenings. Between the island and the city pass and repass the unremitting ferries.

Toronto, the "Queen City," as we Canadians fondly call her, slopes very gently from the lake's edge back to the wooded line of the Davenport Hills. The almost level expanse of her sea of roofs is broken with many spires and with the green crowns of innumerable elms and horse-chestnuts. All through her temperate summers her streets are deliciously shadowed; all through her mild winters the sunlight streams in freely through the naked branches.

From the Don's mouth on the E. to the Humber on the W., a distance of 8 miles, the city stretches an unbroken front along the rim of the lake. Between these limits is gathered a population of about 200,000 —a population which is increasing at a rate with which few other cities on the continent can compare. Already she begins to reach out beyond her containing streams. All Ontario and much of our Northwest, regions growing rapidly in wealth and population, are tributary to her, and must continue to nourish her growth. No other city on the lakes, with the exception of Chicago, has fairer prospects for the future than Toronto.

The very name Toronto signifies "a place of meeting," a place where men are gathered together. The first mention of the name is in some French memoirs of 1686, where it is applied to the Portage from the Humber to Lake Simcoe. In the sheltered harbor at the Ontario end of the trail the French erected a fort, the remains of which are yet to be seen in the exhibition grounds. To this post, at first called Fort Rouillé, the name Fort Toronto was afterward given.

THE HISTORY OF TORONTO.

Ontario, as a separate province, is the creation of the United Empire Loyalists, and Toronto was the creation of Governor Simcoe, the first governor of the new province. These United Empire Loyalists, whose experiences and whose work in province-building we shall again refer to when writing of New Brunswick and Nova Scotia, were inhabitants of the thirteen colonies to the south who remained loyal to the mother-country during the American Revolution. They were an energetic and fearless people, possessing fully the courage of their convictions, and not unnaturally the feeling between them and their insurgent fellow-countrymen was implacably bitter. When the independence of the Thirteen Colonies was acknowledged, their position was difficult in the extreme. They could not accept the new order, and to the new order they were hopelessly unacceptable. They had staked everything on the triumph of England, and to England they now looked for help. They were given lands in Canada and Nova Scotia; and their splendid energy and courage carried them through difficulties and hardships under which a weaker people would have succumbed. A very large proportion of them belonged to the educated and cultured classes. Their great exodus from under the shadow of the new flag took place in the years 1783 and 1784; but when the new province of Upper Canada was organized under the wise supervision of Governor Simcoe, additional parties flocked in, and in the four years from 1791 to 1795 their numbers increased in that province from 12,000 to 30,000. Prominent among the United Empire Loyalists were the Indians of the Six Nations, under their great and humane warrior-chieftain, Joseph Brant or Thayendanagea. These faithful allies were granted a fertile territory along the course of the Grand River.

As we have already mentioned, Niagara-on-the-Lake was the first capital of Upper Canada. Gradually it was borne in upon the provincial authorities that a town like Niagara, within range of American guns, was ill adapted to be the seat of government. Thereupon the capital was shifted to the "Place of Meeting," across the lake, and the infant executive felt more secure. The significant and musical name, however, was changed, and Toronto became York. What are significance and beauty when weighed in the balance against a compliment to the heir-apparent? This was in 1793; but though the old name was exiled from the village it seemed to cling in the hearts of the inhabitants. The name of York was worn like an ill-fitting garment. "Muddy York" it was called by derisive but not unenvious neighbors. And when, in 1834, the village took unto itself the title and the dignity of a city, the name of York, with its contumelious epithet, was eagerly sloughed off, and the "Place of Meeting" resumed its ancient title. In 1794 there were but 12 houses at Toronto, and when the War of 1812 broke out this provincial capital, now the second city in the Dominion, contained but 900 inhabitants.

In the War of 1812 Toronto was twice captured by the Americans, who destroyed the fortifications and sacked the town, after a struggle lasting from early morning to sundown, when the English general, considering the position untenable, abandoned it when he found himself confronted with a vastly superior force. The Canadian militia, who bore the brunt of the war, preferred to select some more advantageous battle-ground than the exposed provincial capital. All through this war the chief honors, in the land battles, fell generally to the Canadian arms. On the American side the war was strongly disapproved of by the best men; its object being thus sarcastically characterized by Randolph of Virginia: "The people of Canada are first to be seduced from their allegiance, and converted into traitors, as a preparation for making them good American citizens." The spirit with which the Canadians went into the contest is thus described by

Colonel G. T. Denison: "In 1812 every able-bodied man went to the frontier to fight, leaving the old men, the boys, and the women to till the fields. One might travel a day's journey in this province during that war without meeting an able-bodied man, as they were all on the frontier."

In 1837 occurred the rebellion of William Lyon Mackenzie, who called himself "Chairman *pro tem.* of the Provisional Government of the State of Upper Canada." The foolish self-styled patriots established what they called a Provisional Government on Navy Island in the Niagara River; but the rebel rendezvous was a place known as "Montgomery's Tavern," on Yonge St., a few miles north of the city limits. With a force of about 900 men the rebels threatened Toronto; but when the "Men of Gore" arrived, under Colonel McNab, the rebel bands were scattered after a short but sharp struggle. Soon afterward took place the destruction of the steamer Caroline, already referred to. This exploit has been thus described by Dr. Bryce:

"The Provisional Government was now organized on Navy Island, in the Niagara River. The patriot flag, with twin stars and the motto, 'Liberty and Equality,' was hoisted, and planted in the face of Colonel McNab, who held the Canadian shore. A daring action was performed on December 29 by Captain Drew, R. N., one of McNab's command. The insurgents had made use of a vessel, the Caroline, in carrying supplies from the American shore to Navy Island. The vessel lay moored for the night under the very guns of Fort Schlosser; indeed, the shadows of the fort enveloped the Caroline. With 7 boats, carrying some 60 men in all, who were armed with pistols, cutlasses, and pikes, the captain boarded the ill-fated vessel, captured her, but not being able, on account of the current, to bring her to the Canadian side, sent her flaming over the Niagara Falls. The vessel proved to be an American bottom, and so Britain was compelled to disavow the seizure, but nothing could blot out the bravery of the deed."

THE TORONTO OF THE PRESENT.

Hotels, etc.—The *Queen's Hotel* ($3 to $4), in Front St.; the *Rossin House* ($2.50 to $3), cor. King and York Sts.; the *Walker House* ($2 and $2.50), Front and York Sts.; and the *Arlington*, cor. King and John Sts. Street cars (fare, 5c.) render all parts of the city easily accessible. Cab rates are $1 an hour. From station or Niagara steamer's dock to hotel, 25c. The chief clubs are the National, Toronto, and Albany Clubs; also the Victoria, Granite, Athenæum, Golf, and the various political clubs. Theatres: Grand Opera-House, Shaftesbury Hall, Princess, Toronto Opera-House, Horticultural Gardens, and Robinson's Musée.

The Toronto of the present offers many attractions to the visitor.
It is the best possible place to pause and lay one's plans. It may fairly
claim to be called the intellectual center of the Dominion. Filled with
a homogeneous and successful population, looking back upon a past of
wonderful achievement, and forward to a future bright with all possibilities, it is instinct with the sanguine and self-reliant spirit of this
young Canadian people. Its hotels are of the best; its open water-
front and quiet harbor offer every facility for boating, canoeing, and
yachting. There is charming scenery in the immediate neighborhood,
and within easy reach are the gigantic maskinonge and swarming trout
and black bass of the wild Muskoka waters.

The principal street of Toronto, as it was of the original village, is
King St., running E. and W. between the Don and the Humber.
Where now stands the old jail were erected the first Houses of Parliament of Upper Canada. These were wooden buildings and of no
great architectural distinction. During the War of 1812 they were
burned with the Library and the provincial records, by the American
invaders. This injury was avenged a few months later, when a British force destroyed the public buildings at Washington. Opposite the
spot where now towers the noble structure of St. James's Cathedral was
once the market-place. Here stood the stocks and pillory, which were
in use up to 1834. Either the men of Toronto were less gallant in
those days, or her women less deserving, for we find in the town records that one Elizabeth Ellis, convicted of being a public nuisance, was
condemned to stand in the pillory for two hours at a time on two successive market-days. The women of Toronto are still held up to the
gaze of the world, but it is for the world's admiration, as they display
some of the most attractive types of Canadian beauty. Next in importance to King St. is **Yonge**, which runs at right angles to it.
If we may accept the authority of George Augustus Sala, this is the
longest street in the world. It runs N. from the water's edge, and
was laid out in 1793, to be used as a portage to the upper lakes.
The object of this was to avoid the necessity of ascending Lake Erie
and passing under the guns of the American fort at Detroit. For the
first 46 miles of its extent Yonge St. became the main artery of the
province, and was speedily lined with homesteads. Apropos of the
" magnificent distances " of this thoroughfare the following anecdote
may be quoted from an entertaining and valuable work by Dr. Scad-
ding, entitled " Toronto of Old ": A story is told of a tourist, newly

arrived at York, wishing to utilize a stroll before breakfast by making out as he went along the whereabouts of a gentleman to whom he had a letter. Passing down the hall of his hotel he asked, in a casual way of the book-keeper, " Can you tell me where Mr. So-and-so lives ? " (leisurely producing the note from his breast pocket); " it is somewhere along Yonge St. here in town." " Oh, yes," was the reply, when the address had been glanced at, " Mr. So-and-so lives on Yonge St., about 25 miles up ! "

At the corner of King and Yonge Sts. throbs the heart of the city.*

From King St. northward to the city limits Yonge St. is lined with fine retail establishments. From King St. S. to the water it is built up with massive warehouses. This applies equally to Front St., which skirts the harbor. At the water-front of Yonge stands the Custom-House, a piece of elaborately decorated Italian architecture. Between Front St. and the water to the W. of Yonge lies a low flat known as the Esplanade. Here the various converging railways enter the city and here at the foot of York St., where in 1851 the Countess of Elgin turned the first sod of the Ontario, Simcoe and Huron R.R., stands the Union Station. The interest of Front St. may be said to terminate at the old Parliament Buildings, which have given place to the splendid structures erected in Queen's Park. Toronto is a city of churches, there being over 150 churches and chapels within its borders. This being the case, it goes without saying that Sunday is religiously observed as a day of rest. Except when the churches are drawing in or pouring forth their demurely pacing throngs, the city seems

---

* This is the most convenient point from which to calculate distances when arranging for drives through the suburbs. The following table of ways and distances I take from Mr. Barlow Cumberland's useful handbook to " The Northern Lakes of Canada." :

Distances out and back from Corner of King and Yonge Streets.

EAST.—The Lake Shore Road, Woodbine, Ben Lomond, Don and Danforth Road, and the Necropolis—8¼ miles.

NORTHEAST.—Necropolis, Todmorden, Don Valley, Eglington, Mount Pleasant—6¼ miles.

NORTH.—Queen's Park, Deer Park, Ridge Road, St. Albans St., St. George St.—6 miles.

NORTHWEST.—College St., Bloor St., Slattery's High Park, Queen St., and Subway—8¼ miles.

WEST.—King St., Lake Shore Road, Humber Bay and back—9 miles.

asleep; and from seven o'clock on Saturday evening until a seemly hour on Monday morning no one can gain admittance to the bar-rooms —except by the back door! A little E. of the corner of Yonge is **St. James's Cathedral**, at the junction of King and Church Sts. This building is of simple and noble design, in what is known as perpendicular Gothic. Its spire, soaring to a height of 316 ft., is with one exception the loftiest on the continent; the newly completed spires of St. Patrick's Cathedral in New York reach the height of 328 ft. Within the tower of St. James's Cathedral is an exquisite chime of bells, and all Toronto prides itself on the celebrated clock of St. James's, which won the first prize at the Vienna Exhibition. The interior of the cathedral contains monuments to some of the distinguished sons of Ontario, and to that strong old ecclesiastic, Bishop Strachan, than whom few pastors have been better able to rule their flocks. The chancel windows are fine examples of the best stained-glass work of Munich. St. James's Cathedral is the fourth church which has occupied the present site, fire having removed its three predecessors. From the tower a magnificent view may be had of Toronto and her surroundings.

Some important buildings in the neighborhood of St. James's Cathedral are the St. Lawrence Hall and Market, the old City Hall, the admirably managed Public Library, at the corner of Adelaide and Church Sts., and the Post-Office, on Adelaide at the head of Toronto St. This short thoroughfare is the Wall St. of Toronto. A little to the W. of the Post-Office is the Grand Opera-House, on whose spacious stage have moved the most brilliant modern actors. This theatre has a seating capacity of 2,300. There are also three other theatres.

Moving westward along King St., we come to a stately piece of Norman architecture, the Presbyterian **Church of St. Andrew's**, at the corner of King and Simcoe. Opposite St. Andrew's is **Government House**, a handsome building of modern French design. The main entrance is on Simcoe St., under a spacious and elaborate carriage porch. The gardens are broad and well kept, and the little valley winding through them was once Russell's Creek, up which Governor Simcoe used to row when the infant capital was but a lake-side clearing. The dining-room at Government House contains a fine collection of portraits. Permission to view the interior must be obtained from the A. D. C. Just beyond Government House, in the midst of ample grounds, are the old Upper Canada College buildings, which, having outgrown their usefulness, are now deserted, and this famed seat of learning is now located in a magnificent structure in Deer Park, another part of the city. Close by is John St., at the head of which is the fine old colonial mansion of The Grange, the home of Goldwin Smith. On the carriage-way of the Grange estate, some threescore years ago, tradition hath it that the owner's horses were attacked by bears as they were being driven up to the doorway. Continuing along King St. to the Central Prison, one may turn S. again to the water and visit the old and new forts, parade-ground, and well-kept exhibition-grounds with their Crystal Palace. Still moving W., we pass through Parkdale, where stand the Home for Incurables and the Mercer Reformatory; and we end our wanderings in this direction among the picnic-grounds of High Park on the Humber.

If we return by way of Queen St., we pass the Provincial Lunatic Asylum and the graceful buildings of **Trinity University** in their ample and park-like grounds. Trinity is a Church of England institution, and was founded by the indomitable Bishop Strachan when old King's College of Upper Canada was secularized and became the University of Toronto.

On Queen St., between Yonge and College Ave., is **Osgoode Hall**, the seat of the Superior Courts of the Province, of the Law Society, and the Law School. The building is named after the first Chief-Justice of Upper Canada, and cost $300,000. The exterior has an air of solid magnificence. The interior is of unusual beauty, and contains a library of 30,000 volumes. A little farther along Queen St., at the head of Bay St., is the magnificent pile of the new **Civic Buildings** and **Law Courts,** which have been in progress for the past seven years, and which will cost when complete upward of $2,000,000. Immediately north of Osgoode Hall are the fine **Armouries** which are the headquarters of the local regiments of the militia. This is the largest **Armoury** in America, and 2,500 men have been formed up in parade within its walls.

College Ave. is a broad boulevard running N. from Queen St. to **Queen's Park**, Toronto's chief pleasure-ground. At the head of it is a fine statue of Sir John Macdonald in bronze. Turning to the left the carriage-way skirts the edge of a ravine and passes the Volunteers' Monument, erected to the memory of Canadians who fell in the Fenian raid of 1866. Opposite stands the bronze statue of the Hon. George Brown, one of the chief statesmen of Canada, and founder of the Toronto Globe. This statue is a fine piece of sculpture, and was done by Burch, of London. Queen's Park is a portion of the estate of **Toronto**

University, and was handed over to the city on a perpetual lease. The university grounds and buildings adjoin the park on the W. The buildings were destroyed by fire a few years ago, but the loss was one that was soon repaired. It is not too much to say that the main building is the finest piece of college architecture in the New World. In design it belongs to the Norman period, and the square central tower was of peculiarly noble and satisfying proportions. The deep carved porch is famous for its solidity and richness. The buildings, completely restored, are fully equal in all respects to the original buildings. Across the lawn stands the Observatory, the home of the meteorological department of the Dominion, commonly known as "Old Probabilities." Not far from the University are the new **Government buildings,** a very massive and handsome block, of stone, containing the Legislative chamber and the Departmental offices. Alongside of the Observatory stands a distressingly crude structure of red brick, the eyesore of the lovely neighborhood. This is the School of Technology. At the head of the park is a fine structure of brown Credit Valley stone, faced with red brick. This is McMaster Hall, of **McMaster University**, and was presented to the Baptist denomination by the late Senator McMaster. A little W. of McMaster Hall stands the graystone pile of Knox College, belonging to the Presbyterian Church; and in the immediate neighborhood stands Victoria University, of the Methodist Church.

Though the growth of Toronto is chiefly toward the west and north, the handsomest residences are probably east of Yonge, on Jarvis and Sherbourne Sts., and on various cross-streets connecting them. On the corner of Gerard and Sherbourne are the **Horticultural Gardens,** which were opened by the Prince of Wales in 1860. They occupy a square of 10 acres, and were presented to the city by the Hon. George Allan. On the west side of the gardens stand the Pavilion and the Conservatories. The Pavilion has seating accommodation for 3,000 people. At a short distance west stands the **Massey Music Hall,** a gift to the city by the late Hart A. Massey. It will seat 4,000 people. A short distance down Church St. is the great **Metropolitan Church** of the Methodists. Its organ is the largest in Canada and one of the finest in the world, containing as it does 3,315 pipes and 53 stops. The famous organ of Strasburg Cathedral has 46, and that of Westminster Abbey 32. Near the Metropolitan Church stands **St. Michael's Cathedral**, the seat of the Roman Catholic Archbishop. On Church St. also is the **Normal School**, with the offices of the Department of Education. The buildings occupy the center of an open square, covering 7 or 8 acres. The gardens are attractive and of special interest to the student. The Normal School contains a fine gallery of paintings and statues, where the visitor will find many valuable originals and reproductions of most of the masterpieces of ancient art. Entrance to the art galleries of the Normal School is free on weekdays from 9 A. M. to 5 P. M. Tourists who are interested in art will do well to visit the exhibition-rooms of the Ontario Society of Artists, 14 King St., West. Whatever they may be interested in, they will do well to visit the lovely and aristocratic suburb of Rosedale; and they will do well to pay this visit at a time when Canada's national game is being played at the Rosedale Lacrosse Grounds. Lacrosse is a game lacking most of the defects of foot-ball, but possessing all the pre-eminent merits of that most manly sport. Toronto has produced some of the most skillful Lacrosse players of Canada—that is to say, of the world; and Toronto boys, one might almost say, are born with a "stick" in their hands. The Toronto Base-ball Grounds are situated on Kingston Road.

The Muskoka District.

The best side-trip to be taken from Toronto is that to the lake country of Muskoka lying N. of Toronto, between Georgian Bay and the Ottawa River. Fares are as follows: Toronto to Beaumaris and return, $5.55; Pt. Cockburn and return, $7.05; Rosseau and return, $6.55; Magnetawan and return, $8.20; Burk's Falls and return, $6.95. A quarter of a century ago this region was a total wilderness; but now its tangle of lakes and streams is dotted with villages and summer hotels. The G. T. R. traverses it as far N. as Lake Nipissing, and steamboats ply upon its principal waters. The innumerable lakes are of all sizes, from 40 miles in length down to as many rods. All are clear, deep, and cool, and swarm with brook trout, lake trout, black bass, and perch; while the covers and reed beds abound with feathered game, and deer are fairly numerous. In some of these northern waters may be taken that fish of many *aliases*, the "Tiger of the Lakes," the gigantic maskinonge, or muscalonge. The Muskoka district proper lies to the N. of the high divide at Gravenhurst, and comprises a territory about the size of Belgium. Within this area lie something over 1,000 lakes. The district south of Gravenhurst is long settled, but contains some excellent fishing and shooting grounds, about the lovely waters of Lakes Simcoe, Sparrow, and Couchiching.

Taking the Grand Trunk Railway, we skirt the city to the W. and turn N. to the water-shed, where streams diverge toward Lake Huron. Emerging from the hills the train winds through the pleasant vale of Aurora, with its sweet old-country landscapes. Passing the little country town of Newmarket, we catch a glimpse of the infant stream of Holland River, which was of old the path of Indians and *voyageurs* who had just made the portage from Toronto. By Holland River also came the war parties of the Iroquois to slaughter the Hurons on Lake Simcoe and Georgian Bay. The drowsy village of **Holland Landing** was once a busy mart, when, before the days of railroading, all the traffic of the northern settlements passed in heavy wagons through its streets. In 1825 Sir John Franklin called at Holland Landing on his first expedition overland to the north pole. On the village green may be seen a huge anchor, which was brought from the Royal Dockyards in England, and hauled hither from the lake by 16 yoke of oxen. It was destined for the Provincial Navy-Yard at Penetang, where a fleet was being built for warfare on the lakes. The great anchor was stopped in the middle of its journey by the declaration of peace between England and the United States.

At Bradford, a little farther down the river, there is good trolling for maskinonge, and there are some fine snipe covers in the neighborhood. At Lefroy we get the first glimpse of **Lake Simcoe**, a splendid sheet of water, 30 miles long by 16 broad; and a little beyond is Allandale Junction, whence three lines radiate northward—the Muskoka Branch to Muskoka and Lake Nipissing, the Penetang Branch, and the Collingwood Branch. Just N. of Allandale Junction lies the county town of **Barrie**, set picturesquely on the hillside sloping down to the lake. Barrie (population, about 6,000; hotel, Queen's, $2) is a charming summer resort, with good fishing streams in the neighborhood and innumerable boats and yachts. Nine miles down Kempenfeldt Bay is a great summer hotel at Big Bay Point. Joined to Lake Simcoe by a channel called the Narrows lies the breezy water of **Lake Couchiching**, which, being interpreted, is the "Lake of Many Winds." At the head of the lake is the pretty town of **Orillia** (hotels, Orillia House and Russell House, $1.50), with its beautiful pleasure-grounds of Couchiching Park. This is the highest region in Ontario, being 750 ft. above Toronto. The air here is very clear and pure, and the waters of the lake are excellently stocked with black bass, pickerel, and salmon-trout. At Rama, on this lake, is a settlement of Ojibway Indians, the last remnants of the once powerful tribe that peopled the shores of Lakes Simcoe and Couchiching to the number of at least 25,000. At Orillia the tourist may, if he prefers, take the steamer 14 miles down the lake, and rejoin the train at Washago. Here begins the splendid fishing stream of the **Severn**, which runs through deer, duck, and grouse grounds, through wild rapids, and over Severn Falls, and drains the whole Simcoe region into Georgian Bay. A short distance below Washago the Severn widens out into Sparrow Lake, famous for its maskinonge and black bass, and its duck and grouse shooting. A good canoe trip, for which Indians and canoes may be hired at Rama, is that from Couchiching to Gravenhurst, with short portages, through Beaver, Legs, and Pine Lakes. A more exciting trip, through some sharp and intricate rapids, is down the Severn River to its outlet. Guide and canoe may be obtained at Rama or Orillia, at a cost of about $2 a day.

Crossing the river by a lofty bridge, the railroad forsakes the pale limestone formations of the Simcoe region and enters a land of red granite. Hither and thither amid the high and glistening bluffs of the "divide" winds the train, till at last through **Granite Notch** it emerges upon the highlands of Muskoka. At the southernmost extremity of Lake Muskoka, the largest of the series, stands the busy town of **Gravenhurst**, 112 miles from Toronto. Gravenhurst is very picturesquely situated on the high shores of an inlet. It has a population of about 2,000, and good hotels, the Albion, Windsor, and Grand Central, at $1 to $2. From this point, which may be regarded as the gateway of the Muskoka region, the tourist may continue N. by rail *via* Bracebridge, the Muskoka River, Huntsville, where connection is made with steamers for the Lake of Bays district, including Mary, Fairy, and Vernon Lake; to North Bay and the Canadian Pacific R. R. at Lake Nipissing; or he may take the steamers of the Muskoka Navigation Co., through Lakes Muskoka, Rosseau, and Joseph, and the Muskosh River. A side excursion up the S. branch of the Muskoka River to the Lake of Bays will enable the tourist to visit a lake which rejoices in the title of Kahweambotewagamog.

From Muskoka wharf the steamers go to Bala, Bracebridge, Beaumaris, Port Carling, Windermere, Rosseau, Rosseau Falls, Port Sandfield, Craigielea, Port Cockburn, Juddhaven, and several other villages, all of which are full of attraction for sportsman and tourist. One of the loveliest of these is **Beaumaris**, which has a large and excellent hotel situated on Tondern Island. Immediately opposite is a group of small islands called the "Kettles," where may be found the best bass fishing and fine trolling for salmon-trout. In the neighborhood of Brace-bridge, the chief town of the Muskoka district, are the lovely cataracts known as High Falls and the Great South Falls. The most central town on the lakes is Port Carling, where all the steamboat routes converge, and where Lakes Muskoka and Rosseau are connected by locks.

Lake Rosseau has an extreme length of 14 miles, and presents a great variety of charming landscape. In its southern portion it is set thick with the loveliest of islands. As many of these islands are inhabited, and the dwellers thereon may be said to spend the most of their time in boats, that section of the lake carries the appellation of Venetia. Into the bay near Port Rosseau flows the mystic and incom-parable **Shadow River**, on whose flawless surface one floats as if suspended midway between two lovely worlds of summer foliage. On a small stream stealing into Shadow River resounds the clear tinkling of the Bridal-Veil Falls. A conspicuous landmark on Lake Rosseau is the headland of Eagle's Nest. The third of the series of the Muskoka Lakes, Lake Joseph, was till very lately almost unknown. Now it is coming into repute as possessing a bolder beauty than its fellows. Most tourists will probably decide that the difference is less of degree than of kind, for it would be hard to say which of the three waters is the fairest. An advantage afforded by all alike is that the tourist here may "rough it" charmingly in tent and canoe, or, if he so prefer, enjoy all the conveniences of civilized life in well-kept but unostentatious inns. The round trip, combining both the Muskoka Lakes District and the Georgian Bay, can be made in both directions, either *via* the Grand Trunk to Muskoka Wharf Station and from there by steamer through Muskoka Lake to Port Cockburn, at the head of Lake Joseph, or to Rosseau, at the head of Lake Rosseau, and thence by stage line to Maple Lake Station, and rail from there to Parry Sound, where steamer is taken for the trip through the 30,000 islands of the Georgian Bay to Midland or Penetang, connection being made at these points with the Grand Trunk Railway for Toronto and all points east and west; or, taking steamer at Midland and Penetang, the tourist can travel in the opposite direction and proceed *via* Parry Sound, Maple Lake Station, and Port Cockburn or Rosseau to the Muskoka Lakes.

The traveler who wishes to visit the **Magnetawan** waters and Parry Sound will follow the railroad north to Burks Falls and there

3

take the steamer Wenona down the Magnetawan through Cecebre, Ahmic, and Wahwaskesh Lakes to Byng Inlet at the mouth, and thence down the coast of Georgian Bay through Parry Sound and the Archipelago to historic **Penetang**, where under the waters of the harbor lie the remains of four British gunboats. Here is one of the finest summer resorts and hotels in Canada—"*The Penetanguishene.*" The first settlement of the Jesuits in Ontario was established in 1634 at Penetang, then called Ihonatiria, and in commemoration of this the Jesuits have built there one of the finest ecclesiastical structures on the continent. In the almost virgin waters of the Magnetawan, which one traverses on this trip, are plenty of trout, and on their banks many kinds of game.

Between Parry Sound and the mouth of Moon River lie the desert waters of Crane and Blackstone Lakes, favorite haunts of the maskinonge. The capture of this splendid fish in these lakes is thus described by a writer in the Toledo Post :

" The shores of Crane and Blackstone Lakes are capital specimens of the primitive wilderness, and long may they so continue ! The few who have visited their teeming waters have mostly been genuine fishermen who are happiest when far away from conventionalism and habitations. But one clearing broke the majestic sweep of the grand old forests, within the sheltered bays the loons laughed undisturbed, and the wild birds splashed in the marshy edges or upon the sandy shores with none to molest or make them afraid.

" We were out for maskinonge, and took no account of either black bass or pickerel. It seems strange to talk of shaking off black bass and making disrespectful remarks about these gamy gentry when they insisted in taking the hook, but they were so plenty as to be really troublesome.

" When an angler goes forth to catch the maskinonge it is necessary to be careful lest the maskinonge should catch him. The native method of taking the maskinonge in the primeval waters of Canada is by a small clothes-line, hauled in by main strength when the fish bites ; but we proposed to troll, as should an angler, with the rod. Ours were split bamboo rods 9½ ft. long, quadruplex reel, and braided linen line, 2 ft. of medium-sized copper wire, a No. 4 spoon with double hooks, and finally a good gaff.

" Our guide, as we started over to Crane Lake the first morning, indulged in sundry smiles and remarked that we should break our rods, so that, although placid in outward mien, I felt inwardly a little nervous ; but I didn't mean to back down until compelled.

" Swinging around a little point, with some 20 yards of line astern, before fishing a great while I felt a sudden movement at the spoon that was more like a crunch than a bite. It took only a second to give the rod a turn that fixed the hooks, and another second to discover that I had hung something. Scarcely had I tightened the line when the fish started. I do not know that I wanted to stop him, but I felt the line slip rapidly from the reel as though attached to a submarine torpedo. The first run was a long one, but the line was longer, and the fish stopped before the reel was bare. This was my opportunity, and I had the boatman swing his craft across the course, and, reeling in the slack line, I turned his head toward the deeper water. Forty-five minutes of as pretty a fight as one could wish to see left my new acquaintance alongside the boat, and before he recovered his surprise the gaff was in his gills and the boatman lifted him on board.

"He weighed 14 pounds on the steelyards, and was my heaviest fish. There were other encounters of a similar character, but none quite so protracted."

Tourists for the upper lakes take the train at 1.10 P. M. on Tuesdays, Thursdays, and Saturdays, and Thursdays for Owen Sound during the tourist season, and at 7.30 Saturday mornings for Windsor (during July and August), where one of the C. P. R.'s Clyde-built steamers awaits the train before starting for Sault Ste. Marie, and Fort William, at the head of Lake Superior. Here connection is made with the transcontinental train going to or coming from the Pacific, and here sportsmen bound for the Nepigon and the other famous trout-streams north of Lake Superior disembark. All these routes are fully described in The Canadian Guide-Book, Part II, Western Canada.

From Toronto eastward.

From Toronto to Ottawa and Montreal one has a liberal choice of routes. One may take the C. P. R., by way of Peterboro and Smith's Falls to Ottawa, and thence to Montreal (fare, $10). This is the direct route between Montreal by way of Ottawa. It runs through a newer country than that traversed by the Grand Trunk R., which, however, is the most direct route between Toronto and Montreal, and which skirts the lake and the St. Lawrence all the way to Montreal (fare, $10). Or a tourist may travel by the C. P. R. to Tweed, and there take the Bay of Quinté road to Kingston, where connection is made with the Richelieu Steamship Company's boats, or at Sharbot Lake, on the C. P. R., passengers for Kingston take the Kingston and Pembroke Railway, running direct to Kingston (see page 41). The route we would recommend, however, is that by water, by the boats of the Ontario and Richelieu Navigation Company, which traverse almost the whole length of Lake Ontario, the fairy landscapes of the Thousand Islands, and the famed St. Lawrence rapids (fare, $10, meals and berths extra). Arrived at Montreal the tourist may go to Ottawa by either of the railroads which connect the cities, the Canadian Pacific and the Canada Atlantic, and return by boat down the Ottawa River.

The tourist who elects to go to Ottawa by the C. P. R. will travel by one of the best-equipped and most reliable railroads in the world. He takes the train at the Union Station. The first town of importance after leaving Toronto is **Peterboro** on the Otonabee River, a thriving city of about 10,000 inhabitants. This is the birthplace of the famous "Peterboro" or "Rice Lake" canoe; and the tourist who loves fishing and canoeing will do well to linger at this point. The shores of Rice Lake have been made illustrious by the residence of three of those Strick-lands whose names are so well known in the world of letters—Colonel Strickland, and his sisters, Mrs. Moodie and Mrs. Traill. The country about is a tangle of lakes and water-ways, a fisherman's paradise, and it all lies at the feet of the skillful canoeist. Railway lines center at Peter-boro from half a dozen directions, and the Otonabee affords an immense water-power which is utilized by many mills and factories. Among the manufactures of the city are lumber, flour, cloth, agricultural implements, machinery and engines, pottery, and leather. The river is spanned by six bridges, and the public buildings are numerous and handsome. The best hotels are the Oriental, Snowdon House, and Grand Central.

For 100 miles, between Peterboro and Perth, the road runs through a broken country rich in iron, phosphate, asbestos, and other valuable minerals. At the town of Tweed we cross the Moira River, whose waters are freighted with logs from the lumber regions. At **Sharbot Lake**, a famous resort for sportsmen, the Kingston and Pembroke R. R. is crossed. Perth, with a population of 4,000, is a prosperous milling town, with rich quarries of building-stone and phosphates in the vicin-ity. Twelve miles beyond Perth is Smith's Falls on the Rideau River, a junction town with a population of 4,500. Here the main line between Toronto and Montreal is crossed by the line of the Ottawa and Brock-ville division, whose cars we take at this point. Thirteen miles farther on, at Carleton Junction, we first strike the main transcontinental line of the C. P. R. From Carleton Junction to Ottawa is a distance of 28 miles. Before entering the city the road follows the S. bank of the mighty **Ottawa River**, and the traveler may look down from the car windows upon vast stretches of logs which, enchained in the long cir-cuits of the "booms," almost hide the water.

The Grand Trunk Ry. between Toronto and Montreal is set thick with towns and cities from start to finish, and gives one a good idea of the general prosperity of Canada. About 23 miles from Toronto the road skirts a lovely landlocked mere, on which of old stood a village of the Senecas. The entrance to this unruffled water was so concealed by a growth of flags and rushes that none knew of its existence save the dwellers on its banks, who called their village by the name of Gandatsetiagon. Here now stands the town of Pickering, the sheltered mere has become Pickering Harbor, and the reed-grown entrance has been widened and deepened to admit the traffic of the lake. In the neighborhood of Pickering are some fair pike and black-bass waters. Just beyond Pickering is Whitby, the seat of the Ontario Ladies' College, whence a branch line runs north, past the town of Lindsay, to its terminus at Haliburton. Haliburton stands in the midst of an admirable hunting and fishing region. The lakes and streams around the town are well stocked with brook trout and salmon trout, which take the fly freely from the middle of May to the end of June. Within easy reach of Haliburton the hunter will find deer, bear, moose, and partridge fairly abundant, and guides with dogs may be hired in the neighborhood.

About 4 miles east of Whitby is the busy manufacturing town of Oshawa, with good fall duck-shooting in the neighborhood. Here, in old days, was the beginning of the portage from Ontario to Scugog Lake; and the name *Oshawa* simply means the carrying-place.

"The map of Lake Ontario has, within historic memory, been overwritten with five series of names and settlements—those of the Huron-Algonquin era, those of the Iroquois domination, those of the French occupation, those of the Mississaga or Ojibway conquest, and those of the English occupation. Of the Huron-Algonquin period but slight trace survives on Lake Ontario beyond the name of the lake itself. After alternate *fanfares* and *disgrâces* it had been rechristened Lake St. Louis and Lake of the Iroquois, Frontenac's Lake and Lake Cataraqui; but the grand old lake went back to the simplicity—the majestic simplicity—of its ancient name. Even in Charlevoix's day—a hundred and sixty years ago—the undisputed name was once more Ontario, 'the Great Lake.'"

Of the Iroquois domination also but few traces remain—a few sonorous names like Niagara and Toronto. The race of athletes who lorded it over half the continent, whose alliance was eagerly courted by France and England, were, after all, unable to maintain their foothold against the despised Ojibways. Of these, the Mississagas became specially numerous and aggressive, so that their *totem*, the crane, was a familiar hieroglyph on our forest trees from the beginning of the last century. One of the oldest of Greek legends relates the war of the cranes and pygmies. Though the foes of our northern cranes were not pygmies but giants, they possessed not the craft of the little ancients who lived by the ocean-shore. The Mississagas so multiplied in their northern nests that presently, by mere numbers, they overwhelmed the Iroquois. Most desperate fighting there was, and the battle-fields were still clearly traceable when English pioneers first broke ground.

The Mississagas, though not endowed with either the Mohawk verve or intellect, were no more destitute of poetry than of valor. Take the names of some of their chiefs. One chief's name signified "He who makes footsteps in the sky"; another was Wawanosh, "He who ambles the waters." The Rev. Peter Jones was, through his mother, descended from a famous line of poetic warriors; his grandfather was Waubuno, "The Morning Light." On occasion, the Mississaga could come down to prose. Scugog describes the clay bottom and submerged banks of that lake, which, taking a steamer at Port Perry, we traverse on our summer excursion to Lindsay and Sturgeon Lake. Chemong aptly names the lake whose tide of silt sometimes even retards our canoe when we are fishing or fowling. Omemee, "the wild pigeon," has given its name not only to Pigeon Lake and its chief affluent, but to the town where Pigeon Creek lingers on its course to the lake.

"On Rice Lake, the chief Indian settlement is Hiawatha, named after the Hercules of Ojibway mythology, whom the American poet has immortalized in his melodious trochaics. At Hiawatha and on Scugog Island you may still find, in the ordinary language of the Ojibway, fragments of fine imagery and picture-talk, often in the very words which Longfellow has so happily woven into his poem. And the scenery of this Trent Valley reproduces that of the Vale of Tawasentha. Here are 'the wild rice of the river' and 'the Indian village' and 'the groves of singing pine-trees—ever sighing, ever singing.' At Fénelon Falls we have the 'Laughing Water,' and not far below is Sturgeon Lake, the realm of the 'King of Fishes.' Sturgeon of portentous size are yet met with, though falling somewhat short of the comprehensive fish sung by Longfellow, which swallowed Hiawatha, canoe and all!

"Among these forests, too, dwelt once Meggissogwon, that 'mightiest of magicians,' who, 'guarded by the black pitch-water, sends the fever from the marshes.' Our fathers and grandfathers knew this magician only too well; felt him, far off, and shook at his coming.

They fought him, not like Hiawatha with jasper-headed arrows, but with the woodman's axe. Like the Indian hero, our pioneer was often 'wounded, weary, and desponding, with his mittens torn and tattered.' "—*Picturesque Canada.*

Leaving Oshawa, we pass through Bowmanville, Newcastle, Newtonville, and reach the important town of **Port Hope** (chief hotels, *St. Lawrence Hall*, $1.50 to $2; and *Queen's*, $1.50), picturesquely situated in a deep ravine, and busy with a large lake traffic. There are good hotels at this point, and within easy distance are the waters of Rice Lake, which swarm with maskinonge, black bass, and green bass. On Rice Lake the best month for maskinonge is June; for bass, from July to September. Seven miles beyond Port Hope is the university town of Cobourg, formerly the seat of **Victoria College**, which is now amalgamated with Toronto University. Fortunately for Cobourg, it is something more than a university town. Cobourg must rely henceforth entirely on her manufactures and her trade, her car-works and her breweries. The next important point after leaving Cobourg is Trenton, on the river Trent. Here the Grand Trunk is crossed by the lines of the Central Ontario, which runs down the beautiful peninsula of Prince Edward County to Picton. The Trent River is the outlet of Rice Lake, and empties into the Bay of Quinté at its head.

Beyond Trenton lies the city of **Belleville**, beautiful in its surroundings and in its handsome and shaded streets. Belleville has a population of about 12,000, and is full of activity and enterprise. Its chief hotels are the *Quinté*, $2; *Anglo-American*, $1.50; and *Queen's Hotel*, $1.50. It has fine public buildings, and is the seat of Alexandra College and of the Provincial Institution for Deaf-Mutes. The city was named in honor of Arabella, wife of Governor Gore. It stands on the shores of the exquisite Bay of Quinté, whose waters teem with all delights for the fisherman, and whose changeful and delicious landscapes will long delay the traveler.

The best way to visit Picton, at the extremity of Prince Edward Peninsula is by boat from Belleville down along the Quinté shores. This is a region of glamour and romance, away from the beaten paths of trade. It is a land of waving barley-fields, and of merry picnic parties. In the heart of the peninsula is the lovely and romantic Lake of the Mountain, which occupies the highest point on the peninsula, and is kept ever full to the brim, with no visible sources of supply. Its surface is on a level with that of far-off Lake Erie, a circumstance which has given rise to many conjectures of a mysterious communication between them. Over the changing shores and headlands hang memories of Huron and Jesuit, Iroquois and Sulpician, Mississaga and loyalist pioneer. The Belleville steamer touches at the stirring port of Deseronto, where the mainland thrusts itself forth into the bay. Deseronto is a center of the flour and lumber trade, and in its saw-mills the logs of the Trent, Moira, and Napanee Rivers are cut up into planks and boards and laths and shingles to be consumed across the border. The town is named after a famous Mohawk chief of the last century, a cousin of the great Brant, and the signification of the title is "Thunder and Lightning." Leaving Deseronto the steamer enters the magnificent expanse of placid water known as the Long Reach. At the southern extremity of the Reach the high shores draw together to form Picton Bay, at the head of which the town of Picton (chief hotel, the *Royal*, $1.50 to $2) beautifully terminates the vista. On the lakeward side of the peninsula is an interesting phenomenon known as the "**Sandbanks**." The strange scene is thus described in *Picturesque Canada:* "Lofty ridges of sand, appearing from a distance as white as snow, were originally in some obscure way thrown up at the water's edge; but, by a kind of glacier movement, which proceeds only in the winter, they have now withdrawn from the shore and are encroaching on the adjacent farms at the rate of about 150 feet a year. The active agent in the movement appears to be the drifting snow which entangles the sand and carries it forward. On the hottest day snow may be found a short distance down, as we proved by repeated trials at various points of the banks. Historically, too, Big Sandy Bay is most interesting. It was on the cove within, now called West Lake, that in 1668 the Kenté Mission was established."

About 22 miles E. of Belleville, on the Grand Trunk, is the ancient town of Napanee. The name is derived from the Mississaga word *Nau-pau-nay*, which signifies "flour." As bread-stuffs are the staple of Napanee's trade, the name is highly appropriate. The town is situated on a strange river, whose deep and somber waters are swayed by a mysterious tide every two hours. This tide represents a variation of 16 inches in mean level, and sometimes attains a fluctuation of 30 inches.

Kingston.

Population, 25,000. The chief hotels of Kingston are *The Hotel Frontenac*, $2 and $3; *British-American*, $2 and $3; *City Hotel*, $1.50

and \$2; and *Anglo-American.* Livery charges, \$2.50 a day for single horse and carriage. Hacks are to be hired at usual rates. The only theatres are the public halls.

The next town of importance after leaving Napanee is **Kingston**, which is known as the "Limestone City," standing guard at the foot of the lake where the channel of the St. Lawrence begins to define itself. This gray and enduring little city, with its 25,000 inhabitants, has a beautiful and commanding situation, and its spacious harbor is fenced by islands from the storms of Lake Ontario.

Where the olive waters of the Cataraqui flow into the blue expanse of the bay came Frontenac, greatest of the Governors of New France, to establish a fort and trading post on what he considered "one of the most beautiful and agreeable harbors in the world." Frontenac pitched his tents where now stand the *Tête du Pont* Barracks, commanding the mouth of the Cataraqui. This was in July of 1673. The command of the fort, which speedily rose under the energetic directions of Frontenac, was assigned to the illustrious Robert Cavalier de la Salle. The settlement grew speedily in wealth and importance, till La Salle departed to discover the route to the Gulf of Mexico, and die by the hands of a traitor in Texas. Under the next Governor, M. de Denonville, Fort Frontenac was the scene of an act of treachery on the part of the French toward the Indians which brought down terrible vengeance upon New France. A number of Iroquois chiefs, under pretext of a conference, were enticed into the fort, where they were loaded with chains and then sent to France to wear out their lives in the galleys. The retort of the Iroquois was the harrying of the French settlement, the capture and destruction of Fort Frontenac, and the midnight massacre of Lachine. When the weakness and treachery of De Denonville had brought New France to these straits, Frontenac came back and saved the colony, and rebuilt his favorite fort; and fifty years of peace began their brooding over the mouth of the Cataraqui. The fort was captured by Colonel Bradstreet in 1758. Thereafter the place fell into forgetfulness, from which it did not emerge till the end of the Revolutionary War, when a party of United Empire Loyalists chose the fair site for a settlement, and in their zeal Cataraqui became Kingstown, afterward shortened to Kingston. When the War of 1812 broke out, Kingston came into prominence as the strongest Canadian post on the lake, the chief rival to the American stronghold of Sackett's Harbor. Fort Henry was begun, and a for-

midable battle-ship, the St. Lawrence, was built in the Kingston Dockyard. So hard was it for the mother-country to realize that any good
thing could come out of a colony, that this ship was built, at a cost
of £500,000, with timbers sent out from England for the purpose.
At this period the town was surrounded by a chain of block-houses
connected by a picket stockade. These block-houses subsequently
were supplanted by stone batteries and martello towers, which, however ineffective they might be against modern artillery, nevertheless
add greatly to the martial air of Kingston as seen from the water.
When Upper Canada was erected into a province, Governor Simcoe
was sworn into office at Kingston, and from this point were issued
writs for the convening of the first Provincial Parliament, which met,
however, as has been already stated, at Niagara. When Upper and
Lower Canada were united in 1840, Kingston was made the seat of
government, and the Legislature occupied the building now employed
as the City Hospital. Only for four years, however, was Kingston suffered to enjoy this proud distinction; and in 1844 the departure of the
Government and its officials left the "Limestone City" in a slough of
commercial and social despond.

Now, however, Kingston has entered anew upon an era of prosperity. She is the outlet for the traffic of the Rideau Canal, and, which
is vastly more important, for that of the Kingston and Pembroke R. R.,
which opens up a district of immense mineral wealth. She has become
a great educational center. Here is Queen's University, which has become, under Principal George M. Grant, one of the most successful and
well-conducted institutions of learning in Canada. Here also is the
Royal Military College, the West Point of Canada, where the cadets
get a training the efficiency of which is well recognized in sister colonies
and in the mother-country. Kingston is also the seat of the Royal
College of Physicians and Surgeons, and of the Women's Medical
College, both of which are affiliated with Queen's University. The
buildings of "Queen's" are the chief architectural ornament of Kingston. The individuality of Kingston is thus effectively described by a
distinguished Canadian writer:

"Still Kingston contains a military look, not unpleasing to the tourist's eye. There is the fort crowning the glacis. Full in front, a
round tower covers the landing. At its base, a semicircular bastion
pierced for artillery is ready to sweep the water. The embrasures of
the fort look askance at the foundries and the enginery on the opposite

side of the harbor. The cannon confronts the locomotive; and, fit emblem of our time, a solitary warder guards the decaying fort, while in the locomotive-shops between 400 and 500 skilled workmen are employed. The tower, with its conical red cap and circling wall of compact ball-proof masonry, looks well. It would have scared the Iroquois. It could have defied the raiders of 1812. Against modern artillery it is as good as an *arquebuse.* Hard by is the Military College, with its 100 or 120 red-coated, white-helmeted cadets. Where the olive-green of Cataraqui Creek blends with the blue of the bay, still stand the old naval barracks, where Tom Bowling and Ned Bunting were wont to toast 'sweethearts and wives.' A little up the creek is Barriefield Common, once gay with the pomp and circumstance of glorious war, but now seldom marched over by anything more militant than the villagers' geese. From the common a causeway, nearly half a mile long, extends across the creek to the *Tête du Pont* Barracks, the headquarters alternately of the very efficient A and B Batteries. Thanks to the gentlemen cadets and battery-men, the streets of Kingston still have a sprinkling of red, white, and blue."

Six miles up the placid windings of the Cataraqui stream we enter a deep gorge, whose rocky banks, almost overhanging, are richly clothed with vines. Here we meet the foamy rush of a little cascade; and here is the entrance to the **Rideau Canal**, whose sedgy waters, the haunt of innumerable mallard and teal, afford the canoeist an enchanting path through the Rideau Lakes to Ottawa. On Long Island, in one of these lakes, is erected a fine building called the *Anglers' Club House.*

The tourist who is not in an inordinate hurry to reach Montreal will take the steamer at Kingston if he has come thus far by rail; for the river trip between Kingston and the commercial metropolis of Canada is one of the most attractive on the continent. As the steamer rounds Fort Hill, and passes Cedar Island, we find ourselves fairly in the channel of the St. Lawrence, at this point about 14 miles in width. If one wishes to "do" the Thousand Islands thoroughly, it is best to stop off at the village of Gananoque, around whose shores the islands appear to swarm. The name Gananoque signifies "rocks in deep water." The town stands on a small river of the same name, is well supplied with hotels, and has good maskinonge and black-bass fishing in its neighborhood.

The Thousand Islands.

The **Thousand Islands** are really many more than a thousand in number, there being about 1,800 of them large and small, in a stretch of about 40 miles. The Indians call the region Manatoana—"the Gar-

den of the Great Spirit." The islands are all of that formation which
the geologists call gray gneiss. Through the innumerable labyrinths
that divide them the current of the great river flows with varying
rapidity. In some of the channels it is a foaming torrent, while in
others the gently-moving tide is as smooth as a summer pool. The
islands present the greatest variety of effect. Some are high and
precipitous, others barely lift their heads above the lily-pads that encircle them. Some are 'as naked as if their granite frames had just come
from the primeval fires; others are topped with pine and fir, or softly
rounded with the foliage of vines and shrubbery. Some are dotted
with cottages, or the tents of camping parties. Several of the islets
are built up with fantastic structures, pagodas, and fairy bridges, till
they look as if they had just stepped off an old blue " willow-pattern "
plate. Hither and thither among them dart the trim craft of the
canoeists, for here it is they most do congregate; and in many a
sluggish eddy or sheltered bay may be seen the punt of him that lies
in wait for maskinonge.

As might be expected, the scenery of the Thousand Islands is
touched with the charm of many an old romance. They inspired the
song of Tom Moore, and one of them is the scene of Cooper's story,
The Pathfinder. Among their mazes a British ship, the Sir Robert
Peel, was burned in 1838 by a band of American outlaws under the
leadership of one "Bill Johnson," who aspired to establish a Canadian
Republic. This romantic desperado was saved from the indignant
clutches of the law by a picturesque and dauntless girl, his daughter
Kate, who rowed him from one hiding-place to another as each in succession grew too hot for him.

Gananoque is situated in the heart of the Thousand Islands, and
is one of the best points from which to make the journey through this
scenic paradise. Gananoque also boasts of a first-class hostelry, recently built and called the " Gananoque Inn," and which is one of the
finest hotels on the St. Lawrence River. The commodious passenger
steamers running on the Thousand Islands route call daily at the Inn
wharf. Tourists can stop over and spend a few days at this point with
much profit, and the fishing in the locality is within a stone's throw of
the hotel.

The steamer leaves Gananoque at six in the morning for the trip
through the Thousand Islands, and passengers in the sleeping-car
arriving at this point by the Grand Trunk Railway from the west are

In the Thousand Isles.

permitted to remain in the car until a few minutes before the departure of the steamer.

Stave Island, in close contiguity to Gananoque, has been chosen several times as the camping ground of the American Canoe Association, and has been selected for the 1899 meet. This locality is decided upon owing to the freedom from swift currents, its health-giving pine woods and forests, and its suitable shores and bathing beaches. It is an unequaled spot for camps, boating, and canoeing.

Leaving the Thousand Islands we pass Morristown and Ogdensburg, while on the opposite shore are Brockville and Prescott, where connections are made for Ottawa, Montreal, and the east and south.

On one of the largest of the islands, known as Wells's Island, is the swarming summer resort of the **Thousand Island Park,** with its post-office, public buildings, and stores, and its water-side street of boat-houses. This is the famous camp-meeting ground of the Methodists, and here religion and relaxation are most alluringly combined. At the lower end of the island is the somewhat quieter resort of Westminster Park, also under religious control; and directly opposite the island, on the American mainland, and not under religious control, is **Alexandria Bay,** the "Saratoga of the St. Lawrence." Hence, it may be seen that the Thousand Islands stand in little need of the romance of old, for the makers of romance are among them the summer long, and turn out their enchanting though transitory product in an abundance that beggars reckoning. On a promontory, near the landing at Alexandria Bay, stands the villa known as Bonnie Castle, the residence of the late Dr. J. G. Holland.

After the steamer emerges from the clustering isles it swings up to the wharves of **Brockville,** the Thousand Island City. Brockville is the river terminus of the Ottawa and Brockville branch of the C. P. R. This beautiful little city, whose gilded towers and spires glitter fairly above the billows of foliage that screen its comely thoroughfares, was named after the hero of Queenston Heights. Brockville is supplied with excellent hotels, such as the *St. Lawrence Hall, Revere House,* and *Central Hotel.* In the river, at this point, and in the neighboring lakes of Charleston and Ridout, there is good fishing for black bass, salmon trout, pickerel, pike, and maskinonge; and duck, plover, woodcock, snipe, and partridge are fairly abundant in the surrounding country.

Twelve miles beyond Brockville stands the town of Prescott, whence a branch line of the Canadian Pacific runs direct to Ottawa. On a point of land about a mile below Prescott stands the historic "**Wind-**

mill," a white stone tower pierced with loopholes, and now serving as a lighthouse.   In November, 1837, the "Windmill" was the scene of a foolish but pathetic tragedy.   It was seized by a little band of self-styled "Patriots" under the leadership of a Polish exile named Von Shultz.   Being made the tool of knaves and adventurers in safe refuge across the border, Von Shultz was deceived into the belief that Canada was groaning under an intolerable tyranny, and that he was called to deliver her from the yoke.   With his brave but lamentably misguided followers he held the mill for some days against the Canadian forces under Colonel Dundas.   During the fight the American shore opposite was crowded with spectators, who lent the insurgents the safe and cheap assistance of their sympathy.   Compelled at length to surrender at discretion, the unhappy Von Shultz, with 9 others of the 110 prisoners, was tried by court-martial at Fort Henry and put to death on the gallows.

Below Prescott the calm blue reaches of the river present little variety till the **Galoups Rapids** are reached.   Here the awakening water writhes and foams, and we feel a tremor in the timbers of our sturdy craft; but the rapids are not violent, and merely serve as a foretaste of those to be encountered farther on.   Parallel with the "Galoups" runs a small canal, at the lower end of which lies the thriving village of Cardinal.   Soon the spires of Morrisburg rise above its embowering trees, and round a curve of the shore, between islands softly wooded with white birch, our steamer sweeps through the low, green, singing waves of the Rapide du Plat.   Two miles and a half below the village, near a little promontory, the shore is broken by an irregular ravine. The country all about is a vision of peace, of orchards and quiet homesteads and meadows deep with grass, and bits of woodland spared discreetly by the axe.   Yet the scene is one of heroic memories, and every Canadian heart thrills to look upon it.   In the ravine, and on the uplands about it, was fought the bravely contested battle of **Chrysler's Farm**, on November 11, 1813.   On the one side was the American invading force, on the other a little army of Canadian volunteers with a handful of British regulars.   The issue of the battle was long uncertain, but the final result was a decisive victory for the Canadians.

The Rapids of the St. Lawrence.

From Chrysler's Farm onward we pass a succession of pretty villages and bits of peaceful landscape, till, just as the monotony of sweetness is beginning to pall upon the eye, the current quickens and high rocks appear along the shores.   We are entering the splendid rapid of the **Long Sault**, by far the grandest, if not the most exciting rapid of the chain.   It is a novelty indeed to find a large steamer tossed to and fro like a little cockboat, and buffeted by huge billows which make her quiver from stem to stern.   Other rapids have swifter sweeps or sharper turns, but this bears away the palm from all in the size and glory of its waves.   The roaring channel is divided by a somber and thickly wooded island.   The northern passage is called Lost Channel, and there is no path through its shouting rabble of high white waves that clamber upon each other and seem to race up-stream.   The steamer dashes into the white and emerald turmoil of the South Channel, and, drenched with spray, plunges with a galloping motion down the long incline, till it rests in smooth water under the steep sides of the island of St. Regis.

Boats ascending the St. Lawrence get around the Long Sault by means of the Cornwall Canal, at the lower end of which stands the busy manufacturing town of Cornwall.   At this point we pass into the province of Quebec, and at this point also the St. Lawrence ceases to form the boundary between Canada and the United States, for the dividing line recedes sharply to the eastward.   The shores of the river spread apart to form Lake St. Francis, with the little town of Lancaster on the left coast and the settlements of Dundee and Fort Covington on the right.   In the distance rises a blue range of mountains, the hills of Chateauguay, on which the eye rests with delight after the low horizons of Ontario.   In the vicinity of those blue heights lies the battle-field of **Chateauguay**, where De Salaberry and his handful of French Canadian volunteers won a decisive victory over a much superior force of American militia.   At the foot of the lake is the quaint French Canadian village of Coteau du Lac, with its straggling brown street, its long, brown wooden pier, its old-fashioned boats, and the gilded spire of its great stone church shedding a glory over the scene. Away to the south lies cotton-spinning Valleyfield, at the head of the Beauharnois Canal.   When the lake is fairly left behind, the shores grow more abrupt, the current dips and begins to dart and twist ; and we plunge through the rapid of " **The Cedars**," where the rich foliage sweeps down to the flying waters.   Then more quiet reaches are traversed, and we come to the beautiful " **Cascades**," where the clamoring waves flash high and thin among the rocky islets that break

the channel. Ere the excitement of the descent has died away we
come out on the broad breast of **Lake St. Louis**, where the St. Lawrence widens to give fitting reception to its mighty tributary the Ottawa.
The waters of this great stream, drawn from its somber hills of pine and
fir, are of a brown color that defines itself sharply against the clearer
and bluer tide of the St. Lawrence. Away to the left is the village
of St. Anne, made forever musical by the Canadian Boat Song of Tom
Moore :

> Faintly as tolls the evening chime,
> Our voices keep tune, and our oars keep time.
> Soon as the woods on the shore look dim,
> We'll sing at St. Anne's our parting hymn.
> Row, brothers, row ! the stream runs fast,
> The rapids are near, and the daylight's past !
>
> Why should we yet our sail unfurl ?
> There is not a breath the blue waves to curl.
> But when the wind blows off the shore,
> Oh ! sweetly we'll rest our weary oar.
> Blow, breezes, blow ! the stream runs fast,
> The rapids are near, and the daylight's past !
>
> Ottawa's tide ! this trembling moon
> Shall see us float o'er thy surges soon.
> Saint of this green isle ! hear our prayers ;
> Oh, grant us cool heavens and favoring airs !
> Blow, breezes, blow ! the stream runs fast,
> The rapids are near, and the daylight's past !

On the horizon ahead rises a bold, blue mass which we recognize as
"the Mountain" of Montreal. Soon other purple masses emerge to
keep it company, the summits of Mounts Shefford, Belœil, and St. John,
and we reach the Indian village of **Caughnawaga**, the home of the famous Lacrosse-players. The steamer slows up to take aboard a pilot,
and our hearts beat quicker as we realize that the great **rapid of
Lachine** is at hand.

This famous rapid is less impressive in its surroundings than the
Long Sault; it lacks the absolute beauty of the chiming and dancing
"Cascades"; but it is far more awe-inspiring than either. It makes
one catch one's breath with a sense of imminent peril. The descent
has been thus vividly described: "Suddenly a scene of wild grandeur
bursts upon the eye. Waves are lashed into spray and into breakers
of a thousand forms by the submerged rocks, which they are dashed
against in the headlong impetuosity of the river. Whirlpools, a

storm-lashed sea, the chasm below Niagara, all mingle their sublimity in a single rapid. Ere we can take a glance at the scene, the boat descends the wall of waves and foam like a bird, and in a second afterward you are floating on the calm, unruffled bosom of 'below the rapids.'"

Presently we pass the wooded shores of Nun's Island, and the stately city of Montreal lies before us.

Ottawa.

Toward dayset, where the journeying sun grown old
Hangs lowly westward darker now than gold,
With the soft sun-touch of the yellowing hours
  Made lovelier, I see with dreaming eyes,
  Even as a dream out of a dream, arise
The bell-tongued city with its glorious towers.

A. LAMPMAN.

Hotels.—The chief hotels of Ottawa are the *Russell, Cecil, Windsor House,* and *Grand Union*; rates from $2 to $4 a day. The clubs are the Rideau and West End. Chief restaurants: The *Bodega, Chambers's, Queen's, Walker's, Burns's.* Reading-rooms: *The Parliamentary, Y. M. C. A.,* and *St. Patrick's Literary and Scientific Society.* Theatre: The *Grand Opera-House.* Street cars connect the city with towns across the river (fare, 5c.). Population, 55,000.

We will suppose that the tourist has taken the direct route from *Toronto* to **Ottawa**—that by the Canadian Pacific, already described. If he has gone first to *Montreal*, he may go thence to Ottawa by the Canadian Pacific, the Canada Atlantic, or *by boat* up the *Ottawa River.* We should advise the route up by rail, and the return by boat. The Canadian Pacific has two lines between Montreal and Ottawa —one along the Ontario bank of the Ottawa River, and the other along the Quebec bank. By the former one passes through Ste. Anne de Bellevue and Vandeville, where the line turns north, and, passing the famed Caledonia Springs and Plantagenet, lands its passengers in Ottawa at the Central Station, a few minutes' walk from the Parliament Buildings. By the other (or transcontinental) line the first branch of the Ottawa is crossed at Ste. Rose, a pleasant summering resort. From Ste. Theresa a branch line runs to the excellent fishing waters in the Laurentian Mountains. There are numerous interesting places *en route.* By the Canada Atlantic the route is by Coteau Landing. Ottawa, the capital of the federated provinces of Canada, is in the province of Ontario, on the south shore of the Ottawa River, 126 miles

4

from its mouth. For picturesque grandeur the site of Ottawa is second only to that of *Quebec*. At this point the great river roars down into the terrific caldron of *Chaudière Falls*, to whose vindictive deity the Indians of old were wont to make propitiatory offerings of tobacco. At this point also the Ottawa is joined by its tributary, the *Rideau River*, which flows in over a fall of wonderful grace and beauty. The shifting, curtain-like folds of this cascade give the river its name of Rideau, or the "Curtain."

Like Quebec, Ottawa consists of an *Upper* and a *Lower Town*. In the double city flows a double life—the life of a rich capital and the life of a rafting and milling center—the life of that society that clusters around the government and the life of the French-Canadian lumberman. Ottawa is not only the seat of government but a hive of industry as well. It is the city of laws and saws. Its Upper Town rings with the eloquence of our legislators; its Lower with the shriek of our unremitting saw-mills. It is growing as no mere bureaucratic center can grow, and has a population of over 50,000, where, forty years ago, there were but 7,000 or 8,000 inhabitants. It is a city of deeps and heights, of sharp contrasts alike in its landscapes and its life; and both are alike dominated by the truly splendid pile of the *Parliament Buildings*, which imperially crown the loftiest point of the city.

In the days of the "old régime," when the Ottawa River was the chief path of the fur-trade, on which New France subsisted, the place of portage around the falls of the Chaudière had not even a wigwam to mark it as the site of a future city. It was a place of horror and of lying-in-wait; for here the Iroquois came to intercept the Algonquins of the north country, on their way to Quebec, with their canoe-loads of peltries. In 1693 so closely did the Iroquois bar the stream that a three-years' gathering of beaver-skins was held up at *Michilimackinac* unable to make its market; and it took Frontenac himself, the *Deus ex machina* of New France, to break the dread blockade. Most of the romantic history of Old Canada, however, went by the other way, and left the difficult passes of the Ottawa unhaloed. Not till 1800 did the spot where the Rideau spills its stream attract the regard of pioneers. In that year one Philemon Wright, of Woburn, Massachusetts, led a little colony to the spot, and founded a prosperous settlement, which is now the city of *Hull*, on the Quebec side of the river, immediately opposite Ottawa. The War of 1812 impelled the Imperial Government to build the Rideau Canal, for strategic purposes, and on the unpromis-

Parliament Buildings, Ottawa.

ing cliffs, across the river from Hull, arose the community of *Bytown*, named for a colonel of the Royal Engineers, who had charge of the canal construction. The village grew and became a town; and at length the seat of government, after having been made the shuttlecock of politicians and bandied between Niagara and Kingston and Toronto and Quebec and Montreal, was planted here by order of the Queen, and found a secure abiding-place.

The **Parliament Buildings** are designed in a modified twelfth-century Gothic, and are an admirable combination of simplicity, grace, and strength. The material of which they are constructed is a cream-colored sandstone, whose richness of tone grows under the touch o time. The door and window arches are of red Potsdam sandstone with dressings of Ohio freestone. The great central block occupies a stone terrace with broad, sloping carriage approaches, and is surmounted by a well-proportioned tower 220 ft. in height. This building stands at the back of a spacious square, of which the eastern and western blocks form the two sides. In the central block are the two Houses of Parliament, the Commons and the Senate. The side-blocks contain the offices of the various departments. Facing the Parliament square is the Langevin block. Behind the Chambers stands the beautiful building of the *Parliamentary Library*, its lofty dome supported by flying buttresses of admirable design. From a number of points of view the buildings "compose" in a way that gives the keenest pleasure to the eye. The first stone of the buildings was laid by the Prince of Wales in 1860, and in their present form they have cost about $5,000,000. The beautiful grounds of Parliament Hill, seated high above the river and commanding an unrivaled view, are laid out in broad walks, which form the favorite promenade of the citizens.

Ottawa contains other fine buildings such as the *Post-Office* and the great Roman Catholic *Cathedral* in the interesting French district of Sussex St. and its neighborhood, and some massive and magnificent commercial buildings; but they are so overshadowed by the noble structures on Parliament Hill that one is apt to ignore them. On one side of the ample breadth of Cartier Square is the fine stone pile of the *Normal School*, and not far off the enormous red brick block of the *Drill Shed*.

Rideau Hall, the residence of the Governor-General and the center of the brilliant social life of Ottawa, stands about two miles out of the city, on the road that leads past *Rideau Falls* and through the suburb

of *New Edinburgh.* It is a most unpretentious and hap-hazard con-
glomeration of plaster, brick, and stone, but withal a very comfortable
and home-like place to live in. The "season" at Ottawa is during
the winter months, when Parliament is in session; and then the ample
grounds of Rideau Hall become the scene of such a typically Canadian
merry-making that one can hardly realize that the dispenser of vice-
regal hospitalities is not a Canadian, but a five-years' visitant from
over seas. The skating-pond and the long toboggan-slides are thronged
with Canada's manliest and fairest; and the visitors from the mother
country take very kindly to the exhilarating Canadian pastimes.

A species of summer-tobogganing, but vastly more thrilling and with
a more piquant flavor of novelty and peril, is the descent of the "lumber-
slides "—an experience which none but the very timorous tourist should
omit. The "slides" are long, flat-bottomed, sharply-sloping channels
of massive stone-work and timber. These are built for the passage of
great logs which have been hewn square in the woods, and which
would be damaged by such merciless grinding and battering as the
ordinary rough logs are subjected to in their plunge over the falls.
The squared logs are made up, for the descent, into "cribs" of about
20 sticks, exactly fitting the slides. As these are but slightly fastened
together, there is always the fascinating possibility of a break-up; and
the pace of the descent is eminently exciting. The experience of the
slides—an experience through which all illustrious visitors, such as the
Prince of Wales, Prince Arthur, the Grand Duke Alexis, and the
Princess Louise have passed with dutiful heroism—is thus effectively
described by Mr. F. A. Dixon:

"Just at the head the adventurous *voyageurs* hurriedly embark, the
crib being courteously held back for a moment for their convenience.
Under direction they perch themselves upon the highest timber in the
rear, out of the way as far as possible of uprushing waters, and the
huge mass is cleverly steered, by the immense oars which are used for
the purpose, toward the entrance of the chute. Ahead for a quarter
of a mile appears a narrow channel, down which a shallow stream of
water is constantly rushing, with here and there a drop of some 5 or 8
feet; the ladies gather up their garments, as the crib, now beginning to
feel the current, takes matters into its own hands; with rapidly-quicken-
ing speed the unwieldy craft passes under a bridge, and with a groan
and a mighty cracking and splashing plunges, nose foremost, and tail
high in the air, over the first drop. Now she is in the slide proper,
and the pace is exhilarating; on over the smooth timbers she glides
swiftly; at a bridge ahead passers-by stop, and waving of friendly

Timber afloat at the Saw-mills, Ottawa.

handkerchiefs is interchanged. Now comes a bigger drop than the last, and the water, as we go over, surges up through our timbers, and a shower of spray falls about us. A delicate 'Oh!' from the ladies compliments this effort. Never mind ; a little wetting was all in this day's march. Another interval of smooth rush, and again a drop, and yet another. Ahead, there is a gleam of tossed and tumbled water, which shows the end of the descent ; down still we rush, and with one last wild dip, which sends the water spurting up about our feet, we have reached the bottom, cleverly caught on a floating platform of wood, called the ' apron,' which prevents our plunging into ' full fathoms five.' We have ' run the slides.' "

The most interesting part of **Lower Town** is crowded about *Chaudière Falls*. This is the lumber region—a city of deals, but not such deals as are to be had in Wall St. The air is full of the smell of fresh-cut pine and fir, and the shop-windows are stocked with saws and axes, chains and pike-poles, "cant-dogs" and gigantic leg-boots, and indestructible raiment. Sawdust is the pervading element. As we approach the water our ears tingle under the shrieking *crescendo* and *diminuendo* of the innumerable saws. The mills crowd half-way across the river. Every point of rock is packed with structures, and out from every point of vantage are thrust great embankments of stone and timber, on which more mills are heaped. Besides the saw-mills, there are flour-mills and cement-mills, and wool-mills ; and, on the other side of the cataract, reaching out from the Hull shore, a gigantic structure where matches are made, and wooden-ware. There, also, are yet more mills. The great river has been caught and put in harness. A portion of its water is permitted to thunder over the falls, which form a great semicircular chasm in mid-channel, and are crossed by a suspension bridge. The rest of the current is forced to labor in the mills, ere it may continue its journey to the sea ; for a thousand sluices have begun

" To hem his watery march, and dam his streams,
And split his currents."

In the saw-mills the chaos of strange and strident noises is indescribable, and the scene is beyond measure novel and impressive. By day in the yellow gloom, by night in the white glare of the countless electric lights, go on the rending and the biting of the saws. In the dark, sawdust flecked water about the foot of the dripping slides wallow the rough brown logs. Great chains and hooks descend, and the logs are grabbed and dragged up the slide into the dens where the myriad teeth await them. What are known as the upright saws are set together to the number of two or three dozen, in a combination called a "gate" which keeps darting up and down in a terrible and gigantic dance. Against their teeth the logs are driven; steadily and irresistibly the steel bites its loud way from end to end; and the logs pass forth on the other side in the shape of yellow planks and boards. On every side, and of all sizes, hum the circulars, revolving so fast that they appear stationary and can not show their teeth. A log or plank approaches the innocent-looking, humming disk; it touches, and there rises a soaring shriek which may quaver through the whole gamut. The timber divides swiftly, as if it were some impalpable fabric of a dream, and behind the saw shoots up a curving yellow spray of sawdust.

From Ottawa to Montreal.

Every week-day morning, at 7.30, a steamer of the Ottawa River Navigation Company leaves Ottawa for *Montreal*, and makes the run in about 10 hours. The scenery on this trip is strong and picturesque. The river rolls its brown tide between the stern hills of the Laurentians, over mad rapids, and through wide, many-islanded reaches. There is no monotony on this trip. The chief traffic of the river is in lumber, and we overtake and pass fleets of roomy barges piled high with the yellow deals and towed by gasping and laboring steam-tugs.

A mile below Ottawa we run past the mouth of a great river, the *Gatineau*. This stream, draining a vast extent of country, discharges an immense volume of water into the Ottawa; but the last 7 miles of its course are rendered unnavigable by a succession of fierce rapids. A few miles below the Gatineau is the mouth of the *Lièvre*, a much smaller stream, yet boasting a course of nearly 400 miles. This is the land where the canoeist, besides all the sport with rod and gun that his heart can wish, may conveniently taste the rapture of running rapids in his frail craft. This is a very different experience from the descent in a great steamer, which lifts you so far above the waves that you fail to realize all their fury. Yet another experience is to make the descent of the rapids on a raft of logs, amid the oaths or pious ejaculations of the French lumbermen. The men surge desperately on their long sweeps, but the unwieldy craft appears to wallow in utter helplessness amid the terrific surges; and when the descent has been accomplished the traveler wonders how he came through alive. The life of the river, in its combination of the homely and the picturesque, its mixture of adventure and pathos, has been crystallized into an exquisite lyric by the lamented Mr. Lampman :

BETWEEN THE RAPIDS.

The point is turned ; the twilight shadow fills
  The wheeling stream, the soft receding shore,
And on our ears from deep among the hills
  Breaks now the rapid's sudden quickening roar.
Ah ! yet the same, or have they changed their face,
  The fair green fields, and can it still be seen,
The white log cottage near the mountain's base,
  So bright and quiet, so home-like and serene ?
Ah, well I question ; for, as five years go,
How many blessings fall, and how much woe !
   .   .   .   .

The shore, the fields, the cottage just the same,
  But how with them whose memory makes them sweet ?
Oh, if I called them, hailing name by name,
  Would the same lips the same old shouts repeat ?
Have the rough years, so big with death and ill,
  Gone lightly by and left them smiling yet ?
Wild, black-eyed Jeanne whose tongue was never still,
  Old wrinkled Picaud, Pierre, and pale Lisette,
The homely hearts that never cared to range
While life's wide fields were filled with rush and change.

And where is Jacques and where is Verginie ?
  I can not tell ; the fields are all a blur.
The lowing cows, whose shapes I scarcely see,
  Oh, do they wait and do they call for her ?
And is she changed, or is her heart still clear
  As wind or morning, light as river-foam ?
Or have life's changes borne her far from here,
  And far from rest, and far from help and home ?
Ah, comrades, soft, and let us rest awhile,
For arms grow tired with paddling many a mile.
   .   .   .   .

Blacker and loftier grow the woods, and hark !
  The freshening roar ! The chute is near us now,
And dim the cañon grows, and inky dark
  The water whispering from the birchen prow.
One long last look, and many a sad adieu,
  While eyes can see and heart can feel you yet,
I leave sweet home and sweeter hearts to you,
  A prayer for Picaud, one for pale Lisette,
A kiss for Pierre, my little Jacques, and thee,
A sigh for Jeanne, a sob for Verginie.

Oh, does she still remember ? Is the dream
Now dead, or has she found another mate ?
So near, so dear ; and ah, so swift the stream !
Even now perhaps it were not yet too late.
But oh, what matter ? for before the night
Has reached its middle we have far to go :
Bend to your paddles, comrades ; see, the light
Ebbs off apace ; we must not linger so.
Aye thus it is ! Heaven gleams and then is gone.
Once, twice it smiles, and still we wander on.

The next point of interest below the mouth of the *Lièvre* is the *Château of Montebello*, the home of the great French-Canadian *Papineau*. This man, whom the stress of a patriotic struggle misled into rebellion, was one of the ablest and most eloquent of Canada's sons. The principles he fought for have triumphed by constitutional means, and his name is held now in all reverence. The château, in which he spent his days after his recall from exile, is a picturesque and beautiful structure, embowered in elms and savoring of Old France.

Below Montebello we pass the town of *L'Orignal*, and not far off is the mouth of the *Kinonge*, the outlet of the enchanting mountain-girt lake of *Comandeau*. This water, which teems with trout, is best reached by a portage from *Grenville* (the next place at which the steamer arrives) to the river *Rouge*, which must be ascended in canoes some miles to the Comandeau portage. The beauty of the scenery will well repay the tourist who turns aside for this trip.

At Grenville we leave the steamer and take the train for *Carillon*, to avoid the great rapids known as the *Carillon, Long Sault*, and *Chute au Blondeau*. These three rapids are further circumvented by three canals, used chiefly for the freight traffic. They were built by the Imperial Government for military purposes, for which it is to be hoped they may never be required. That which passes the Long Sault is known as the *Grenville Canal*, and was excavated for six miles out of what is mainly solid rock.

The *Pass of the Long Sault*, on the western shore, is to Canadians holy ground, for there was enacted a deed of heroism than which the pages of history can show none more magnificent. In 1660 the whole force of the Iroquois confederacy bent itself to the destruction of the French colonies of Villemarie and Quebec. The doom appeared inevitable. But there were heroes of the ancient type in New France.

Long Sault Rapids.

A young nobleman, the Sieur Daulac des Ormeaux, familiarly known as *Dollard*, gathered a band of sixteen comrades, who devoted their lives, with the most solemn ceremonial of the Church, to the task of breaking the attack of the invaders. They intrenched themselves at the Pass of the Long Sault. With them went some twoscore Huron allies, all of whom but two chiefs deserted them when the enemy appeared. Five hundred yelling savages, the best of all Indian warriors, swarmed upon the frail barricade; and again and again they were beaten off with tremendous slaughter, till they drew back to await reenforcements. For three days the handful of heroes held the post, sleepless, and parched with terrible thirst; and when the last man of them had struck his last blow, the Iroquois had no more stomach for the fight. Their losses had been so heavy that they had to give up all thought of attacking Villemarie, as Montreal was called; and Daulac had saved New France. The story has been woven into a glowing romance by Mrs. Catherwood, under the title of The Romance of Dollard.

At *Carillon*, where we resume the steamer, the Ottawa ceases to be the boundary-line between the two provinces, and from this point on we are in Quebec. Soon we enter the *Lake of Two Mountains*, an irregular sheet of water from 3 to 4 miles in width and about 24 miles long. Into this lake flows the *Rivière à la Graisse*, past the pretty village of *Rigaud*. This neighborhood was the scene of many conflicts between the so-called "Patriots" and the Loyalists in the difficulties of 1837. Near Rigaud rises a hill called the *Montagne Ste. Magdalaine*. On the summit is a square field several acres in extent, whose surface is covered with bowlders. These stones, by some strange freak of Nature, have been set in long, orderly lines, so as to resemble a newly plowed field, and the name of the place is called *Pluie de Guérets*. In this mysterious spot one can hear distinctly underground murmurs as of flowing water; but the digging of curious investigators has failed to reveal the cause of this phenomenon. Far down the lake is a charming summer resort, the Indian village of **Oka**. Some of the Indians have been removed and settled in a new domain in the Muskoka country. There is now a monastery of Trappist monks at Oka, to which visitors are admitted and shown over the establishment. Of the two mountains which give the lake its name, the larger was called *Calvaire* by the pioneers of New France. On the summit of the steep were seven chapels, memorials of the mystic seven of St.

John's vision; aud hither, on many a pious pilgrimage, came the people of Villemarie, taking their lives in their hands when they quitted the shelter of their palisades. Below the Lake of Two Mountains is the village of *Ste. Anne*, which we saw in our descent of the St. Lawrence, and in the quaintly dressed crowd that gathers on the wharf we see an epitome of the picturesqueness of the *habitants*, as the French Canadian country folks are called. At this point the Ottawa splits his mighty current into three streams, the largest of which helps furnish the expanse of *Lake St. Louis*, while the two smaller flow north of *Laval* and *Montreal Islands*. At *St. Anne* the steamer enters a short canal of one lock to avoid a dangerous rapid. Here the Canadian Pacific and Grand Trunk cross on to *Montreal Island* by splendid and massive viaducts under which the steamer passes with lowered funnel. On a point of the island, a little beyond, we note the ruins of a castle built after a mediæval pattern as a defense against the Iroquois. There are two such castles standing close together, with a circular tower on the hill-tops watching over their approaches. Within the high walls of the castles was space enough to shelter all the women and children of the ancient settlement.

At the drowsy and picturesque old town of *Lachine*, 8¼ miles from Montreal, is the head of the canal by which the *Lachine Rapids* are avoided on the upward trip. Before the canal was built, Lachine was a place of great commercial importance; now it is chiefly a place of summer residence for citizens of Montreal. Its steep gables and old-fashioned dormer-windows nestle amid the green of ancient trees. All its neighborhood is historic ground, but the memories that cluster most thickly about it are those of the great La Salle. Its site was granted by the Sulpician Fathers to La Salle that he might establish there a fortified outpost for the more effective defense of the city. La Salle named his settlement La Chine, thus embalming his dominant idea of a passage across the continent to the Indies and Cathay. La Salle soon left it to follow his adventures, but the settlement continued to flourish till the dreadful massacre of 1689, which we referred to in our account of Kingston. The cause which led to this catastrophe has been already related; the catastrophe itself has thus been described by a Canadian writer, Mr. C. V. Rogers:

"Nearly two centuries ago, on the night of August 5, 1689, as the inhabitants of Lachine lay sleeping, amid a storm of hail upon the lake, which effectually disguised the noise of their landing, a force of

Running Lachine Rapids.

many hundred warriors, armed and besmeared with war-paint, made a descent upon Lachine. Through the night they noiselessly surrounded every building in the village. With dawn the fearful war-whoop awoke men, women, and children to their doom of torture and death. The village was fired; by its light, in the early morn, the horror-stricken inhabitants of Montreal could see from their fortifications the nameless cruelties which preceded the massacre. It is said the Iroquois indulged so freely in the fire-water of the Lachine merchants that, had the defenders of Villemarie been prompt to seize the favorable moment, the drunken wretches might have been slaughtered like swine. Paralyzed by the horrors they had witnessed, the French let the occasion slip. At nightfall the savages withdrew to the mainland, not, however, without signifying by yells—repeated to the number of ninety—how many prisoners they carried away. From the ramparts of Villemarie and amid the blackened ruins of Lachine the garrison watched the fires on the opposite shore, kindled for what purposes of nameless cruelty they knew too well. The fate of Lachine marks the lowest point in the fortunes of New France; by what deeds of heroism they were retrieved is not the least glorious page in Canadian history."

PROVINCE OF QUEBEC.

Quebec, the senior province of the Canadian confederation, occupies the greater portion of the St. Lawrence Valley. It has an extreme length, E. and W., of 1,000 miles, and a great diversity of scenery and resources. For a long time it monopolized the name of Canada; and for a far longer period its history was practically the whole of Canadian history, save for what was being enacted in the narrower sphere of the Acadian Peninsula. The following extremely condensed abstract of the history of the province is taken from Dr. Stewart's article on Quebec in the Encyclopædia Britannica:

" Quebec was first visited by the French, under Jacques Cartier, in 1535, and a second time in 1536, though it is said that Sebastian Cabot discovered the country in 1497. The regular settlement of the province, however, was not made until 1608, when Samuel de Champlain landed at the site now occupied by Quebec City. Here he established military and trading posts, and it was not long before the new possession became the seat of the Jesuit and Récollet missions, which were zealously carried on under the most trying circumstances for nearly a century and a half. The early settlers endured countless hardships from the incursions of the Indians, and the frequent wars in which they were forced to engage with the English and Dutch. In

1759 the Marquis of Montcalm was defeated at Quebec by an English army under General Wolfe. A year later the French surrendered all their important posts, and the colony passed under English rule. In 1763 the Treaty of Paris was signed, by the terms of which, and the conditions laid down a few years later in the memorable Quebec Act of 1774, the French were guaranteed by England their laws, language, and religion. In 1791 the colony was divided into Upper and Lower Canada; but in 1841, after a series of internal dissensions, including the rebellion of 1837, and several political quarrels, the country was again united. In 1867 the provinces of Old Canada, under the names of Ontario and Quebec, were erected, with New Brunswick and Nova Scotia, into the Dominion of Canada."

Under the indulgent protection of England, Quebec has grown and prospered, and developed a civilization unique in the modern world. The province is in many respects a piece of Old France. In its religious homogeneity it is almost mediæval; and along with this goes a conservatism, as far as custom and tradition are concerned, which gives the life of the *habitant* a marked individuality and local color. At the same time the French Canadian has grown up under the responsibility of self-government and British institutions, to which he very readily adapted himself, and which have given him a certain political alertness. Vividly conscious of his power in the confederation, he is not at all diffident in the exercise of it; but, underlying a good deal of self-assertive glorification of the illustrious race from which he is sprung, there is a sound loyalty not only to the flag under whose shelter he has so prospered, but also to the young federation in which he plays so important a part.

To the romancer and the student of character, the province of Quebec offers a field of almost unparalleled richness, which has as yet been but little worked. To the lover of outdoor sports it offers almost virgin woods and waters of unlimited possibilities. To the idle tourist, who is so unfortunate as not to be preoccupied by any hobby, it offers the attraction of novel scenes, unfamiliar customs, fresh experiences, and an invigorating climate.

JACQUES CARTIER.

No flame of war was he, no flower of grace,
No star of wisdom ; but a plain, bold man,
More careful of the end than of the plan.
No mystery was he afraid to face ;

No savage strategy, no furious storm,
  No stings of climate, no unthought disease,
  His master purpose would not bend to these,
But saw, through all, achievement's towering form.

He first beheld the gloomy Saguenay,
  And Stadacona's high, forbidding brow ;
His venturous vision, too, did first survey
  Fair Hochelaga, but not fair as now.
St. Malo holds his dust, the world his fame,
But his strong, dauntless soul 'tis ours to claim.
                              MATTHEW RICHEY KNIGHT.

Montreal.

Hotels, etc.—The leading hotels are the *Windsor*, on Dominion Sq. ;
the *Place Viger Hotel*, on Place Viger, at the east end; *St. Lawrence
Hall*, on St. James St.; the *Balmoral*, on Notre Dame St., West; the
Queen's, cor. St. James and Windsor Sts.; *Carsley's* and the *Richelieu
Hotel*, on Jacques Cartier Sq., the latter the favorite French hostelry.

Modes of Conveyance.—Electric street cars traverse the city in
every direction, and afford easy access to principal points. Carriages
wait at the depots and steamboat-landings, and at various stands in
the city. Their charges are :

One-horse Vehicles.—One or two persons, 15 minutes, 25 cents; 30
minutes, 40 cents; the first hour, 75 cents, and 60 cents for every subsequent hour. Three or four persons, 40 cents for 15 minutes, 60
cents for 30 minutes; $1 for the first hour, and 75 cents for every
subsequent hour.

Two-horse Vehicles.—One or two persons, 50 cents for 15 minutes ;
65 cents for 30 minutes, and $1 per hour. For three or four persons,
65 cents for 15 minutes, 75 cents for 30 minutes, and $1.25 per hour.

Clubs.—Metropolitan, on Beaver Hall Hill; St. James, on Dorchester St.; and Montreal.

From *Windsor Station* the C. P. R. express trains leave for New
York, Boston, Toronto, Sherbrooke, St. John, N. B., Halifax, Ottawa,
Detroit, Chicago, Sault Ste. Marie, St. Paul, Minneapolis, etc., Winnipeg,
and Vancouver. From *Place Viger Station* the C. P. R. trains leave
for Ottawa, Ste. Agathe, and Quebec. Suburban trains leave from both
stations. The trains of the G. T. R. all leave from the *Bonaventure
Depot ;* as do also the trains for Ottawa boat at Lachine. Steamers
running down the St. Lawrence to Quebec and intermediate points, as
well as for Toronto and the Lakes, leave from wharves of the Richelieu and Ontario Navigation Co.

Trains leave Montreal at 5 P. M. to connect at Lachine with boats
about to run the rapids. Round trip, 50 cents.

Population, with suburbs, 325,000.

Montreal is a microcosm of Canada. Here is the Old Canada side
by side with the New ; here French Canada and English Canada come

into close and perpetual contact, and yet maintain their individuality. She stands between French Quebec, 172 miles east, and English Toronto, 338 miles west. With a quarter of a million inhabitants, an unrivaled site at the head of ocean navigation, yet in the heart of the continent, with enormous wealth, and with all the resources of the Northwest seeking an outlet through her port, Montreal is the commercial metropolis of Canada, and a city with the securest possible future. She has a past also, heroic, romantic, and brilliant beyond that of most cities of this New World, and a present in which all Canada takes just pride. To Montreal the trade of the Northwest has been tributary from its beginning. First, it was the fur-trade, whose merchant-princes, building their homes on *Beaver Hall Hill*, gave Canada its fit emblem, the wise and capable beaver. Then came the lumber, grain, and cattle trades, all pouring their wealth into the city's lap; and now the great transcontinental railway, the Canadian Pacific, with its headquarters at Montreal, reaches out for the trade of "the gorgeous East," and realizes the dream of La Salle and those old explorers who shattered their forces in the effort to find a route to Cathay.

The city takes her name from the mountain which stands guard over her. ˙ The peculiar form of the name, "Mont Réal," seems to point to Portuguese influences somewhere in the dawn of her history. In a succession of terraces the streets climb the mountain, all the summit of which is reserved to the citizens as a matchless park. Business has gradually worked itself back, street by street, from the water-front, till now the once aristocratic exclusion of *St. Catherine St.* is a main artery of trade.

MONTREAL IN HISTORY.

In spite of the strongly differentiated elements of which Montreal's population is composed—English Protestant and French Roman Catholic—race and religious antagonisms are kept subdued by much mutual good-will and forbearance. For some time after the conquest, Protestants were allowed the use of a Roman church after the morning mass. Every Sunday afternoon, from 1766 to 1786, a Church of England congregation occupied the Church of the Récollets. The same privilege was afterward extended to the Presbyterians, up to 1792, when that denomination moved to a church of its own. At this time this exceedingly Protestant congregation, to show its good-will and sense of gratitude, made a parting gift to the Récollet priests, in the shape of candles for the high altar and wine for the mass. A few years ago the picturesque and historic Bonsecours Church was about to be torn down to make room for a railway station; but a few Protestants, holding in honor the associations of the building and the memory of the devoted Sister who founded it, made a strong protest, and roused the bishop to forbid the sale.

It was in the autumn of 1535 that Jacques Cartier, with a forty-ton galleon and two open boats, ascended the St. Lawrence to seek the city Hochelaga, of which the Indians had told him at Quebec. On the 2d of October they reached the landing-place of Hochelaga, where hundreds of Indians crowded about them in eager delight, and welcomed them with gifts of fish and maize. The Indian city lay some way back from the water, at the foot of the mountain. Around it rustled fruitful corn-fields, and around the corn-fields rose the black masses of the ancient woods. The town was fenced with a triple row of heavy palisades formed of the trunks of trees. In the center of the town was an open square, wherein Cartier was received as a demigod, and besought to heal the sick with his touch. This he could not do, but he could bestow gifts, which is a semi-divine function; and after this ceremony he ascended the mountain, followed by a troop of adoring natives. When the full magnificence of this unrivaled landscape unfolded itself before him, he very fittingly gave the Mount the name of Royal. Not till seventy years after Cartier's visit did European eyes again behold the site of Montreal. Then Champlain undertook the work that Cartier had begun. But he found no town of Hochelaga. There had been war among the tribes, the maize-fields had been laid waste, and the city wiped out by fire. The story of its destruction was detailed to Champlain by two old Indians who guided him up the mountain. The tale is a romantic one, and tells how " Hurons and Senecas lived in peace and friendship together at Hochelaga for many generations. They intermarried and had no cause for quarrel, till, for some reason, a Seneca chief refused his son permission to marry a Seneca maiden. Enraged at the action of the stern parent, the lady refused all offers of marriage, and declared she would only wed the warrior who should slay the chief who had interfered with her happiness. A young Wyandot, smitten by her charms, attacked and killed the old chief and received the coveted reward. The Senecas, however, adopted the cause of their chief, and a terrible fratricidal war spread desolation throughout the Huron country, nor did it cease till the Iroquois had completely broken up and almost exterminated the Hurons."

In 1611, having founded Quebec, Champlain selected the site for a trading-post at Montreal. It was on a small stream which enters the St. Lawrence where the Custom-House now stands. He called the spot Place Royale. Though coming after Cartier, Champlain is rightly called the father of Canada. Parkman says of him: " Of the pioneers of the North American forests, his name stands foremost on the list. It was he who struck the deepest and foremost stroke into the heart of their pristine barbarism. At Chantilly, at Fontainebleau, at Paris, in the cabinets of princes and of royalty itself, mingling with the proud vanities of the court; then lost from sight in the depths of Canada, the companion of savages, sharer of their toils, privations, and battles, more hardy, patient, and bold than they; such, for successive years, were the alternations of this man's life."

On the 14th of October, 1641, Montreal was founded by Maisonneuve, for the Company of Montreal, who had obtained a cession of the whole island. In the following spring the city was consecrated, under the name of Ville-Marie. With the expedition of city builders, numbering 57, went one Mlle. Jeanne Mance, of unfading memory, carrying with her, to assist in the founding of the city, a sum that would be equivalent now to a round quarter of a million. This was the donation of a wealthy widow in France, Madame de Bouillon. Not till 1643 did the Iroquois learn of this new settlement; but then, and for half a century thereafter, the city found itself engaged in an almost incessant struggle for its existence. On what is now known as the Place d'Armes, Maisonneuve had a hand-to-hand contest with the savages. All through this terrible half-century of trial the garrison of Ville-Marie consisted of never more than 50 men. In 1663 the rights of the Company of Montreal were purchased by the Seminary of St. Sulpice, which still holds certain seignorial rights over the island. In 1665 the Marquis de Tracy arrived on the scene with a portion of the famous Carignan Regiment, and broke the power of the Mohawks. By 1672 the population of the city had increased to 1,520, and suburbs began to appear outside the walls. But, though the Mohawks had been crushed, war was still the heritage of this city, whose foundation had been under the auspices of a religion of peace. In 1690 a little army of 200 French and Indians made an expedition from Montreal on snowshoes southward through the wilderness, and laid waste with fire and sword the Dutch settlement at Schenectady. The retort of the English colonies was an expedition in force under Governor Winthrop and Major

G   **H**   **I**

Colleges, Hospitals, etc.

29. Mc Gill University, E 2
30. Redpath Museum, D 2
31. Montreal College, C 1
32. High School (Pro.), D 2
33. Victoria Hospital, E 2
34. General Hospital, E 4
35. Western Hospital, B 2
36. Hotel Dieu, F 2
37. Grey Nunnery, C 2
38. Notre Dame Hospital, E 5
39. House of Refuge (Pro.), E 3

Churches.

ROMAN CATHOLIC.
40. Notre Dame de Lourdes, F 4
41. Jesuit's, E 3
42. St. Peter's Cathedral, D 3
43. Notre Dame, D 4
44. St. James', F 4
45. St. Patrick's Cathedral, D 3

EPISCOPAL.
46. Christ Church Cathedral, D 3
47. St. George's, D 3
48. Trinity, E 4
49. Grace, B 4

METHODIST.
50. St. James', D 3
51. St. Charles', E 3
52. West End, B 3

PRESBYTERIAN.
53. St. Andrew's, D 3
54. St. Paul's, D 3
55. American, C 3

BAPTIST.
56. French, E 3
57. Olivet, C 3

CONGREGATIONAL.
58. Calvary, C 3
59. Emmanuel, D 2

SYNAGOGUES.
60. German and Polish, D 3
61. Spanish and Portuguese, D 2

Miscellaneous.

62. Custom Examiners' Warehouse, D 4
63. Harbor Office, D 4
64. Montreal Jail, G 5

Schuyler, which advanced on Montreal by way of Lake Champlain, while a fleet under Sir William Phipps was sent against Quebec. But in those days the star of New France was in the ascendant, and both forces were triumphantly repulsed.

After the victory of Wolfe on the Plains of Abraham, Montreal was the spot in which the power of France in America made its last stand. About its walls the armies of England closed in swiftly and surely. When they met, there was nothing for Montreal to do but capitulate.

During the American War of Independence Colonel Ethan Allen, with 200 of his "Green Mountain Boys," advanced to the attack of Montreal, but was defeated and taken prisoner by Governor Carleton. Later came Montgomery, and forced the city to capitulate. Montreal was taken possession of in the name of the Continental Congress, and Benjamin Franklin came north and endeavored to persuade the Canadians to join in the rebellion. In this attempt he failed signally; but he left behind him a memorial of his presence by establishing a newspaper. This journal, the Gazette, which enjoys to this day a prosperous existence, is now marked by a sturdy loyalty which belies the circumstances of its foundation. In the spring of 1777, after the defeat and death of Montgomery at Quebec, the American forces evacuated Montreal; and never since have her streets known the tread of hostile feet.

A quaint episode in the early history of Montreal is connected with the Carignan Regiment already mentioned. These veterans, when their time had expired, were disbanded and settled in Canada. In embracing a farmer's life they found themselves in need of many things not formerly deemed essential. Above all, they needed wives—for what is a farmer without the farmer's wife? A lot of girls were thereupon selected in France and shipped to Canada to supply this long-felt want. Baron La Hontan has left us an amusing account of the consignment of prospective brides which were sent out in 1684: " After the reduction of these troops many vessels loaded with girls were sent out under the direction of some old beginners, who divided them into three classes. These damsels were, so to speak, piled up, the one on the other, in three different chambers, where the husbands chose their wives, in the same manner as the butcher goes to choose his sheep in the midst of the flock. There was material to content the fantastical in the diversity of girls in these three seraglios—for there were to be seen there tall and short, fair and brown, lean and fat; in short, every

5

one found a shoe to fit his foot. At the end of fifteen days not one remained. I am told that the fattest were the soonest carried off, because it was imagined that, being less active, they would have more trouble to leave their housekeeping, and would better resist the cold of the winter; but many people who went on this principle were taken in by it. . . . Those who desired to marry addressed themselves to the directresses, to whom they were bound to declare their property and faculties before choosing from these three classes her whom they found to their taste. The marriage was concluded on the spot by the aid of the priest and the notary, and the next day the Governor caused to be distributed to the married a bull, a cow, a hog, a sow, a cock, a hen, two barrels of salt meat, eleven crowns, and certain acres."

POINTS OF INTEREST.

Before undertaking to "do" the city one should view it as a whole from the top of the mountain, and so possess one's self of the "lay" of the streets and chief points of interest, and equip one's self with a proper realization of the magnificence of the city's island throne. Gaining the summit by beautifully winding drives, or more directly by an incline railway, we stand on what was once an active volcano. Far below, between the mountain and the river, lies spread out the broad confusion of the city roofs and streets and towers, fringed along the shining water-limits with the masts and funnels of its shipping. Beyond the water lie great breadths of flat country, bounded on the far horizon by the twin mountains of *St. Hilaire*. In another direction we see a silent city clinging to the steep—the cemeteries of *Côte-des-Neiges* and *Mount Royal*. Away to the westward over *Nun's Island* the surges of *Lachine* are glittering in the sun. Straight across the river, almost in the center of the panorama, ran the famous **Victoria Bridge**, regarded at the time of its construction as the eighth wonder of the world, and which has now been replaced by an open-work steel bridge, made necessary by the enormous amount of traffic which passes over this portion of the Grand Trunk Railway system. Some distance to the left *St. Helen's Island* divides the giant stream; and in the middle distance, dominating the roofs of the city, rise the majestic twin towers of *Notre Dame*. On the other side of the mountain, fenced by the reaches of *Back River*, lie the opulent villages, farms, and orchards which have earned for Montreal Island the title of the Garden of Canada.

Descending the mountain and re-entering the mazes of the streets, we make our way first to the historic *Place d'Armes*. This was the first burying-ground of the pioneers. Now it is a railed space of trees, cool with the spray of its fountain and with the shade of the stately buildings surrounding it. Here is erected a magnificent statue of Maissoneuve, the founder of the city. On the south side stands the parish church of **Notre Dame**, one of the largest ecclesiastical structures on the continent. It accommodates 10,000 people easily, and has been known to contain 15,000 within its walls. Its towers are 227 ft. high. It has a magnificent chime of 11 bells, of which one, called the Gros Bourdon, is the largest in America, and weighs 29,400 pounds. From the summit of the tower which contains the bells a splendid view is obtained. The cost of this church was about $6,000,000.

Alongside of Notre Dame stands the ancient *Seminary of St. Sulpice*, built more than two centuries ago, its massive wall, pierced with loopholes, looking grimly down on the thronged and peaceful street. The seminary shares with the *Bank of Montreal*, whose pillared abode rises on the opposite side of the square, the distinction of being the wealthiest institution in America. In the immediate vicinity of the Place d'Armes throng the splendid structures of the Post-Office, the Jacques-Cartier Bank, the Banque Nationale, and the buildings of the New York Life and other insurance companies.

As far as situation goes, and perhaps in other respects as well, the finest square in the city is *Dominion Square*. It is high and spacious, and about it gather several fine churches; the vast pile of the Windsor Hotel, the handsome pile containing the station and general offices of the Canadian Pacific Railway, resembling the keep of a Norman castle; the Y. M. C. A. building; and, overshadowing them all, the great Roman Catholic Cathedral, which is known as *St. James's* from the fact that St. James is its patron saint. This noble structure is a *facsimile* of St. Peter's at Rome, with its dimensions reduced about one half. The extreme measurements of this cathedral are: length 333 ft., breadth 222 ft., height 258 ft., circumference of dome 240 ft. It is in this square that the fine memorial statue to Sir John Macdonald was unveiled on June 6, 1895.

Of the other Roman Catholic churches of the city the most interesting to tourists are the beautiful *Church of Notre Dame de Lourdes*, on the corner of St. Catherine and St. Denis Sts. ; the *Jesuits' Church* on Bleury St., with its unrivaled frescoes and exquisite music; the *Chapel of Notre Dame de Nazareth*, with its fine paintings; and the famous old *Bonsecours Church*, which was built in 1771.

Of the Anglican churches the finest, from an architectural point of view, are *St. George's*, the *Church of St. James the Apostle*, and the stately *Christ Church Cathedral* at the corner of University and St. Catherine Sts. This latter structure is, perhaps, with the exception of Christ Church Cathedral at Fredericton, the most perfect specimen of pure Gothic architecture on the continent. A noble and massive structure is the St. James Methodist church on St. Catherine St. The Presbyterians have a number of fine churches, of which the most noteworthy, architecturally, are *St. Paul's*, the *Crescent Street*, *Erskine*, and the *American Presbyterian*. The old *St. Gabriel's Church*, the first Protestant place of worship in the city, was erected in 1792 at the west end of the Champ-de-Mars, and is still standing, being now used as an office for the revenue police. Montreal has three Jewish synagogues, one of which, on Stanley St., is an impressive structure.

Besides the Place d'Armes and Dominion Square, already referred to, Montreal has other parks and squares. She is well supplied with breathing-places. There is the historic *Champ de Mars*, on Craig St., still used as a parade-ground. Near the City Hall is *Jacques-Cartier Square*, adorned by two Russian guns from the spoils of Sebastopol, and by a column and statue erected in 1808 in memory of Nelson. At the junction of McGill and St. James Sts. is *Victoria Square*, formerly the haymarket, presided over by a colossal bronze statue of the Queen. On St. Denis St., the aristocratic French residence quarter, is *Place Viger*, opposite which is the new C. P. R. hotel and station. *St. Helen's Island* is now used as a public park, though belonging to the English Government. It is the favorite resort of the city picnickers, and forgets its martial experiences of old times. Champlain's wife, in whose honor the island is named, was the first European woman of gentle birth to cast in her lot with Canada. A place of resort which the tourist should not fail to visit is the **Bonsecours Market.** The great market-days are Tuesday and Friday when the broad space is thronged with *habitants*,* and one comes into close contact with the quaint material of which French Canada is really made up.

Montreal is not only a city of churches, but of hospitals and benevolent institutions as well. The largest and wealthiest of these is the *Hôtel-Dieu*, under the management of the Black Nuns. This institution was founded in 1644. The famous **Grey Nunnery**, founded in

---

* French Canadian country-folk.

1738, is not a convent, but a hospital, under the management of the Grey Nuns. According to Murray's Guide to Montreal, "The name 'Grey Nuns' was first given them in derision. The malicious reports circulated against the ladies, especially that of furnishing the Indians with alcohol, and making too free a use of it themselves, gave rise to the epithet 'Sœurs Grises,' the word *grise* bearing a double meaning in French, viz., a gray color, or tipsy." The Sisters who were thus cruelly assailed have made the once opprobrious epithet a title of the highest honor. The best time for visitors to call at the Grey Nunnery is at the noon hour, when callers are always made welcome. The *Royal Victoria Hospital* is the gift of two of Montreal's chief citizens, Lord Mount-Stephens and Lord Strathearn. Just below Hochelaga, beyond the eastern limits of the city, stood the vast structure of the *Longue Pointe Asylum*, which was burned to the ground in the summer of 1890. This institution was in charge of a Roman Catholic religious order. Sixty of the inmates, including several of the nuns in charge, perished in the conflagration.

Among the educational institutions are **McGill University**, the *Presbyterian College*, the Montreal College or *Seminary of St. Sulpice*, the *Veterinary College*, St. Mary's or the *Jesuits' College*, the Montreal branch of *Laval University*, whose parent institution is at Quebec, the *Villa-Maria Convent School for Girls*, and the Girls' School of the *Nuns of the Sacred Heart*. Of these the most important is of course McGill University, which, under the presidency of the renowned Sir William Dawson, has grown to a world-wide fame and influence. The pride of the city, it receives munificent gifts from wealthy citizens, and is ever reaching out to wider spheres of usefulness. Its buildings, which are on *Sherbrooke St.*, the "Fifth Avenue" of Montreal, stand in the midst of fine grounds, and contain a good library and the famous Redpath Museum. Affiliated with McGill are the Presbyterian, Congregational, Wesleyan, and Anglican Colleges of Montreal, together with Morrin College at Quebec and St. Frances College, Richmond. The tourist will do well to visit the *Art Gallery* on Phillips Square, and the rooms of the *Natural History Society* on University St. The museum of this society is the best in Canada. Among its treasures are the "Ferrier Collection" of Egyptian antiquities, the most perfect of its kind on the continent. Here also may be seen the first breech-loading gun ever made. We read in Murray's Guide that "it was sent out to this country by the French Government. It was used by the French in one of their expeditions against the Indians of Lake Oka. The Indians attacked the canoe in which the cannon was placed and upset it. The cannon lay for a while in the bottom of the lake, and one part of it was lost there and never found." The museum also contains the best existing collection of Canadian birds.

One of the chief "lions" of Montreal is the magnificent **Victoria Jubilee Bridge**, crossing the St. Lawrence River at this point, and which was built to replace the old and famous Victoria tubular bridge, already mentioned as "the eighth wonder of the world," and which had become unable with its single track to cope with the enormous traffic which the Grand Trunk Railway now handles.

The present bridge was designed by the chief engineer of the Grand Trunk Railway, Mr. Joseph Hobson, was commenced in October, 1897, by the erection of the first span on the west end, the structure being built completely around the tube of the old bridge, the latter being cleverly utilized as a roadway on which a temporary steel span was moved out to the first pier, and the new structure then erected outside the temporary span.

While the old bridge entire weighed 9,044 tons, the new bridge weighs 22,000 tons. The total length of bridge is 6,592 ft., number of piers 24, number of spans 25, length of central span 330 ft., length of side spans 242 ft.

While the width of the old bridge was 16 ft., the width of the new bridge will be 65 ft. The height of the old bridge was 18 ft., the height of the new bridge over all is 28 ft.

The total cost of the new bridge, which provides double track for railroad trains, driveways for vehicles on each side, and footwalks on the outside of driveways, will be about two million dollars. The contract price of the old Victoria Bridge was $6,813,000.

The flooring of the present bridge will weigh 2,800 pounds per lineal foot, and each span has been so erected that it will carry not only a train on each track, moving in opposite directions, but going at a rate of 45 miles an hour, with a total weight of 4,000 pounds to the lineal foot, moving at the rate of 25 miles an hour—as well as driveways and footwalks crowded with vehicles and pedestrians.

The new bridge will rank, from an engineering standpoint, with the foremost structures of the age, as the bridge which it replaced ranked the foremost as a monument to the skill of the engineers and bridge builders of the period in which it was built.

The opening of the double track on the new bridge marks an era in the handling of traffic over the Grand Trunk Railway system, for, whereas the old bridge could accommodate a maximum of but 100 trains per day—as they were required to travel at a low rate of speed, and one train could not follow another until the preceding one was out, thus losing a considerable amount of valuable time during a day—the present bridge has almost an unlimited capacity in this respect, as trains can be moved rapidly, and follow each other in rapid succession, owing to the establishment of a modern electric block system, which will permit two or three trains on the bridge at the same time. This enables the Grand Trunk to handle with facility the large freight business passing through Canada and the city of Montreal for export to Europe—which has heretofore been more or less hampered, owing to the limited capacity of the old bridge—as well as handling in a proper manner the large passenger business which annually comes to and through Montreal during the summer tourist season.

The current of the St. Lawrence at this point has a speed of about 7 miles an hour. Close by the bridge, at *Point St. Charles*, is the burying-ground of 6,000 immigrants who died in 1847-'48 of a frightful epidemic of ship-fever. In the center of the burying-ground is a huge bowlder known as the *Immigrants' Memorial Stone*, which was taken from the bed of the river and raised on a column of masonry by the workmen engaged in the construction of the bridge.

In sharp contrast with the gigantic tube of the Victoria Bridge is the aërial structure by which the Canadian Pacific Railway crosses the St. Lawrence at *Lachine*. This bridge is built on the most modern design, and is a brilliant application of the cantilever principle. Its spans appear like clusters of great steel cobwebs. They offer little resistance to the winds, and combine the greatest strength with the least possible weight.

Prominent among the buildings of Montreal are the Royal Victoria Hospital, the Board of Trade, Bank of Toronto, the capacious *Bonaventure Depot*, belonging to the Grand Trunk Ry., and the splendid stations of the Canadian Pacific on Windsor St. and Place Viger. These latter edifices may honestly be called palatial, resembling as they do a palace far more than railway stations.

In connection with the water-supply of Montreal there is a point of interest for the tourist. This is the great reservoir, which is hewn out of the solid rock far up the side of the mountain. The reservoir has a capacity of 36,500,000 gallons. It is supplied by an aqueduct which leads the water of the St. Lawrence from above the Lachine Rapids to a point on the western limit of the city, whence it is pumped up the mountain to the reservoir.

The tourist who is interested in athletics and outdoor sports will see some splendidly contested Lacrosse matches at the grounds of the Shamrock, National, and Montreal Clubs, and he will do well to visit the admirably equipped gymnasium of the Montreal Amateur Athletic Association and the Y. M. C. A. building on Dominion Square, or the fine baseball grounds on St. Catherine St. West. At the Lacrosse Grounds matches are usually being played on Saturday afternoons, or other days as advertised, and admission is by ticket. If he is at all touched with Anglomania he will be enraptured with the Montreal Hunt Club, the best-conducted establishment of the kind on the continent. In respect of sports, Montreal is as well off in winter as in summer. Hockey is the favorite pastime, and perhaps the best skaters and snow-shoers in the world are the sons and daughters of Montreal.

The following eminently practical bit from Murray's Illustrated Guide may be found useful by some travelers :

How to visit the Principal Places of Interest in the Shortest Time for the Least Money.

In whatever quarter of the city you are lodging, the first place to visit is the *Notre Dame Church.*

From the hotel either hire a cab or take the street-cars, and tell the conductor to let you off at Place d'Armes Square, and then a few paces from you is Notre Dame Church and several other places of interest. A few blocks E. from there is the *City Hall,* the *Court-House, Nelson's Monument, Château de Ramezay,* St. Gabriel St. old *Presbyterian Church,* and not far away is the *Bonsecours Market* and *Bonsecours Church.* While there you may visit *the harbor* and the *New Custom-House,* about a half-mile farther W. Then walk up Mc-Gill St. to Victoria Square, whence you may get the street-cars to take you to the principal places of interest up town. First visit the *Notre Dame de Lourdes,* near the corner of St. Catherine and St. Denis Sts. Thence retrace your steps westward till you come to Bleury St., and there is the old *Jesuits' Church* and *College.* Then turn up to St. Catherine St., W., till you come to the *Art Gallery,* corner of Phillips

Square. Then visit the *English Cathedral* and the *Museum of the Natural History Society*. Then take the street-cars till you come W. as far as Guy St., and visit the *Grey Nunnery* at noon. After dinner, hire a cab to take you to the *McGill University* (there is a very interesting museum in connection with the college, which visitors may enter on payment of a small entrance fee), and close by are the two city reservoirs; and you can hire a cab to take you to the top of the mountain, or you can go up by the incline railway. Then, after you have taken a good view of the surrounding country from the top of the mountain, and visited the two cemeteries, you can come back to the city by street-cars, and you have a day well spent, and not over $1 of necessary expense, besides your hotel bill. To this must be added the fact that the new electric car system will carry the traveler to almost any part of the city.

From Montreal to St. John.

From Montreal the tourist, who has already visited Quebec, may go direct to the *Maritime Provinces* by the Canadian Pacific Short Line (fare, $13.50; return, $19) which traverses the so-called Eastern Townships, the great hunting and fishing districts about *Lake Megantic* in N. E. Maine, and thence, almost as the crow flies, to *St. John, New Brunswick*. By this route we cross the St. Lawrence by the new Canadian Pacific R. R. bridge at *Lachine*, and run through the Indian village of *Caughnawaga*, where dwell the remnants of the Iroquois. These Indians are magnificent boatmen, and in the late Egyptian war a band of fifty of them did splendid service for England in the rapids of the Nile. At *Brigham Junction* the Montreal and Boston Air-Line diverges for the *White Mountains*. Soon we come in sight of *Memphremagog's* shining waters, watched over by the famous peaks of Elephantis and Owl's Head. From *Magog Station* a steamer departs daily on a circuit of the lake's winding shores, stopping at the many summer resorts for which the region is famous. After passing Magog, the next important station is *Sherbrooke*, the metropolis of the Eastern Townships, a pretty city at the junction of the Magog and St. Francis Rivers. Sherbrooke has a population of over 10,000, and is building up a large manufacturing interest. The falls of the Magog are well worth a visit. The chief hotels are the *Sherbrooke House, Magog House*, and *Grand Central*, charging from $1.50 to $2 a day. From Sherbrooke the Quebec Central R. R. runs through a rapidly developing country to Quebec. On the Quebec Central are the interesting and valuable asbestos mines of *Thetford*. Three miles beyond Sherbrooke is the pretty little university town of *Lennoxville*, the seat of the Church of England institutions of Bishop's College and Bishop's College School. These institutions have of late been making very great progress under the principalship of Dr. Adams; but the corporation has lately suffered a severe blow in the destruction by fire of the fine university building. In the neighborhood of Lennoxville a point of interest is *Spider Lake*, sometimes called the Geneva of Canada, where the club-house of the Megantic Fish and Game Club is located. Then we come to Lake Megantic, a body of water 12 miles long, from 1 to 4 in width, and a veritable Mecca of sportsmen. The name Megantic signifies " the resort of fish." There is fair accommodation at *Megantic Station*, and competent guides may be procured on the spot. Direct rail connection is made here with Levis (opposite Quebec) by the Quebec Central. A few miles beyond Megantic we cross the boundary-line, and find ourselves in the State of Maine. Twenty miles from Megantic Station we run into the village of *Lowelltown*. Then comes *Greenville*, on the shore of the grandest of all Maine waters, the famous *Moosehead Lake*. This water is 40 miles long and from 1 to 15 wide. Its scenery is magnificent and varied. Its waters are splendidly stocked with trout of great size, and around its shores are admirable shooting-grounds, where one may bag such game as moose, bear, deer, and caribou, to say nothing of grouse innumerable. At Greenville are guides and canoes, and several comfortable hotels. From *Greenville Junction* the Bangor & Aroostook R. R. diverges to Oldtown and Bangor, Me. Steamers run to all the points of interest on the lake, including the *Kineo House* at the foot of Mount Kineo. Moosehead Lake is the source of the *Kennebec River*, which flows out of the lake at *Askwith Station*. In the 100 miles of comparative wilderness between Moosehead Lake and *Mattawamkeag* the chief points of interest are Boarstone Mountain and the lovely Lake Onawa. At *Brownville Junction* we cross the line of the Katahdin Iron Works Railway. At *Mattawamkeag* the C. P. R. unites with the line connecting *Bangor* and *St. John*. At the same point the track crosses the *Penobscot River*. From this point to *Vanceboro*, on the New Brunswick boundary, we pass through a rugged country, full of lakes and streams, and dotted here and there with crude little lumbering villages. Vanceboro is on the *St. Croix River*, the outlet of the boundary, or Chiputneticook Lakes. The region of these lakes is a good one for the sportsman, and Vanceboro is a convenient point from which to reach them. Six miles beyond Vanceboro is *McAdam Junction*, a village whose houses are perched in such vacant spaces as can be found between the huge bowlders which cover the face of the land. At McAdam connections are made for *Woodstock* and *Presque Isle* to the N., and for *Calais*, *St. Stephen*, and the lovely summer resort of *St. Andrew's* to the S. Forty miles beyond McAdam is the little village of Fredericton Junction, 20 miles from Fredericton; and a run of 44 miles beyond Fredericton Junction, through scenes to be described in later pages, brings us to the city of *St. John*.

Montreal to Quebec by the St. Lawrence.

If the tourist has not seen *Quebec*, then assuredly he will not take the short line to the Maritime Provinces. By one of four routes he will certainly betake himself to a city that is perhaps, in many respects, the best worth seeing on the continent N. of Mexico; and from Quebec he will seek the Maritime Provinces probably by the Quebec Central and C. P. R. short lines, or the Intercolonial R. R., or, if very much addicted to the water, by steamer around the Gulf coast. From Montreal, one may go to Quebec either by the Grand Trunk or Intercolonial down the S. shore of the St. Lawrence, or by the Canadian Pacific down the N. shore, or by steamer down the mighty stream itself. As it is to be presumed that the traveler has plenty of time, and desires plenty of scenery, we would recommend the last-named route. The splendid palace steamers that ply between Montreal and Quebec belong to the Richelieu and Ontario Navigation Company. The distance is 180 miles; and the first-class fare, not including supper or berth, is $3.

As the steamer leaves Montreal we pass the village of *Longueuil*, on the S. shore, where many of Montreal's citizens have their summer abodes. At Longueuil, in 1775, Governor Carleton was defeated by the American forces. On the N. shore, a little beyond, is *Longue Pointe*, with the ruins of the great asylum already mentioned. Nine miles from Montreal we pass *Point-aux-Trembles*, with its old French church, which was built in 1709. A little farther on, and we are among the flat and reedy Isles of *Boucherville*, where admirable are the pike-fishing and duck-shooting in their seasons. Among these shoals and islands and reaches of slow water, the ice, in the spring breaking-up, is apt to run aground and jam, causing floods which

Montreal finds very troublesome. Fifteen miles from Montreal is the charmingly situated health-resort of *Varennes*, made important by its mineral springs. The fields of Varennes are washed in front by the St. Lawrence, and in the rear by the arrowy tide of the lovely and historic *Richelieu*. Thirty miles beyond Varennes the Richelieu flows into the St. Lawrence. At this point stands *Sorel*, which has lately been promoted to the dignity of a city. Here in 1665 a fort was established by De Tracy. Sorel was for a long time the summer residence of the Governors of Canada. There is good fishing among the islands which cluster at the Richelieu's mouth, and in October the neighborhood affords capital snipe-shooting. The population of Sorel is about 7,500.

In the towns and counties along the *Richelieu* are perpetuated the names of the officers of the old Carignan-Salières Regiment, who were stationed on seignories throughout this region to guard the approaches to Villemarie. As Mr. Hunter picturesquely puts it, they are "picketed around the ancient rendezvous at the confluence of the Richelieu and St. Lawrence, . . . as though still guarding the Iroquois River-Gate." Here, besides Varennes, we have Berthier, Lavaltrie, Boucher, Contrecœur, and Verchères. One of the most illustrious of Canada's heroines is Madeleine, daughter of Lieutenant Verchères. Verchères's fort was called "Castle Dangerous," being so exposed to the assaults of the Iroquois. On one occasion Madeleine, with a force of three men and two little boys, sustained the attacks of the Iroquois for a whole week, till help came from Quebec. The girl was at this time but fourteen years of age. Her followers, on the first attack, were for killing themselves, to escape the torture of the Iroquois, but her dauntless courage and energy gave them new heart, and her wisdom taught them to conduct the defense successfully.

The valley of the *Richelieu* was for two centuries a pathway of war, along which fire and sword, Iroquois and Abenakis, French and Dutch and English, Canadian and American, streamed alternately on errands of vengeful hate. The tourist who wishes to travel this blood-stained track will ascend through landscapes of blended sublimity and peace, and find himself at length on the bosom of that magnificent lake, no longer Canadian, which yet perpetuates the name of the Father of Canada, Samuel de Champlain. Like the war parties of old, he will find himself in the very heart of the State of New York. Unlike those ancient visitors, however, his visit will be not unwelcome. He will have found his ascent of the rushing Richelieu made easy by the *Chambly Cana'*,

Fort Chambly, on the Richelieu River, near Montreal.

He will have traversed the rich and lovely Eastern Townships and caught their distinctive flavor. He will probably delay his trip, and linger long and wander hither and thither in this delightful land of lake and mountain. Besides Lakes *Memphremagog* and *Megantic* he will visit the lovely waters of *Brome* and *Massawippi*. Through the wild, maple-wooded hills he will trace the path by which, in 1759, the avenging band of Rogers's Rangers swept to the slaughter of the Abenakis—after which the homes of New England had peace for a little.

The earliest recorded name of the Richelieu River, as found in Champlain's narratives, is *Rivière des Yrocois ;* so called because it led to the land of the Mohawks. The chief town on the Richelieu is the pretty little garrison city of *St. John*, with a population of about 5,000. Chief hotel the *Canada Hotel*.

A few miles below the mouth of the Richelieu the St. Lawrence opens out into the great expanse called *Lake St. Peter*. Cartier named this water, when first he ascended the St. Lawrence, Lac d'Angoulême ; but sixty-eight years later it was visited by Champlain on St. Peter's Day, and named in pious commemoration of the festival. The lake is 25 miles in length by 9 miles in breadth, and is shallow except in the channel, which has been dredged to afford safe passage to the largest ocean steamers. The shallow waters are subject to sudden and violent storms, by which the great rafts on their leisurely way to Quebec are frequently wrecked. The wide waters of Lake St. Peter were once famous for the songs of the raftsmen delayed on the sluggish current. Dr. W. H. Drummond has introduced this locality in his delightful book " The Habitant " :

> " On one dark night on Lac St. Pierre
> The wind she blow, blow, blow,
> An' the crew of the wood scow, Julie Plante,
> Got scairt and ran below.

> " The capiteen walk on the front deck,
> He walked the hin' deck too,
> He called the crew from up the hold,
> He called the cook also."

At the foot of Lake St. Peter is a sharp bend called *Pointe Platon*, with a little island over against it whereon of old stood a fort. It was called Fort Richelieu, and was established by Champlain in 1683. All vestiges of the fort have vanished, but its memory lingers in the name of the swift and broken water below Pointe Platon, which is known as the Richelieu Rapid.

A little below Lake St. Peter flows in from the north the great *St. Maurice River*, which will be referred to later on. At its mouth stands the city of **Three Rivers,** ranking third in importance and population among the cities of the province. This city stands midway between Montreal and Quebec, at the head of tide-water on the St. Lawrence. It has a population of about 10,000, and is the center of a heavy trade in lumber and iron. Around the city lie vast deposits of bog-iron ore, and the great lumbering interests of the upper St. Maurice find an outlet through its port. Three Rivers is the see of a Roman Catholic bishop, whose cathedral is an imposing structure. The city derives its name from the fact that the river on which it stands enters the St. Lawrence by three mouths. It was founded in 1618, and played an important part in the early history of Canada. The smelting of iron was begun at Three Rivers as early as 1737. The city is rendered the more interesting by the masses of legend and romantic tradition that cluster about it, offering a field which has hardly been touched save by the pen of the French-Canadian author, Benjamin Sulte. It will well repay an extended visit. Steamers ply from the city wharves to the adjacent river villages. Within easy reach are many large mountain brooks, swarming with trout; and from the city one may conveniently visit the splendid fishing waters of the upper St. Maurice. A stage-ride of 26 miles from Three Rivers takes one to the famous mineral springs of *St. Leon.* On the south shore of the St. Lawrence, opposite Three Rivers, is the village of *Doucet's Landing*, the terminus of the Arthabaska and Three Rivers branch of the G. T. Ry., which connects the city with the Eastern Townships.

A short distance below Three Rivers we pass the village of *Batiscan*, at the mouth of the Batiscan River. River and village are named after an Indian chief famous in the early history of Canada. The next village commemorates the apparently omnipresent Ste. Anne—in this case called *Ste. Anne de la Perade.* Beyond St. Anne's lies the ancient settlement of *Pointe-aux-Trembles*, where, during the final siege of Quebec in 1759, took place several encounters between French and English. The following incident is taken from the entertaining pages of Mr. J. M. Le Moine:

"A party of 1,200 of Fraser's Highlanders and Grenadiers," says Panet, "were dispatched to Pointe-aux-Trembles, commanded by General Wolfe in person, under the guidance of Major Robert Stobo, on July 21, 1759, and captured three men and a bevy of Quebec French ladies, who had sought a refuge there during the bombardment. The English were fired on by about 40 Indians, but succeeded, about half-past three in the morning, having surrounded the houses round the church, in capturing about thirteen ladies. Among the fair captives were Mesdames Duchesnay, De Charny, with her mother and her sister, and Mdlle. Couillard. The Joly, Malhiot, and Magnan families formed part of them. They were treated with every kind of respect. Young General Wolfe headed the detachment under the guidance of Major Robert Stobo, who, it seems, made several pretty speeches to the ladies —'qui a fait bien des compliments.'

"What was worse," remarks Panet, "was that while the British soldiery did them no harm, the Indians (allies of the French) pillaged the houses and property of nearly all these unfortunate refugees. (Panet's Journal du Siège, p. 13.) Each captive for the day bore the name of her captor.

"It sounds odd that it should have seemed necessary to detail 1,200 Highlanders and British Grenadiers, etc., to capture thirteen French ladies! One likes to recall this romantic incident in the career of Miss Lowther's admirer, James Wolfe—the chivalrous gallantry of the young soldier toward beauty in distress. Next day the fair Quebecers were brought home in boats and landed at Ance des Mères, at 3 P. M., orders having been sent by the General to the English fleet to stop firing on the city until 9 P. M., so as to afford the captives time, after their release, to retire to a place of safety. Who were on that July 21, 1759, Madame Wolfe, Madame Stobo, Madame Frazer? What a lark for the sons of Mars to write about in their next home letters! At Pointe-aux-Trembles occurred, during the spring of 1760, the engagement between the French frigates and an overwhelming force of the British fleet, brave Captain de Vauclain, of the Atalante, winning, by his spirited though unsuccessful defense, the respect of worthy foes."

Next we pass *Jacques-Cartier River*, famous for its salmon-fishing and well stocked with trout. Here the shores of the St. Lawrence begin to grow more bold and picturesque. Lower down we pass, in the clear morning light, the old village of *St. Augustin*, whose first church, built in 1690, enjoyed, according to tradition, a very peculiar distinction. It is told that the devil, in the guise of a gigantic black horse of monstrous strength, hauled the huge stones of the foundation walls. About 12 miles from Quebec is the mouth of the *Chaudière River*, flowing in from the south. This river runs a wild course of about 100 miles, and as it nears the St. Lawrence plunges down a magnificent fall of nearly 100 ft. The cataract is famous for its picturesque grandeur. It was by way of the valley of the Chaudière that Benedict Arnold led his troops on that heroic but disastrous expedition of his from New England to Quebec. The storied heights which loom on either hand as we approach Quebec will be described in subsequent paragraphs. Steaming between the cliffs of Lévis and the guns of that aërial citadel which guards the gate of Canada, we round up to the wharves of Quebec.

To Quebec by the South Shore.

In going from Montreal to Quebec by the Grand Trunk, the traveler is carried far south of the St. Lawrence, and through the romantic and richly storied landscapes already described in connection with the Richelieu River. It is a lovely journey, and should be taken on the day express. The crossing of the *Victoria Jubilee Bridge* occupies between four and five minutes. A magnificent view of Montreal is obtained. From Montreal to *Richmond*, where the Quebec Branch diverges from the main line running through to *Portland, Me.*, the way is thick with thriving towns, and fruitful in historic memories. *St. Hilaire*, 22 miles east of Montreal, has excellent black-bass and pike fishing in June, July, and August. The busy little French city of *St. Hyacinthe*, on the *Yamaska River*, has some points of interest for the tourist, and a population of about 8,000. It has a college, two cathedrals, and a large manufacturing interest in leather, woolens, and machinery. At *Richmond*, important as a junction town, and for the copper-mines in its vicinity, there is a village population of between 1,000 and 2,000. A few miles beyond Richmond is the growing village of *Danville*, with several factories. *Arthabaska* village is of importance chiefly as the starting-point of the branch line to *Doucet's Landing*, already referred to. Near Arthabaska we cross the river *Nicolet*, named for Champlain's brave interpreter, Jean Niclot the peacemaker, who dwelt for nine years among the wizard Nipissings. A little beyond Arthabaska lies the village of *Stanfold*. At *Lyster*, where we cross the *Becancour River*, there is a considerable lumbering business. Twenty miles from *Lévis* is a station with the musical name of *St. Agapit de Beaurivage*. At *Chaudière* we cross the wild river of the same name, already referred to. Nine miles farther on we stop at the station of *Lévis*, whence a ferry carries us over to Quebec.

The Intercolonial has opened a line to Lévis. It runs on the tracks of the Grand Trunk to Rosalie Junction, whence its route lies between the Grand Trunk line and the St. Lawrence River to Lévis.

To Quebec by the North Shore.

The trains of the C. P. R. run between Quebec and Montreal along the north shore of the St. Lawrence, in five and a half hours. This is a rapid and luxurious trip, for the line is unrivaled in management and equipment; but in the way of landscape it offers little variety. Leaving *Place Viger Station* we pass the stations of *Hochelaga, Mile End,* and *Sault aux Récollets,* and reach *St. Martin's Junction,* whence the main line of the C. P. R. swerves off for its long journey across the continent. Passing the junction, we cross the north branch of the Ottawa River at *Terrebonne,* whose limestone quarries have built Montreal. From *Joliette Junction* there are branch lines to a number of small towns—such as *Joliette, St. Felix de Valois,* and *St. Gabriel de Brandon.* From *Lanoraie* and *Berthier Junctions* run short branch lines to villages of the same names on the river-shore. Berthier has a population of 2,500. In the neighborhood of *Louiseville* are the *St. Leon Springs,* already referred to. All these stations are in a level, highly cultivated plain, cut up into the long, narrow fields that characterize the older parts of Quebec. This curious arrangement arises from the French custom of dividing estates equally among the owner's heirs, and giving each portion of the subdivided farms a like river-frontage. Leaving Louiseville the train runs through *Yamachiche* and *Point du Lac,* and reaches the city of *Three Rivers.*

The *St. Maurice River,* third in rank of the tributaries of the St. Lawrence, rises in a maze of lakes and streams 220 miles to the north. In the same wild region rise the Ottawa and the Saguenay. It is a region visited only by a few Indians and trappers, Hudson Bay traders, and the lumbermen whose axes ring on the banks of every stream. Civilization has as yet but touched the skirts of this wilderness. From the banks of the St. Lawrence it has climbed the river about 100 miles, and ends at the roaring falls of the *Tuque.* Between this point and the "Piles," 60 miles farther down, the St. Maurice runs quietly, and is traversed by a small steamer. The lower St. Maurice is a succession of falls and rapids, which are avoided by a railway running from the "Piles" to *Piles' Junction* on the C. P. R. Below the "Piles" the land lies in terraces or "benches." At Grand Mere are extensive pulp-mills. Twenty-four miles above Three Rivers are the famous *Shawenegan Falls,* remarkable for their beauty and grandeur even in this country of cataracts. The Indian name, Shawenegan, signifies "needlework," and was doubtless

6

suggested by the beautiful play of colors on the foaming surface. Just above the falls the river is split by a rocky island. The right branch descends with a direct plunge. The left, roaring around the obstacle, meets the other almost at right angles. Here the reunited torrent finds its way blocked by a rugged point. Hurled back upon itself, the river falls away to one side, and sweeps down a rocky trough into the swirling bosom of a spacious basin. Into this same basin winds peacefully, between quiet glades of elms and river meadows, the Shawenegan River. If one ascends this stream a little way, which may be done very delightfully in a canoe, he will be rewarded by a sight of one of the loveliest and most romantic of cascades, the *Little Shawenegan Falls*. Guides to the fishing and shooting of the St. Maurice may be obtained at Three Rivers and other places. For information as to leased waters, for permits, etc., one should write in advance to the Government Superintendent of the St. Maurice District.

Two miles beyond Three Rivers our train passes Piles Junction, already referred to. Then come *Champlain, Batiscan, Lachevrotière,* and other villages whose names savor of old France. *Portneuf* is a busy little town, devoted to the manufacture of shoes and wood-pulp. Seven miles from Quebec is *Lorette*, a settlement of Christianized Huron Indians, founded about two centuries and a half ago. Beyond Lorette we pass the junction of the Quebec and Lake St. John R. R., the gateway to that sportsman's paradise which lies about the head-waters of the Saguenay. Four miles farther, and our train stops under the citadel of Quebec.

City of Quebec.

Hotels, etc.—The *Château Frontenac* ($3.50 to $5 a day), on Dufferin Terrace; the *Florence* ($2.50 to $4 a day), in St. John St.; the *Victoria Hotel; Henchey's Hotel*, in St. Ann St.; *Mountain Hill House* ($1.50 a day), on Mountain St.; and *Blanchard's*, in the Lower Town.

Modes of Conveyance.—Street-cars (fare 5c.) traverse the streets along the river in the Lower Town and extend to the suburbs. A second line runs along St. John St. in the Upper Town. Carriages or *calèches* may be hired at the livery-stables, and on the cab-stands near the hotels and markets. The *calèche*, a two-wheeled one-horse apparatus, is the usual vehicle, and costs about 75c. an hour. Ferries connect the city with South Quebec, New Liverpool, and Point Levi, on the opposite side of the St. Lawrence, and run three times a day to the Isle of Orleans. An elevator runs from Champlain St. to Dufferin Terrace in the summer only.

Clubs.—Garrison, Union, Castanet, Club de Marchands, Club Montmorency, Le Carillon, Quebec Assemblies, Quebec High-School Museum.

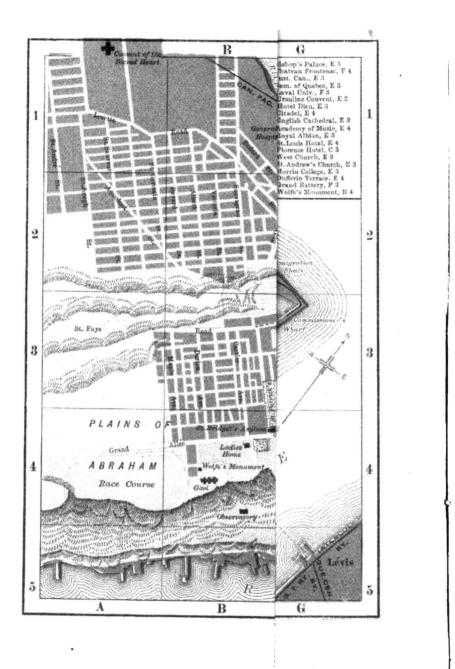

B   G

1   1

2   2

3   3

4   4

5   5

A   B   G

Convent of the
Sacred Heart

Bishop's Palace, E 3
Chateau Frontenac, F 4
Inst. Can., E 3
Gem. of Quebec, E 3
Laval Univ., F 3
Ursuline Convent, E 3
Hotel Dieu, E 3
Citadel, E 4
English Cathedral, E 3
General Academy of Music, E 4
Hospital Royal Albion, E 3
St. Louis Hotel, E 4
Florence Hotel, C 3
West Church, E 3
St. Andrew's Church, E 3
Morrin College, E 3
Dufferin Terrace, E 4
Grand Battery, F 3
Wolfe's Monument, B 4

Laurier

St. Andre
Ste.

Road

Road

St. Foye   Road

PLAINS OF

Grand

ABRAHAM

Race Course

Alfee

Ladies
Home

Wolfe's Monument

Gaol

Observatory

Levis

Immigration
Sheds

Commissioner's
Wharf

St. Patrick

Restaurants.—Chien d'Or, Mercantile, Quebec Club, Royal Mail, St. Peter.

Theatre.—Academy of Music.

Population of Quebec, 85,000.

QUEBEC, 1757.

(From the French of Philippe de Gaspé, author of The Canadians of Old. Translated by Charles G. D. Roberts, and published by D. Appleton & Co.)

An eagle city on her heights austere,
  Taker of tribute from the chainless flood,
She watches wave above her in the clear
  The whiteness of her banner purged with blood.

Near her grim citadel the blinding sheen
  Of her cathedral spire triumphant soars,
Rocked by the Angelus, whose peal serene
  Beats over Beaupré and the Lévis shores.

Tossed in his light craft on the dancing wave,
  A stranger where he once victorious trod,
The passing Iroquois, fierce-eyed and grave,
  Frowns on the flag of France, the cross of God.

Among the cities of the New World the grandest for situation, the most romantic in associations, the most distinctive and picturesque in details, is the sentinel city that keeps the gates of the St. Lawrence. Nothing could be more impressive than the view of Quebec from a little distance down the river, unless it be the matchless panorama to be seen from the parapets of *Dufferin Terrace*, within the city. Looking up toward Quebec, or looking down from Quebec, it is hard to say which is the more impressive view. When one is ascending the St. Lawrence he sees on his right the milk-white cataract of *Montmorency*, descending as it were out of heaven over the dark face of the mountains that skirt the north shore of the St. Lawrence. On the left the white villages of *Isle d'Orleans*, with their far-glittering gilded spires, nestle in the deep green of luxuriant groves. In front rises the enchanting city, tier upon tier of steep-roofed houses and quaint, precipitous streets, breadths of gray cliff-front, and again the roofs and towers, and far up, on the summit of the height, the grim eyrie of the ancient citadel. Across the face of the peopled steep run irregularly the massive lines of the city walls, and on a natural terrace midway between the water-front and the *citadel* frown the guns of the *Grand Battery*. Near by is the picturesque *Château Frontenac*, a magnificent fire-proof hotel, modeled on the plan of the sixteenth-century French *châteaux*, and costing nearly $1,000,000. The flourishing suburb of *St. Roch* sweeps off to the right from the lower slopes of the cape, and dwindles into the villages of *Charlesbourg* and *Lorette*. A little lower down the quiet current of the *St. Charles* winds in silver curves through the meadows of *Beauport*. On the high shores beyond the city are the dark fir-groves of *Sillery*, "with its memories of missions and massacres." The water-front of the city is thronged with ships whose masts and funnels obscure the warehouses. Ships are anchored thickly in mid-channel, and between them dodge the puffing tugs and the high two-decker ferries making their hasty way to the lofty and huddling town of *Lévis*, whose heights resound all day to the shrieks of locomotives. The picture is one whose sublime lines and masses are brought out to the full by the fresh coloring that plays over it. Under the vivid and flawless blue come out sharply the pale gray of the citadel, the duller gray of the cliff-face streaked with rust-color and splashed with light green, the black guns bristling on the ramparts and batteries, the brown streets, roofs of shining tin, and gilded steeples, with here and there a billow of thick foliage, the blue-green flood of the St. Lawrence, the white and emerald of the tributary farms and villages, and the somber purple setting of the remote surrounding hills. A famous American bishop declares, "Only Heidelberg in Germany, Stirling and Edinburgh in Scotland, and Ehrenbreitstein on the Rhine, can contend with Quebec for grandeur of situation and the noblest beauty." The vast promontory which the city occupies is called *Cape Diamond*, from the innumerable quartz crystals which once glittered over its surface.

Her *Winter Carnivals*, with their ice castles stormed by torchlight, their gay skating tournaments and masquerades, their unrivaled snowshoe parades, have become world-famous. The climax of the Carnival is the assault upon the ice-castle, which, illuminated within by electric light, flames with a white and ghostly radiance recalling the dream-palaces of Kublai Khan. Down the mountain wind the assailing lines of torch-bearers, their strange costumes more strange in the lurid light; and the spectral citadel is carried with tumult, amid a many-colored storm of rockets, Roman candles, and all the most gorgeous of pyrotechnic devices.

THE HISTORY OF QUEBEC.

The site of Quebec, when visited in 1535 by Jacques Cartier, was occupied by the Indian town of Stadacona, which signifies "The narrowing of the river." Cartier was received by the Indians with generous hospitality, and by their aid continued his explorations up the river to Hochelaga. Before starting on his return voyage to France he repaid their kindness by kidnapping their head chief Donnacona, with several others of the tribe, to take home as trophies and proofs of his adventure. In 1541 Cartier came again with five ships, but found no friendly welcome. His treachery was not to be forgotten in five years. He attempted to found a settlement at Cap Rouge, but the hostility of the Indians lay heavy upon him and the effort was abandoned. A little later the attempt was repeated by the Sieur de Roberval, nicknamed by Francis I "The little King of Vimieu." This was in 1549. The enterprise of De Roberval, which came to a disastrous end after a winter of terrible sufferings and strange disease, has been made the subject of a picturesque and brilliant historical drama by the Canadian poet John Hunter Duvar. With the remnants of his little colony De Roberval set sail for France, and nothing more was heard of him thereafter. It is supposed that the ships went down in a storm off the coast of Newfoundland.

The real founding of Quebec was in 1608, when Champlain established a post at the foot of the steep. Stadacona had passed away. Soon a tiny village stood upon its site. Champlain was a practical colonizer, and he succeeded where Cartier and Roberval had failed. In the winter came the scourge of that strange and dreadful disease, the scurvy, and of his little band of 28 but 8 survived to greet the spring. In the following year Champlain made an alliance with the tribes of the Algonquins and Hurons, and committed New France to a hundred years of war with the Five Nations. For some years Quebec was but a military and fur-trading post, but Champlain's purpose was to found an empire, and the foundation of that, he well knew, must be laid in farming. He brought out one Louis Hébert, with his son-in-law Couillard, to till the soil of New France. The families of these men struck deep root into the virgin soil, and now their descendants are to be found all over the province. Two of the quaintest and most mediæval-looking of the streets of Quebec are *Hébert* and *Couillard Sts.*, which are said to run where ran the first furrows plowed in Canada. They are straighter than those old streets in Boston which follow the devious paths worn by the cows of the Pilgrim Fathers. Had the farmers come to Quebec in as great numbers as did the Récollets and Jesuits, and with half the zeal and energy of these latter, New France would have grown as rapidly as New England. As it was, however, its growth was comparatively slow, and the policy of the great fur-trading company which controlled it for a long while checked its development. In 1629 the infant stronghold was captured by Sir David Kirke; but it was restored to France by the Treaty of St. Germain-en-Laye, and Champlain again became its Governor. In 1635 the "Father of Canada" died, and, strange to say, we know not his exact resting place, for the records of Quebec were burned in the great fire of 1640. It is enough to know that he lies somewhere within the city, and Quebec is his all-sufficient monument. Quebec may be said to have been born under the auspices of two strangely incongruous powers —religion and the fur-trade—and the former, fortunately, got the best of it in the long run. It moved rich and devoted women to found such institutions in the new colony as the *Hôtel Dieu* and the *Ursuline Convent*. The former was established by the Duchess d'Aiguillon, with the help of the Hospital Nuns of Dieppe; the latter by a rich and beautiful young widow, Madame de la Peltrie, who devoted her fortune and her life to the welfare of New France. To this day Quebec is full of churches, ecclesiastical establishments, and institutions of charity. In 1663 the whole population of New France was not above 2,000, scattered thinly along the river from the Saguenay to Montreal. Of these Quebec contained 800. Then came better days; and Louis XIV, destroying the monopoly of the fur company, took the colony under his own control. Immigration was energetically promoted, and under the management of the wise Intendant, Talon, Quebec rose into a commercial importance which it took his incompetent and unscrupulous successors a long while to destroy. After Talon's time New France was ruled by several excellent governors, chief of whom was the great Frontenac; but the business management of the colony was in the hands of the intendants and abominably conducted. In October, 1690, came Sir William Phips with an English fleet, and, anchoring off Isle d'Orleans, demanded the capitulation of the city. Very short was the answer of the fiery old Governor, Frontenac, and emphatic was his repulse of the hostile squadron; but New France was ever a thorn in the side of the English-speaking colonies along the Atlantic seaboard, and the citadel on Cape Diamond was a wasp's nest, by whose stings they were goaded all too frequently. Not unnatural was their demand for its destruction, and in 1711 the task was again undertaken, this time by Admiral Sir Hoveden Walker. His fleet, however, was shattered by a storm in the Gulf of St. Lawrence; and for

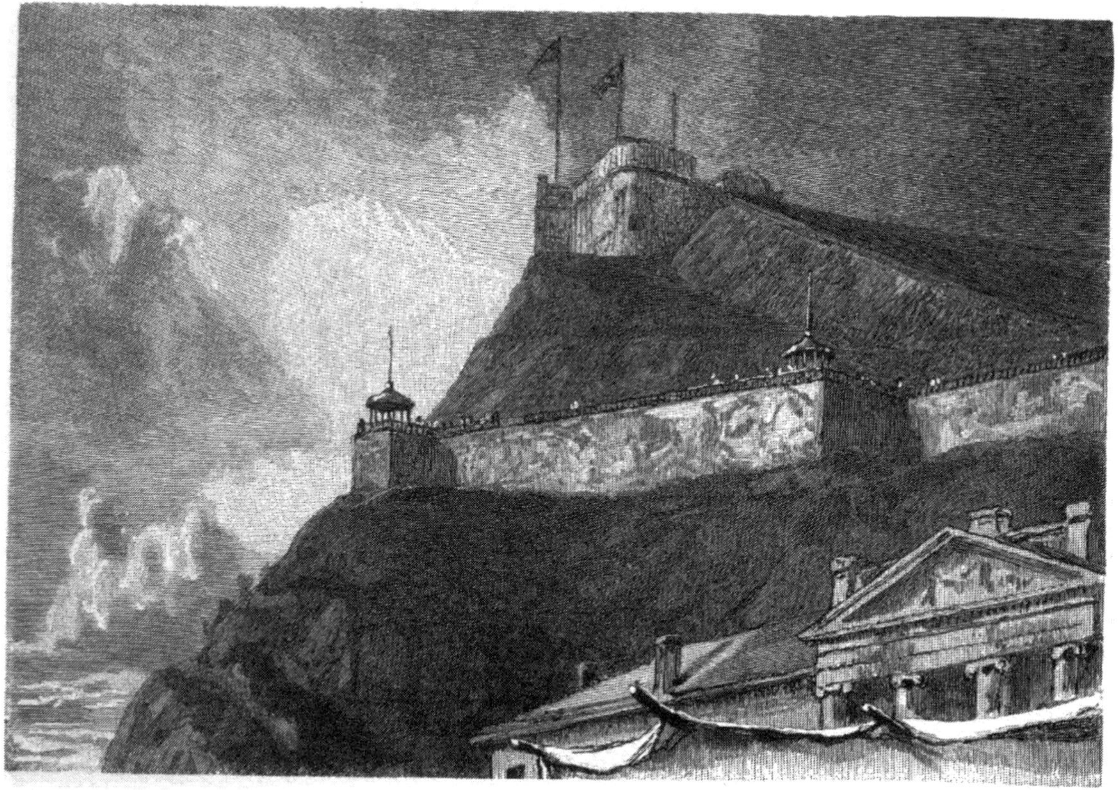

Citadel at Quebec.

these two deliverances the parish church in the *Lower Town* was dedicated to *Notre Dame des Victoires*. During the Seven Years' War between France and England, Quebec was finally captured, and the leopards of England supplanted the lilies of France. This took place in 1759. The splendid victory of General Wolfe against heavy odds has been brilliantly narrated by Parkman. On the 26th of June came a fleet under Admiral Saunders, with transports carrying Wolfe and the English army. The fleet anchored off *Isle d' Orleans*, which at that time retained the name given it by Cartier, Isle de Bacchus. The French army, of about 13,000 men, under command of the illustrious Montcalm, was occupying the *Beauport* shore. General Moncton took possession of the *Lévis Heights* and bombarded the city. On the 31st of July Wolfe effected a landing near the *Montmorency River* and attacked the French lines. He was defeated with severe loss. Then followed a long and weary delay caused by Wolfe's illness, and not until September could the attack be renewed. Under cover of night the English forces stole up river, under the guns of the citadel. At dawn of September 13th a landing was gained at a place now called *Wolfe's Cove*, below *Sillery*. The heights above appeared inaccessible, but they were scaled successfully, Wolfe's Highlanders leading the way. A small French guard on the summit was promptly overcome, and by the time it was clear day the British line of battle was formed on the *Plains of Abraham*. Montcalm was outgeneraled. He was still in camp at Beauport, on the scene of his victory, awaiting another attack. In hot haste he threw his forces across the *St. Charles*, and by 10 o'clock the armies were engaged. The battle was short. Wolfe fell mortally wounded, on the spot now marked by Wolfe's monument; and almost at the same moment the French lines broke, and Montcalm, who had received his death-wound, was carried by the fugitives into the city, where he died and was buried in the Ursuline Convent. The French army drew off to *Cap Rouge*, and on the 18th Quebec was surrendered to the English. In October the fleet sailed for England, and General Murray was left in the city as governor, with a garrison about 6,000 strong. Now, under the very walls of the citadel, just back of the Dufferin Terrace, stands a monument in joint commemoration of the opposing generals who fell on the Plains of Abraham.

> " Montcalm and Wolfe ! Wolfe and Montcalm !
>   Quebec, thy storied citadel
>   Attest in burning song and psalm
>   How here thy heroes fell ! "

In the following spring the besiegers became the besieged. The French general De Lévis, with an army of about 10,000 men, defeated Murray on the Plains of Abraham; and the English were shut up behind the fortifications till relief came in the shape of an English fleet on the 15th of May. De Lévis withdrew; and soon afterward Canada became an English colony. In 1775, during the American Revolution, General Benedict Arnold, with a small army, made his famous march by the *Chaudière Valley*, scaled the heights at Wolfe's Cove, and laid siege to the city. Two weeks later General Montgomery arrived. On the 31st of December the American forces advanced to the assault, but were repulsed with heavy loss. The brave Montgomery fell before a barricade on *Champlain St.* The house on *St. Louis St.* to which his body was taken is now an Indian curiosity-shop, and one of the points of interest of the city. Montgomery was buried at the foot of *Citadel Hill*, but the body was afterward removed to New York.

POINTS OF INTEREST.

Quebec is often called the Gibraltar of America. The base of the citadel is 333 feet above the water. Its fortifications cover about 40 acres. The city is divided into the *Upper* and *Lower Town*, which are connected by an elevator ascending the face of the cliff, and by a steep, winding street called *Côte de la Montagne.* The cliff face is in places insecure, and not long since an immense mass of rock fell away, overwhelming a portion of the street below. Many persons perished in this catastrophe; and now, though costly engineering operations have been undertaken to reinforce the cliff, wayfarers who pass along *Champlain St.* do so in fear and trembling. Most of the business is in the Lower Town, by the water-side. The Upper Town lies within the city walls and beyond them to the *Plains of Abraham*, and comprises also the suburbs of *St. Louis* and *St. John.* The walls run west from the citadel to the heights overhanging the *St. Charles*, and thence around the face of the promontory till they rejoin the cliffs of *Cape Diamond* near the Governor's garden, a circuit of nearly 3 miles. Some years ago the old city gates, five in number, were removed, but two new ones, far more substantial and ornamental, have replaced them. These are *St. Louis Gate* and the *Kent Gate* in *St. Patrick's St.*

"The point to which the attention of the stranger in Quebec is first directed is *Dufferin Terrace*, which lies along the edge of the cliff, towering 200 feet above the river, and overlooking the Lower Town.

Part of it occupies the site of the old Château of St. Louis, built by Champlain in 1620, and destroyed by fire in 1834. Dufferin Terrace, which was opened to the public in June, 1879, by the Marquis of Lorne and Princess Louise, is an unequaled promenade over ¼ mile long. The outlook from the Terrace is one of the finest in the world, and is of itself worth a trip to Quebec. The *Esplanade*, near the St. Louis Gate, is another attractive promenade, and the walk along the Ramparts between the St. Louis Gate and St. John's Gate, affords prospects rivaled by few in America. The view from the *Grand Battery*, near the *Laval University*, is considered by many to be finer even than that from Dufferin Terrace; and that from the vast balcony of the University building is still more impressive. The new hotel, *Château Frontenac*, must be counted one of the sights of Quebec. The *Place d'Armes*, or Parade-ground, is a pretty little park adorned with a fine fountain, lying between Dufferin Terrace and the Anglican Cathedral, which is a plain gray-stone edifice surmounted by a tall spire, standing in St. Ann St. on the site to which tradition points as the spot where Champlain erected his first tent. Adjoining the cathedral is the rectory, and the pretty little *Chapel of All Saints*. Des Carrières St., running south from the Place d'Armes, leads to the *Governor's Garden*, containing an obelisk 65 feet high, to the memory of Wolfe and Montcalm. Des Carrières St. also leads to the inner *glacis* of the *Citadel*, a powerful fortification, covering 40 acres of ground, on the summit of Cape Diamond." *

The old *Market Square*, on which has recently been erected a beautiful bronze fountain, is in the center of the Upper Town, surrounded by more or less striking buildings. On the E. side is the *Basilica* of Quebec (formerly the Cathedral), a spacious cut-stone building, 216 ft. long and 180 ft. wide, and capable of seating 4,000 persons. The exterior of the edifice is very plain, but the interior is richly decorated, and contains several original paintings of great value by Vandyke, Caracci, Hallé, and others. Adjoining the Basilica on the N. are the quaint buildings of the **Seminary of Quebec**, founded in 1663 by M. de Laval, first Bishop of Quebec. The Seminary Chapel was destroyed by fire in 1887, but it is now being rebuilt. All the rare and priceless works of art were burned. The **Laval University**, founded in 1852, occupies three very imposing buildings. They are

---

* Appletons' General Guide to U. S. A. and Canada.

of cut stone, 576 ft. long (the main building being 286 ft.), five stories high, and costing $240,000. The chemical laboratory is spacious, fire-proof, and provided with complete apparatus; the geological, miner-alogical, and botanical collections are very valuable; the museum of zoölogy contains upward of 1,300 different birds and 7,000 insects; and the museum of the medical department is especially complete. The Library numbers nearly 95,000 volumes, and the Picture Gallery (always open to the public) is one of the richest in Canada, and contains many important works of art. On the W. side of Market Square is the site of the old *Jesuits' College* buildings. *Morrin College* occupies the old stone prison at the cor. of St. Ann and Stanislas Sts. In this building are the library (14,500 volumes) and museum of the Quebec Literary and Historical Society, with its rich collection of MSS. relating to the early history of the country. The High School on the Cape has 200 students, an excellent library, and a small natural history collection.

In Donnaconna St., off Garden, is the **Ursuline Convent,** a series of buildings surrounded by beautiful grounds. It was founded in 1639, and now has 40 nuns, who are devoted to teaching girls, and also to painting, needlework, etc. The parlor and chapel are open to visitors, and in the latter are rare carvings on ivory and some fine paintings by Vandyke, Champagne, and others. The remains of the Marquis de Mont-calm are buried here in an excavation made by the bursting of a shell within the precincts of the convent. His skull is preserved in the par-lor of the chaplain. The *Grey Nunnery* is a spacious building on the glacis W. of the ramparts, and contains about 75 Sisters. The Chapel adjoining the nunnery is a lofty and ornate Gothic edifice, with a rich interior. Near by (in St. John St. near St. Clair) the new Roman Catho-lic church of St. John replaces the large structure destroyed by fire a few years ago. The **Hôtel Dieu,** with its convent and hospital, stands on Palace St., near the rampart, and in 1875 comprised 45 Sisters of the Sacred Blood of Dieppe, who minister gratuitously to 10,000 patients yearly. In the Convent Chapel are some valuable paintings. The *Black Nunnery* is in the suburbs of St. Roch's. Application to the Lady Superiors will usually secure admittance to the nunneries.

The *Post-Office* is a handsome stone edifice at the corner of Buade and Du Fort Sts. On its face is the historic effigy of "the Golden Dog," *Le Chien d'Or,* with its menacing inscription—"Je suis un chien qui ronge l'os," etc. (I am a dog that gnaws the bone), commemorating a bitter feud between the infamous Bigot and the merchant Philibert, and the long-delayed vengeance of the latter. The tale has been amplified in Mr. Kirby's romance of "Le Chien d'Or." Immediately opposite is the *Chien d' Or Restaurant*, famous for the circumstance that the niece of its first proprietor captivated the fancy of Nelson, then captain of the Albemarle, whose attempted elopement with the "maid of the inn" was frustrated by a friendly Quebec merchant. The incident is, perhaps, the foundation of that rough sailor-song called "Shannodor." Near by is the *Cardinal's Palace*, a stately and handsome structure. Other noteworthy buildings in the Upper Town are the City Hall, the Quebec Academy of Music, the Masonic Hall, and the Garrison Clab, in St. Louis St. On Grande Allée are situated the Skating-Rink, the *Parliament* and *Departmental Buildings*, which were begun in 1878, and the Armory and Exhibition Building, a beautiful structure. The Court-House, finished in 1888, is on the corner of St. Louis St. and Place d'Armes. Among noteworthy churches are the Methodist Church in St. Stanislas St., a fine specimen of the flamboyant Gothic style; St. Matthew's (Episcopal), in St. John St.; St. Andrew's (Presbyterian), at the intersection of St. Ann and St. Stanislas Sts., a spacious stone structure in the Gothic style; Chalmers (Presbyterian), in St. Ursule St.; St. Patrick's (Roman Catholic), in McMahon St., and St. Sauveur and St. Roch's, in the suburbs. The fine and spacious Y. M. C. A. Hall is in St. John St., just without St. John's Gate. There are a good library, lecture-room, and reading-rooms, etc., opposite to which is the Montcalm Market Square and Hall. The Institut Canadien is in Fabrique St., and in Ann St. is situated the Woman's Christian Association.

Just N. of Dufferin Terrace is the head of Mountain Hill St., which descends to the Lower Town. To the right is a picturesque stairway, called the *Champlain Steps*, or *Côte de la Montagne*, which leads down to the church of Notre-Dame des Victoires, erected in 1690 on the site of Champlain's residence. S. of the church is the *Champlain Market*, a spacious structure on the river-bank, near the landing of the river steamers. St. Peter St., running N. between the cliff and the river, is the main business thoroughfare of this quarter, and contains the great commercial establishments, banking-houses, wholesale stores, etc. St. Paul St. stretches W. on the narrow strand between the cliff and the St. Charles, amid breweries and manufactories, till it meets, near the mouth of the St. Charles, St. Joseph St., the main artery of the large suburb of St. Roch's. On the banks of the St. Charles are the principal ship-yards, once so thriving; and the numerous coves of the St. Lawrence, from Champlain St. to Cap Rouge, are filled with acres of vast lumber-rafts. On the opposite shore of the St. Lawrence are the populous towns of *South Quebec*, *New Liverpool*, and *Levis*, which present a scene of activity scarcely surpassed by the city itself. The *Custom-House* is reached from St. Peter St. by Leadenhall St., and occupies the very apex of the point made by the confluence of the St. Lawrence and the St. Charles Rivers. It is an imposing Doric edifice, with a dome, and a façade of noble columns, approached by a long flight of steps. The Marine and Emigrants' Hospital, built on the model of the Temple of the Muses, on the banks of the Ilissus, is near the St. Charles River, and half a mile farther up the river is the General Hospital. This institution was founded in 1693, and is under the charge of the nuns of St. Augustine. Overlooking St. Roch's suburbs is the Jeffery Hale Hospital. The Finlay Asylum is on St. Foye road.

The suburbs of St. Louis and St. John stretch S. and W. along the plateau of the Upper Town, and are constantly encroaching on the historic *Plains of Abraham*. They contain many handsome private residences and several large conventual establishments and churches. The best approach to the Plains of Abraham is by *Grande Allée*, which begins at the St. Louis Gate and the Martello Towers, four circular stone structures erected in 1807-'12 to defend the approaches to the city. On the spot where Wolfe fell in the memorable battle of September 13, 1759, stands *Wolfe's Monument*, a modest column appropriately inscribed. A short distance to the left is the path by which his army scaled the cliffs on the night before the battle; it is somewhat shorn of its rugged character, but is still precipitous and forbidding. On the Plains, near the Ste. Foye road, stands the monument commemorating the victory won by the Chevalier de Lévis over General Murray in 1760. It is a handsome iron column, surmounted by a bronze statue of Bellona (presented by Prince Napoleon), and was erected in 1854. About 3 miles out on the St. Louis road are *Mount Hermon Cemetery*, 32 acres in extent, beautifully laid out on irregular ground, sloping down to the precipices which overhang the St. Lawrence, and St. Patrick's (R. C.) Cemetery.

In its surroundings Quebec is more fortunate than any city in Canada. In whatever direction one turns, some point of interest will appear. The great island below the city, already mentioned as **Isle d'Orleans**, is rich with history and romance, and is a favorite summer resort for the citizens of Quebec. It was called *Isle de Bacchus* by Cartier, and *Minego* by the Indians. By the superstitious *habitants* it is still called *Isle des Sorcières*, and is piously believed to be the favored resort of every kind of hobgoblin. This superstition, however, has not hindered the fruitful island from becoming the seat of many flourishing villages, such as *St. Pierre, St. Jean, St. Laurent, St. Féréol, St. François*. The island is reached by a ferry-steamer from Quebec.

The Falls of Montmorency.

From Quebec to the **Falls of Montmorency**, 9 miles below, is a delightful drive over the *Beauport meadows* and through an almost continuous street of cottages and farm-houses. The tourist who prefers to make the trip more speedily and less expensively may go by the Quebec, Montmorency and Charlevoix R. R., which runs 21 miles down the St. Lawrence shore to the famous shrine at *St. Anne*, whither the pilgrims flock by thousands every season. Fare to Montmorency, 20c.; return, 30c. To St. Anne, 60c.; return, 85c. "The Montmorency Falls," says Mr. Le Moine, in his charming Tourist's Note-Book, "are still known to old French peasants as *La Vache* (the Cow) on account of the resemblance of their foaming waters to milk, though others have attributed the name to the noise, like the bellowing of a cow, which is made by the roaring torrent during the prevalence of certain winds. They present, when swollen by spring floods or by autumnal rains, a most imposing spectacle. The volume of water, though much less than that of Niagara, falls from a much greater height—viz., 275 ft. Beauport's wondrous cataract may be seen under various attractive aspects. . . . I also remember, on a bright, starry night amid winter, contemplating in dreamy-rapt silence a novel spectacle, seldom vouchsafed to Quebecers. The snowy cone at the foot of the cataract had been scooped out by an enterprising city *restaurateur*, to represent a vast, glittering palace, provided with icy couches, seats, etc.—a cold, bright but fitting throne for the Frost King, illumined by Chinese lamps, reminding one of Cowper's glowing description of Imperial Catharine's Russian ice-palace of 1787:

> 'a scene
> Of evanescent glory, once a stream,
> And soon to glide into a stream again.' "

The Falls should be viewed both from above and from below. To see them well from above one must cross the *Montmorency Bridge*, traverse a field, and descend an interminable stairway to a platform which thrusts itself out over the very face of the cataract. The view from this point is most effective. To see the Falls from below one must pass through a property formerly occupied by the Duke of Kent, and descend the precipitous path called *Zigzag Hill*. From the foot of the hill we move along the beach till suddenly we find ourselves in the midst of the spray and tumult of the Fall, and a gorgeous rainbow, so close that we can almost touch it, is flashing in our eyes. The volume of water flowing away from the foot of the Fall seems much less than that of the river before it has taken the plunge. There is a belief current in the neighborhood to the effect that most of the river passes by an underground channel beneath the bed of the St. Lawrence, and rises near the foot of Isle d'Orléans. At this point there is a bit of angry water known as *Le Taureau*, which is considered very dangerous, and is popularly supposed to be the Montmorency escaping from its subterranean prison. On the banks of the Montmorency, above the crest of the Fall, stand the remnants of a suspension bridge. About forty years ago this structure fell into the abyss, carrying with it an unfortunate *habitant* and his family who were driving over it at the time. The tourist must not fail to visit, while at Montmorency, the famous *Natural Steps*, about a mile and a half above the bridge, where the river rushes madly over a series of cascades, each three or four yards in depth. On each side rises a perpendicular wall of somber cliff whose summits are fringed with pine-trees. Here and there beside the ledges are green and ferny nooks, the delight of retiring picnickers. Between the " Steps " are black and swirling pools whence one may coax a few fine mountain trout. The peculiar formation extends for over an eighth of a mile; and every here and there some *chute* more tumultuous than its fellows sends up a cloud of spray. Hard by is the *Fairy River*, or *L'Eau Tenue*, whose small stream buries itself in the earth to reappear a little farther down. The beach at the foot of Montmorency Falls is the scene of Wolfe's disastrous attack on July 31, 1759. In attempting to scale these perpendicular heights, which were defended by the most expert of French-Canadian marksmen, Wolfe lost no less than 500 men in killed and wounded.

Places of Interest near the City.

Four miles beyond Montmorency is the village of *l'Ange Gardien*, with some nice trout streams in the neighborhood, and good snipe and partridge shooting in the autumn months. Yet 5 miles farther, and we come to the lovely plum and apple orchards of *Château Richer.* Here, also, are good snipe-grounds, and there is excellent trout-fishing above and below the romantic falls of *Sault à la Puce.*

The *raison d'être* of the Quebec, Montmorency and Charlevoix R. R. is the village of **Ste. Anne de Beaupré**, otherwise known as *La bonne Ste. Anne.* In 1887 the parish church of Ste. Anne was raised by the Pope to a shrine of the first order. Of late years the shrine has been brought into great prominence on account of the many miraculous cures which are said to have been wrought there by the relics of the saint. The railroad is kept busy by the thousands of devout pilgrims and more or less pious tourists who flock to visit a shrine of such renown. Of the pilgrims, however, great numbers come afoot, from motives either of penitence or economy; and they come in all stages, from robust and grateful health to the extreme of piteous and supplicating decrepitude, and they come from all parts of Canada, the United States, and even from Europe. The church is a repository for innumerable crutches which have been left there by the maimed and the halt, who, having experienced the healing influence of the sainted relics, had no more need of a staff to support their steps. Even the blind, it is said, return from the shrine of St. Anne with seeing eyes. The great day for pilgrimages, and the most interesting time for the tourist to visit the village, is on the feast-day of St. Anne, which is the 26th of July. The curative powers of the shrine are to be experienced by kissing the relic of the saint, provided the act of devotion is done with faith. In the church is a really fine painting by Le Brun, representing Ste. Anne and the Virgin. This picture was presented to the church, in 1666, by the Marquis de Tracy. Less than 3 miles from the village are the wildly beautiful *Falls of Ste. Anne,* made up of a series of seven plunges. Trout and salmon are fairly abundant above and below the falls.

Leaving Quebec by the *Dorchester Bridge* and turning to the left we come to the estate of *Ringfield,* lying near the spot where Jacques Cartier, with his three ships, La Grande Hermine, La Petite Hermine, and L'Emérillon, passed the winter of 1535–'36, and where still may be seen the remains of mounds and earthworks thrown up by the daring little company. About 4 miles farther out, along the same road, lies the beautiful village of *Charlesbourg.* Eastward of Charlesbourg stand the ruins of a famous or notorious château of the old French type, variously known as *Beaumanoir*, *Château Bigot*, or the *Hermitage*. The romance of this historic structure has been reproduced for us by such writers as M. Amédée Papineau; M. Marmette, in his story of L'Intendant Bigot; and Mr. Kirby, in Le Chien d'Or. It is given briefly as follows in Holliwell's Guide to the City of Quebec:

" At the foot of La Montagne des Ormes are the ruins of Château Bigot, ruins which can now but faintly give an idea of what the original building was, of its grandeur, of its extent, of its secret passages, or its form. Two gables and a center wall, or rather the remnants of them, are visible, and from the fact of there being a sort of clearance, now partly overgrown, we may presume that there was a garden. Ensconced in the midst of a forest on one of the slopes of the Lawren tides are these relics of the past, and one can not but be impressed with deep melancholy as his eyes rest upon this deserted spot and his fancy repeoples the shattered halls and chambers with the giddy and guilty throngs which once crowded them. History has given some few indistinct data, and imagination has done the rest for this story of the past.

" The Intendant Bigot, whose profligacy and extravagance were unlimited, and whose rapacity supplied his requirements, constructed this château in the wilds of the mountains; and hither, with companions as graceless as himself, he was wont to adjourn in every excess of dissipation. The intendant was a man fond of field sports, and the château was the headquarters of his hunting expeditions. It is said that on one of these he lost his way, and met a young Algonquin squaw of singular beauty, who led him to the château, and, being induced to enter its walls, its strong doors were closed against her egress, and she remained there a prisoner either to love or to fate. But the intendant was a man of mark in the colony, a man to satisfy the longings of any ambitious girl who might wish for power, and such a one there was in the city of Quebec who was determined to have the intendant as her lord, that she, as his wife, might rule in New France and punish those who had slighted her. Such a one, it is said by Mr. Kirby, in his historical romance, The Golden Dog, was Angelique des Moloises; and she had heard of the Indian maid at Beaumanoir. Murder is a trifle to such natures as hers, wholly absorbed by ambition; and one night a piercing cry was heard echoing through the halls and corridors of Beaumanoir, and Caroline, the unhappy Algonquin, was found stabbed dead. Not long since was to be seen her grave-stone in a vault of Beaumanoir, with but the letter C. engraved thereon. It is said that the unhappy Caroline was not of full Indian race, but that her father, by marriage, was an officer of high rank in the army of France. Such is the story, not the first nor the last, connected with this place, which has been replete with guilt and caused much sorrow."

Quebec to Lake St. John.

A grand side trip to be made from Quebec is that by the Quebec & Lake St. John Railway to Chicoutimi, and down the Saguenay and back to Quebec by the steamers of the Ontario and Richelieu Navigation Co.

The distance from Quebec to *Roberval*, the chief town on Lake St. John, is 190 miles. The fare is $5.70; return, $7.50. The express runs through by day, which gives the tourist an opportunity to see the landscape. The journey, and the conclusion of the journey, have been thus described in a small book entitled Where the Trout hide, by Kit Clarke:

"A vast country, crowned with a pristine forest, dotted with countless lovely lakes and rivers where the furred, the feathered, and the finny nations hold high carnival. It is a land of trackless tangled woods, of myriads of dainty lakes, and he who loves the stately solitude of nature or the music of rippling crystal waters, will find here an absolute Utopia of delight.

"This glorious wilderness, strange as it may appear, has been ruptured by a railroad. For 200 miles directly N. it sends its snorting iron messenger back and forth, and the majestic moose, the pompous caribou, and the ruminant *cervus* stand appalled at the hideous shriek of the brazen fiend.

"But they don't stand long—at least, not to any alarming extent.

"The path of the railway winds its tortuous labyrinth from beginning to end through a magnificent unbroken forest—an endless, wild, romantic, fantastic spectacle. For more than a hundred miles its path is carved between majestic trees, with no semblance of a dwelling, nor even a hunter's cabin to break the monotony of its thrilling isolation. For 40 miles it finds its crooked way along the shores of the Batiscan River, whose turbulent waters sweep over immense bowlders, and dash with unbridled fierceness between towering wooded mountains, while no indication of human life is visible along its entire intrepid course.

"It is a journey to thrill the very soul of a man whose days have been hemmed by the busy hum of the noisy city, and a breath of the perfect breeze that sweeps in unencumbered freedom through the valley, laden with the odors of balsam, is health-giving and bracing beyond measure and price.

"'What a beautiful view!' exclaimed an occupant of the car.

"'Give us two for that euchre first,' was the reply.

"'In the early evening we reach the journey's end, and, after supper, stroll upon the bluff and gaze enraptured upon a magnificent sheet of clear, white water. As far as the eye can reach it rests like a mirror, as quiet and calm as if never a breeze had rimpled its sleeping surface.

"What a delusion! No more insolent inland sea can be found upon the continent; none more roaring, saucy, and turbulent, none more audacious and tumultuous than this impudent sheet of water,

7

now so bland, docile, and polished. Let but a few careering winds
fondle its surface, and the very essence of stormy savageness holds
ferocious carousal. This is Lake St. John, the source of the marvelous Saguenay, and the home—the only home—of the peerless ouana-
nish, the grandest game-fish, the most prodigious warrior that plows
niche water."

About 10 miles from Quebec, close to the line of this railway, is the
lovely village of *Indian Lorette*, where dwells a remnant of the *Huron*
tribe. These Indians are civilized and self-respecting, and their village will well repay a visit. The station for Lorette is known as *Indian
Lorette*. Lorette occupies a breezy height 450 ft. above tide, and from
this point of vantage we get an unrivaled view of Quebec, Lévis, Isle
d'Orleans, and the valley of the St. Charles. Beside the village thunders
the picturesque cataract known as the *Falls of Lorette*. Sixteen miles
from Quebec we cross the lovely *Jacques-Cartier River*, already referred to as famous for its trout and salmon pools. In the valley of
this river is the village of *Valcartier*, which was chiefly settled by re-
tired English officers and soldiers. In the village cemetery, deep in
the heart of the Laurentian Hills, lie no fewer than nineteen of the
veterans of Waterloo.

A few miles farther and we reach *Lake St. Joseph*, a fair water
much frequented by Quebecers in the summer-time. The lake is 22
miles long by 8 miles wide, and the mountains that encircle it, clothed
richly in birch and maple, beech and ash, come down to the water's
edge. Hither and thither over its bosom, for the delight of the summer traveler, plies the steamer Ida. The waters of the lake, of a wonderful transparency and depth, abound in black bass, trout, and the
voracious "togue"—a species of thick-set lake-trout sometimes reaching 30 pounds in weight, and to be captured by trolling. There are
good summer hotels on Lake St. Joseph. Five miles beyond, the railway touches the shores of *Lake Sargeant*, once famous for its black
bass, but at present spoiled by over-fishing. At *St. Raymond* we cross
the river St. Anne, whose valley widens here to receive the charming
village. St. Raymond is the center of a great fishing and shooting
district, and may profitably delay for a time the tourist whose passion
is for angling. The village is built on three plateaus, and contains the
workshops of the railway company. A little below the village the
river is joined by its north branch, which is known, on account of its
severe and colossal scenery, as the *Little Saguenay*. About 68 miles
from Quebec the railway enters the valley of the *Batiscan*, whose course

it follows for a distance of 30 miles. Here the scenery is surpass-ingly fine, especially at the points where the river is joined by the *Miguick*, and a little farther on by the *Jeannotte*. It is impossible to enumerate all the rivers and lakes which offer inducements to the sportsman, but those mentioned will be found sufficient for most travelers.

In the same neighborhood is a chain of well-stocked trout lakes, leased by the *Laurentides Fish and Game Club*. This is a region of fish and game clubs, many of which have commodious club-houses on their respective waters. Among them may be mentioned the *Tou-rilli, Little Saguenay, Lac au Lard, Stadacona, Fin and Feather, Para-dise, Metabetchouan, Jacques Cartier*, and *Lake Quaquakamaksis*. In-formation as to these leased waters and the possibility of obtaining fishing privileges thereon may be obtained from the authorities of the railway, or from Mr. A. Waters, 22 Fabrique St., Quebec. About 112 miles from Quebec we reach the waters of *Lake Edward*, which is more than twice the size of Lake St. Joseph and splendidly stocked with a peculiarly fine and impetuous trout. The lake is somewhat more gen-erally known by the name of *Lac des Grandes Iles*. It is leased by the railway company, and fishing permits may be obtained free by all patrons of the railway. There is an excellent hotel on the lake, the *Laurentides House*, where camp outfits, guides, canoes, etc., may be obtained. The waters of the lake are traversed by the little steamers *Swan, Ripple*, and *Emma ;* but in its 100 miles of winding coast-line lurk deep bays and inlets, as yet practically unexplored. The lake is a veritable maze of islands, in whose labyrinths the heedless canoeist may readily lose himself.

A hundred and thirty-five miles from Quebec the railroad skirts *Lake Kiskisink ;* and, indeed, all the way from *Lake Edward* to *Rober-val* there are lakes innumerable on either hand, chief among which may be mentioned *Lakes Bouchette* and *des Commissaires*. At *Chambord Junction* we come in view of **Lake St. John** itself. Here a branch diverges eastward to *St. Jerome ;* but we continue up the west shore of the lake 13 miles farther to *Roberval*.

Lake St. John.

The Lake St. John Territory extends from the head of navigation on the *river Saguenay*, at *Chicoutimi*, to the northern boundary of the province of Quebec, a distance of 220 miles, and from the sources of the waters flowing into Lake St. John, from the east, to the *river St. Maurice*, embracing the valley of the *river Batiscan*, a distance of 200 miles, the whole forming an area of 44,000 square miles, or about 28,000,000 acres. Comparatively little is known of this great country, with the exception of the valley of Lake St. John, which, within the last few years, has been colonized with great rapidity, and now contains a population of some 40,000. The soil is almost universally composed of rich, gray clay, whose fertility seems well-nigh inexhaustible. The climate of the region resembles that of Montreal, being more temperate than that of Quebec, and with a much less heavy snow-fall. The lake itself, called by the Indians *Pikouagami*, or "*Flat Lake*," is 28 miles long by 25 miles broad, but for the most part not more than 80 ft. in depth. There flow into it no fewer than 19 rivers, chief of which are the mysterious *Peribonca*, 400 miles long, the *Mistassini*, 300 miles long, and the *Ashuapmouchouan*, the "river where they watch the moose," 150 miles in length. These are navigable for steamers for distances of from 10 to 20 miles from their mouths, after which they are obstructed by rapids and cataracts. The river *Ouiatchouan* is famous for its magnificent falls, which lie in a most conspicuous and impressive situation about a mile from the lake shore. This cataract is estimated to possess a height of 280 ft. All these gathering waters find an outlet by one great stream, called **La Décharge du Lac St. Jean**, which at Chicoutimi becomes the Saguenay. This stream is divided by Alma Island, for the first 8 miles of its course, into two branches, called respectively the "*Grande Décharge*" and the "*Petite Décharge*"—the former of which divides with the Peribonca the honor of being the favorite resort of the "**ouananiche**."

This famous fish, whose name is spelled with a truly Chaucerian breadth of variation, has quite eclipsed in reputation the other denizens of these well-stocked waters. It is thus effectively and exactly described by Messrs. L. M. Yale and J. G. A. Creighton in Scribner's Magazine for May, 1889:

"In appearance a fresh-run salmon and a fresh-run ouananiche do not differ much more than salmon from different rivers. The back of the ouananiche is green or blue, and in a fish just out of water can be seen to be marked with olive spots, something like the vermiculations on a trout; the silvery sides are more iridescent, the X-marks are more numerous and less sharply defined; the patches of bronze, purple, and green on the gill-covers are larger and more brilliant, and with them are several large round black spots. As the water grows warm the bright hues get dull, and toward autumn the rusty red color and hooked lower jaw of the spawning salmon develops. As the ouananiche, unlike the salmon, feeds continuously, and in much heavier and swifter water than salmon lie in, it has a slimmer body and larger fins, so that a five-pound ouananiche can leap higher and oftener than a grilse, and fight like a ten-pound salmon. The variety of its habits, which are a compound of those of the trout and those of the salmon, with some peculiarities of its own, gives great charm to ouananiche-angling, and opportunity for every style from the ' floating fly ' on tiny hooks to the ' sink and draw ' of the salmon cast. It takes the fly readily when in the humor, though wary and capricious like all its relations, and fights hard, uniting the dash of the trout with the doggedness and ingenuity of the salmon. In railway and hotel prospectus the ouananiche weighs from five to ten pounds. In Lake St. John and the Décharge the average is two and a half pounds; four-pounders are large and not too plentiful, while six-pounders are scarce. The ouananiche is, however, much longer than a trout of the same weight; a five-pounder, for example, is twenty-five inches long, twelve inches in girth, and looks like an eight-pound salmon. Now and then solitary fish of great size are seen, old *habitants* dating from ' *les premières années*,' when ' *ça en bouillait, monsieur, des gros comme des carcajous*' ('It just boiled, sir, with ones big as wild-cats'), but they are intensely wary and carefully guarded by the demon of ill-luck.

"Another writer, Kit Clarke, says that 'as a game fish, affording stimulating sport and fomenting excitement in his capture, he is the absolute sovereign of the watery kingdom. The sportsman whose hook for the first time impales the fish will be dumfounded at the tremendous leaps and fiery struggles of this heroic antagonist. His vigorous contentions are astounding, while at every leap into the air he turns a complete somersault, all the while shaking his head with the fierceness of an enraged tiger. These terrific leaps are so continuous that one seems to be fighting the fish in the air as much as in the water. . . . In the spring they are baited with raw beef or the white meat of suckers, and I was told they took the fly in June, but although I tried various kinds of flies I did not get a ' strike ' or see a rise. Afterward I learned that July was the proper time for fly-casting, and that then the fish rise with avidity. The lightest fish that fell to my rod weighed two pounds, and the heaviest a trifle under five pounds. In six days I took thirty-eight, and could readily have taken many more, but I had enough.'"

At *Pointe Bleue*, on the shores of the Lake St. John, is a reserve of **Montagnais Indians**, a most interesting tribe, of whom Mr. W. H. H. Murray (Adirondack Murray), writes : "They are the ' mountaineers ' of ancient times and wars, and dwelt among the Laurentian Hills. They were a brave stock, and they and the Esquimaux of Labrador were never at peace. The mounds of Mamelons, at the mouth of the Saguenay could tell of wars fought on them for a thousand years, could their sands but speak. The Montagnais at Roberval are very dark of skin. They are great hunters, skilled trappers, great canoemen, and runners. They are a racial curiosity and worthy of study on the part of the intelligent tourist, and the sight of them and their peculiarities will be entertaining to all." The tourist who contemplates doing the Lake St. John region and the Saguenay will do well to procure Mr. Murray's romances of " Mamelons " and " Ungava."

The accommodations on Lake St. John are all that could be desired. The *Hôtel Roberval* is excellent in all respects. Its proprietor has secured from the Provincial Government the exclusive fishing rights of the lake and its tributaries, with the double purpose of protecting the fish adequately and of affording the guests of the house free fishing facilities. A branch of the hotel, called the *Island House*, has been established on an island in the Grande Décharge, in the midst of the fishing-pools. If one does not wish to go by rail, a fascinating and thrilling canoe trip may be taken from the Island House down the tumultuous river to Chicoutimi, to meet the Saguenay stream. This trip—not designed for the timorous-hearted—may be made for $10, which includes the hire of birch canoe and two Indian guides. The Hotel Co. keeps on hand a supply of camp outfits, which may be obtained by tourists who wish to go into the wilderness. Such a wilderness may be reached by ascending almost any of the inflowing rivers for a very few miles from their mouths. Here are regions where not even the lumberman's axe has gone, and where one may follow no footsteps more civilized than those of the Montagnais trapper. The close season for ouananiche begins on September 15th, and lasts till December 1st. The return ticket from Quebec to Roberval costs $7.50 ; and for sportsmen, in parties, there are special reductions made, with certain privileges as to dogs, equipments, etc., to be enjoyed on application to the General Passenger Agent at Quebec. Besides the ouananiche, the fish of the Lake St. John region, speaking broadly, include salmon, maskinonge, speckled trout, great gray trout (or togue, or touládi), bass, pickerel, white-fish. The Quebec and Lake St. John R. R. is a new road, excellently constructed, and equipped luxuriously in the most modern style ; and one may ride in a palace car into the very heart of these ancient northern wildernesses, so long imagined to be a region of endless snow. A branch of the railroad extends from Chambord Junction to Chicoutimi, enabling tourists to make the round trip from Quebec and back in twenty-four hours,

Down the St. Lawrence and up the Saguenay.

The steamers of the Richelieu and Ontario Navigation Co. leave Quebec at a comfortable hour in the morning, arrive at *Tadousac*, at the *Saguenay* mouth, some little time after dark, ascend the mysterious river by night to *Chicoutimi*, and then, leaving Chicoutimi in the early morning, descend the Saguenay by daylight and afford the traveler a perfect view of the terrific scenery. The fare to Chicoutimi and return is $8. The trip is one never to be forgotten. If the day be fine —and if it is not, the wise tourist will delay his departure and await the return of sunshine—the journey begins under delightful auspices. The transparent morning light and crisp air bring out the full glory of the enchanting city. Greener than ever appears Isle d'Orléans, more beryl-bright the St. Lawrence tide, more white and cloud-like the skyey curtain of the Montmorency Falls. When Ste. Anne's is passed the dark mountains crowd forward yet more forbiddingly upon the northern rim of the river, rising hundreds of feet, in places, sheer from the water's edge. These Laurentide Hills are sometimes naked, sometimes clad with somber forests; but here and there they suffer a little valley in their iron fronts, and every such valley has its tiny French village and glittering chapel spire. It is a sterile corner, indeed, where the hardy and frugal *habitant* will not make himself a home, and multiply till he has no cause to dread a meeting with his enemy in the gate. These little secluded settlements are primitive in the extreme, and reproduce the Norman-French life of two centuries ago. The atmosphere of the Laurentian Hills is not hospitable to change, and most of the influences of mutability pass by on the other side of the river.

A little below the foot of Isle d'Orléans we pass, on the N. shore, the promontory of *Cap Tourmente*, towering nearly 2,000 ft. from the water's edge. Then come the granite masses of *Cap Rouge* and *Cap Gribaune*, more than 2,000 ft. in height. The summit frowning over *Sault au Cochon* (surely the swine of the Gadarenes, when they rushed violently down a steep place and perished in the sea, had no such leap as this) is 2,370 ft. in altitude. Beyond *Cap Maillard* comes in the *Bouchard River*, up whose valley extends the populous village of *St. François Xavier*. After passing *Cap Labaie*, the steamer heaves to, to meet the boats which come out from the thriving settlement of *St. Paul's Bay*. Some of the finest scenery of the river's northern shore is about this point. The valley lies open before the traveler's eyes.

The rivers *Gouffre* and *Moulin* open magnificent vistas into the strange country back from the coast, which seems a sea of mountain-peaks. The district is a volcanic one, subject to tremblings and shocks, and abounding in curious salt and sulphur springs. It is said that in 1791 a peak to the north of the village vomited smoke and flame for several days, while the country round about was tormented with earthquakes. In 1663 the disturbances of this region were much more violent and terrifying, and at *Les Éboulements* (well named), a few miles farther down the coast, may still be seen the tracks of the frightful land-slides which made such changes in the face of the landscape. "The St. Lawrence ran white as milk as far down as Tadousac; ranges of hills were thrown down into the river, or were swallowed up in the plains; earthquakes shattered the houses, and shook the trees till the Indians said that the forests were drunk; vast fissures opened in the ground; and the courses of streams were changed. Meteors, fiery-winged serpents, and ghastly specters were seen in the air; roarings and mysterious voices sounded on every side; and the confessionals of all the churches were crowded with penitents awaiting the end of the world. . . . An earthquake rooted up a mountain and threw it upon *Isle aux Coudres*, which was made one half larger than before; and in the place of the mountain there appeared a gulf, which it is not safe to approach."

This *Isle aux Coudres* lies with its head off *Bay St. Paul* and its lower extremity off *Les Éboulements*. Between its shores and Bay St. Paul is *Le Gouffre*, where the water suddenly attains a depth of 30 fathoms, and where the meeting of the flood tide with the river currents makes a vast series of eddies and miniature whirlpools. Of old, ere *Le Gouffre* had got filled up with sand deposits, there was a mighty whirlpool, or succession of whirlpools, at the spot, and it was indeed "not safe to approach," as the ancient chronicle declared. The district is rich in iron, graphite, limestone, and garnet-rock. The island, which is between 5 and 6 miles long and about half as wide, is thickly peopled with a thoroughly mediæval farming population, the quaintest of the quaint. It belongs to the Seminary of Quebec, to which it was granted in 1687.

The *village of Les Éboulements*, which we come to next, commands from its lofty perch a magnificent view up and down the river. Lofty as it is, the dark mass of Mt. Éboulement overlooks it, rising 2,600 ft. from the water. As we emerge once more into the open St. Lawrence, here about 15 miles wide, we are in a region much frequented by the white whales, and may catch sight of the great beasts gamboling in the waves. If we do, we shall certainly hear them greeted on all sides as "porpoises," which they are not. They are hunted extensively for their blubber and for their skins, which make an exceedingly valuable leather. They range from 15 to 22 ft. in length.

Broad and sweeping is the base of Mt. Éboulement, and on its eastern skirt lies the village of *St. Irenée*. Then, passing *Cap Sain*, we draw up at the long pier of *Point à Pique*, the landing-place for **Murray Bay**, which is the most popular summer resort on the north shore of the lower St. Lawrence. The bay is very shallow, and the village proper (population upward of 3,000) lies at the head of it on the Murray River. The summer hotels and cottages, however, are at the pier or across the harbor, at the foot of the opposite promontory, *Cap à l'Aigle*. The French name—and the preferable one—for the place is *Malbaie*, handed down from Champlain himself, who called it *Malle Baie*, on account of "the tide that runs there marvelously." It is a fine fishing center, as the *Murray River* and the *Gravel* and *Petit Lakes* are abundantly stocked with trout. Of this resort Mr. Le Moine says:

"Of all the picturesque parishes . . . none will interest the lover of sublime landscape more than Malbaie. One must go there to enjoy the rugged, the grandeur of nature, the broad horizons. He will not find here the beautiful wheat-fields of Kamouraska, the pretty and verdurous shores of Cacouna or Rimouski; . . . here are savage and unconquered Nature, and view-points yet more majestic than those of the coasts and walls of Bic; precipice on precipice; impenetrable gorges in the projections of the rocks; peaks which lose themselves in the clouds, and among which the bears wander through July in search of berries; where the caribou browse in September; where the solitary crow and the royal eagle make their nests in May—in short, Alpine landscapes, the pathless highlands of Scotland, a Byronic nature, tossed about, heaped up in the north, far from the ways of civilized men, near a volcano that from time to time awakens and shakes the country in a manner to frighten, but not to endanger, the romantic inhabitants."

From Murray Bay the steamer crosses the St. Lawrence diagonally to **Rivière du Loup** (so called from the droves of seals, or *loups-marins*, that of old frequented its shoals), a distance of about 30 miles. Rivière du Loup is a thriving town of about 5,000 inhabitants, and is the point where the Intercolonial R. R. is joined by the Temiscouata R. R. The town is picturesquely situated on high land near the river-mouth. Near the town are the picturesque *Rivière du Loup Falls*, where the stream makes a fine plunge of 80 ft. into a deep, quiet basin in the rocks. Rivière du Loup is a pleasant summer resort, and is well supplied with hotels and boarding-houses. Six miles from Rivière du Loup is the famous summer resort of **Cacouna**—probably the most famous in Canada. It has admirable hotel accommodation, fine beaches and scenery, and a remarkably cool, bracing climate in the hottest months. The chief hotel of Cacouna is the *St. Lawrence Hall*, which accommodates 600 guests. The *Mansion House* is comfortable, and very moderate in its charges. Still cheaper are the numerous summer boarding-houses. Anything but moderate, however, are the cab charges for the drive from Rivière du Loup to Cacouna, unless one takes the wise precaution to arrange terms before starting. Cacouna stands on a remarkable rocky peninsula nearly 400 ft. high.

From Rivière du Loup the steamer strikes diagonally across the St. Lawrence again, for the mouth of the Saguenay, passing between *Red Island* and the *Brandy Pots*. **Tadousac**, the ancient village at the Saguenay mouth, lies about 135 miles from Quebec. It was visited in 1535 by Cartier, who saw many Indians fishing off the point, and heard from them a marvelous story to the effect that by "ascending the Saguenay you reach a country where there are men dressed like us, who live in cities, and have much gold, rubies, and copper." In 1543 Roberval explored the river and left most of his company in its awful solitudes. The mystery hanging over the fate of Roberval and his brother Achille, who undertook another expedition in 1549, is not lightened by the intelligence that remains of an ancient stockade and post have lately been found on one of the wild rivers emptying into Lake St. John, and that these are supposed by some to mark the last resting-place of the daring but unfortunate explorers. One can understand the dread fascination that must have been exerted on those adventurous spirits by the Titanic gloom of the great river, together with the strange tales of the Indians and the reputation of one of the tribes, the Nasquapees, for marvelous and invincible powers of magic. These Indians are thus described in Mr. Murray's romance already referred to:

"The Nasquapees are one of the most remarkable families of Indians on the continent, and of whom but little is known. Their country extends from Lake Mistassini eastward to Labrador, and from Ungava Bay to the coast mountains of the St. Lawrence. They are small in size, fine featured, with mild, dark eyes and extremely small hands and feet. The name Nasquapees—Nasqupies—means 'a people who stand straight.' They have no medicine-man or prophet, and hence are called by other tribes atheists. Their sense of smell is so acute that it rivals the dog's. Spirit-rappings and other strange manifestations peculiar to us moderns have been practiced immemorially among them, and carried to such a shade of success that one of our Boston *séances* would be a laughable and bungling affair to them. Their language is like the western Crees, and their traditions point to a remote Eastern origin."

In 1599 a trading-post was established at Tadousac by Pontgravé, and a mere trading-post and fishing-station the place remained till modern times, in spite of many attempts to make it a more permanent settlement. Now it boasts a good summer hotel, with a cluster of cottages for summer visitors. There is good trout-fishing in the neighborhood, and sea-trout are caught in the deep water off the shore. A point of interest near the hotel is the quaint old *Jesuit Mission Chapel*, built in 1746.

Tadousac lies in a semicircular hollow among rounded knobs of granite and huge round hills or "mamelons" of sand. These gigantic sand-mounds, which rise in tiers to the height of 1,000 ft. or more above the Saguenay, are supposed to be the geologic beaches of the morning of the world, and to mark in their successive terraces that shrinkage of the waters by which the earth's surface came to view. A little east of the village lie the red granite masses of *Point Rouge*, and beyond them the white marble of *Moulin à Baude*. In the ravines behind and on the gentler slopes are forests of spruce and birch, and the fathomless sand of the "mamelons" slides down through the village to the sea-green water of the St. Lawrence. Close on the western edge of the village yawn the black jaws of the *Saguenay*. As the steamer, crossing from *Rivière du Loup*, approaches *Tadousac* wharf by moonlight, the scene is one never to be forgotten.

The Saguenay.

If the night is fine, and the moon high in the heavens, the traveler will linger late on deck. A detailed impression of the Saguenay he will receive while descending it by daylight on the following day; but during this night ascent he may experience to the full the influence of its monotonous and awful majesty. Over the still surface of ebony and silver, between the endless and unvarying walls of soaring rock, the boat climbs northward deeper and deeper into this land of mystery. Wrapped in one's rug—for, though it is July, an icy wind draws down out of the north through this great trough—and crouching high in the prow, one feels as if he were on a journey never before attempted by man—as if he were about to explore the fabled lake of Mistassini, or venture with Jason and his fellows on the ship Argo. Here and there a great star peers curiously down through some high notch in the river-wall, or some far cascade, the overflow of a mountain-pool, flashes whitely in the moonlight for a moment as it plunges from one darkness to another. When the colossal gloom and grandeur of the scene have begun to oppress the spirit, the traveler will do well to turn into his berth, leaving directions to be called as the steamer approaches *Chicoutimi*. This will be about daybreak; and as the steamer usually remains an hour or two at the wharf, there is time to go ashore and see the village. The best possible thing to do is to climb the rocky height behind the village, and watch the sun rise in severe splendor over the bald Saguenay hills. But, before undertaking this, find out from the captain *exactly* how long the steamer is going to stay on that particular trip, lest it happen, as it did once to the present writer, that while you are admiring the sunrise from the hill-top the steamer depart without you, and leave you, perchance in marked *deshabille*, to linger shivering in Chicoutimi till the coming of the next boat, or to drive wildly over the hill-tops in a mad French-Canadian "buck-board," to endeavor to overtake the truant steamer at *Ha Ha Bay*. When this mishap befell me, with a friend who was in the same predicament, the latter course was chosen; the drive was a cold one, for our attire was hasty and informal, and a desperate one, for the road was astoundingly precipitous and diversified, the Canadian pony as nimble and erratic as a goat, and the "buck-board" driver regardless of consequences so long as he earned the promised fee. But the experience was novel and thrilling; and we got there in time to sit on the wharf at St. Alphonse and smile at the steamer blandly as she came in.

The town of *Chicoutimi*, now connected with Roberval, on Lake St. John, by rail, is a center of the lumber-trade. It is a growing place and possesses good hotel accommodations. Its trade is largely in the hands of the great lumbering firm of the Prices, the head of which, Senator Price, of Quebec, is known as the "King of the Saguenay." Close to the town the Chicoutimi River joins the Saguenay by a fall about 50 feet in height. This river is an outlet of *Lake Kenogami*, and affords capital fishing for trout and salmon. The name Chicoutimi signifies deep water.

From Chicoutimi to the Mouth.

The Saguenay can hardly be called a river. It is rather a stupendous chasm, from 1 to 2½ miles in width, doubtless of earthquake ori-

gin, cleft for 65 miles through the high Laurentian plateau. Its walls
are an almost unbroken line of naked cliffs of syenite and gneiss. Its
depth is many hundred feet greater than that of the St. Lawrence;
indeed, if the St. Lawrence were drained dry, all the fleets of the
world might float in the abyss of the Saguenay, and yet find anchorage
only in a few places. Of mere soft beauty the Saguenay landscape
can show none, save in one or two valleys where tributary streams
flow in. It has been called, indeed, the River of Death. Silence,
nakedness, and awe brood over it. Its grim solitudes are shunned
by bird and insect. The profound unmoving waters, on account of
their great depth, appear as black as pitch, with purple gleams in
the sunlight, and are broken only where the back of a white whale
rises for a moment into view. Its overpowering sublimity and meas-
ureless desolation become oppressive to some visitors. A writer in the
London Times calls it "Nature's sarcophagus," and declares that,
"compared to it, the Dead Sea is blooming." The same writer continues as follows: "The Saguenay seems to want painting, blowing
up, or draining—anything, in short, to alter its morose, quiet, eternal
awe. Talk of Lethe or the Styx—they must have been purling brooks
compared with this savage river; and a picnic on the banks of either
would be preferable to one on the banks of the Saguenay." The name
Saguenay is variously and most unsatisfactorily derived from "St. Jean
Nez" and from the Indian Saggishsekuss, meaning a "river whose
banks are precipitous." We are prepared for any derivation, however,
when we remember that the village of Des Joachims on the Upper
Ottawa is popularly called "Swishaw."

From Chicoutimi, as far as the mighty inlet of *Ha Ha Bay*, the
scenery is bold indeed, but less gigantically so than that which greets
the traveler farther down. Ha Ha Bay runs 7 miles in between
the mountains, and ends in a spacious haven whose shores are lined
with the meadows of St. Alphonse. The mountains that encircle the
harbor are bright with red and orange stains dashed capriciously across
their bare front. A little way below Ha Ha Bay we pass, on the right
shore, a cliff 900 feet high, called *Le Tableau* from its great, perfectly-
smoothed, square front, like a canvas stretched for painting. Farther
down on the same shore is *Statue Point*, "where, at about 1,000 feet
above the water, a huge, rough Gothic arch gives entrance to a cave,
in which, as yet, the foot of man has never trodden. Before the entrance to this black aperture, a gigantic rock, like the statue of some

dead Titan, once stood. A few years ago, during the winter, it gave way, and the monstrous statue came crashing down through the ice of the Saguenay, and left bare to view the entrance to the cavern it had guarded perhaps for ages."

Cape Trinity and Cape Eternity.

Having left behind Statue Point we approach the climax of Saguenay scenery, the twin Capes **Trinity** and **Eternity**. These giant cliffs, the one 1,600 the other 1,800 ft. in height, watch each other across the black gulf of Eternity Bay, a narrow fiord wherein the sounding-line must descend 1,000 ft. to reach the bottom. The dreadful sublimity of these promontories, springing sheer from the black depths of the mysterious river, compels the reverence of the most indifferent. The northernmost cape justifies its name of Cape Trinity as we approach it from up the river and observe that it consists of three mighty precipices, each 500 or 600 ft. in height, piled one upon the other, and fringed along the beetling top with wind-blown pines. On the side overlooking *Eternity Bay* the aspect of the cape is different and vastly more terrible. The steamer rounds in so close to the base of the precipice that one feels as if he could toss a pebble up against the wall of rock; but for a time no one is so hardy as to attempt it—it would seem like sacrilege. The noisy crowd on the steamer's deck is hushed with awe as all eyes strain upward toward the dizzy height which seems to reel and topple above them, as if it would descend and close the gap. When the instinctive tremor of apprehension has somewhat passed away, a few of the passengers usually attempt to throw a stone across the intervening space. As the missile is launched vigorously into the air, it seems as if it would strike well up on the face of the cliff, but the eye is utterly deceived by the stupendous mass before it, and the stone cast by the most vigorous thrower falls into the water, as if repelled by the cliff, before it has traveled half the distance. Cape Eternity is perhaps 200 ft. higher than its terrible sister, but it deigns to slope a little back from the water and to clothe its sublime proportions in a wealth of forest green. After having been staggered by the imminent horror of Cape Trinity the eye rests with delight on the serene and stable grandeur of its colossal mate. Between the capes there is a remarkable echo, which is usually tested by blowing the steamer's whistle or discharging a gun. When the Flying-Fish conveyed the

Prince of Wales up the river, one of her heavy 68-pounders was discharged near Cape Trinity. "For the space of half a minute or so after the discharge there was a dead silence, and then, as if the report and concussion were hurled back upon the decks, the echoes came down crash upon crash. It seemed as if the rocks and crags had all sprung into life under the tremendous din, and as if each was firing 68-pounders full upon us in sharp, crushing volleys, till at last they grew hoarser and hoarser in their anger, and retreated, bellowing slowly, carrying the tale of invaded solitude from hill to hill, till all the distant mountains seemed to roar and groan at the intrusion."

About 6 miles below Cape Trinity the cliffs part to make room for *St. John's Bay*, which has a little village at its head, and water shallow enough to give ships an anchorage. Four miles farther down flows in a second *Little Saguenay River*, which drains a wilderness swarming with trout and game. Then comes *Rivière aux Canards*, with a number of grim and inhospitable islands clustered off its mouth. A little farther down is *Isle St. Louis*, a ridge of granite half a mile in length thrust up out of 1,200 ft. of water. These deeps swarm with salmon-trout. Over against the islet, on the right shore, stand out the grand promontories of *Cape Victoria* and *Cape George*. Looking northward from this point one of the most magnificent views on the rivers is opened before us. Two miles below we are astonished by the sight of some low land, bordering the mouth of the *Ste. Marguerite*, which is the Saguenay's chief tributary and a splendid salmon stream. Passing the mouth of the *St. Athanase* and *Point Crêpe* we come to *St. Etienne Bay*, with a little tilled soil about its rim. Now the cliffs draw closer together, and the views are more restricted; and leaving behind the *Passe Pierre Isles* we reach a towering cape of granite called *Pointe la Boule*, which thrusts itself out as if to bar our way. Toward dusk we pass **L'Anse à L'Eau**, then *Tadousac*, and find ourselves once more upon the breast of the St. Lawrence, having descended from Chicoutimi 67 miles exactly. *From Tadousac to Quebec* is a distance of 135 miles, and we traverse it by night, arriving at Quebec in comfortable time for breakfast.

To the Maritime Provinces by Rail.

The railway routes to the Maritime Provinces are by the **Intercolonial Railway** from Montreal, which runs down the south shore of the

St. Lawrence as far as Rimouski, then turns south and follows the valley of the wild *Metapedia* to the junction of this river with the *Restigouche*, crossing which we are in New Brunswick, and by the Quebec Central to Megantic, where connection is made with the C. P. R. Short Line. Another route to be described presently is by steamship *via Gaspé* and the gulf coast. The three Maritime Provinces of Canada are **Nova Scotia, New Brunswick**, and **Prince Edward Island**, and the Intercolonial Ry. traverses them all. It is a government road, admirably built and equipped, and most moderate in its charges. It runs through some of the best fishing and shooting districts of the continent and some very beautiful landscapes. The cars on through express trains are lighted by electricity and heated by steam from the locomotive. The head-offices of the railway are at *Moncton*, New Brunswick, and information may be obtained by communicating with the General Passenger Agent at Moncton, or the District Passenger Agent, Montreal or Halifax, and General Traveling Agent, Toronto.

Passengers for the Maritime Provinces leave Montreal by the Intercolonial Ry., which now operates the shortest line between Montreal and Quebec (163 miles), by way of Lévis. As the train leaves Lévis we get a last glimpse of the Falls of Montmorency across the river. Five miles from Lévis we pass *Harlaka Junction*, and 9 miles farther *St. Charles Junction*. The next half-dozen stations are named for as many saints. The most important of them are the lumbering village of *St. Michel*, whose church contains some valuable paintings, and *Montmagny*, a town of about 2,000 inhabitants, the seat of a convent and of Montmagny College. High over the town towers its great parish church. At this point there is a fine though not lofty cataract, where the *Rivière du Sud* falls into the St. Lawrence. These falls are the scene of a thrilling episode in De Gaspé's romance, The Canadians of Old." The villages of *Cap St. Ignace*, *L'Islet*, and *Trois Saumons* are interesting for their connection with the same romance, the scene of which is laid chiefly about the next stopping-place, the romantic little village of *St. Jean Port Joli*, 59 miles from Lévis. The next station of importance is at the thriving town of *Ste. Anne de la Pocatière*, the seat of a large educational institution known as Ste. Anne's College, which is attended by several hundred students, and has an Agricultural College and Model Farm connected with it. The so-called porpoise fisheries of *Rivière Ouelle*, the next stopping-place, have been already referred to. Here dwells the well-known French-Canadian

Cape Gaspé.

historian, the Abbé Casgrain.   In 1690 the *curé* of Rivière Ouelle, at
the head of a band of his parishioners, defeated the New-Englanders of
Sir William Phipps's expedition.   Here the railway leaves the shore
for a few miles, and when it rejoins the river the *Kamouraska Islands*
are in sight just off the coast.   The lovely village of *Kamouraska*, with
its great church and convent, was a favorite summer resort before the
stream of travel turned to *Cacouna*.   The station on the Intercolonial
nearest to Kamouraska is *St. Paschal*.   The next important stopping-
place is Rivière du Loup, which has been already described.   This
town is 115 miles from Lévis.   The traveler who wishes to go directly
to the upper waters of the *river St. John*, and the splendid trout-
streams of *Lake Temiscouata* and the *Squattooks*, may here branch off
by the Temiscouata R. R., which runs through the district in question and joins the Vanceboro, Woodstock, and Edmundston line of
the Canadian Pacific at *Edmundston*, on the St. John.   Five miles
beyond Rivière du Loup is *Cacouna*, already described.   Then the
next station of importance is *Trois Pistoles*, 142 miles from Quebec.
Here the trains stop for refreshments, and in the well-kept dining-
hall of the station one may often feast on delicious fresh-caught trout.
The village stands on a river of the same name, and there is a tradition in regard to this name.   It is said that in the year 1700, while
the river was yet nameless, a traveler rode up to its shore and asked a
solitary fisherman what he would take to ferry him across.   "Trois
pistoles," was the reply.   "What is the name of this river?" asked
the traveler.   "It has none," said the fisherman.   "Then name it
Trois Pistoles," said the traveler.   Trois pistoles means three ten-
franc pieces.

At *St. Fabien*, 18 miles beyond Trois Pistoles, there is good trout-
fishing from early in June to the end of August in small lakes a mile
or two from the station.   The next stopping-place is at the summer
resort of **Bic**, situated on a picturesque and beautiful bay.   The hills
around Bic are 1,800 ft. high, and out of their ravines descend, in
many cascades, two small rivers to mingle with the waters of the bay.
Off the coast is Bic Island, once intended to be made an impregnable fortress as a harbor of refuge for the French navy.   In 1861,
when the Trent difficulty threatened to cause a rupture between England and the United States, English troops were landed at Bic.   Near
by is *L'Islet au Massacre*, where once 200 Micmac Indians, while asleep
in a cave, were surprised by their inveterate enemies the Mohawks,

8

The Mohawks stealthily filled the mouth of the cave with dry wood, then set it on fire, and slew every Micmac that succeeded in making his escape through the flames. Ten miles beyond Bic is the important station of **Rimouski**, an incorporated town with a large and growing trade, a popular summer resort, and a port of call for ocean steamers, where passengers and mail from the Maritime Provinces embark or land as the case may be. Rimouski has good hotels, a fine Roman Catholic cathedral, a college, and important public buildings. In the Rimouski River and lakes in the neighborhood of the town there are excellent trout and salmon fishing. Rimouski is the seat of a Roman Catholic bishop, and is sometimes called the metropolis of the Lower St. Lawrence. Five miles beyond Rimouski is *St. Anaclet*, the station for *Father Point*, where outward-bound vessels discharge their pilots. At *Ste. Flavie*, a railway divisional center 198 miles from Quebec, the railway sweeps off southward from the St. Lawrence. There is excellent trout-fishing in July in lakes about Ste. Flavie. Presently it crosses the famous fishing waters of the *Metis*. At the station of *Little Metis*, 5 miles back from the St. Lawrence, one is within easy reach of a number of excellent trout lakes. The best months for fishing in these waters are April and July, and the hotel, like the guides, will charge about a dollar a day. Two hundred and twenty-seven miles from Quebec lies the little village of *Sayabec*, near which we strike the waters of *Lake Metapedia*. There are no regular hotels in the village, but board may be obtained of some of the villagers, who also may be hired to act as guides. There is good trout-fishing in the lake, in the winter months through the ice, and also in June. The next two stations, *Cedar Hall* and *Amqui*, 8 miles apart, both afford excellent fishing. The village hotel charges are moderate. At Cedar Hall the fishing is in Lake Metapedia and the *Metane River*, and the best months are June, July, and September. At Amqui the fishing, both for trout and salmon, is in the *Amqui* and *Metapedia Rivers*, and the best months are June, July, and August. Fourteen miles beyond Amqui is the famous fishing resort of **Causapscal.** Here there is splendid salmon-fishing in the *Metapedia River*, which flows close by the station; and in Lakes *Angus*, *Michaud*, and *Causapscal* the trout are large and abundant. The Metapedia, like most other really famous salmon streams, is leased to private persons. Names of leaseholders, and limits of their respective territories, etc., may be obtained by communicating with the *Fisheries Commissioner* of the Province in which the

GULF OF ST. LAWRENCE
ST. LAWRENCE
Pte de Monts
St. Maxime
St. Francois Xavier
Manicouagan
Ste Anne de Monts
St. Martin
St. Joseph
49°
Ste Felicité
Ste Anne
la Madeleine
York
St. Jean
Gaspé B.
Pet. Cascapedia
Bonaventure
Gr. Cascapedia
Riv. Nouvelle
L. Metapedia
Percé
C. d'Espoir
New Port
New Richmond
St. George
L. Mitis
Patapedia
48°
Ste Anne
Campbelltown
Bay of Chaleur
I. Miscou
68°
West of Greenwich

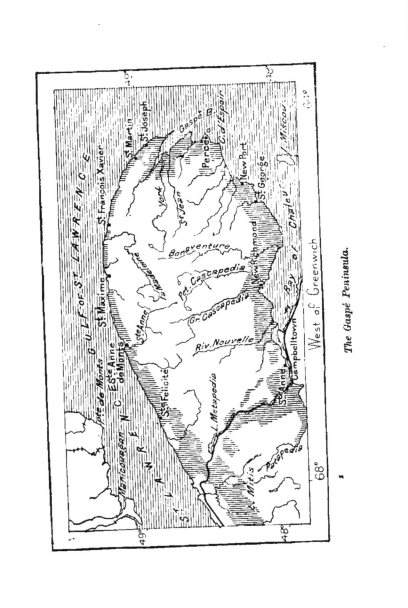

The Gaspé Peninsula.

water lies.   June is the best month for the salmon, while the trout rise
best to the fly in June and August.   Board is to be had in private
houses.

As the train winds for hours down the tortuous valley of the *Metapedia*, the scenery from the car-window is enchanting.   Sometimes
close beside the track, sometimes far below, the amber river foams
and darts, now leaping a low fall, now swirling slowly in a deep and
salmon-haunted pool, now laughing and rippling over wide, shallow
reaches, where the white quartz pebbles shine through the sunlit water.   The river is fringed through most of its course with birch and
elder and moose-wood and mountain-ash; and the hills which rise in
majestic slopes on either hand, cleft here and there by the gorge of
a winding mountain stream, are clothed richly with forests of birch
and fir.   In the autumn these hills are yellow as gold, and the heavy
clusters of the mountain-ash berries shine along the water's edge in
vivid vermilion.   Along this valley the stations are few and far between.   The nearest to Causapscal is *Pleasant Beach*, and then comes
Assametquaghan.   Passing *Mill Stream* we come to *Metapedia*, 290
miles from Quebec, and enter the magnificent valley of the far-famed
Restigouche, the boundary between the provinces of Quebec and
New Brunswick.   In crossing the railway bridges here we get a fine
view from the car-windows up and down the valley.

An interesting route to the Lower Provinces is by the Quebec
Central from Lévis down the beautiful valley of the Chaudière and
through a picturesque country to Megantic, where connection is made
with the C. P. R. Short Line from Montreal.

From Quebec to the Maritime Provinces by Steamship around Gaspé and the Gulf Coast.

The route between Quebec and **Gaspé** is served by the steamer
Admiral; but on every alternate Tuesday morning a fine boat of the
Quebec Steamship Company leaves Quebec for Gaspé and adjacent ports,
and continues down the New Brunswick coast to *Point du Chêne*, thence
to *Summerside* and *Charlottetown* in Prince Edward Island, and to
Pictou in Nova Scotia, where she arrives on Saturday.   This is a
comfortable salt-water voyage, lying nearly all the way through
waters that are rarely rough.   The coast scenery is fine, particularly
about the wild cliffs of Gaspé.   The fare to Gaspé is $10; return,

$15. The fare to Pictou is $16; return, $24. These rates include meals.

The voyage down the St. Lawrence as far as *Father Point* has been already described. A little way beyond is the whaling village of *Metis*, situated right opposite the strangely shaped Manicouagan Peninsula, which fills up the spacious bay at the mouths of the great Labrador rivers, Manicouagan and Outarde. Beyond Metis is the farming and lumbering village of *Matane*, whose broad, sandy beach affords delightful opportunities for bathing. Here flows in the Matane River, famous for its trout and salmon. Far off to the southwest, rising out of the heart of the Gaspé wilderness, we note the lofty summits called the Caps of Matane. The St. Lawrence here is over 40 miles in width, but it narrows again to 35 miles as we approach *Cape Chatte*, 33 miles east of Matane. At Cape Chatte is an important lighthouse. Near here took place, in June, 1629, a naval battle between the English ship Abigail and a French war-ship commanded by Emery de Caen, which resulted in a victory for the Englishman. The Cape is named for Eymard de Chaste, Governor of Dieppe, who in 1603 sent out an exploring and colonizing expedition which was led by Pontgravé and Lescarbot. Twelve or 15 miles eastward we round Cape St. Anne to the village of *Ste. Anne des Monts*, the center of extensive mackerel, cod, and halibut fisheries. In the adjoining river, the St. Anne, trout and salmon literally swarm. A few miles back from the coast rise the lofty St. Anne Mountains, whose chief peak reaches the height of 4,000 feet. These mountains are a spur of the great Gaspesian range called the Shick-shock or Notre Dame Mountains. The old chronicler Lalemant in 1648 wrote as follows : "All those who come to New France know well enough the mountains of Notre Dame, because the pilots and sailors being arrived at that part of the great river which is opposite to those high mountains, baptize ordinarily for sport the new passengers, if they do not turn aside by some present the inundation of this baptism which is made to flow plentifully on their heads."

\   From Cape St. Anne to *Point Pleureuse*, a distance of 28 miles, the coast is but a wall of towering cliffs. Eleven miles beyond is *Cape Magdelaine* at the mouth of the Rivière Magdelaine. All this region has furnished themes for the wildest legends. The name *Pleureuse* is suggestive enough in itself. The superstitious sailors and fishermen of these haunted coasts tell of the piteous lamentations they hear— *Le Braillard de la Magdelaine*—which they ascribe to a damned soul

Gaspé Residents returning from Church.

seeking to tell its torments.   It is usually supposed to be the soul of a murderous wrecker—for some of the old Gaspesian wreckers earned a reputation as black as that which clings to the wreckers of the west coast of Newfoundland.   Others again, of a more ecclesiastical turn of imagination, declare that the wailings are the penitential cries of a priest who willfully suffered a little one to die unbaptized.   The most piteous of the tales is that of a wreck on this iron coast in which only one person came to shore alive.   This was a baby boy, who lay crying all night in the horrible desolation, and died because no help came.   A probable explanation of the weird voices may be found in the wave-eaten caverns of the cliffs, in which the sea moans and cries incessantly.

Quitting this grim haunt of mysteries we pass *Grande Vallée* and come to *Cloridorme*, an important settlement, and the seat of a large branch of the great fishing firm of Robin & Co., which has its head-quarters in the Isle of Jersey.   Then we pass the fishing hamlet of *Fox River*, and find ourselves off *Cap des Rosiers*, sometimes called "the Scylla of the St. Lawrence."   Here lies the village of Cape Rosier, which, with the neighboring settlements of *Griffin's Cove* and *Grand Grève*, are dependent on the great Gaspé fishing firm of W. Hyman & Sons.   At this point we may be said to pass out of the gates of the St. Lawrence, which is here 96 miles wide.   On the cape stands a light-house of stone 112 ft. high.   Due N., like a stern sentinel guarding the riches and loveliness within, stands the grim *Isle of Anticosti*, in the middle of the river's giant mouth.   The isle is no less than 135 miles long by 40 in width; but this great area must be regarded as hopelessly inhospitable.   The coast is perilous, the climate cruel, the soil sterile.   Within a year or so there were a thousand or more inhabitants on the island; but these, having come to the verge of starvation, were lately removed to the mainland and kindlier surroundings.   Now the only dwellers in this wilderness are the lighthouse-keepers.   Seal-fishers visit the spot in the fishing season; and the island streams abound with trout and salmon, as do its barrens with feathered game.

Six miles beyond *Cap. des Rosiers*, we reach the vast projecting promontory of **Cape Gaspé,** which thrusts out into the Gulf of St. Lawrence a towering rampart of sandstone 690 ft. in height.   The name of the cape, and thence of the whole great peninsula, is derived from the Indian word "Gasépion," applying to a lonely detached rock 100 ft. high which once rose out of the waves off the extremity of the cape.   From its resemblance to a statue the *habitants* called this rock

"*La Vieille.*" The ceaseless battering of storms has at length over-thrown this picturesque and historic landmark. Seven miles and a half S. of Cape Gaspé rises the promontory of *Point St. Peter ;* and between them lies the deep inlet of *Gaspé Bay,* which runs 20 miles inland, and keeps at its head the secure harbor of Gaspé Basin.

As we run up the bay we pass on our right the perilous shores of *Grand Gréve,* on which the seas pile furiously when the wind draws up the coast. On the left shore of the bay is the village of *Douglus-town,* at which flows in a famous salmon river called the *St. John.* Then the bay narrows, and round the natural breakwater of Sandy Beach we enter the harbor of Gaspé Town. This is a growing place, the headquarters of immense cod and mackerel fisheries, and the chief town on the whole Great Gaspé Peninsula. It has between 800 and 900 inhabitants, and its noble and unique scenery, matchless summer climate, and the magnificent trout and salmon fishing of the adjacent *York* and *Dartmouth Rivers,* have attracted the attention of travelers. The town is possessed of a comfortable hotel, the *Gulf House.* Its fishing operations are chiefly in the hands of the great firm of Le Boutillier Bros. From its wharf a fortnightly mail steamer runs to *Esquimaux Bay* on the coast of *Labrador.* Its piers are thronged with schooners and an occasional whaling-ship. The surrounding fields are fruitful and well peopled, and petroleum has been found in the neighborhood by boring. On a hill overlooking the town are the guns of *Fort Ram-say.* The Indians who of old inhabited this region had made consid-erable advances in civilization, perhaps from intercourse with the Norse-men, who are supposed to have visited the country frequently in the eleventh, twelfth, and thirteenth centuries. In 1534 Cartier landed here and took possession in the name of the King of France, erecting a cross 30 ft. high with the *fleur-de-lis* upon it. In 1627 a French fleet of 20 ships of war and transports, carrying emigrants and a great quantity of stores for the colony at Quebec, was driven by a storm to take shelter in Gaspé Basin. Hither they were followed by Admiral Kirke with three English ships. The battle resulted in the utter defeat of the French. Kirke burned ten of the ships, and sailed the others, laden with captives and treasure, back to England. In 1760, Gaspé was taken by Admirable Byron. At one time the peninsula of Gas-pesia was erected into a separate province, and Gaspé made the seat of government ; an honor which it did not long enjoy, as the peninsula, on account of its scanty population, was soon reannexed to Quebec.

Running out of Gaspé Bay the steamer rounds Point St. Peter and crosses the mouth of Mal Bay, 9 miles wide, to the village of *Percé*. The port of Percé may be likened to that Salmydessian Harbor which Æschylus called "a step-mother to ships." It lies open to northeasterly storms, and was formerly called *La Terre des Tempêtes*. The village has between 400 and 500 inhabitants. It fairly lives and breathes codfish. It is divided by *Mont Joli* into two settlements called North Beach and South Beach. From the rugged top of *Mount St. Anne*, rising behind the village to a height of 1,200 ft., with rich fossils and agates upon its bleak red slopes, may be had one of the finest views in eastern Canada. The most famous landmark of the whole peninsula lies just off the village Percé. This is the renowned **Percé Rock**. It is thus described by Mr. J. G. A. Creighton in Picturesque Canada :

La Roche Percé, "the pierced rock," stands bold and firm to the end, though the cliffs of Mont Joli, on the mainland, and of Bonaventure Island, 2 miles out at sea, confirm the Indian tradition, given by Denys, that once there was no break in these perpendicular walls of rich-hued conglomerate, where the reds and browns of sandstone, the bright olives and grays of limestone, greens of agate, purples of jasper, white quartz, and deep-orange stain of iron blend together, and, seen against brilliant blue sky and emerald sea, form a wondrous combination of color; but the waves, with unbroken sweep from the open ocean, beat fiercely on this marvelous rock and have already battered down the three grand arches Denys saw. Seventy years before Denys, Champlain says there was only one arch, which was large enough for a sloop under full sail to pass through. At present there is but one opening, 40 or 50 ft. high. Many remember the mighty crash with which the immense arch at the outer end of the rock fell just before dawn one morning about forty years ago, leaving as its monument the great monolith that formed its abutment. Slowly and surely wind and sea are doing their work; they have begun another aperture, not more than a couple of feet in diameter, through which the sunbeams flash as the eclipsing wave-crests rise and fall. On the north side is a tiny beach where you can land at low tide on a calm day. It is like a profanation to tread on the piles of agate and jasper glistening with water, whose every roll tosses up millions of pebbles for the sun to turn into rarest jewels. Myriads of fossils give to the face of the rock, that at a distance looks so hard and weather-worn, the appearance of an arabesque in richest velvet. In this little cove, shut in by the cliff from sight of everything but the water and the sky, with no sound but the cries of the countless birds that tenant the dizzy heights and the music of the surf as its thunderous bass dies away in rapid fugues to tenderest treble of clattering pebbles and dashing spray, we might sit and dream till the great, green rollers, through which a mysterious light gleams on weird shapes of trees and grottoes, and castles and palaces, carried us off willing visitors to the enchanted land they reveal.

Everywhere else the rock rises straight from deep water to a height of 300 ft. At its western end it is worn to a wedge as sharp and straight and clear-cut as the prow of an immense ironclad, which it singularly resembles in outline, if any one imagine an ironclad 1,500 ft. long and 300 ft. wide. Its top is covered with grass, but this is barely visible because of the immense flocks of birds, winged armies ranged in serried order. Each tribe inhabits its own territory; the black cormorants never mingle with the white gulls; the great gannets and the graceful terns keep their own places. If any presumptuous bird wanders into the ranks of another tribe there is a tremendous screaming and flapping of wings to drive away the intruder. They come and go incessantly, circling high over the schools of herring, and plunging deep to seize their prey; they swoop around the cod fishers at anchor far out on the banks; they follow the boats into the beach where the packers are at work; they flit like ghosts about the nets when in the silvery moonlight the fishermen go in quest of bait; but they return always to the one spot allotted to them among the densely packed mass of white that from a distance looks like a bank of snow. During a storm their shrieking is almost unearthly, and can be heard for miles.

In 1776 a naval battle took place off Percé Rock between a fleet of American privateers and the British war-ships Wolf and Diligence, in which two of the American ships were sunk. Our steamer passes now between Percé Rock and the towering cliffs, from 400 to 500 ft. high, of *Bonaventure Island*, which stands 2½ miles off shore. Nine miles from Percé we pass the fishing village of *Cape Cove*, and round the promontory of Cape d'Espoir, whose name on the tongues of the English-speaking inhabitants is very antithetically corrupted into Cape Despair. This is a scene of wrecks, and the fishermen say that sometimes when wind and sea are undisturbed, there comes a vision of dreadful waves rolling in upon the cape, bearing on their crests a spectral ship whose decks are crowded with people in the dress of long ago. In the bow stands an officer with a woman in white clinging to his arm; and as the ship is hurled upon the rocks, over the crash and roar and crying of many voices rises the shriek of the woman. Then all is quiet again and the sea lies still and smiling. Seven miles from the cape lies Robin & Co.'s village of *Grand River*. Then we pass *Grand Pabos* and *Petit Pabos*, the little Acadian village of *Newport*, and round *Point Maquereau*, where in 1838 the treasure-ship Colborne was wrecked with the loss of all on board, to the great enriching of the Gaspé wreckers. Beyond Point Maquereau lie the quiet and lovely

Fercé Rock.

waters of the *Bay des Chaleurs.* Our steamer turns south and runs down the gulf coast of **New Brunswick**, into *Northumberland Strait* to *Shediac, Prince Edward Island* ports, and *Pictou,* where she arrives on Saturday; these places will be described in connection with another route, and here we will make a short divergence to point out some places of interest along the Gaspé shore of Bay Chaleurs.

A few miles beyond Point Maquereau is the settlement of *Port Daniel.* Then we come to *Paspebiac* (meaning "broken banks"), an important fishing village of about 500 inhabitants, who are nicknamed locally Paspy Jacks. Here is a little hotel called the *Lion Inn.* In the neighborhood of the village one may pick up fine specimens of jasper known as Gaspé pebbles. The harbor is protected by a natural breakwater in the form of a sand beach 3 miles long. The trim cottages of the village crown the cliffs, along the foot of which stretch the great red and white buildings of the firm of Robin & Co., so often mentioned. The headquarters of this firm, founded in 1768, are in the Isle of Jersey; and the officers of the firm on this side the water are required to live in single blessedness. Paspebiac holds also an important post of the Le Boutilliers, and its yearly export of fish amounts in value to over $250,000. From Paspebiac to the Intercolonial at *Metapedia* runs the Atlantic and Lake Superior Railway, a distance of 100 miles. Beyond Paspebiac, near the mouth of the Bonaventure River, is the little town of *New Carlisle* (the western terminus of the new Canadian Steamship line). Next we come to *Cascapedia Bay,* with the villages of *Maria* and *New Richmond,* whence steamers run across to Dalhousie. Near Maria flows in the *Grand Cascapedia River,* on which are some of the most famous salmon-pools in the world. Here the successive Governor-Generals of Canada have their fishing lodges, and here was a favorite summer resort of the Princess Louise when she dwelt in Canada. President Arthur, also, used to come hither and cast a fly on these unrivaled waters. Beyond Cascapedia Bay lies the important Acadian village of *Carleton,* with a population of 1,033. The village is watched over by the lovely peak of Tracadiegash. It has a large convent, and extensive herring-fisheries. A few miles beyond Carleton we reach the fertile valley of the Nouvelle River, a beautiful stream of ice-cold water descending from the mountains. Its trout are famous for their size and strength. Above the settlement the river is leased by an American. Continuing for a few miles over a range of hills we reach the Escuminac River, a smaller stream than the Nouvelle, which

contains trout of unusual size. This may be fished by arrangement
with the warden of the river at Escuminac station. A little beyond
lies the mouth of the *Restigouche*, and either at *Metapedia*, *Campbellton*,
or *Dalhousie*, we may bring to an end our journey in this direction.
The fare by rail from Metapedia station to Carleton is $1.62; return,
$2.81; to New Richmond and return, $3.81; to Paspebiac and return,
$6.31.

PROVINCE OF NEW BRUNSWICK.

New Brunswick is first of all a lumbering, ship-building, and fishing
province. She also has heavy agricultural interests, and her great mineral wealth is beginning to find development. In shape the province is
nearly a square, the seaward sides of which are washed respectively by
the Gulf of St. Lawrence and the Bay of Fundy. The center of the
province is yet for the most part a wilderness, threaded and dotted in
all directions with lakes and brooks and rivers, and abounding with fish
and game. Till about a century ago New Brunswick formed a portion
of Nova Scotia or the old Acadian territory. In 1784, on the influx of
the United Empire Loyalists, it was erected into a separate province.

The history of Canada may be said to open on the St. Lawrence
coast of this province, not very far from where we entered it in our
descent by rail from Quebec. It began on June 30th, when Cartier
sighted *Cape Escuminac* on the gulf-shore of New Brunswick. Coming
from the bleak, forbidding coasts of Newfoundland, which he deemed
to be Cain's portion of the earth, this harsh corner of Acadia appeared
to Cartier a paradise. The wide water in which he found himself was
Miramichi Bay. Not discovering the Miramichi itself, whose mouth
lay hidden close at hand, behind long ranges of sand-spits, chains of
islands, and intricate shoals, he landed on the banks of a lesser river,
not identified among the thousand such that overlace that region with
their silver courses. This stream rippled shallow over its gleaming
pebbles, and swarmed with trout and salmon. The woods about were
of pine and cedar, elm and oak, birch, willow, fir, maple, and tamarack,
and the sailors' hearts rejoiced over such unlimited possibilities of ships.
Where the woods gave back a little space, the ground was covered with
wild fruits. Great, melting strawberries betrayed themselves to the lips
by their red gleams piercing the grass. The bronze-green blackberry
thickets were heavy with their yet unripened fruitage, and the wild pea

The Beach at Paspebiac.

A View of the Bay.

trammeled his footsteps with its ropes of purple and pale green. This prodigal land was populous with game. When wild pigeons in innumerable flocks streamed past and darkened the air, the heavens seemed as thick with wings as the sea and streams with fish. The men lay awake at night and listened with wonder to the noise of the countless salmon passing the shoals. Every sedge-grown marsh was noisy with ducks. Plover and curlew piped clearly about the edges of the pools. And the people possessing this land were friendly and few.

Bearing northward Cartier's weather-darkened sails were soon wafting him over the fairest bay his eyes had yet rested upon. Its waters were clear and green, and scarce rippled under the steep sun of mid-July. No reefs, no shoals, but here and there a dark-green island asleep on the sleepy tide. On either hand a long, receding line of lofty shores drawing closer together toward the west, and shading gently from indigo to pale violet. So great was the change from the raw winds of the gulf to this sultry sea that Cartier named it **Baie des Chaleurs**. Here they passed some days very sweetly in indolent exploration, in trading with the hospitable Micmacs, in feasting on seal-flesh and salmon. So commercial were the natives of this land that they bartered the clothes they wore for trades and trinkets. Then Cartier sailed on to the north to discover the St. Lawrence. The first attempt at settlement, however, was in the extreme southwest of the province, and was undertaken by Champlain and the Sieur de Monts in 1604. This attempt, as well as the successive immigrations of French, of New England pioneers, and of the United Empire Loyalists, will be referred to in other connections.

The Restigouche.

The name **Restigouche** signifies the five-fingered river—so called from the five great branching tributaries which spread abroad through Quebec and New Brunswick like the fingers of an open hand. Of these branches the Upsalquitch is a marvelous trout and salmon stream, but difficult of access on account of its almost continuous rapids, and somewhat hard to fish successfully by reason of the preternatural clearness of its currents. The ample stream of the *Quah-ta-wah-am-quah-davic* has had its name providentially condensed by the lumberman into *Tom Kedgewick*. The course of the Restigouche is nowhere broken by falls or impassable rapids; and its strong, full, unflagging current makes it a magnificent stream for the canoe-man. Its salmon-fisheries are famed the world over, and are for the most part in the hands of fishing-clubs made up of wealthy Canadian and American anglers. The Restigouche salmon is remarkable for his size. He is a very different fish from his fellows of *Nepisiguit* and *Miramichi*. He does more of his fighting under water, and usually takes the fly when it is below the surface. He has been made the subject of a bright article in Scribner's Magazine for May, 1888. Gigantic and magnificent as he is, he is capricious in his appetite, and frequently when he is most wanted he is not there. His fame has quite eclipsed that of the noble Restigouche trout, who is always on hand to console the disappointed fisherman. The killing of a Restigouche salmon is thus vividly described in the article just referred to:

We pass around two curves in the river and find ourselves at the head of the pool. . . . First cast, to the right, straight across the stream, about 20 ft.; the current carries the fly down with a semicircular sweep until it comes in line with the bow of the canoe. Second cast, to the left, straight across the stream, with the same motion; the semicircle is completed, and the fly hangs quivering for a few seconds at the lowest point of the arc. Three or four ft. of line are drawn from the reel. Third cast, to the right; fourth cast, to the left. Then a little more line. And so, with widening half-circles, the water is covered gradually and very carefully, until at length the angler has as much line out as his two-handed rod can lift and swing. . . . This seems like a very regular and somewhat mechanical proceeding as one describes it, but in the performance it is rendered intensely interesting by the knowledge that, at any moment, it is liable to be interrupted by an agreeable surprise. One can never tell just when or how a salmon will rise, or just what he will do when he has risen.

This morning the interruption comes early. At the first cast of the second drop, before the fly has fairly lit, a great flash of silver darts from the waves close by the boat. Usually a salmon takes the fly rather slowly, carrying it under water before he seizes it in his mouth. But this one is in no mood for deliberation. He has hooked himself with a rush, and the line goes whirring madly from the reel as he races down the pool. Keep the point of the rod low; he must have his own way now. Up with the anchor quickly, and send the canoe after him, bowman and sternman paddling with swift strokes. He has reached the deepest water; he stops to think what has happened to him; we have passed around and below him; and now with the current below to help us we can begin to reel in. Lift the point of the rod with a strong, steady pull. Put the force of both arms into it. The tough wood will stand the strain. The fish must be moved; he must come to the boat if he is ever to be landed. He gives a little and yields slowly to the pressure. Then suddenly he gives too much, and runs straight toward us. Reel in now as swiftly as possible, or else he will get a slack on the line and escape. Now he stops, shakes his head from side to side, and darts away again across the pool, leaping high out of water. Drop the point of the rod quickly, for if he falls on the leader he will surely break it. Another leap, and another! Truly he is "a merry one," as Sir Humphry Davy says, and it will go hard with us to hold him. But those great leaps have exhausted his strength, and now he follows the line more easily. The men push the boat back to the shallow side of the pool until it touches lightly on the shore. The fish comes slowly in, fighting a little and making a few short runs; he is tired and turns slightly on his side; but even yet he is a heavy weight on the line, and it seems a wonder that so slight a thing as the leader can guide and draw him. Now he is close to the boat. The boatman steps out on a rock with his gaff. Steadily now and slowly lift the rod, bending it backward. A quick, sure stroke of the steel! a great splash! and the salmon is lifted high and dry upon the shore. Give him the *coup de grâce* at once, for his own sake as well as ours. And now look at him, as he lies there on the green leaves. Broad back; small head tapering to a point; clean, shining sides, with a few black spots on them; it is a fish fresh run from the sea, in perfect condition, and that is the reason why he has given us such good sport.

The fishing rights to many of the best pools on the Restigouche are held by gentlemen owning the adjacent shores, and it is usually easy to get permission for a cast in one or another of the pools.

From the bridge the railroad follows down the S. shore of the Restigouche a few miles to *Campbellton*. Immediately behind the village of Campbellton rises a peculiar mountain called the *Sugar-Loaf*, about 1,000 ft. in height. The face of Sugar-Loaf is inaccessible on the side next the village. Its base on this side is strewn thick with mighty bowlders, which have detached themselves on slight provocation. The view from the summit is remarkably fine. Yonder lies the park-like amphitheatre wherein the Restigouche and Metapedia meet, coiling hither and thither in bands of azure. Beyond, towering over innumerable lesser hills, the peaks of Squaw's Cap and Slate Mountain; and over the shining waters of the *Baie des Chaleurs* the blue ranges of the *Tracadiegash* in *Gaspé*, the practically unexplored terminations of the Alleghany system. Below our feet the white cottages of Campbellton shine in the transparent atmosphere.

Within the mouth of the Restigouche there stood in old times a French town called *Petite Rochelle*. Across the river from Campbellton lies the Micmac settlement of *Mission Point*, where the remains of two

French vessels may still be seen at low water. The Micmac village stands upon a good coal-field. In 1760, when the French Government was seeking to regain Quebec, 22 store-ships were sent out from France under a strong convoy. In the gulf they learned the distasteful intelligence that an English fleet had gone up the St. Lawrence ahead of them. Thereupon they took shelter in the *Baie des Chaleurs*, where they were followed by Admiral Byron, commander of the British naval forces at Louisburg. The British squadron, consisting of five ships, captured two of the French vessels on the way up the bay. The French fleet, fleeing into the Restigouche, took refuge under the batteries of Petite Rochelle, whither the English followed, and after silencing the batteries brought on a general engagement. At length the explosion of a French powder-ship brought the battle to a close; and the English destroyed not only the whole squadron but the fortifications and the 200 houses of *Petite Rochelle*. On the site of the ruined town relics of various kinds are yet from time to time unearthed. Nine miles from Campbellton the train stops at *Dalhousie Junction*, whence a run of 7 miles brings us to the lovely watering-place of *Dalhousie*, with its famous summer hotel, the *Inch Arran*. Dalhousie lies on the beautiful and placid waters of the *Baie des Chaleurs*. It is the capital of Restigouche County, and has a population of between 2,000 and 3,000, with a considerable trade in lumber and fish. In the deep sheltered harbor of Dalhousie the boating and bathing facilities are all that could be desired. The Indian name of the *Baie des Chaleurs* is *Ecketuam Nemaache*, which signifies " a Sea of Fish," and is in the highest degree appropriate. The waters of the bay are brooded over by the charm of many legends, chief among which is that of the " Phantom Ship," whose lurid shape is said to appear at times off the coast, and to be associated in some indeterminate manner with the omnipresent Captain Kidd. Here lies the scene also of the brutal deed of Skipper Ireson, the subject of a spirited ballad by Whittier:

> " Small pity for him !—He sailed away
> From a leaking ship in Chaleur Bay—
> Sailed away from a sinking wreck,
> With his own town's-people on her deck !
> ' Lay by ! lay by ! ' they called to him ;
> Back he answered : ' Sink or swim !
> Brag of your catch of fish again ! '
> And off he sailed through the fog and rain."

Valley of the Metapedia.

From the Restigouche to Moncton.

From Dalhousie Junction to *Bathurst* the traveler gets some noble and spacious views from the car-windows. Ten miles from the Junction is Charlo, beside the *Charlo River*, a small stream which has not been leased for several years, though it is a capital trout-stream, and one may kill a few salmon on it in the early part of the season. Sixteen miles farther on we cross *Jacquet River*, a famous fishing stream, which a few years ago was nearly depleted by poachers, but which is rapidly regaining its old status under judicious protection. Beyond Jacquet River we pass the unimportant stations of *Belledune* and *Petite Roche*, at the latter of which we cross the little Nigadou River. As we approach the fine harbor of *Bathurst* we cross the *Tatagouche River.* Then we come to the town of Bathurst, where flows in the *Nepisiguit River.* The name Nepisiguit signifies foaming waters. Besides this river and the Tatagouche, two other streams empty themselves into the lovely basin of Bathurst Harbor—namely, *Middle River* and the *Little Nepisiguit.* All are fishing streams, but the fame of the lesser three is quite eclipsed by that of the Nepisiguit. The name Tatagouche is a corruption of the Indian Tootoogoose, which signifies Fairy River. The town of Bathurst is beautifully situated on two high points, separated by a shallow estuary. It has a population of about 3,000, and a considerable trade in fish and lumber. The chief hotel is the *Kearey House.* The settlement of Bathurst was begun in 1638 by a wealthy Basque, M. Jean Jacques Enaud, who took to himself as wife a Mohawk princess. But difficulties arose between the French and the Indians, and the latter at length destroyed the infant settlement. The district was an old battle-ground of the Mohawks and the Micmacs. At different times settlements were begun on the harbor, only to be destroyed by the savages or by American privateers. The present town was founded in 1818 by Sir Howard Douglas.

The reputation of the *Nepisiguit* as a salmon-stream is second only to that of the Restigouche and Miramichi. It rises in a number of lakes in the high central plateau of the province, separated by only a short portage from the head-waters of certain of the St. John's chief tributaries. The course of the Nepisiguit is tumultuous and broken. Twenty miles above its mouth it plunges in four leaps over a magnificent cataract 140 ft. in height, known as the *Grand Falls* of the *Nepisiguit.* Below the fall the river glides through a narrow channel between high cliffs. Above its *débouchement* it rolls over a bed of great granite bowlders. Though the river is leased, and a good deal of money spent on its protection, its salmon-fisheries are deteriorating, owing, it is said, to a system of trap-nets below tide-water, so arranged as to prevent fish entering the river. This difficulty, it seems, can hardly be remedied, as tidal waters are not under the control of the provincial authorities. Throughout the whole of its upper course, however, the river simply swarms with trout of large size, which are rarely disturbed owing to the comparative inaccessibility of the waters they occupy. The best way to reach them is from the other side of the province, by a canoe trip up the *Tobique* and down the Nepisiguit from its source. This is a trip to delight such bold canoe-men as long for the complete wilderness and a little spice of danger. The salmon of the Nepisiguit are smaller than those of the Restigouche, but a very fierce and active fish.

Five miles beyond Bathurst lies *Gloucester Junction*, whence the Caraquet and Gulf Shore Railway runs down to the *Baie des Chaleurs* shore to the magnificent harbor of *Shippigan*, the port of refuge of the Canadian and American fishing fleets. The fare to *Caraquet* and return is $2.25. This harbor is situated at the extremity of a cape which thrusts itself far out into the gulf. It occupies an important point in a scheme known as the ocean ferry, by which it is proposed to shorten the transatlantic passage. The idea is to run a fast express between New York and Shippigan, swift steamers from Shippigan across the Gulf of St. Lawrence to St. George's Bay in Newfoundland, thence fast express again across Newfoundland to St. John's, whence it is but 1,640 miles of ocean voyage to Valencia. This scheme is yet *in nubibus*, and may remain so; but just beyond Shippigan lies the wide flat island of *Miscou*, whose shooting-grounds are perhaps the best in the Dominion. The seasons are August and September for plover, September, October, and November for geese, ducks, and brant. The shooting privileges of Miscou are held by Lee Babbitt, Esq., of Fredericton, who may be addressed on the subject. Miscou Island is about 20 miles in circumference, and is reached by boat from Caraquet. The distance between Caraquet and Bathurst by rail is 45 miles. The district about Shippigan was once a favorite resort of the walrus.

Between Gloucester Junction and the town of *Newcastle* on the Miramichi, a distance of 39 miles, we pass but three stations, namely,

Red Pine, Bartibogue, and *Beaver Brook.*   Newcastle is at the head of deep water navigation on the Miramichi.   It is a ship-building center, with a population of between 2,000 and 8,000, and a considerable trade in lumber and in canned and frozen fish.   The chief hotel is the *Waverly.*   Five miles down the river, on the south shore, lies **Chatham**, the chief town of the gulf coast of New Brunswick.   Almost midway between them, on the same side of the river as Newcastle, is the lumbering village of *Douglastown.*   Chatham is about 12 miles from the mouth of the Miramichi.   Its population is nearly 10,000, its harbor is safe and roomy, and its lumbering, fishing, and ship-building interests are large.   It is the terminus of the Canada Eastern Railway, which runs to *Fredericton,* 120 miles, and it is the see town of a Roman Catholic bishop.   Between Newcastle and Chatham one may go by rail by way of *Chatham Junction ;* but much the more direct and pleasant trip is by the steamers that ply on the river, though as far as the scenery is concerned the Miramichi, in its lower portions at least, has little to boast of.   The view of Chatham is dominated by the lofty piles of the Roman Catholic institutions *St. Michael's Cathedral* and *College,* and the Convent and Hospital.   The chief hotels of Chatham are the *Adams House* and *Bowser's.*

Besides the Miramichi itself, to be referred to presently, the traveler who halts at Chatham finds himself within convenient distance of many fine fishing waters.   It is a short drive to the *Bartibogue,* whose wide shallow reaches abound in season with splendid sea-trout.   It is an easy stream to fish, and at the head of tide may be had good sport with the striped bass.   Stages run from Chatham to the famous *Tabusintac,* "the place where two meet," a distance of 34 miles.   As a trout-stream this narrow river, full of pools, is almost unrivaled.   The sea-trout swarm up its waters, and run very large.   A trip to the Tabusintac is the great delight of Chatham anglers.   Fifteen miles beyond this river lies the *Big Tracadie River,* a broad, shallow stream well stocked with salmon and trout, and running through a sandy region. The district about the river is thickly settled with Acadian French, whose farming and fishing are alike prosperous.   The mouth of the Tracadie, as of most streams flowing into the gulf along this coast, is sheltered by a long, low, sandy island, forming a shallow lagoon.   These lagoons are frequented in the autumn by vast flocks of ducks, wild geese, and brant.   At Tracadie is the famous *Lazaretto,* an object of most painful interest, where a colony of lepers is secluded and cared

9

for. Some time in the course of last century a French vessel was
wrecked on this coast, certain of whose sailors were afflicted with the
virulent leprosy of the Levant. By close association and intermarriage
the disease spread rapidly among the Acadians, but it is now being
stamped out by the precautions of the Government.

. From Chatham excursion steamers run frequently down the river to
the settlements of *Bay du Vin* on the south shore and *Burnt Church*
on the north shore of Miramichi Bay. Both these settlements are on
small trout rivers. Burnt Church is the capital of the Micmac Indians,
and they gather to the spot in great numbers every summer on the
festival of Ste. Anne. They celebrate the festival with religious ceremonies, sports, and dances. Governor Gordon says, " I was surprised
by the curious resemblance between these dances and those of the
Greek peasantry."

The Miramichi.

The *Miramichi* is the second river in the province, ranking next to
the St. John in size and importance. The head-waters of some of its
tributaries interlace with those of streams that flow into the St. John.
A short distance above *Newcastle* the river forks into what are known
as the *Nor'west Miramichi* and the *Sou'west Miramichi*, of which
the latter is really the main stream. The name is Micmac, and means
" the happy retreat." The Sou'west Branch is the more thickly settled, and its valley is traversed by the Canada Eastern R. R. as far
as Boiestown. The course of the river, as of most of its tributaries,
is comparatively unbroken, and offers every facility for both fishing
and canoeing. The Nor'west Branch is more difficult of access and
has perhaps fewer first-rate salmon-pools. Nearly all these waters,
however, are justly renowned for trout and salmon. Particularly
famous are such tributaries as the *Big* and *Little Sevogle*, the *Renous*,
and the *Dungarvan ;* and in the latter stream, owing to the rigid sup-
pression of poaching, the fish become yearly more numerous. Perhaps
the most famous salmon-pools are those on the upper waters of the
Sou'west Branch, above *Boiestown*, at the mouths of Burnt Hill Brook,
Rocky Brook, and the Clear Water. For information as to fishing
privileges in New Brunswick generally, one would do well to communicate with the Commissioner for the Province, J. Henry Phair, Esq., of
Fredericton. An excellent canoe trip may be made by ascending the
river St. John by steamer, canoe, or rail some distance above *Woodstock*

and portaging over by a short carry to the head of the Sou'west Branch, whence the run is easy all the way to Chatham.

A good deal of history has been made on the lower portion of the Miramichi and about its mouth. The early settlers were usually unfortunate in their relations with the Indians. An interesting point is *Beaubair's Island*, at the confluence of the Nor'west and Sou'west Branches. Here once stood a flourishing French town, most of whose inhabitants perished by disease and famine in 1758. The destruction of the town was completed by a British fleet in 1759, and now its site is woods and picnic-grounds. In October, 1825, the greater portion of the river valley was visited by an awful calamity which occupies a very prominent place in New Brunswick history under the name of *The Great Miramichi Fire.* This conflagration destroyed 3,000,000 acres of forest and 160 human lives. Those who escaped only saved themselves by taking refuge in the lakes and rivers. The catastrophe is thus described by Dr. Bryce:

For two days preceding the 7th of October, 1825, the air had been intensely close; there was a dead calm. Toward evening a rumbling sound was heard, then a breeze, and last a hurricane bringing flames, cinders, ashes, and hot sand, so that simultaneously several hundreds of square miles were wrapped in one blaze. The town of Newcastle was swept away almost entirely. Vessels in the river were cast ashore and a number burned. Hundreds of men, women, and children were overtaken in the flames and perished. The Governor-General advanced upward of £2,000 for relief, which was cheerfully assumed by Lower Canada, Nova Scotia appropriated £750, and military stores to the value of many thousands of pounds were sent to the miserable survivors.

The Intercolonial crosses the Miramichi above the forks by two fine bridges. Between Newcastle and *Kent Junction* it passes the small stations of *Derby, Chatham Junction, Barnaby River,* and *Rogersville.* At Kent Junction the Kent Northern R. R. may be taken for the quiet little town of *Richibucto,* the capital of Kent County, near the mouth of the *Richibucto River.* The neighborhood is interesting to tourists chiefly for the typical Acadian town of *St. Louis,* with its sacred well and grotto, 7 miles by rail from Richibucto. The fine summer hotel of Richibucto, known as " The Beaches," is now closed. The name Richibucto means " the river of fire," and was applied not only to the river but to a fierce tribe of savages that dwelt upon its shores. In 1724 this tribe, under the leadership of their chief, the Great Wizard, made an expedition to *Canso* and captured seventeen Massachusetts vessels. With this fleet they were sailing homeward in triumph when they were overtaken by two ships of war which had been sent in pursuit of them from Boston. In the strange sea-fight that followed the Indians fought desperately, but were defeated and slain to a man. After leaving Kent Junction we pass the stations of *Weldford*, *Adamsville*, *Coal Branch*, *Canaan*, and *Berry's Mills*, in the run of 45 miles which brings us to the city of Moncton.

Moncton.

Moncton is important as a railway center. It is a prosperous and rapidly growing town of about 10,000 inhabitants, but is not a pretty town as regards either its situation or its buildings. It has a sugar refinery, cotton-factory, and the works and offices of the Inter-colonial R. R. It lies in a flat, inexhaustibly fertile farming region at what is known as "The Bend" of the *Peditcodiac River*, a remarkable tidal stream flowing into the Bay of Fundy. The extreme variation · between high and low tide sometimes reaches 70 ft.; and the flood tide sweeps up the channel in a foaming wall·of water from 4 ft. to 6 ft. high, which is known as the Bore of the Petitcodiac. The shores of all these tidal rivers emptying into the Bay of Fundy are lined with vast breadths of salt meadows, consisting of an alluvial deposit of wonderful depth and inexhaustible fertility. They are reclaimed from the sea by an elaborate system of dikes, and produce fabulous crops of hay. There are several good hotels in Moncton, of which the best are the *Brunswick*, the *Commercial*, and the *Royal*, recently rebuilt; rates, $2 per day. From Moncton a railway runs to the town of *Buctouche* (famous for its oysters), a distance of 32 miles. Return tickets cost $1.50. The chief hotel at Buctouche is the *Bay View*.

Routes from Moncton.

Moncton to St. John, $2.67; return, $4.00. Moncton to Charlotte-town, $3.50; return, $5.30.

In the way of choice of routes from Moncton the traveler now experiences an *embarras de richesses*. If he wants to do New Brunswick thoroughly before going outside of the province, his best route is as follows: By Intercolonial (western section) to **St. John**; thence up the *river St. John* to *Fredericton*, *Woodstock*, *Grand Falls*, and the fishing districts of the *Tobique*, *Green River*, and the *Squattooks*.

From Woodstock or Fredericton by rail to *St. Stephen, St. Andrews, Campobello*, and the lovely region of *Passamaquoddy ;* thence by boat or the cars of the Shore Line Ry. back to St. John. From St. John one may cross the Bay of Fundy to *Digby* and thence up the far-famed *Annapolis Valley*, through the land of Evangeline, by the Dominion Atlantic R. R. to **Halifax**. From Halifax as a center one may conveniently do the eastern end of the province, with *Prince Edward Island, Cape Breton*, and the far-off ancient colony of *Newfoundland ;* then, when ready to set his face for the land of the eagle, he may take the splendid steamers City of Halifax and Olivette, of the Canada Atlantic and Plant Line, for **Boston**. This latter is a luxurious and delightful voyage, skirting the bold Atlantic coast of Nova Scotia and avoiding the choppy seas of the Bay of Fundy mouth.

Another good route is to retrace one's steps from St. John to Moncton after having finished the western portion of New Brunswick. If one intends to do *Prince Edward Island* and *Cape Breton*, it will be best to follow the main line of the Intercolonial from Moncton to *Sackville*, and thence across the *Isthmus of Chignecto* to *Amherst*, where one may visit the famous *Chignecto Ship R. R.* From Amherst he will return by Intercolonial, a distance of 40 miles, to *Painsec Junction*, whence a branch line runs to the charming little watering-place of *Shediac*, where there is unrivaled sea-bathing in the warm waters of *Northumberland Strait*. From Shediac one goes by boat to *Summerside*, in Prince Edward Island ; thence by rail down the island to the city of **Charlottetown**, its capital ; thence by boat again to *Pictou, Nova Scotia*, and by rail from Pictou to *Mulgrave*, where we cross the *Gut of Canso* into *Cape Breton*. After having tasted the fishing and scenery of Cape Breton, then back by rail to Pictou and *Truro*, and on to **Halifax**. By this course one misses the country between Amherst and Truro along the line of the Intercolonial, which is, however, neither beautiful nor historic, but interesting mainly for its great coal-mines and iron-works at *Spring Hill* and *Londonderry*. The latter town, however, may be visited by a short run from Truro, and the former by the Cumberland Railway from *Parrsboro* on *Minas Basin*. Having reached **Halifax** by this route a traveler may then take the Dominion Atlantic Ry. to *Digby*, making, if he will, a *détour* from *Middleton* by the Nova Scotia Central to *Bridgewater* and *Lunenburg* on the Atlantic coast. From Digby he may cross the bay to **St. John** by the Prince Rupert, a magnificent and speedy steamer, and thence to

Boston either by rail or by the splendid coast steamers of the International Steamship Co.; or he may go by the Dominion Atlantic Ry. to the city of *Yarmouth*, at the extreme southwest corner of Nova Scotia, and thence by one of the fine new steamers of the Yarmouth Line—the Yarmouth or the Boston—by a pleasant ocean voyage of sixteen hours to the metropolis of New England.

From Moncton to St. John.

From Moncton to St. John, a distance of 89 miles, the Intercolonial runs for the most part through a rich farming country, and, as we approach St. John, we catch many beautiful views from the car-windows The fare to St. John is $2.67; return, $4. At *Salisbury*, 13 miles from Moncton, the Intercolonial is joined by the Salisbury and Harvey R. R., which runs 45 miles through the small fishing and ship-building villages of Albert County to its terminus on *Shepody Bay*, an inlet of the Bay of Fundy. *Hillsboro* is an important village on this line, and has a heavy plaster trade. At *Albert Mines* was once procured the most valuable species of coal which the world has known. This mineral, called Albertite, fetched enormous prices; but the supply is now exhausted, and the village is falling to decay. The coast villages of Albert County are largely engrossed in the shad-fisheries. The peak of *Shepody Mountain*, called originally " Chapeau Dieu " from its crown of clouds, commands a truly sublime view. The region it overlooks is rich in minerals and game.

Five miles from Salisbury is the village of *Pollett River*, with good trout-fishing and fine scenery at Pollett Falls. Five miles farther we come to the important village of *Petitcodiac* (chief hotels, *Mansard House* and *Central*) in a district settled by Dutch loyalists from Pennsylvania. Not far from Petitcodiac are the famous fishing waters of *Canaan River*. Leaving Petitcodiac we pass small stations with the picturesque names of *Anagance, Penobsquis,* and *Plumweseep*. Then we reach the growing town of *Sussex*, the center of the rich agricultural district of Sussex Vale, which contains the head-waters of the lovely *Kennebecasis*, and was settled by loyalists from New Jersey. Between Sussex and *Hampton*, a distance of 21 miles, we pass the stations of *Apohaqui* (famous for its mineral waters), *Norton, Bloomfield,* and *Passekeag*. From Norton a new railroad, the Central, runs northward across the *Washademoak* through the coal regions at the head of *Grand Lake*. Hampton is a growing town on the Kennebecasis, 22 miles from St. John, and is a favorite summer resort for the people of that city. From Hampton the Central Railway of New Brunswick runs about 30 miles southeast to the small town of *St. Martins* or *Quaco* on the Bay of Fundy. Quaco is one of the chief ship-building centers in the province; its harbor is exceedingly picturesque, and is surrounded by lofty cliffs of sandstone. The promontory of Quaco Head is an important landmark to Bay-of-Fundy navigators. Not far from the town of Quaco are *Tracy's Lake* and *Mount Theobald Lake*, famous for their trout.

Between Hampton and *St. John* the Kennebecasis opens out into a deep and wide estuary of the *river St. John*, with both shores fringed with wooded uplands in which nestles many a quiet village. The summer climate about this beautiful water is, like its boating and its bathing, not to be surpassed. After passing the stations of *Nauwidgewauk*, *Model Farm*, and *Quispamsis* we come to the lovely little town of *Rothesay*, where many of St. John's wealthy citizens have their summer homes. *Rothesay Hall* is a good summer hotel. Across the wide water of the Kennebecasis from Gondola Point lies the secluded and beautiful village of *Clifton*, famous for its strawberries. Leaving Rothesay, the train skirts the Kennebecasis, passing the stations of *Riverside*, *Torryburn*, and *Brookville*. On the farther shore, across from Torryburn, is the peculiar cliff called the "Minister's Face." Torryburn House stands near the famous Kennebecasis Rowing Course. Between Torryburn and St. John, on what is known as the Marsh Road, is the race-course of *Moose-path Park*. A few miles east of Torryburn, toward the coast, lies the favorite fishing resort of *Loch Lomond*, with good shooting in the neighborhood. Loch Lomond properly consists of three lakes, and in their waters may be caught not only the ordinary brook-trout, but what is known as the white trout. *Bunker's* and *Dalzell's* are hotels on the lake. The railway keeps along the river shore to within 2 or 3 miles of the city, when it leaves the water and runs through a marshy valley, through the manufacturing suburb of *Cold-brook*, and into the splendid new Intercolonial station at St. John.

St. John.

The population of St. John is over 46,000. The chief hotels are the *Royal*, *Victoria*, *Dufferin*, and *New Victoria ;* rates from two to four dollars a day. Electric cars (fare 5 cents) traverse the principal streets. The city is well supplied with hacks—fare 30 cents between depot and hotels, 50 cents per half-hour. Opera-House, the Academy of Music. Chief club, the Union. The ferry and bridge tolls, for carriage, are 15 and 20 cents respectively each way. The ferry leaves every fifteen minutes from the foot of *Princess St.* The up-river steamers of the Star Line leave *North End* daily for *Fredericton* at 9 A. M. The steamship Prince Rupert of the Dominion Atlantic Railway leaves for *Digby* at 8.30 A. M. and 1 P. M. The steamers of the International S. S. Co. leave at 2 P. M. on Mondays, Wednesdays, Thursdays, Fridays, and Saturdays, and 6 P. M. on Tuesdays, during the summer months. During the winter they run one and sometimes two steamers a week. On Wednesdays and Saturdays the Fawn leaves Indiantown at 8 A. M. for *Grand Lake.*

The city of St. John, the commercial metropolis of New Brunswick, has a population of something over 46,000, and ranks as the sixth city of the Dominion. It is an important winter port, and as a ship-owning center heads the list. St. John is a creation of the United Empire Loyalists. The site of the city is historic ground. The first settlements at the mouth of the St. John River were made by the French early in the seventeenth century. The most stirring episode in the early history of the spot is that of the feud between Charles La Tour, who had a fort at the head of St. John Harbor, and his rival D'Aulnay Charnisay, who had his headquarters across the bay at *Port Royal.* Trading with the Indians, and fishing and hunting, Charles La Tour prospered in his fort in the St. John's mouth. The story of the disasters that at length overtook him has been thus told by the present writer in another work:

"But La Tour's chief good fortune lay in the possession of a woman, who appears to have been in all ways the fit wife for a man of his stamp. Her ability, no less than his own, contributed to his prosperity, and losing her he lost also, for the time, all his life-long efforts had availed to gain. It was through the vindictive jealousy of La Tour's brother-lieutenant in Acadia, D'Aulnay Charnisay, that an end came to these fair prospects. Holding undisputed authority over half the territory of Acadia, Charnisay had no joy in his possessions while his hated rival was in prosperity near him. Craving the rich trade that flowed through the post on the St. John, and conscious of his strength at the court of France, he was soon in open hostilities against La Tour in Acadia, and intriguing against him at Versailles. As a result La Tour was charged with treason, and Charnisay was authorized to seize and hold him for trial. But La Tour was behind his walls and secure in the justice of his cause. He mocked at the royal mandates and made ready for a struggle. The city of Rochelle came promptly to his assistance, while Charnisay drew re-enforcements from Paris. In the spring of 1643 Charnisay suddenly, with a large force, blockaded the mouth of the St. John. Supplies were low in the fort, and a ship was daily expected from Rochelle. When this arrived it was signaled to keep at a safe distance; and one cloudy night a boat slipped silently out of the harbor upon the ebb-tide. Invisible in the gloom along the Carleton shore and beneath the rocky heights of Partridge Island, it passed under the very guns of the blockading ships, and La Tour and his wife were off for Boston in the Rochelle vessel. The next development of the situation was the appearance of La Tour in the harbor, at the head of five New England ships; and Charnisay was driven across the bay to Port Royal, and sharply punished on his own ground. Again he essayed the attack, closely investing Fort La Tour in the hope of starving its defenders into submission. But from two spies, who, in the disguise of friars, had succeeded in penetrating the fort, only to be unmasked by Lady La Tour and contemptuously dismissed unpunished, he learned that La Tour was absent, and that the post was under command of his wife. Expecting an easy and speedy victory, he straightway ordered an assault, but was met unflinchingly by Lady La Tour at the head of the garrison, and obliged to draw off writhing with shame. But when La Tour was again away on a trading expedition his enemy returned and found the garrison weak. For three days his assaults were re-pulsed, but through the treachery of a sentry he at last gained an entrance. Even then the brave woman did not yield, but met him so intrepidly at the head of her faithful handful that the dastard offered honorable terms of capitulation. She accepted them, to save the lives of her brave followers. No sooner had the articles been signed, and the garrison laid down their arms, than Charnisay hanged every man of them but one, whom he forced to act as executioner to his com-rades; and Lady La Tour he led to the gallows with a halter round her neck, and compelled her to witness the execution. Her home destroyed, her husband ruined and in exile, and the horrible fate of her followers ever present in her memory, Lady La Tour's health gave way and she died within a few months. This story has been made the subject of a spirited ballad by Whittier."

From the days of La Tour to 1763 the mouth of the St. John was the scene of several naval encounters between French and English. In the latter year the territory of northern Acadia, now New Brunswick, was finally ceded to England. Three years earlier Mr. James Simonds had started fisheries on the harbor, but had been driven away by the Indians. In 1764, however, with Mr. James White, Captain Peabody, and a party of fishermen, he repeated his attempt, and succeeded in establishing a little settlement. In 1775, during the American Revolu-tion, an expedition of Americans from Maine plundered the village and destroyed the old French fort. Then in the gray morning of May 18, 1783, took place the " Landing of the Loyalists "; and on the grim peninsula of gray rock arose, as it were in a night, a city of nearly

5,000 inhabitants. Its first name was Parrtown, which, fortunately, was soon discarded for the present more dignified and musical appellation.

The nursling of the waters and the fogs, St. John has found her most relentless adversary in fire. In 1837 she suffered from this scourge the loss of over a hundred buildings; and thereafter like calamities fell upon her from time to time, till the climax was reached in the great fire of June 20, 1877, which wiped out a full third of the city. This catastrophe has been described elsewhere by the present writer, as follows:

Nine hours sufficed for the swallowing of 1,612 buildings in the fiery vortex. The rocks held and multiplied the furious heat till the streets glowed as a furnace, and the most massive structures of granite crumbled to powder, melting away swiftly like hoar-frost. The smoke was vomited up to the tops of the steeples, and there, driven on a level before the wind in rolling surges, formed a lurid roof which shut in the perishing city. The ships in the harbor were many of them burned before they could escape from their moorings. Coals and hot ashes were rained upon the villages miles about. In Fredericton, 84 miles distant, the sky to the southeast was like a wall of hot copper until daybreak. When the flames died out along the water's edge, all the city south of King Street had gone down. In a day or two the centers of the streets and open squares were cool; and as one walked, ankle-deep in the soft, white ashes, at early morning, the scene was one of most weird and desolate grandeur. The sun shone over the dazzling ripples of the bay, over the silvered and soundless spaces which had been streets, and against the unclouded blue the thin smoke-wreaths rising from the cellars and masses of ruin took a soft saffron color. Here and there stood bleak, tall chimneys, red and black and gray, or thin fragments of high walls, loop-holed and ragged. At intervals the silence was broken by the crash of some masonry that had held itself up through the stress of the trial and now toppled reluctantly to its fall. In the center of the squares, and in the open country about the city, were hundreds of tents and sorry cabins, wherein reigned a sort of sullen tumult; and in spots a louder excitement, with piles of bottles and flasks close in view, testified that some treasures had been recovered out of the ruin by the endeavor of willing volunteers. On the site of one isolated liquor-store, the *débris* of which still glowed most fervidly, stood a pitiable old figure poking, with a long-handled rake, among the ruins, his eyes gleaming with delight whenever an unbroken bottle was resurrected. St. John received prompt and liberal aid in her calamity, and rose from her fall with an energy and vitality that were marvelous. All that had been laid waste was rebuilt with added splendor, and the new city will compare more than favorably in its architecture with cities many times its size. But even yet, with so much of her capital locked up in costly blocks, she feels too vivid reminders of that grievously staggering blow.

In 1889 the city of St. John and the adjoining city of *Portland* were united under one civic government—a step which has given a great impulse to the city's prosperity. The harbor of St. John is perfectly sheltered and kept clear of ice in the severest winters by the tremendous Fundy tide and the great current of the St. John River. It is always thronged with shipping of all kinds, from the stub-nosed wood-boats—and the little red tugs that rush hither and thither with a great black scow on each arm, as it were—to the stately square-rigged ships that trade around Cape Horn, and the great iron steamers that carry lumber across the Atlantic. Occupying a high, rocky peninsula, crowned with spires, the city shows up admirably as one approaches it by water. As the artists say, it composes well. Behind it lies the broad, shallow, empty expanse of *Courtney Bay*, across which we see the grim pile of the *Penitentiary*. The city is remarkable for its sober coloring. All is gray stone or brownish-gray wood, producing a color effect which is good under a clear sky, but dismal enough when the fog has rolled its dense curtain over the city, to hang, sometimes, for days together, and touch the complexions of the St. John women with that bright yet delicate bloom for which they are renowned. There is much to be said in favor of the fog; but most depressing is the deep, sepulchral voice of the fog-horn at the harbor mouth, whose periodic note seems to issue with painful effort from a throat which the fog is choking. About the head of the harbor, where all available space by the water's edge is occupied by shrieking saw-mills, the bank sweeps in a lofty ridge till it seems to meet the *Carleton* shore. Carleton is a dingy and busy and superlatively rocky suburb of St. John, occupying the western side of the harbor.

One of the most effective streets in Canada is *King Street*, St. John. Truly magnificent in its breadth, and lined on both sides by fine shops, it climbs straight up a steep hill from the harbor, and terminates in the dark foliage of King Square. At its water-foot is "Market Slip," where, at low tide, a flock of wood-boats, fishing-smacks, and small schooners, are gathered on the long, black slope of ooze. Next in importance to King is *Prince William Street*, running southward at right angles to it to the water's edge at *Reed's Point*. On Prince William Street are many fine buildings, chief of which is the splendid *Custom-House*, the finest building of the sort in the Maritime Provinces. It is built of a rich-toned sandstone, from the quarries near Dorchester. The *Post-Office, City Hall*, and *Banks* of *New Brunswick* and *Montreal* are exceedingly handsome new buildings, all put up since the fire. Near Prince William, on the corner of Germain and Princess Sts., stands the handsome new building of St. John's chief club, the Union. On *Germain St.*, and extending through to Charlotte, is the magnificent pile of *Trinity Church*, built of a light-gray stone, and rendered doubly effective by the long and steep approach that leads to its main entrance. In the steeple is a remarkably fine chime of bells. Near by is *Queen Square*, commanding a lovely view seaward, and faced by some stately private residences. Just off this square is a veritable palace of gray stone, the home of one of St. John's wealthiest merchants. This building, in its simple, massive, and harmonious proportions, is, perhaps, from an architectual point of view, the best private house in St. John. A little east of the square is the *Wiggins Male Orphan Institution*, a really beautiful structure of red and gray sandstone. By a short walk southward, toward the water, we reach the spacious *Military* and *Exhibition Grounds*, formerly occupied by British troops, but now the resort of cricketers and ball-players.

King Square, already mentioned, is the most popular of the city's breathing-places. Its three acres are set with shade-trees, and in the center plays a fountain. Just beyond and adjoining it is the old Burying-Ground, whose tombstones are of interest to the antiquarian and the searchers of epitaphs. North of King St., between Germain and Charlotte, lies the fine, spacious building of the city market. On Charlotte St. also is the Young Men's Christian Association building, whose library and reading-room are open from nine in the morning till ten at night. At the head of Germain Street, on an imposing site, stands the old *Stone Church*, and close beside it Calvin Church and the wooden building of the *Mechanics' Institute*. Some distance east from King Square, on Waterloo St., stands the Roman Catholic *Cathedral*, the largest church in New Brunswick. This is a beautiful structure in pointed Gothic, built in a striking combination of freestone and marble. Its spire soars magnificently over the surrounding buildings. The interior is massive and severe, and the stained-glass windows are exceedingly good. The length of the cathedral is 200 ft. and its width at the transepts 110 ft. Over one of the great doors is a fine marble bas-relief of the Last Supper. Adjoining the cathedral are the Bishop's Palace and the Orphan Asylum, on Cliff St., and on the other side the grim, brick pile of the Nunnery. By way of Waterloo St. we reach the conspicuous building of the General Hospital, which occupies the crest of a rocky hill, overlooking the valley by which the Intercolonial gains access to St. John. At this point the valley is a deep and thickly-peopled ravine dividing the main portion of the city from the lofty line of *Portland Heights*, among whose barren rocks perch airily many handsome villas, and the ambitious pile of Reed's Castle. In the valley lie the skating-rink, the Owen's Art School, the brick Church of St. Stephen, and the tall, wooden structure of St. Paul's, familiarly known as the *Valley Church*. Besides the churches already mentioned, there are a number of other handsome ecclesiastical structures in the city.

Conspicuous among the Portland Heights is the bald eminence of *Fort Howe Hill*, surmounted by a battery of heavy guns, and commanding a magnificent view of the city and harbor. On its naked slopes one may conveniently observe the character of the rocks on which St. John is built; and one ceases to wonder that the hand of man has not yet reduced St. John to a level. Many of the city streets, as it is, have been blasted and hewn at great cost out of the solid rock, which in many places towers high and black above the roofs, and greatly restricts the citizens' back yards. In walking about St. John one is always going up or down hill—a circumstance which most visitors find wearisome, but which perhaps accounts in some degree for the elastic and well-balanced figures of St. John women.

Carleton, across the harbor from St. John, and reached by way of the ferry, or the Suspension Bridge over the Falls, is interesting for its Lunatic Asylum, its Martello Towers, its sea-bathing, and its unusual ugliness. Far down the Carleton shore of the harbor stretches a long line of rocky flats, left naked at low tide, and adorned with the long, picturesque gray lines of the herring-weirs. At the extremity of the flats rises a lofty white structure known as "The Beacon," which resembles at high tide a high-decked river steamer. A little way out beyond the Beacon lies the black, steep mass of *Partridge Island*, the home of the fog-horn and the lighthouse, and the bulwark that shields the harbor from the rage of Fundy's waves.

The chief business of St. John is ship-building, and the shipping of lumber and plaster; but besides these industries it has large manufacturing interests, particularly in iron castings, and the manufacture of nails, boots and shoes, cotton, and cars and machinery. The city also conducts important herring, gaspereaux, and shad fisheries. From the port of St. John run steamship lines in every possible direction—across the Atlantic; along the American coast to Eastport, Portland, Boston, and New York; around the Atlantic coast of Nova Scotia; up the Bay of Fundy to Parrsboro and Windsor; up the river St. John and its navigable tributaries. Of these lines, those of special interest to the tourist are the International S. S. Co., whose fine side-wheel steamers (including the new palace steamship *St. Croix*) run along the coast to Portland and Boston; the Dominion Atlantic Railway, whose superb steamer *Prince Rupert* runs across the bay to Digby; and the Star Line, plying between St. John and Fredericton. The railways centering at St. John are the Intercolonial, the Canadian Pacific, and the Shore Line.

Up the River St. John.

From St. John to **Fredericton** we may go expeditiously by the trains of the C. P. R., a distance of 67 miles; but the tourist should go by boat to Fredericton, and there take the C. P. R. for the upper portions of the river. To Fredericton by water the distance is 84 miles, through such varied and beautiful scenery as has earned for the river St. John the somewhat extravagant and misleading appellation of the Rhine of America. The scenery of the St. John possesses indeed diversity, breadth, and magnificence; but it lacks the "castled crags" which give their chief charm to the banks of the Rhine.

The steamers of the Star Line are the *David Weston* and the *Victoria*, which leave St. John on alternate days. Both are comfortable steamers, but the *Victoria* is the newer and faster boat, and the traveler will do well to await her day. Passengers are taken aboard at the suburb of *Indiantown* (now *North End*) above the Falls; but at certain times of the tide the steamer runs down through the falls to take on freight at the city wharves. It is well worth one's while to find out the hour, varying with the tide, at which the boat goes back to North End, and make the trip up through the gorge and beneath the bridges. The fare by boat to Fredericton is $1; by rail $2; by steamer to Fredericton and return by C. P. R., $2.15.

The gorge is spanned at its narrowest portion by a suspension bridge and by a splendid new railway bridge built on the cantilever system. Just above the bridges are the *Falls*.

This remarkable phenomenon was described as follows by the present writer in the pages of Picturesque Canada: This cataract is of interest even to one satiated with cataracts. It is worth getting up at daybreak to become acquainted with, for it stands almost alone among waterfalls in being reversible. At one time it falls in one direction, in a few hours it is falling in the other direction. You go away marveling. You return, of course, to settle the matter finally, and behold, there is not a vestige of a fall. You look down from the suspension bridge, and instead of a seething tumult of mad surges assaulting the gray walls of the gorge, you see a placid surface, flecked here and there with gently wheeling foam-bubbles. This peace is but temporary; it passes away swiftly. And it is not strange that vessels on their way up river seek to catch this happy moment of mid-tide. The whole volume of the great St. John River, which is nearly 500 miles long, and 4 or 5 in breadth half a dozen leagues above the city, at this point finds its way to the sea through a deep ravine a couple of stone-throws across, spanned by a suspension bridge. When the ebb-tide has emptied the harbor, the accumulated river-waters fall through this ravine as through a mighty sluice-gate. As the tide returns the fury of the escape is diminished, the river is gradually checked, till a level is reached on either side of the great gate, and quiet reigns while the antagonists take a breathing space. But soon the tremendous Fundy tide overpowers the river, bears it down, and roars triumphing through to brim the upper basin. Before it can accomplish much in this direction, however, its retreat is ordered, and the recovering river presses on its rear. This battle is fought twice every day; and the river is so far successful that it holds its freedom, and can never be subjugated into a tidal river with drowned shores and banks of ooze. The St. John is able to guard its narrow pass. Were the gate to be thrown wide open, as are those of other rivers, the barbarous hordes of the tide would overwhelm miles on miles of the low-lying center of New Brunswick.

Leaving the wharf at *North End*, and passing the high limestone quarries of Boar's Head, we steam up through the narrows, whose precipitous walls of many-colored rock resemble, in all but hue, a somewhat diminished bit of Saguenay scenery, though the deep river flowing between them teems with traffic. The cliffs are jagged and splintered and piled up magnificently; and we recall the theory that the path we are now following is not the outlet by which the St. John in old times sought the sea. It is surmised that the river had anciently two mouths, the one leading from Grand Bay through the low lands west of Carleton, the other from the Kennebecasis down through the "Valley" between St. John and the Portland Heights. The present channel seems to have been formed by a violent rending asunder of the hills, which was probably accomplished by the same terrific convulsion which raised all the coast west from St. John 30 ft. above its former level. The Indians say that the Great Spirit once grew angry with the river for its arrogance and closed the passes against it. They have another legend to the effect that a great beaver appeared upon the earth and in one night built a dam across the outlet and drowned all the people of the inland regions. The country about the mouth of the river (called by the Etchemins "Oolastook" and by the Micmacs "Ouangondy") is rich in traditions of the demigod Gluskâp, who had his chief abode here and called it Menagwes.

MENAGWES.

Gluskâp, the friend and father of his race,
From Menagwes, his kindly dwelling-place,
With help in need went journeying three days' space;

And Menagwes, left empty of his arm,
Naked of that wise might, its shield from harm
Leaned on his name and dreaded no alarm.

But evil spirits watched his outward path—
Such enemies a good man always hath—
And marked his fenceless dwelling for their wrath.

With shock of thunder and the lightning's slings,
And flame, and hail, and all disastrous things,
They came upon the tempest's midnight wings.

When home at length the hero turned again,
His huts were ashes and his servants slain,
And o'er the ruin wept a slow, great rain.

His own heart wept for sorrow; but no word
He spent in wailing. With dread anger stirred
He cried across the sea—and the sea heard—

And sent great whales, that bare him from the strand,
And, bending to the guidance of his hand,
Made swift and sure his path to Newfoundland.

In vast morass, and misty solitude,
And high cliff-cavern lurked the evil brood,
Mocking at vengeance in derisive mood.

But scarce the hero's foot had touched the coast
When horror seized on all the wizard host,
And in their hiding-places hushed the boast.

He towered before them, gathering like a cloud
That blackens day; and when their fear grew loud,
His vengeance came about them like a shroud.

Then seeing that his utmost vengeance kept
No spell to break the sleep his servants slept,
Gluskâp returned to Menagwes and wept.

The St. John River, so called by Champlain because it was discovered on St. John's Day, 1604, has a course of about 450 miles, of which the lower 225 miles lie within the province. It is navigable to *Fredericton*, 84 miles from the mouth, and for light-draught stern-wheel steamers 75 miles farther, to *Woodstock*. It receives a number of large tributaries, and drains a highly fertile farming and timber country.

About 3 miles above St. John, North End, our steamer emerges from the narrows into the 9-mile-broad expanse of *Grand Bay*. On our right, between two high rounded headlands, lies the mouth of the Kennebecasis, on whose splendid rowing-course took place the famous boat-race between the "Paris crew," of St. John (so called from its conquest of the world's championship at Paris), and the Tyne crew, from the north of England—a struggle in which Renforth, the stroke of the Tyne crew, lost his life. Behind us, to the left, stretches the ample basin of South Bay, ever crowded with rafts and set about with saw-mills.

As we cross Grand Bay the river shores again draw together. In the fresh light of the morning wonderfully beautiful is the contrast between the high shores of vivid green, dotted with glittering white farm-houses, the fringing yellow beach, and the deep blue of the ruffled river. Soon after passing the landing-place, called *Brundage's*, we enter the *Long Reach* where, for a distance of 20 miles, the river pursues an almost straight course between high shores from 3 to 5 miles apart. These shores consist of beautiful rounded hills, some cultivated, some richly wooded, diversified by fairy valleys and sleepy villages and bits of meadow. The magnificent expanse of the river is dotted with the sails of wood-boats, yachts, and schooners; and there are usually several little steamers in sight, busy hauling rafts of logs to the saw-mills. As we near a point of land a boat puts out to meet us, and the steamer, with a hoarse whistle, slackens speed. As the boat approaches, its bow high out of water, we see that it is propelled by a solitary waterman, and carries in its stern a woman, dressed in her best, and holding an ancient, black parasol over herself and a box of codfish, which latter is probably a consignment for some secluded grocery farther up stream. Vigorously our paddles reverse as the little craft closes in perilously beneath our high, white side. Her bow is grappled with the iron beak of a pike-pole, she is held firmly to the gangway for a moment, and codfish and female are nimbly transferred

10

to our lower deck.   In another minute we are once more throbbing onward, while the skiff dances in our wake like an eccentric cork.

On the western shore of Long Reach, 17 miles from St. John, lies the lovely summer resort of *Westfield*.   Two miles farther is the landing of Greenwich Hill.   Six miles beyond is *Oak Point*, a hamlet of most unusual beauty.   Between Greenwich Hill and Oak Point, on the same shore, is the lofty wooded ridge called the Devil's Back.   At the head of the reach is a cluster of high, rocky islands covered with birch and fir.   The typical Island of St. John, of which we shall pass so many that we may as well dispose of them all at once, is a large or small fragment of alluvial meadow called " interval," fringed with alder and Indian willow, and dotted with here and there a splendid elm, and here and there a haystack.   One of these islands which we shall pass is little more than the bushy rim to a broad pool, where ducks and herons chiefly congregate.   " The Mistake " is a long, narrow peninsula much resembling an island, and when the unwary navigator has traveled 2 or 3 miles up the inlet which separates it from the western shore he realizes vividly the appropriateness of the name.   Just above the Mistake, on the east shore, is the deep inlet of Belleisle Bay, a mile wide and 14 miles long.   An arm of this bay is Kingston Creek, at the head of which among the hills lies the secluded and romantic village of *Kingston*.   Near Kingston is a remarkable little lake called Pickwaakeet, which occupies the crater of an extinct volcano.   River landings at which the steamer calls after leaving the village of Tennant's Cove (29 miles) at the mouth of Belleisle Bay, are Hampstead (33 miles), Wickham (34 miles), and Otnabog (40 miles), at the outlet of Otnabog Lake.   Then we pass the Lower Musquash Island, behind which, on the east shore, hides the deep mouth of the Washademoak, which is a sort of a compromise between a river and a lake, and has a rich farming region about its shores.   After passing the Upper Musquash Island the steamer turns into a cove on the west shore and draws up to the wharf of *Gagetown*, 50 miles from St. John.   This sleepiest of river villages is the shire town of Queen's County, and seems the exact counterpart of Robert Buchanan's " Drowsytown ";

> " Oh, so drowsy ! In a daze
> Sweating 'mid the golden haze,
> With its one white row of street
> Carpeted so green and sweet,
> And the loungers smoking still
> Over gate and window-sill ;

A Moose Family.

Nothing coming, nothing going,
Locusts grating, one cock crowing,
Few things moving up or down,
All things drowsy—Drowsytown."

Leaving Gagetown the steamer heads down river a short distance
in order to round the foot of Grimross Island, and passes on the east
shore the mouth of the Jemseg River, which the inhabitants call the
"Jumsack." This deep, narrow, and sluggish stream is the outlet of
Grand Lake, a fine body of water 30 miles in length, surrounded by a
rich agricultural and coal-bearing region. The shores of the lake
abound in fossils. The Jemseg banks are clothed with historic associations. In 1640 a strong fort was erected at the mouth. This was
captured by an English expedition in 1654, but restored to the French
in 1670. In 1739 the Seigniory of Jemseg contained 116 inhabitants.
Under M. de Villebon it was made the capital of Acadia, an honor
which was afterward transferred to Fort Nashwaak, opposite the point
of land now occupied by Fredericton. In 1776 an army of 600 Indians gathered on the Jemseg, to lay waste all the settlements of the
St. John Valley; but the firmness of the Oromocto settlers overawed
them, and they suffered themselves to be mollified with presents. A
little above Gagetown we enter the county of Sunbury, which once
comprised the whole of New Brunswick, but is now the smallest of her
counties. It is also the most fertile. Its low, rich meadows are covered with water in the spring freshets, when the inhabitants move about
in skiffs, the row-boat instead of the carriage is brought to the front
door, the children explore in wash-tubs the farthermost recesses of
the farm-yard, and the farmer sets his nets for gaspereaux where a
little later he will be plowing and planting in a hot sun with no drop
of water in sight save what he carries in his tin bucket. Passing
Mauger's Island we see on our left the village church of Burton, on our
right the white walls of Sheffield Academy, now the County Grammar
School. A little beyond, on the right shore, lies the scattered village
of *Maugerville* behind its willows, the first English-speaking settlement
established in New Brunswick. It was planted in 1763 by pioneers
from the parishes of Rowley, Boxford, and Andover, in Massachusetts,
and speedily became a flourishing community. During the Revolution
the inhabitants declared for the Americans, and all but twelve of them
signed resolutions repudiating Great Britain. Massachusetts sent them
arms and ammunition, and in an outburst of warlike fervor the Mau-

gervillians organized an expedition against Fort Cumberland on the
Isthmus of Chignecto. There they found a schooner stranded on the
mud, and this easy prize they captured ; but the sight of the fort dis-
mayed them, and they altered their intention of carrying it by storm.
The schooner they took away and sold. They were afterward compelled to make restitution to the vessel's owners ; but, this done, a
lenient Government indulgently overlooked their folly.

Just above Maugerville, on the opposite shore, lies the county town
of Sunbury, the village of *Oromocto*, at the mouth of the Oromocto
River. Here of old stood a fort for protection against the Indians.
The Oromocto is a deep and narrow stream, navigable for small craft
a distance of 22 miles. On its upper waters, and particularly in Oromocto Lake, there is excellent trout-fishing. In its lower reaches pickerel abound. Off the mouth of the river lie Thatch Island and the great
meadowy expanse of Oromocto Island. Here we are 74 miles from St.
John and about 10 miles from Fredericton. Five miles farther up the
boat calls at the interminable booms of *Glasier's*, where logs from up
river are put together into rafts to be towed to St. John. Along toward
the middle of the afternoon we catch sight of the smoke which rises
over " The Mills," a mile below Fredericton. Then the river widens
out, and over its shining expanse we see the long bridges, the spires,
and the billowy foliage of the city of elms, Fredericton, which is called
by New-Brunswickers, in affectionate banter, the " Celestial City."

Fredericton.

The population of Fredericton (estimated) is 8,000. The chief hotels
are the *Queen's* and *Barker House*. Cab fares are 25 cts. for a course
within the city. The livery stables of Fredericton are good and much
patronized, and the charges very moderate. The fare between Fredericton and St. John by boat is only $1. Fare by rail to Woodstock,
$2 ; Grand Falls, $3.80 ; Edmundson, $4.80 ; return, $3, $5.70, and
$7.20. Fare to St. Stephen, $3.15 ; St. Andrews, $3.25 ; return, $4.75
and $4.90.

The history of Fredericton begins at the mouth of the *Nashwaak*,
an important tributary of the St. John, which flows in immediately opposite Fredericton. Hither in 1692 came Villebon, from the Jemseg,
to be nearer his Melicite allies. Here he built a large and well-stock-
aded fort, which in the autumn of 1696 was attacked by the New-Englanders, under Colonel Hawthorne and old Benjamin Church. Villebon,

being forewarned, was forearmed. That redoubtable ecclesiastic, Father Simon, brought thirty-six of his *Medoctec* warriors to swell the garrison, and all was enthusiasm within the fort. The New-Englanders landed with three cannon near the S. shore of the stream, on a point now much frequented by the schoolboys of Fredericton in the cherry season. Truly it is a charming spot, and its cherries are marvelously great and sweet and abundant. But the New-Englanders found little pleasure therein. The fire from the fort by day dismounted one of their guns, and suffered them not to work the others with any degree of comfort, while by night a plentiful hail of grape upon all such watch-fires as they lighted drove them to sleep unwarmed and wet, whence came in the morning much rheumatism and complaining. The undertaking became unpopular in the invaders' camp, and, under cover of the next night, they forsook it and fled. In the autumn of 1698 the garrison was removed to Fort La Tour, which had been rebuilt at the mouth of the St. John, and after Villebon's death in 1700 the Nashwaak fort was demolished. Nothing now remains to remind us of those exciting though uncomfortable times save some green mounds where once stood Villebon's ramparts, or a few rust-eaten cannon-balls which the farmer gathers in with his potato-crop.

In the year following the erection of New Brunswick into a province the capital was, for strategic reasons, removed from St. John to what was then known as St. Anne's Point, now Fredericton. For a long while Fredericton was the headquarters of a British regiment. Now it is the seat of a military school, and the post of a company of Canadian regulars. Being a military, political, judicial, educational, and ecclesiastical center, Fredericton was for a long time, from a commercial point of view, rather unprogressive; but within the last few years she has begun to throw off her lethargy, and enlarge both her trade and her population. She has become a railroad center, no fewer than four lines radiating from this point; and additional lines are proposed, with every prospect of their construction. She is the distributing point for a large and rich agricultural section, the headquarters of an immense lumber-trade, of cotton and leather manufacturing, and of extensive canning operations. With a population of only about 8,000, Fredericton has a disproportionate share of public institutions and fine buildings, and her society derives special individuality and charm from the influences which there concentrate themselves.

The streets of Fredericton are broad and level, overarched for the most part with elms of stately growth, and wearing generally an air of quiet prosperity. The main business street is *Queen St.*, running the whole length of the city near the water front. One side of this street is lined with shops. The other side has business houses on its upper and lower blocks, but is occupied along its central portion by the *Officers' Square* with its lawns and tennis-grounds and battery of little cannon, the gray-stone buildings of the Officers' Quarters, the handsome Post-Office and Custom-House, the Barracks and Parade Ground, the graceful red brick structure of the Provincial Normal School, and the brick block of the City Hall, with its clock-tower over the front and a ludicrous little perky appendage, like a rudimentary tail, sticking up on its rear. From just above the Post-Office the long white structure of the passenger bridge runs across the river to the suburban village of *St. Mary's*, on whose outskirts hangs an interesting little settlement of Melicite Indians, some of whom are famous hunters, guides, and canoe-men. Near the lower end of Queen St., where it is joined by King and Brunswick, stands the beautiful little Anglican cathedral of the diocese of Fredericton. This is a harmoniously proportioned structure in pure Gothic, built of gray-stone with window-casings of white Caen stone. It occupies the center of spacious triangular grounds, beautifully wooded. Just below it the river is crossed by the splendid steel bridge which connects the Canadian Pacific with the Canada Eastern R. R. at the busy village of Gibson on the opposite shore. In the block above the Cathedral stand the new *Parliament and Departmental Buildings*, taking the place of the old buildings which were destroyed by fire. The main building is a handsome and solid structure of freestone and light gray granite, which would be entirely satisfactory but for the attenuated dome which surmounts it and much resembles a pepper-pot. In its rear is the fire-proof library, containing an invaluable collection of the plates of Audubon's "Birds," once owned by Louis Philippe. On the side of the block facing St. John St. is the handsome purple sandstone structure containing the Government offices. In winter, when the Provincial Parliament is in session, this is a busy quarter of Fredericton.

At the extreme upper end of the city are the new *Victoria Hospital*, and the severe stone pile of *Government House* in its spacious grounds. Scattered through the city are many churches, of various denominations. The most noticeable of these are the handsome stone structures belonging to the Baptists and the Presbyterians, standing within a block of each other on York St.; and the exquisite little parish church, called Christ Church, on the corner of George and Westmoreland Sts. This edifice is of an Old English pattern, and carries a silvery chime of three bells. Back of Fredericton rises a line of wooded heights, whereon are some good private residences, and the massive old building of the New Brunswick University, crowning a succession of terraces. This was of old King's College of New Brunswick, established by royal charter in 1828, under the auspices of Sir Howard Douglas. It is now a Provincial Institution, and is doing good work under the management of President Harrison. From its cupola we get a wide and lovely view. At our feet lies the city in its billows of green, bounded by the broad and shining arc of the St. John. Above and below extends the river, dotted in the one direction with islands, in the other with the sails of wood-boats. Straight across opens the fair Nashwaak Valley, with the village of Marysville in the distance. Opposite the upper end of the city we mark the mouth of the Nashwaaksis, or little Nashwaak, which boasts a pretty cataract some 10 or 12 miles from its mouth.

On the outskirts of Fredericton, half a mile above Government House, stands a picturesque old mansion called "*The Hermitage*," which is rapidly falling to ruin. In the gay old days of British military and "family compact" rule, "The Hermitage" was a famous social center. Now its deserted chambers are romantically supposed to be haunted, and its spacious and well-wooded grounds are a favorite resort of the city's picnic parties. Continuing on past The Hermitage, a very lovely drive extends up the river shore some 4 m. or more to the village of *Springhill*. Another interesting drive is across the river to Gibson, and thence up the valley of the Nashwaak about 3 miles to the growing town of *Marysville*, the creation of the gigantic cotton and lumber mills of Alexander Gibson. This trip may be made, if one prefers, by the Canada Eastern R. R., which runs through the town on its way to the Miramichi and its salmon-pools. After the vast cotton-mill, the chief point of interest in Marysville is the beautiful little church erected by Mr. Gibson.

With all the beautiful and accessible waterways that surround it, no wonder Fredericton is the very home of the birch-bark canoe. Her inhabitants easily equal, and often excel, the Indians in the management of this fascinating little craft. An easy and charming canoe-trip may be taken from Fredericton down the river to St. John, an indolent voyage, with no fishing or hard paddling to do, and villages all along the way to supply provisions.

Fredericton to Woodstock.

In spring and autumn, when the river is high, the steamer *Aberdeen* of the Star Line plies between Fredericton and **Woodstock,** a distance of 60 miles. All the points of interest along this route will soon be accessible by rail, as a line is under construction along the western shore of the St. John. It traverses the populous settlements of Prince William and Queensbury, peopled by descendants of disbanded loyalist soldiers. The finest scenery on the trip is at the mouth of the Pokiok River, by which the waters of Lake George find outlet to the St. John. The *Pokiok Falls* are about 40 ft. in height; and after this plunge the river roars and leaps through a gorge 1,200 ft. in length, whose perpendicular walls, 75 ft. high, are less than 30 ft. apart. The signification of Pokiok is "The Dreadful Place." Lake George is somewhat renowned for its productive antimony-mines. Near Pokiok is Prince William Lake, and a little beyond the Sheogomuc Lake and River. At **Canterbury** the road crosses Eel River, the outlet of Eel and North Lakes, from which a famous portage (whose deserted paths are worn deep by the many Indian feet that trod them of old) leads to the Chiputneticook Lakes and the St. Croix, and thence to Passamaquoddy Bay. By this route went the troops of Villebon many a time to ravage the New England borders. Five miles beyond Eel River is the site of the old French fort Medoctec, beside the rapids and Melicite village of the same name. This district was of old the Seignory of the Sieur Clignancourt, and was held an important center, owing to the necessity of making a portage at this point to avoid the rapids. These, however, the steamer surmounts, as a rule, without great difficulty. The approach to Woodstock, whether by land or water, is picturesque and charming, the high, rounded hills being well tilled and crowned with groves and cottages. Fare by boat, $2.50.

The best route to Woodstock at present, available at all seasons, is by the C. P. R. R. from Gibson. Or we may take the train on the Fredericton side, at the little temporary Bridge Station, soon to be replaced by a union depot. A mile above the station we pass through St. Mary's, already referred to, and 2 miles farther we cross the Nashwaaksis at *Douglas Station*. For the next 8 or 10 miles we get fine views of river and islands from the car-windows, and at the mouth of the Keswick River (called "Kissaway" by the dwellers on its banks) a splendid expanse of interval country spreads before our eyes. From this point the railroad climbs the pleasant Keswick Valley, passing a number of unimportant stations. Upper Keswick is 17 miles from Keswick. Beyond the road traverses a rather desolate-looking region, till again it nears the rich St. John Valley at Newburgh. In the wilderness it crosses the Nackawic (43 miles from Fredericton) and Falls Brook, both trout-streams. At *Woodstock Junction* a branch diverges and runs down river a short distance to Woodstock, affording varied and delightful views between the rounded hills. Over the high railroad bridge we steam slowly into the progressive little town of *Woodstock*, the shire-town of Carleton County, and the chief commercial center on the river above Fredericton.

Woodstock has good hotels in the *American* and the *Carlisle House*. The town is well situated on the uplands at the junction of the Maduxnakeag stream with the St. John, and has a rich farming country behind it supplying a large local trade. Its 4,000 or so of inhabitants are plucky and enterprising, and have recovered bravely from the losses to which they have been subjected by numerous fires. Around the mouth of the Maduxnakeag is a cluster of saw-mills. A short distance above the town are the now abandoned iron-mines, where a peculiarly dense and hard quality of iron was formerly extracted. The village of Upper Woodstock is familiarly and disrespectfully known as "Hardscrabble." The whole district is peculiarly adapted to the growth of grain and fruit, and is sometimes called "the orchard of New Brunswick." Nineteen miles distant, and reached by a section of the C. P. R. R., is the American town of Houlton, in Maine.

The Upper St. John.

To continue our journey up the St. John we recross the river and retrace our way to Newburg Junction, 6 miles distant. Passing Hartland (13 miles from Woodstock) and Peel (17 miles) we come to the station of *Florenceville* (24 miles). The village lies across the river, and is reached by a ferry. Its situation is remarkably picturesque, on the wind-swept crest of a high ridge. A few miles southwest of Florenceville rises *Mars Hill*, a steep mountain about 1,200 ft. high, which overlooks a vast expanse of forest. This was one of the chief points of controversy during the old border troubles, and its summit was cleared by the commissioners of 1794. Beyond Florenceville the charm of the landscape deepens. The railway keeps close to the river. From the village of Kent, 3 miles farther, where we cross the Shikiti-hauk stream, a portage of 15 miles leads to the upper waters of the southwest Miramichi. Guides and canoes for this trip may be engaged in Fredericton. Passing Bath Station, and the Brook Munquauk, we come to *Muniac*, 15 miles from Florenceville, where the Muniac stream, descending through a rocky glen, brawls beneath the track. In this neighborhood there is a peninsula jutting out from the river shore, around which the channel makes a long *détour*, while the portage across the isthmus is short and easy. The Melicites say that once upon a time, when an army of their enemies was encamped on the shore opposite the point, preparing to attack the villages below, which had been left defenseless while the braves were off on the war-path, a clever *ruse* was practiced here which saved the villages. Six Melicite warriors, returning down river in their canoes, discovered the invaders' camp and took in the situation. First one canoe paddled swiftly down, keeping to the safe side of the river. Then at a short interval came the second, and after another brief space the third. Meanwhile the two Indians in the first canoe, as soon as they were well out of sight around the point, landed, carried their craft in haste across the portage, and embarked again to repeat the performance. The other canoes did likewise in their turn; and this was kept up the greater part of the day, till the hostile band, looking on with lively interest from the farther shore, were so impressed with the numbers of the returning Melicite warriors that they discreetly withdrew to seek some easier adventure.

At the little milling village of *Perth*, 49 miles from Woodstock, the railroad crosses the river to *Andover* (51 miles), a village of 500 inhabitants, and the Tobique branch runs from here along the river 28 miles to Plaster Rock. This is the headquarters for fishermen who are going to make the Tobique trip. There is a homelike country hotel here, whose proprietor will furnish information as to guides, etc. A mile and a half above Andover, on the other shore, comes in the **Tobique**, an important tributary, about 70 miles in length, famous for its trout and salmon fishing. At its mouth is a large Indian reservation, containing a prosperous Melicite village. Some of these Melicites are exceedingly intelligent and capable as guides and canoe-men, and may be hired at from $1 to $1½ a day. From the head of the Tobique one may portage to the Nepisiguit Lake and descend the Nepisiguit to Bathurst. The Tobique trip will be treated in detail in succeeding pages.

Five miles above Andover is *Aroostook Junction*, whence a branch line runs 34 miles up the fertile Aroostook Valley to the Maine towns of Fort Fairfield (7 miles from the Junction), Caribou (19 miles), and Presque Isle (34 miles). These towns have each from 2,000 to 3,000 inhabitants. The district in which they lie is enormously productive, and was the subject of the boundary dispute between New Brunswick and Maine which nearly brought on a war between England and the United States. Indeed, in the year 1839, there was a little outbreak of hostilities between the province and the State most concerned. This skirmish is known to history as the Aroostook war. Troops were called out on both sides, and a band of Americans, who had gone into the disputed territory to arrest alleged trespassers, were captured by a party of New Brunswick lumbermen and their leaders carried captive, on a horse-sled, to Fredericton. Maine called out her militia. Sir John Harvey, the Governor of New Brunswick, summoned the provincial troops and the few regulars within reach. Nova Scotia voted all her men and all her revenues to the help of the sister province, and Upper and Lower Canada made haste to send aid. There was excited oratory at Washington, and (seeing that New Brunswick was but a colony) more temperate discussion at London, and finally war was averted by the arrival on the scene of an English commissioner, who with easy generosity yielded to the American commissioner, Mr. Webster, all New Brunswick's claims; and the Aroostook Valley, largely settled by New Brunswickers, became American territory. By a similar piece of astute British diplomacy Canada was deprived of broad and rich territories on the Pacific coast as well. In the Aroostook country there is fine bear, deer, moose, caribou, and duck shooting, and excellent fishing in the Aroostook and Presque Isle Rivers and the Squawpan Lake. There is also available from this point a good round trip through the Eagle Lakes.

From Aroostook Junction the main line follows the heights overlooking the river St. John to the village of **Grand Falls**, seated on a high plateau 72 miles above Woodstock. The village, with its cool airs and the really sublime scenery of the Falls and Gorge, has become a popular summer halting-place. The *Grand Falls Hotel* is a good hostelry, and there are also the *American House* and *Glasier's Hotel.*

Through the village runs the street ambitiously named Broadway—which is indeed so broad and grassy that it might be mistaken for a meadow. Though the inhabitants are few—not more than 700 or 800—there is stir in the village, caused by the busy geese and pigs. There are several churches; but the chief architectural distinction of the village is the Grand Falls Hotel, already referred to, which, with its pretentious front of tall, white, fluted pillars, suggests at first sight that a Greek temple has captured a whitewashed modern barn and proudly stuck it on behind.

The Grand Falls of the St. John.

In magnitude the *Grand Falls of the St. John* can not be compared to Niagara; but in impressiveness of surroundings they will endure the comparison. A little above the cataract the river loiters in a wide basin, where boats from up stream make a landing. Then the shores suddenly contract, and the great stream plunges into the gorge by a perpendicular leap of 73 ft. At the foot of the fall, in its center, rises a sharp cone of black rock on which the descending waters break and pile up magnificently. The scene varies greatly with variations in the height of the river. It is peculiarly awe-inspiring when the logs are running through, and one may see mighty timbers shattered into fragments, while others at times shoot high into the air in the fury of their rebound. From the foot of the cataract the river is volleyed off, as it were, with an explosive force that hurls huge foam-white masses of water into the air. The bottom of the terrific trough is sometimes bared for a moment as the river sways madly up one or the other of its imprisoning walls. The gorge is about a mile in extent, and walled by contorted cliffs from 100 to 250 ft. in height. The rocks are dark Upper Silurian slate, whose strata have been twisted and turned on end, and their seams filled with white interlacing veins of quartz. Throughout the extent of the gorge there are several lesser falls, which are swallowed up in one roaring incline when the river is at freshet. One descends into the gorge by a series of precipitous stairs. On the wild and chaotic floor one may clamber some distance, and visit " the Cave," whose jaws remind one of the mouth of a gigantic alligator; one may get a near view of the curious "Coffee-Mill," where a strange eddy, occupying a round basin beside the channel, slowly grinds the logs which it succeeds in capturing as they dash past. "The Wells" are a strange phenomenon, smooth, circular pits several feet in diameter, bored perpendicularly deep into the rock, and leading nowhither. It will take some days to exhaust the attractions of the gorge. At its lower end, reached by a wonderfully picturesque and precipitous road from the village, is the lovely, quiet expanse of the Lower Basin, where logs are caught and made up into rafts for the voyage down to Fredericton. At low water one may be poled in a lumberman's "bateau" for a short distance up the gorge to the foot of the towering cliff called *Squaw's Leap*, over whose face a small stream falls silverly. Over this steep the Indians used to hurl their victims.

One of the best views of the cataract is obtained from the old mill, which occupies a rocky ledge thrust out into the very face of the fall. Here one is in the midst of the spray and the rainbows. Another good view may be had from the *Suspension Bridge*, which swings from crag to crag across the gorge a couple of hundred yards below the falls. The spot has been the scene of many a tragedy. Lumbermen have been sucked down, and never a trace of their bodies found thereafter. The first bridge built across the gorge fell into the awful depths with several teams upon it. The most heroic story, however, comes to us from Melicite tradition. An invading army of Mohawks entered the country by the head-waters of the St. John. Their object was to surprise the chief village of the Melicites at Aukpak, far below Grand Falls. Descending the upper reaches of the river, they took a little village at the mouth of the Madawaska, whose inhabitants they slew with the exception of two women, whom they saved to pilot them down the river. The women guided them safely through some rapids. Toward evening they told their captors that the river was clear of falls and rapids for another day's journey, after which they would have to make a portage. The Mohawks lashed together their fleet of canoes, placed their captive guides in the middle, and resigned themselves to the current. The falls are buried so deep in the gorge that, as you approach them from up river their roaring is not heard until one is close upon them. At the first sound of it some of the watchers inquired the cause, but were assured by the captives that it was only a tributary stream falling into the main river. As the fleet swept round the point, and quickened for the plunge, and the full blast of the cataract's thunder roared suddenly in their ears, the Indians sprang in desperate horror to their paddles. But it was too late; and the women raised their shrill war-cry as they swept with their captors into the gulf, and saved their tribe.

Above the Grand Falls.

Just above Grand Falls the railway crosses once more to the right bank of the river, and enters the Acadian French county of Madawaska. About this point the river becomes the boundary-line between the United States and Canada. Fourteen miles from Grand Falls is the Acadian village of *St. Leonards.* Four miles beyond is the mouth of *Grand River,* where one may begin a fine hunting, fishing, and canoeing trip. Guides and canoes may be brought from the Melicite village, at the Tobique mouth, or they may be hired from one or another of the Acadian settlements. The route lies by poling up Grand River to the mouth of the Waagansis, and up that meager stream through dense and interminable alders to its source in the water-shed dividing the streams of the St. John from those of the *Restigouche.* A portage of 5 or 6 miles leads to the Waagan, a wretched stream down which one forces his way till he comes out on the lovely and well-stocked waters of the "Five-fingered River." On this trip the present writer heard from his Indians the following picturesque legend, which may. be called a Melicite "Passing of Arthur":

THE DEPARTING OF GLUSKÂP.

It is so long ago ; and men well-nigh
Forget what gladness was, and how the earth
Gave corn in plenty, and the rivers fish,
And the woods meat, before he went away.
His going was on this wise :

All the works
And words and ways of men and beasts became
Evil, and all their thoughts continually
Were but of evil. Then he made a feast.
Upon the shore that is beside the sea
That takes the setting sun, he ordered it,
And called the beasts thereto. Only the men
He called not, seeing them evil utterly.
He fed the panther's crafty brood, and filled
The lean wolf's hunger ; from the hollow tree
His honey stayed the bear's terrific jaws ;
And the brown rabbit couched at peace within
The circling shadow of the eagle's wings.
And when the feast was done he told them all

That now, because their ways were evil grown,
On that same day he must depart from them,
And they should look upon his face no more.
Then all the beasts were very sorrowful.

It was near sunset and the wind was still,
And down the yellow shore a thin wave washed
Slowly ; and Gluskâp launched his birch canoe,
And spread his yellow sail, and moved from shore,
Though no wind followed, streaming in the sail,
Or roughening the clear water after him.
And all the beasts stood by the shore, and watched.
Then to the west appeared a long red trail
Over the wave ; and Gluskâp sailed and sang
Till the canoe grew little like a bird,
And black, and vanished in the shining trail.
And when the beasts could see his form no more,
They still could hear him, singing as he sailed,
And still they listened, hanging down their heads
In thin row, where the thin waves washed and fled.
But when the sound of singing died, and when
They lifted up their voices in their grief,
Lo ! on the mouth of every beast a strange
New tongue ! Then rose they all and fled apart,
Nor met again in council from that day.

Thirty-one miles above Grand Falls we cross the rushing emerald waters of *Green River*, which contrast sharply with the amber current of the St. John. This is an unrivaled trout-stream in its upper waters, but somewhat difficult of access, owing to the shoals and rapids that obstruct its course. It is severe poling all the way up, and all the latter part of the journey is through complete wilderness. The trout, however, are large and very fierce, well worthy of the effort one must make to get them. Typically Acadian are the farm-houses, in their fields of buckwheat and flax, along the lower course of Green River. Governor Gordon has thus described the home of the Madawaska Acadian :

The whole aspect of the farm was that of a *métairie* in Normandy ; the outer doors of the house gaudily painted, the panels of a different color from the frame ; the large, open, uncarpeted room, with its bare, shining floor ; the lasses at the spinning-wheel ; the French costume and appearance of Madame Violet and her sons and daughters, all carried me back to the other side of the Atlantic.

The town of *St. Basil*, 34 miles from Grand Falls, has nearly 2,000 inhabitants, an immense Roman Catholic church, and the Convent and

School of the Sacred Heart. Six miles farther we cross the mouth of
the Madawaska River, and enter the little town of *Edmundston*, sometimes called Little Falls, from the low cataract by which the Madawaska, descending through a narrow ravine, plunges to meet the St.
John. The chief hotels of Edmundston are *The Adams* and the *Hôtel
Babin.* The *Temiscouata R. R.* runs 81 miles, along the Madawaska
River, *Lake Temiscouata*, and over the divide to Rivière du Loup. The
best view of Edmundston is obtained from the top of the old block-
house. At this point the best of fishing waters lie all about us. Within
easy reach are the *St. Francis*, with its lakes Welastookawagamis,
Pekaweekagomic, Pohenegamook, well stocked and little fished.
Across the river is the round trip by the Eagle Lakes and Fish River
to the American village of Fort Kent. Into the Temiscouata Lake
flows the Cabineau, a noble trout-stream ; and the *Tuladi*, the outlet of
the Squattook and Tuladi chain of lakes.

Routes for the Sportsman.

One of the best round trips in New Brunswick, or, I should say, in
the Maritime Provinces, is what is known as the "Squattook trip";
much of which, indeed, lies in the province of Quebec. The route is
as follows : Take the canoes (either poling them up stream or putting
them on a flat car) up the Madawaska, 15 miles, to a place called Griffin's. Then portage 5 miles to the ugly little pool called Mud Lake,
with its desolate and fire-ravaged shores. From Mud Lake descend
Beardsley Brook (pronounced Bazzily), catching a few trout by the way,
and squeezing through many alder thickets, till the *Squattook River*
is reached. Run with thrilling speed down the rapids of this river, till
you come to *Big Squattook Lake*, where one should stop and fish at the
outlet. From this down there is fishing everywhere. Passing through
Second, Third, and Fourth Squattook Lakes—Second Lake known as
"Sugar-Loaf Lake," from the fine peak that overshadows it—the *Horton branch* is reached, which should be ascended for the sake of the
wonderful abundance and good size of its trout. The Squattook River
enters the *Tuladi Lakes*, two almost contiguous sheets of wilderness
water, wherein the great lake-trout, called "Tuladi," are numerous,
and to be taken by trolling. Out of the lower Tuladi Lake flows the
Tuladi River, whereon are the *Tuladi Falls*, round which, except at certain stages of the water, one must make a portage. The falls are just

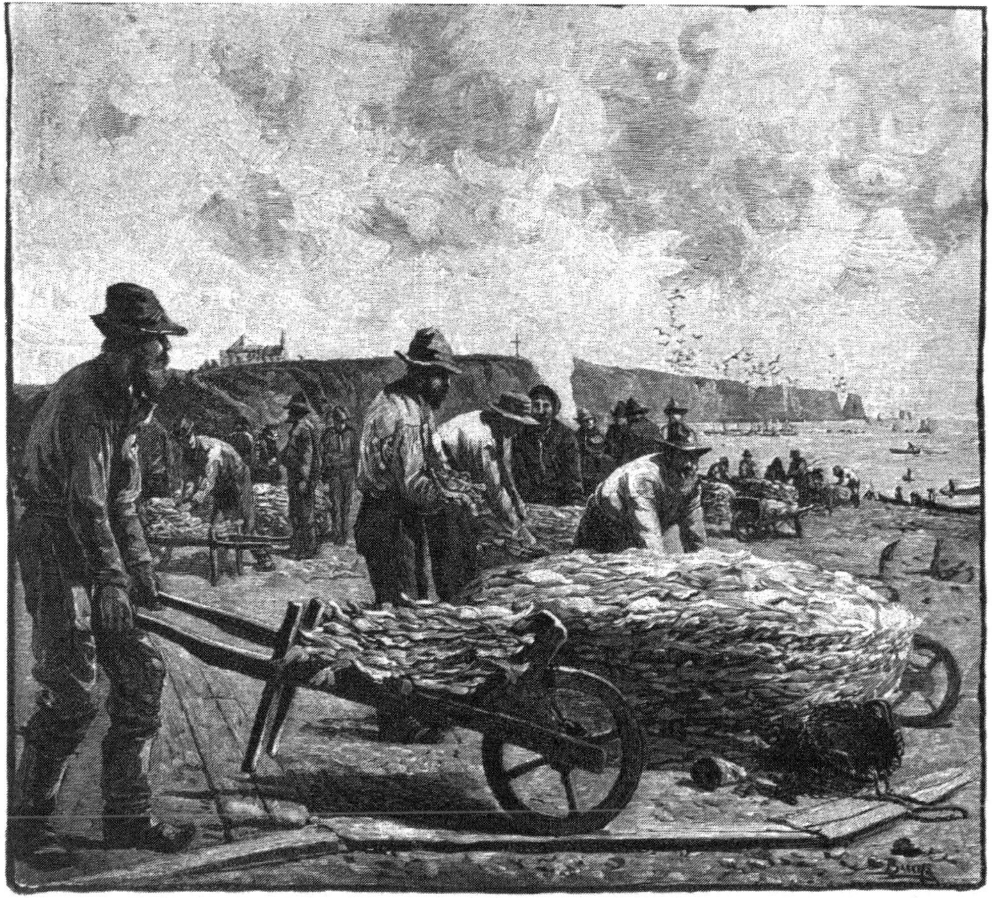

Curing Fish at Percé.

below the lake. Thence there is a clear run, with swift but not dangerous water, to Lake Temiscouata, which must be crossed to reach the village of *Détour du Lac*. Here one may put up at *Clouthier's Hotel*, if tired of camping. Temiscouata Lake is 30 miles long, 1½ miles in breadth, and remarkable for its depth. There is good fishing in its waters at times, especially for the great gray trout called " togue "; but it is not as good a fishing water as the streams and smaller lakes surrounding it.

THE BIRCH-BARK CANOE.

The birch canoe of the Melicite is filled with mystery for the uninitiated, who may be known beyond a shadow of doubt by the way they talk. If a man begins dilating on the perils of the bark canoe, you may be assured at once that he is either totally ignorant of his subject, or is making a bid for your admiration at the cost of truth itself.

I can not make you love the bark as I do—at least not through these pages—but if you seek out Jim Paul at Fredericton he'll give you a taste of the dreamy delight for a very small sum. Many men of Fredericton who do not live in a hut and wear moccasins summer and winter can not be beaten, either in skill or endurance, by any Indian on the river. The probabilities are that you will be charmed with your first experience, and if Jim is in the stern of the canoe you'll ask him if it's difficult to paddle—to which he'll say, " Not much," with a grin— and what you'd have to pay for a nice canoe? To this latter question he may answer, anywhere from $20 to $40. It all depends on the impression he gets of your wealth and gullibility. If he says $20, you had better offer him $18 and take it. He'll think more of you if you don't give him quite as much as he asks, and you may make your mind easy with regard to the other $2, because he didn't expect $20 anyway.

If you have time, it will interest you to watch your canoe being built. Jim Paul builds as good canoes as any one, and he is a good man to deal with. He lives opposite Fredericton, in the Indian village at St. Mary's, already mentioned, and if you walk over the bridge and follow the footpath to your right, along the bank, you'll come to Jim's hut before you've gone 50 yards. If he has begun operations on your canoe, he'll be sitting on the ground by his front door driving wooden pins into the ground. He makes a little fence of these, about 8 in. high and inclosing a space the size and shape of your canoe. After a

11

few last pats on the ground inside the inclosure, to make sure it is level and free from stones and lumps, he brings out the bark and lines the inclosure with it, putting it inside out. The bark of a canoe runs with its grain from bow to stern, and, if his piece is long enough to cover the whole inclosure, so much the better as far as looks are concerned. If not, there will be a seam across near the middle.

When the bark is put into the little inclosure it is pressed smoothly and flatly down to the ground and up against the wooden pins and folded over their tops ; and bricks or other convenient weights are put in upon it to keep it in place.

Next, long, thin strips of cedar, about 4 in. wide and $\frac{1}{4}$ in. thick, are laid over the bark, and are fitted so as to cover all the inside of the canoe, leaving only very narrow cracks here and there. Then the gunwales are put on—or at least the inner strips are put in place and bound tightly with cane (he'll use hackmatack-roots if you must have them). This will give the builder a purchase for the ribs, which are next in order. They may be of any light, strong wood—cedar or spruce, usually. They are broader at their middles than at their ends, so that the bottom of the canoe is well floored over while the silvery bark of the birch is gleaming through at the sides. The midrib is the greatest arc, and from the midrib to each end they gradually diminish in size until at last they are bent almost double. For a short dis-tance—a foot and a half—in bow and stern there are no ribs at all, and the bark of each side is sewed with roots or cane so as to make a sharp, neat prow. The cavity is generally stuffed with shavings, and a shin-gle is cut to fit in and close it immediately ahead or behind the last rib.

So far the bottom of the canoe is flat and the sides stand on it at right angles ; but when the ends of the midrib are pressed under the gunwales on each side and it is pushed into its proper position and a few of its fellows are ranged in place on each side, we see that the bark has left the ground, except at the center, and the sides are as-suming the curve of the finished canoe. Everything is rather loose till the bars are put in. There are five bars in an ordinary-sized ca-noe—a long one in the middle and shorter ones on each side. They are of maple, and are fitted into the gunwales at each end and lashed in snugly, drawing the canoe to its proper shape. Then the top strips of the gunwales are put on, and the seams on bow and stern and mid-ships—if there be a seam there—are covered with cotton and smeared thoroughly with a mixture of resin and grease, and the canoe is ready for trial. It will probably leak, of course, and the leaks must be found and smeared with the resinous mixture. Then your canoe is done, and you must learn to manage it!

If you get in and kneel down in front of the stern-bar and get Jim to sit in front and watch you, you will, after a few attempts, be able to keep her from wabbling in her course—that is, from zigzagging—but you will find that after every two or three strokes of the paddle you *stop and steer*, or else you are inclined to paddle first on one side and then on the other. Both these methods are in nowise allowable. No canoeman stops to steer! No canoeman changes sides—except to rest. If you are paddling on the right side, let your right hand grip the paddle *very near* the top of the blade—the lower down, the more power— and the left a couple of inches below the top. Many good canoemen clasp their fingers over the *top* of the paddle, but it is not so good form nor as good for long work as is the true Indian mode of holding—viz., with the back of the hand toward the face and the *thumb and fingers* reaching around to the front. Dip the whole depth of the blade, so that your right hand goes under water, and pull strongly and slowly. At the end of your stroke, as the blade is rising toward the surface, turn the blade on to its edge by twisting the right wrist toward the side of the canoe. No time is spent in this twisting of the blade, but on it depends the mastery of the canoe and the decision of your course. Practice alone can show you how to make it effective. By the steadiness of his blade in the water and by judgment as to the proper time for a new stroke, the experienced canoeman can defy a chopping white-crested sea that would make short work of a stout row-boat. Be sure and don't sit upon the bar of your canoe unless you are alone or have no room to kneel. Any one on the St. John River will know you are a novice if you are seen perched upon the bar. Kneel, as I said before, and kneel rather low. For ordinary light work you will find it convenient to rest against the bar behind you, but when you go making your 35 miles a day on dead water you'll find that you work best " on your hunkers," as the Indians say—that is, sitting on your heels.

Paddling a canoe is one thing; propelling it by a pole, even against a moderate current, is quite another. But learn to pole you must, if you would explore New Brunswick waters and be independent of your Indian. The first essential is the pole. It will be of spruce, 8 or 9 ft. long, and about the size, in circumference, of the circle made by your thumb and second finger. It will be dry and light and smoothly finished, and, if it is free from knots and flaws as it should be, it will be wonderfully pliable and tough.

You had better get an experienced poler to give you a few instructions before you try your hand, because, of course, you must stand up to pole a canoe, and you will get no support from the pole, and the length of time you remain in the canoe will depend entirely on your luck if you go at it blindly.

Jim Paul poles in good form.   Let him take you up the river a way while you watch him closely.

You will see that he stands with his feet braced apart a little and faces the near shore.   Suppose he is poling on the right side, he grasps the pole near the middle with his right hand and puts it to the bottom of the river just behind him, using his left hand merely to direct the pole to its hold in the hard mud.   Then he surges steadily and strongly back with his right arm, and, as the canoe glides ahead, the left arm gets a chance to shove too and makes the most of its opportunity.   The right hand, so long as he poles on this side, will never leave the pole except in making a long push, in which case the poler will often run the length of the pole hand over hand.   He will always lift from the stroke with his right hand and swing the dripping end out ahead of him in a shining half circle, seize it below with his left to plant it for a new shove, and go on as before.

By setting the pole on the bottom, at some distance out from the side of the canoe, and, during the stroke, drawing the stern close to the pole, the bow will be swung in toward shore, gradually or abruptly, as the poler may desire.   By setting the pole well *under* the canoe, and pushing the stern off from it, a turn in the opposite direction is made.

An experienced canoeman keeps a perfectly straight course and makes his turns and curves with precision and without wabbling or wavering, just as a practiced bicyclist does with his wheel.

In very deep water, sometimes, the pole must be used, for some of the strongest rapids are deep.   But you need not be taken unawares by deep, strong water.   You will know whether or not you are going to encounter any, and will start on your trip armed with a pole of exceptional length.

This long pole will be found of great service, too, in a short, shallow rapid of more than usual strength, when you can not afford to take a full, new stroke.   You will then find it advisable to "swish" the lower end quickly into the air and "snub" down hard with the other, keeping your pole ever ready to gain a step, as it were, by turning a handspring. With a reliable man in the bow and stern, a canoe can be forced up through a foaming, dashing run that looks utterly impassable.

The pole will be indispensable also in shooting rapids—running down over them. On the New Brunswick waters, at many seasons of the year, there is very little water in the principal fishing streams, and the rocks are so thick in the runs that a paddle is useless. Then the bowman must keep his wits about him, and must kneel high with a short, stout pole held ready to "snub" for all he's worth, so that the bows may not be stove in on some bare rock that the sternman has failed to avoid, owing to his natural inability to keep his canoe headed in every conceivable direction at once, without getting in the least "rattled."

If you are going to shoot rapids—full-grown ones—you must be as cool as if your game were elephants. If you are not, you will break your bark's back over a ledge or rip her up with a pointed rock; and will lose a lot of your load, and have to tramp through the woods to the nearest village.

Many a time I have looked from my position by the stern-bar and seen a raging incline hissing and snarling ahead of me, with black rocks bobbing up everywhere. Never a word from the fellow in front of me. He leans peering over the bow, and keeps his pole flashing like a fencer's foil from side to side. He's working like a horse. I pick out the main course and use all the common sense and experience I can lay claim to in choosing the deepest water and keeping clear of the worst rocks. He looks out for the smaller but no less dangerous ones. We come to a sharp turn, and I head her straight for a giant bowlder that stoops in front of us, surging his way against the roaring stream with frothy, jagged shoulders. The canoe shivers and leaps at him, and I give a twist to right, and a side current helps me just in time, and we turn half round and dart for another. The bowman catches her in her jump and holds hard while I slip the stern to the left, and we spring through a line of rolling waves and shoot into the rest and calm of a deep, still pool, and "lie easy" a minute to look back and live those last few seconds over again. Our pipes are smoked to the very heel, and we start again, with every sinew and nerve strung tight, ready for what may come.

That is the kind of strengthening medicine you will get in the wilds with a birch-bark canoe!—strong water that will intoxicate you fast enough and leave no headache!

If you strike the stream when the water is high—say, after the June freshet—you'll find all the rapids full and the water running deep and heavy and covering all the smaller rocks, so that there is not half the risk of being "stove in." Then you can let your bowman sit at his ease, and you can settle yourself with your broadest-bladed paddle and keep things straight, and listen to the shouting of the stream. No work for you now! Nothing but highly-spiced hot puddings and the brightest of the bright champagnes! And all digestible as bread and milk! And no stint!

Try it for yourself, and see whether or not this is exaggerated.

Up the Tobique by Canoe.

A TYPICAL NEW BRUNSWICK TRIP.

Our party consisted of the "Ecclesiastic," the "Artist," and my-self. The Ecclesiastic is a veteran devotee of birch and paddle. The Artist was a novice, but, being of frame and spirit fashioned to with-stand the thousand unnatural shocks which the canoeist is heir to, he soon proved himself one of the initiated. Without much difficulty, and for a consideration of $1 a day, we provided us each with an In-dian, and each Indian provided a birch canoe, warranted unstable but water-proof.

Our supplies we laid in at the Andover grocery. As an essential, they included an open tin baking-oven—an apparatus with which the Melicite bakes excellent bread at the camp-fire.

The start was decreed for Friday morning, but rain and the non-appearance of our Melicites postponed it till the afternoon. A word in regard to these Melicites, whom let me commend to explorers of the Tobique. They were Steve Solace, chief guide, and his two nephews, Tom and Frank.

About 1.30, in a spell of clear sky, we paddled off from Andover and fancied ourselves under way; but the Indians had a stop to make at their village. Here was a delay of nearly two hours, which left us little of the afternoon for journeying. Not far ahead were "The Nar-rows," the toughest piece of navigation which the whole length of the Tobique could bring to bear against us, with the possible exception of Red Rapids. We decided to employ the remnant of our daylight in demolishing the obstacle, that we might have clear poling to look forward to on the morrow.

A mile of easy water, and "The Narrows" were reached. Here the Tobique has chiseled itself a cañon through a range of calciferous slate which had sought to bar its way to the St. John. The little difficulty, I understand, was settled some ages back, but the river still chafes furiously at remembrance of the opposition; the gloomy crags still threaten, as if they brooded over their defeat. Redly into the gate of the gorge streamed the light of the low, unclouded sun, filling the water with fervent greens and olives and flushing the naked faces of the cliffs.

But the gorge is tortuous and the sunshine was speedily shut out, while the rocks drew closer and closer above, as if they would strike their somber foreheads together. The toppling black walls were scrawled over with tracings of white where the thin seams of limestone displayed themselves. Here and there we marked the cordial green of a cedar-tree, swung from some scant root-hold on the steep. Once we came to a spot where the cañon widened, giving room for an eddy which served us for a breathing-place, and for a queer detached rock-pinnacle which must figure as an island at high water. At this season the stream was low, or a passage of the Narrows would have been one of the wildest of impossibilities. Instead of volleying down the gorge in an endless succession of great, white, roaring surges, as is its wont in time of freshet, the current now darted on like a flight of green arrows, splintering into a hiss of foam on every point and ledge, and occasionally dipping under a group of thin-crested, stationary "ripples." Though this devious chasm is not a mile in extent, we occupied two hours and more in its passage. For all that, we had little time to delight in our grim surroundings. We had to snatch our impressions. With straining shoulders and flashing paddles, we aided to our utmost the poles of our sorely-perspiring guides. Sometimes we would grasp a jutting rock, and hold on like leeches while the panting Melicites breathed. We thrust and paddled desperately, now on this side now on that, as a spiteful cross-current would tug fiercely at our bow to drag us into some small but malignant Charybdis. All the while our ears rang with the rushing clamor of the rapids, doubled and trebled and hurled back upon us by the chasm's resonant walls. At last the walls fell swiftly apart before us, revealing a far, bright stretch of placid waters, bedded in low, green shores, with a sundown sky of clear sea-green and amber widening out peacefully above it. Beheld from this cavern of tumult and gloom, the vision came to our eyes like the veritable embodiment of a dream.

Upon a plot of gravelly sward we pitched our tents. As the rains had drenched everything, we had trouble with our fire till a dry stump was found. After supper, while the red glare of the fire wrought strange confusion with the moonbeams among the thickets about us, and on the misty level of the water that neighbored our threshold, we gathered huge armfuls of a giant fern which grew near by, and dried them for our couches and pillows. The Indians, who had their "lean-to" over against the tent-door, preferred their wonted pile of hemlock-branches. As we were running over with noble resolutions concerning an early start, before the morrow's sun should have got his eyes well opened, we sat not long that night about our fire. At a modest hour we were snug in our ferns and blankets.

Fortunately for the fate of our resolutions, the morrow, to all appearance, had no sun. It was rain, rain, rain; now mist, now drizzle, now "pitchforks." When it happened to be for a little in the milder form of mist, about eleven in the morning, we struck tent and got under-way. At once came on the rabid form of "pitchforks." With water-proofs buttoned up to the neck, the skirts thereof spread out to shed the downfall, we endured in silence till we had scored a moist three miles. Then, coming to a farm-house set temptingly close to the stream, we decided to break for cover. The Ecclesiastic was sitting in a pool which chilled, he said, his most deeply-seated enthusiasms; and we agreed that a kitchen-fire, with possibilities of buttermilk *an' sich*, had just now peculiar charms for a canoeist's imagination. Canoes and dunnage safe beneath tarpaulins, we presented ourselves all dripping at the kitchen-door, while the Indians took to the barn.

Soon the weather cleared, and in the afternoon we made good progress. Between the showers the Artist would be busy with his sketch-book, whipping it under his mackintosh at the first sign of a sprinkle. As for the Ecclesiastic, he is an ardent disciple of the gentle Isaac, and had got his rod spliced as soon as we came in sight of the Tobique. We two now kept casting from side to side as the canoe climbed onward, though on this lower course of the stream we had no expectations to be disappointed. The large trout were lying higher up, or in the mouths of the brooks, and one need not look for a salmon at his fly before he reaches the Oxbow. Yet certain of the small fry were on

Caribou Migration.

hand, and we took enough to supply our pan liberally. The Ecclesiastic also, favored among anglers, struck and skillfully landed a small grilse. The fertile soil along the lower Tobique is being rapidly taken up by settlers, so during all this day's poling we were rarely out of sight of some sign of civilization. Now it was a latticed red and white bridge, leaping out of a mass of green on either lofty bank, and putting an airy limit to some enchanted vista before us. Now it was a white village perched on a hill, with a wall of dark fir-trees behind, and the yellow refuse of its now idle saw-mill covering the low level in its front. Toward sunset the showers ceased finally, and in the exquisite air we grew all too indolent to wield or rod or pencil. We dreamed along between the changing shores, and were disposed to grumble when the Indians halted for supper. To the halt, however, we grew reconciled, when the savor of our browning trout stole out upon the hay-sweet breezes. After supper we pushed on through gathering dusk, while the twang and cry of night-hawks filled the upper skies with magic, and we caught a far-off piping of summer frogs, with the lowing of cattle from a farmstead back of the hills. Reaching a wooded island in mid-stream we saw that it was good, and pitched our tents.

The camp was on the east side of the island, under a pair of stately black ash. What a mighty fire we built that night to glare across the water! It served at the same time, truth compels me to add, the less romantic purpose of drying our socks, etc. We were so wet that one *cheep-lah-quah-gan* * could not satisfy our needs. The camp was full of *cheep-lah-quah-gans*. It was also full of sand-flies—the insidious and all-pervasive "*bite-um-no-see-um*"—and with a fine Tobique variety of the mosquito. These troubled the Artist sorely, while the rest of us, knowing them of old, hid beneath a panoply of tar-ointment. This compound, familiarly known as "slitheroo," is tar and grease boiled down, with some unnecessary chemical superadded. The Artist stood in awe of it. He fled to it at last, however, after bitterly inveighing against the Tobique for having brought him "to this pitch." As he stood by the *cheep-lah-quah gan*, alternately turning his socks and daubing on the succulent ointment, he became, on a sudden, inspired. He began:

---

* This is the Melicite name for the green sapling driven into the ground to stand over the camp-fire, for the purpose of holding the pot and kettle. Clothes, etc., are hung upon it to dry.—ED.

> " Tobique, or not Tobique, that is the question.
> Whether 'tis nobler in the flesh to suffer
> The stings and arrows of outrageous midges,
> Or to take arms against a siege of sand-flies,
> And by tar-ointment end them ! "

At this stage he was rudely interrupted.

By a lamentable oversight our tent was pitched with the door there-of toward the east. Therefore we awoke too early, and lay long watching the sunrise over the low, thick-wooded hills. Then the coils of mist, tinged with saffron, pink, and violet, wavered and faded from the uplands; but on the water they clung writhing in pearly ropes for nearly an hour longer. The woods all about were full of the " Canada-bird," or white-throated sparrow, whose limpid, pathetic whistle lacked never an echo. As we watched the crystalline pageant of the morning a blue film stole between our eyes and it, then a dazzling shimmer, and we knew that the camp-fire was lighted. Soon a smell of pancakes and hot coffee invaded our couch, and springing up with alacrity we were fairly launched out upon a delicious Sunday's rest.

. We set off on Monday early, while the mists were yet on the stream, and the elm-branches, in the moveless, cool air, were drooping as if asleep. This was the luxurious time for traveling, and in the heat about noon we could indulge ourselves in a *siesta*. At half-past ten we reached Red Rapids, a spot where the river revels down a wild incline of red sandstone. The day had turned out temperate and cloudy. These rapids being shallow and difficult, we disembarked, and carrying our rods along with us took a settlements-road parallel with the stream, leaving the Indians to navigate the *chutes*, and appointing to meet them later at the mouth of Trout Brook. But a pleasant surprise was in store for us. We soon came within sound of laughter and singing, the neighing of horses, and the shouts of young backwoods swains. A turn of the road brought us out upon a clearing all alive with tethered teams and strolling couples. In the midst of the clearing was a barn, in which was being held what I may define as a picnic tea-meeting. From the mouth, from Arthuret, from Andover even, they had gathered in hilarious parties, in a gorgeous but bewildering whirl of fluttering ribbons and many-colored attire. They received us into their midst with the frankest and heartiest hospitality. It was a gay time for us, till the Ecclesiastic unkindly pointed out that we had consumed nearly three hours in this Vanity Fair. The Artist and I had made a perfect host of acquaintances (especially among the maidens), who did not seem to want us to go away. We had played many games, interesting and more or less *naïve*, in the course of which (I blush to tell it) it had fallen to the Artist's lot to kiss the prettiest damsel present. We had been treated to the dubious delights of the swing, which made us dizzy; and we had laid out a vast amount of precious muscle in assisting to swing fair ladies. This swinging was the darling pastime of the ladies, whose passion for it seemed insatiable, and was indulged with great expenditure of giggling and small shrieks, and with an artless prodigality of spotless stockings. At length the Ecclesiastic was obliged to remind us of our families, and to point out that the rural beaux were looking grim; so, with pockets full of cookies, conversation lozenges, and other tender tributes, we gathered up our tackle and withdrew. Perhaps we imagined it, but it seemed to us a gloom fell over the company as we left.

At the mouth of the brook the Indians were awaiting us. Had we kept them so waiting all day they would never, such is their patience, have dreamed of complaining. We stayed to fish the last hundred yards or so of Trout Brook, getting fine sport with some lively and voracious half-pounders. The brook seemed alive with sprightly and graceful fish, from a quarter to a half pound in weight. The Ecclesiastic said a good many of these would weigh a pound and over; such delicious ambiguity is the safeguard of a fisherman's reputation.

Later on we halted at a ruined mill, where the dilapidated dam seemed a part of the river's bank, and the scanty stream that had supplied it fell over the moss-greened timbers in a diaphanous veil of silver. The mill-pond above was shallow, and muffled in water-lilies, from under which we lured some large but soggy-looking trout. They had little play in them, for all their vast and ferocious black mouths. For the rest of the day we little cared to fish; we were content with the *dolce far niente* which our tireless Melicites and this peerless river conspired to make possible for us. Our journeying was after this fashion. Before embarking, the Indian would heap into the canoe, aft of the front bar, a sweet-smelling armful of ferns, or wild grasses, or hemlock-boughs. This for our seat. For a back thereto he would fix a wide bit of board against the second bar; and over it, for softness, throw a blanket or a coat. Stretched out on such soft couch, our feet in moccasins, our rods thrust into the bow ahead of us, we lolled, or smoked (all but the Ecclesiastic), or read, or took notes, or chatted lazily across the waters that parted canoe from canoe. Or at times, when we preferred it so, how sweet it was simply

> " to watch the emerald-colored water falling
> From cave to cave through the thick-twined vine " ;

or

> " hearing the downward stream,
> With half-shut eyes ever to seem
> Falling asleep in a half dream ! "

We passed the embowered mouth of the quiet Wapskehegan, navigable for 20 miles, but said to contain no fish; and a little farther we discovered what may have been a former channel of this stream. It was a sharply-defined, tortuous green lane, leading from the river's brink back into the wilderness, with alders and poplars and ash-trees dipping into it. Plainly it was not a roadway. It resembled the bed of a river from which the sparkling floods had been shut off, that the influent, liberal, grassy tide of summer might flow in thereby and brighten over the land.

Leaving behind the "Wapsky" and its problematical ancient *debouchement*, we came to one of the lions of the Tobique, the beautiful " Plaster Cliff." The opposite shore is low and luxuriantly wooded, with a mat of vines over trees and underbrush. The cliff itself rises so sheer from the water's edge that only in one or two places was it possible to land; and its face, about 100 ft. in height, is a many-colored rock so soft that we could carve out specimens with our knives. The surface crumbles rapidly under the frost and

> " The stealthy depredations of gray rain " ;

and the settlers, in winter, come from miles about and haul it to their farms as a fertilizer. The naked wall loomed over us, but could not look forbidding with its lovely mixture of cool blues and grays, reds and browns and yellows and umbers, somber purples and rosy or creamy whites. Wheresoever there was a ledge, or fissure, or gentle slope, there would be gathered a rich detritus bearing a perfect hanging-garden of wild flowers. The pendulous cups of the hare-bell swung airily from every crevice, sometimes so thickly as to hang a veil of blue lace-work over many square yards of the rock. From the dizziest shelves drooped the twisted pea-green cables of the vetch, studded with its vivid purple blossoms; and the white aromatic yarrow flung a silvery mantle over the lowermost slopes. I have never seen in nature another color-harmony so exquisite. The Artist was enraptured, and wished his pencil were compounded of the rainbow, rather than of sober graphite. The Ecclesiastic found a sermon of marvelous eloquence in these stones.

Above Plaster Cliff the river runs through a wide belt of red sandstone, remarkable for its depth and strength of tone. The next landmark in my memory—or should I style it a "water-mark?"—is the Oxbow. This is a curious and strongly defined double bend in the river, and we reached it late in the afternoon. Here, instead of the airiness and park-like effects of hard wood shores and grass, we had a sort of warm and cheerful shadow, deep, quiet, olive waters, rich-hued, close-drawn shores of fir and cedar, and rocks all muffled in moss. We paused awhile, in hope of striking a salmon. We tried our most alluring flies, but the salmon, if on hand, were apparently not open to inducements. The trout, however, were very numerous, and rose finely, besides being of a larger size than any we had hitherto taken. The Ecclesiastic chose to fish from shore, whither Steve followed to help land the larger fish; the Artist also went ashore, to sketch; but with Tom's assistance I fished from the canoe. Steve had been evincing some desire to try his own dusky hand at the sport; so at last the Ecclesiastic handed him the rod for a moment, with a few cautionary hints, and betook himself up the bank to a spring he had espied among the rocks. I held my hand to watch Steve, as he stood proudly wielding the unaccustomed lance-wood; and in that posture the Artist immortalized him. All the preliminaries the Indian accomplished with skill; but presently a fair-sized trout took one of his flies, and started off up stream with it. Now Steve was in a piteous quandary. He had forgotten all that he had been told to do. He did not understand the reel, and was afraid the rod was going to break. He simply stood and looked, with an expression of profound concern on his mahogany face. When the trout started back, he pulled in some of the slack with his fingers, gingerly enough, but let it go at once when the fish started off again. No one would go to his assistance uninvited, lest he should wound the Melicite dignity. At last a variation was introduced. A large fish seized the disengaged fly, as it trailed about the pool; and then Steve turned frantically and raised a cry for help. The Ecclesiastic, with immense laughter, ran up and seized the rod; and after a sharp struggle both prizes were brought to basket. The two together weighed a pound and three quarters, and Steve most complacently plumed himself on being their captor. For all that, however, he would not touch the rod again; perhaps dreading lest a more dubious success might cast tarnish upon his piscatorial laurels.

Just beyond the Oxbow we came to the mouth of the Gulquac, one of the Tobique's most important affluents. A little below it we saw a deep, eddying pool, in which lay several salmon. They dispersed at our coming, but we marked the spot. At the Gulquac was a small island, treeless and grassy and stony, on which we encamped. Then, leaving the Artist to sketch, the Melicites to get supper ready, the Ecclesiastic and I took a canoe and dropped down to look for those salmon. They had not yet returned, however; so, promising to call again next morning, we poled back to the Gulquac. This river joins the Tobique in a long, straight, shallow race, just swift enough to dimple and bubble deliciously. The place was alive with trout, of all sizes saving the largest. We used a small, brown fly, and in half an hour took four dozen, ranging from six or seven ounces to three quarters of a pound. As the dusk thickened we put on small moths, and with a lavender-colored fly I killed two fish that closely approached the pound. The Ecclesiastic, just as we decided to reel up, struck a large fish that gave him good fight, and, with his usual slice of luck, brought it safely home. 'It went a pound and thirteen ounces. We reveled in trout henceforward till we began furtively examining our sides and shoulders to see if little rows of vermilion spots were beginning to come out upon us, or fish-bones to stick through our skin. That night we named our halting-place Camp Mosquito.

In the morning the Ecclesiastic and I paid an early visit to the pool, in accordance with our resolve of the evening before. We were fortunate enough to find the salmon at home. Tying the canoe to a projecting branch a little above the pool, we made long and crafty casts right down to the critical spot. We used small, quiet flies, such as are most killing in the Nepisiguit, and played them lightly over the surface. Presently, as my fly fell softly on the outermost edge of the eddy, there came a strange little whirlpool right beneath it, followed by a screech from my reel. The Ecclesiastic dropped his rod as if it had burnt him, slipped the knot, and seized a paddle to be ready for assisting me. Like a bow of silver the salmon shot into the air, straightened himself, and fell slap on the spot where he expected the line to be. But it wasn't there—I had dropped my rod-tip in time. Without a pause, another and wilder leap, right toward the canoe; and we saw him fiercely shake at the tiny feather sticking fast in his jaw. Then, after two more leaps, and an attempt to dart under the canoe, foiled by a strong sweep of the Ecclesiastic's paddle, he hummed off down stream, while the reel sang, and the canoe followed as fast as our paddle could urge it. When he had taken off about sixty yards of my line he turned for an up-stream scurry, which was hard on my paddle but still harder on himself. I dared to check him severely while going in that direction. Then came another series of leaps, and another rush, and not till after twenty minutes of fight did the splendid fish seem to grow perceptibly weaker. At last those mighty rushes became short and of little account; he lay half on his side close by us, and the Ecclesiastic lifted the gaff. But the sight seemed to rouse him to one last effort. He whizzed off and brought up blindly in a shallow pool close to shore. We drew in and cut off his retreat. The Ecclesiastic has a just dislike to the gaff, so he slipped overboard into the shallow water, with a swift motion got both arms beneath the fish, and threw him out upon the grass. Poor salmon, what a gallant fight he had made! We gave him an instant *quietus*, and gazed upon him with respect and admiration. "How about the favored clergy now?" inquired the Ecclesiastic, as we poled homeward. I said nothing; and that salmon went thirteen pounds.

This day's voyaging was pleasant, though about midday the heat was so appalling as to drive us to covert. Early in the day we reached Two Brooks, which is the singular name given to *one* small brook running through a little settlement. At its mouth was a salmon-weir, running out nearly to mid-stream. To our right rose, in hazy grandeur, the twin summits of Blue Mountain, its nearer slopes a stony and fire-scathed wilderness; on our left the brawling brook, some rich groves, the gray little village, and fields of charred stumps, all muffled in deep grasses. The fishing here, for numbers, was superb. There was no limit to it, apparently. The Artist built him a lean-to, that he might sketch in shade; and he penciled a masterpiece. This masterpiece, since rendered permanent with ink and Chinese white, depicts the Ecclesiastic with his trousers rolled far above his energetic knees, the skirts of his clerical coat (donned in deference to the neighboring civilization) dragging in the water, established as near mid-stream as wading would place him, while he throws his whole heart into dropping his fly into the very back-wash of the weir. Myself, averse to exertion, conspicuous by my lightness of attire, am fishing from the canoe. The

Artist himself appears not in the masterpiece, which is so far in-complete.

As through the afternoon we continued

"Ever climbing up the climbing wave,"

we narrowly escaped being run down by a voyaging squirrel. This brave little voyager was making across current diagonally, and seemed to us somewhat exhausted. The Ecclesiastic, being nearest, stretched out his paddle to the bushy navigator, who straightway climbed aboard, and sat up, dripping but "chipper," upon the bow of the canoe. Con-ducted courteously to the other shore, which he reached, by a daring leap, before we had time fairly to land him, he whisked off without a word of acknowledgment or a hint of paying his fare. Later we passed a green snake swimming along complacently, and we concluded the creatures were sanctioning the pernicious practice of bathing in the heat. We accepted his sanction as valid; and at the next pool, in-stead of fishing, we swam. Toward sundown we reached a couple of small islands, below which the fishing was excellent and the fish large. The trout rose all around us, took our flies greedily, and it was most re-luctantly that we tore ourselves away. A mile farther on we encamped on a tempting point of dry, sweet meadow, round which the river swept in a narrowed channel; and Steve, pointing to the deep, rapid curve, said: "Plenty salmon here, mebbe; ugh!" We all tried for these straightway, even the Artist, while supper was getting ready; but we took only two or three trout and a wretched chub. Next morning, however, brought us better fortunes. Standing at the lower corner of the bend, I raised a small salmon at my second throw; but there was some flaw in the casting-line, and he sailed off, to my deep disgust, with two flies and a couple of yards of gut. Thereafter, I suppose, he tried some fishing on his own hook. A few minutes later I heard a shout from the Ecclesiastic on the other side of the point. Rushing to him, I found him busy with what was evidently a first-rate fish; when brought to book, after a quarter of an hour's excitement, it proved an eleven-pounder.

Not far beyond this camp we sighted Bald Mountain, rising some miles back from the river, out of the midst of cedar swamps. Here is the little settlement of Riley's Brook, endowed with the most primitive affair in the way of post-office that I have ever yet discovered. We mailed letters here, exceeding brief ones, consigning them, with certain misgivings, to the care of the primitive postmaster—a rheumatic old lady. Then we pushed on for the Forks, bidding good-by to the last of Tobique civilization. The next few miles were through a fire-stripped country. We sighted here a bald-headed eagle, which, perched on the top of a bleached pine trunk, kept guard over the surrounding desolation. His perch was but a stone's-throw back from the stream, and as we approached he stretched out his lean neck, his flat, sharp, snakelike head, and surveyed our movements inquisitively. When we had got well past he seemed to repent having let us off so easily, and yelped after us some choice maledictions. Then we came to the Forks.

The Forks of the Tobique—this was one of the chief objective points of the expedition. Here is the trout-ground of the river; and here, too, a favorite resort of the salmon. Three large streams at this point flow together. From the southward comes the Campbell River, more commonly called the Right Branch; next, the Mamozekel— "River of Alders," as the Melicite hath it—forming the middle tine of this delectable fork; and from the northward the Left Branch, *alias* the Little Tobique, *alias* the Nictor. Where these waters gather in conclave the shores draw somewhat apart, inclosing a spacious, deep, sandy-bottomed basin, full of quietly-circling eddies and swirls. The southward walls of this watery amphitheatre are low and rankly wooded, but on the north they are high and bare, forming an airy perch whereon we pitched our tent. The tongues of land between the converging streams were, for the most part, of luxuriant weedy meadow, melodiously noisy with bobolinks. While dining on the height we gloated over the liberal-bosomed pool spread out below us, and as soon as dinner was over, leaving the Artist to his pencil, we took two of the canoes and crossed to the side where the Right Branch emptied in. The Ecclesiastic stationed himself upon one side, I on the other, while our Melicites held us in position by thrusting down their paddles into the sand. For a time the sport was merely good, not markedly better than much we had left behind us; and the fish were fastidious, taking nothing but a smallish gray and yellow fly. Our persevering casts for a salmon elicited no response whatever. Then the breeze moderated, as the sun began to cast lengthening shadows, and all at once the pool became alive. Here and there a magnificent trout, of almost any number of pounds, according to our excited eyes, would leap with the complete *abandon* of the smaller fry; and the smaller fry themselves seemed to spend a large part of their time in the air. We shifted our flies a

12

little, but soon found that the trout of Tobique Forks, when bent on making a meal, would make it of whatever might come handiest. Each new fly seemed better than the last. The half and three-quarter pound fish were reeled in with an alacrity which set glistening the eyes of our stoical Melicites. I had already, after a series of brisk fights, taken several lively one-and-a-half-pounders, and in the bottom of my canoe lay a deep-set, solid trout that I flattered myself would go over the two pounds. The Ecclesiastic, to judge from his joyous occasional shouts, was being no less successful. At last, as it drew near sundown, and our wrists had grown well-nigh helpless, I caught a sharp exclamation from the Ecclesiastic, which made me turn to look at him. He was so occupied that I thought he had hooked a salmon. Just then the fish rolled half out of water, and I saw it was indeed a trout, but one of patriarchal proportions. "A five-pounder!" I shouted, frantically; but the fisherman shut his lips and said never a word. He had need of all his faculties. This trout gave him the work of a salmon of more than twice his size. The strife was long and desperate, but kept within the circle of the pool, and, when the Ecclesiastic netted his prize at last, it was without having moved a hand-breadth from his post. Just from the water this trout well cleared four pounds. It was *the* fish of the trip. The Ecclesiastic afterward struck, and lost, one which he considered larger (this was on the following day); and one which I am ready to swear to as the historical five-pounder, rose in a *dilettante* fashion to inspect my "Jock Scott" when I was on the quest for salmon; but I can't deny that these weights are problematical. The fish stayed not long enough to permit of my being more accurate. *My* best trout of the expedition went several ounces short of the three-pound scratch; but, when we came to brag of salmon, I was away ahead of the Ecclesiastic. We put in two more days at the Forks, in the course of which we discovered that the salmon had a *penchant* for the lower part of the pool, where I killed three more, good fish, the Ecclesiastic at the same time scoring a couple of grilse. The Tobique salmon do not rise so freely as those of the Nepisiguit or Miramichi. As for the number of trout which we had taken—and early we stayed our hands—the Indians salted them down in birch-bark crates. We imagined the mahogany youngsters at Tobique mouth reveling in the fruits of our prowess; and we imagined them so vividly that the artist forthwith made a sketch of our imaginings. And thus we felt no scruples on the abundance of our catch.

Before we set out for up the Nictor we had to endure a break in our little party. The Ecclesiastic had duties in town which required him to be back at a certain day, and early on our third day at the Forks he took his departure. We supplied him with rubber blankets for a lean-to, and with sundry of the choicest delicacies from our commissariat; and after a sorrowful farewell we watched him and his faithful Steve glide off with the current. As for us who were left behind, for a while we fell into a kind of melancholy. Rousing ourselves at last we struck tent, shipped our dunnage, and made ready to ascend the Nictor. Our aim was Little Tobique, or Nictor Lake, with its guardian mountain. We got off at about eleven, and our little flotilla appeared to us sadly diminished. We missed the Ecclesiastic's unflagging ardor, and the Artist could find no heart to sketch, the penster to take notes or flourish his lance-wood. The poling at first was difficult, as the Nictor here flows over a formation of flagstones and slate-ledges, affording poor hold to the poles. Passing this we made good headway, and, stopping for lunch at the mouth of Cedar Brook, found the trout large, hungry, and abundant. The Artist became fisherman here, and we tried hard to shake off our depression. We were stayed more than once by windfalls, large trees blown right across the channel, and several of the rapids we scaled were very shoal, as our canoes bore painful witness. Throughout the day a fly, wherever cast, was sure to raise a fish. By sundown we had covered two thirds of our way, and we encamped where a little nameless brook flows in from the north. I shall never forget how the sand-flies swarmed at this camp. They burrowed into our nostrils, our ears, our hair. They developed a most depraved taste, an actual craving, it seemed, for our tar ointment, in which we had fairly soaked ourselves. The evening fishing was utterly spoiled for us. We retreated to the tent, which the Indians walled about with a chain of "smudges"; then, when we had recovered from our panic, we began loudly exulting in the discomfiture of our foes. A roaring fire of dry pine-logs, the pleasant smell of the cedar smudges, a good supper, and a comfortable couch in the glow, soon restored us to something like our wonted cheerfulness. We sang songs, smoked our pipes, and shouted many a warm greeting to the solitary canoe which had forsaken us, and which we pictured as, by this time, possibly sliding down by the Wapskehegan's mouth.

Next day we made never a halt to fish, and in the early afternoon shot out upon the steely mirror of Little Tobique Lake. The scene

was almost oppressive in its stillness and its somber majesty. Round
the lake-shores were masses of dark syenite, with equally dark swamp-
forests intermingled ; and near the lake's head rose Nictor Mountain,
a beetling, naked cone of feldspar, frowning into subjection the lesser
hills which crouched and huddled around. The water was of great
depth, ice-cold, and colorless.   The woods appeared to harbor no
birds or squirrels, and the only familiar sound which greeted us was
the piping of the frogs, which arose toward evening. We scaled Nictor
Mountain, which is some 2,000 ft. high, and from its summit had such
a panorama of hills, and rivers, and lakes, as I have described elsewhere
as seen from the peak of Sugar-Loaf. We noted old Sugar-Loaf on
the bright northwestern horizon. At this place we spent a day and
two nights, finding no lack of sport in the gloomy waters; but the
region proved too severe and chilling for us, and its atmosphere of
stony endurance crept into our very souls.

> " The strange-scrawled rocks, the lonely sky,
>   If I might lend their life a voice,
>   Seem to bear rather than rejoice."

We had not time at our disposal to portage to Nepisiguit Lake and
descend that wild river. As we hastened away with the racing current,
on our downward trip, one morning, we seemed to leave behind us a
whole mountain of vicarious woe. We stopped not till we reached the
Forks that same afternoon.

After a successful evening's sport in the well-loved pool, we found
that now we had little room to spare in the canoes, on account of the
Indians' cargo of salt-fish. Thenceforth we killed but enough for each
meal. On our down trip we made great progress, and traveled luxuriously. My remembrance of it is, for the most part, a confusion of
greens and blues and browns, streaming away behind us as we fled,
with a vivid effect in rose and white at Red Rapids, and a study in
black, with lightning high-lights, when we made the passage of the
Narrows during a thunderstorm. We ran the Red Rapids about noon,
in a reckless mood, with enthusiasm and hair-breadth escapes. At the
Narrows we kept our heads level, for the stream was pretty full; and
the passage, amid the roar of the surges, the volleyings of the ponderous
thunder, the streaming of the rain, and the blue dartings of the lightning from cliff to cliff, was thrilling enough for all reasonable demands.
A half-hour later we were in Andover, at Perley's Hotel, donning the

garb of civilization with a degree of haste marvelously accelerated by a savor of beefsteak and buckwheat pancakes.

By Rail from Woodstock.

From Woodstock the C. P. R. runs, for the most part, through a rather rough country to *McAdam Junction*, passing Debec Junction, whence the Houlton Branch diverges. *Houlton*, in Maine, has between 4,000 and 5,000 inhabitants, and is a progressive little town. Ten miles beyond Debec Junction is the station of Wickham. The landscape seen from the car-windows throughout by far the greater part of this route can hardly be called exhilarating. Sometimes there is a little appearance of cheer around the stations; and among the charred stumps of the half-cleared fields are patches of sweet-smelling buckwheat. As a rule, the forests consist chiefly of gray bowlders and the trunks of dead trees. In late summer, however, the brilliant blossoms of the fireweed touch the desolation with a purple glory. Twenty-six miles from Woodstock is the station of *Eel River.* Five miles beyond is *Canterbury Station*, in the neighborhood of the famous *Skiff Lake.* In this water is taken the landlocked salmon or "shiner," a magnificent game-fish, very much like the ouananiche, but running to a larger size. It is in every way the peer of its more renowned relative, but is at times very capricious in its tastes, refusing to rise to the most seductive fly invented. The station of Deer Lake, 35 miles from Woodstock, is a mere lumbering post. Twenty-two miles beyond the gray bowlders thicken over the face of the landscape, and among them we discover *McAdam Junction,* where one may get refreshments in the station restaurant. Thence, passing the stations of Barber Dam and Lawrence, we come to *Watt Junction,* 14 miles from McAdam; here a branch diverges to *St. Stephen,* a distance of 20 miles.

St. Stephen is a progressive little town at the head of navigation on the St. Croix River. It is a center of the lumber-trade, and has growing manufactures. Contiguous with St. Stephen is *Milltown,* with a large cotton-mill. Together the two towns have a population of between 4,000 and 5,000. Across the river, and forming practically one community with St. Stephen and Milltown, is the little American city of *Calais,* in the State of Maine. Calais has between 7,000 and 8,000 inhabitants. Between these communities, though they differ in their allegiance and their flag, there exist the closest harmony and most intimate social relations; but the bridges connecting them are guarded by the customs officials of both nations. Nevertheless, the neighborhood affords a fine field for interesting and sometimes successful smuggling experiments. In the War of 1812 St. Stephen and Calais refused to come to blows, or to regard each other as enemies. The chief hotel of St. Stephen is the *Queen Hotel*. In Calais the best are the American House and Border City. At Milltown the navigation of the river is closed by falls. A steamer runs daily in summer, semi-weekly in winter, down the river to *St. Andrews* and *Eastport*, connecting with the boats of the *International S. S. Co.* St. Stephen is at present the western terminus of the *Shore Line Railway*, which runs eastward to St. John. From Calais a railway runs 21 miles N. W. to the foot of the *Schoodic Lakes*, whence a small steamer ascends to the famous fishing-grounds of *Grand Lake Stream*, in Maine. The lower lake is occupied by pike, which have cleared out the more valuable game-fish; but the upper waters abound with brook-trout, lake-trout, landlocked salmon, and pickerel. Near the foot of Big Schoodic dwells a tribe of the Quoddy Indians, among whom may be hired guides to the labyrinths of lakes and streams connecting with the Schoodics. By short portages from these waters one may reach tributaries of the Penobscot and Machias.

The main line from *Watt Junction* passes the little stations of Dumbarton (3 miles from the Junction), Rolling Dam (7 miles), and here we touch the Digdiguash River, and follow its course some miles; Hewitt's (8 miles), Roix Road (12 miles), Waweig (14 miles), Bartlett's (16 miles), and Chamcook (22 miles). Here the scenery becomes impressive. We skirt Passamaquoddy Bay. Chamcook Mountain is a steep and solitary mass, overlooking the bay and the quiet bosom of Chamcook Lake. A few miles above Chamcook, on the St. Croix, is the picturesque inlet of Oak Bay. At this point the St. Croix bends at right angles to its course, and forms, with Oak Bay, a figure much resembling a cross, whence, according to tradition, is derived its name. Five miles beyond Chamcook Station we run into the delightful watering-place of *St. Andrews*, a village of two thousand and odd inhabitants, and the shire town of Charlotte County.

Acadian history makes its real beginning at this point. To the St. Croix, in 1604, came Champlain and the Sieur de Monts, and planted a colony on a little grassy island within the river's mouth. A quadrangle of wooden buildings was erected, with a chapel, and the Governor's residence. In spite of the lateness of the season, grain and vegetables were planted, and a garden was laid out, after the fashion, faintly, of those old gardens in France, for which, it may be, the colonists were now a little homesick. But in the bleak days of late autumn their situation was dreary enough; and, because their crops had failed to ripen, they were compelled to live mainly on salt meats, a diet which speedily affected their health and spirits. At last winter came, and the snow, and the freezing winds; such cold as in their own land they had never learned to dream of. The sleet drove in through the chinks of their ill-made buildings. Fuel was hardly to be obtained, and they shivered over their scanty fires, till, in spite of Champlain's indomitable and never-failing cheerfulness, their hearts sank utterly within them. When disease broke out—scurvy in a terrible form, from their unwholesome living—they fell an easy prey. Out of some 80 persons, but 44 survived, and these hardly. When the first warm days came they crawled forth in the sun like shadows. Scarcely could the sick be attended, the dying ministered to, the dead buried. In the spring the island was abandoned, stripped of all that could be carried away; the fortifications were dismantled, and the poor remnant of the colony fled over the bay to Port Royal. Now, the lighthouse-keeper is the one man who makes St. Croix Island his home. When, in 1783, the St. Croix River was fixed upon as the boundary between Maine and New Brunswick, it became a disputed question as to what was the true St. Croix. The Americans claimed that it was the river now known as the Magaguadavic, much farther to the eastward; but after much searching the dispute was laid to rest, and the British claim established, by the discovery of the remains of Champlain's settlement, on Doncet's Island, above St. Andrews.

St. Andrews is commandingly situated on a peninsula between the St. Croix—at this point two miles wide—and Passamaquoddy Bay. It was of old an important shipping center, with a great West Indian trade, but its supremacy has been stolen and divided by St. John and St. Stephen. The town is well laid out, in squares, with wide and well-kept streets, and, besides its charms of scenery and climate, it has interesting remains of old British fortifications.

St. Andrews has expectations of a great commercial future, which may or may not be realized, though her harbor is certainly all that could be desired. As a summer resort her popularity is yearly increasing. She has her cool sea-breezes in the hottest months, her immunity from the Fundy fogs, her fresh and salt water fishing. More-over, she has her bathing, joyously indulged in by gay parties of young men and maidens, old men and children. The water, however, is some-times uncomfortably cool. A favorite diversion at St. Andrews is the sport of lobster-spearing. In the cool of the morning, when the tide suits, there is a novel excitement in being rowed stealthily over the transparent green water, while, spear in hand, one peers eagerly into the masses of brown seaweed that dot the level bottom. In these clumps of seaweed lurks our bottle-green prey, closely resembling his surroundings in color, but betrayed by his red points. The lobster-spear is not a spear at all, but a hook. It does not penetrate the lob-ster's shell, but catches under its belly among the small claws ; and one must be neat-handed and swift to land the nimble crustacean. The excitement reaches its highest pitch after a few active lobsters have been captured and dropped loose in the boat, to investigate the merry fishermen's ankles. In the way of hotels, St. Andrews has a regular hostelry called the *Central Exchange*, also the large summer hotels, the *Argyll House* and the *Algonquin*. Opposite the town is the American ship-building village of Robbinston. Travelers who have come straight through by rail, without diverging to *St. Stephen*, will do well to visit the latter town by the up-river boat. They will find good scenery at Oak Bay, already mentioned, where stands the lovely pastoral village of the same name. Leaving Oak Bay, the steamer passes on the left a promontory called Devil's Head, named in somewhat ambiguous com-memoration of a settler named Duval who once dwelt thereon. Three miles beyond is the ancient fishing village known as The Ledge ; and another 4 miles brings us to St. Stephen.

Campobello and Grand Manan.

To visit the summer resorts of **Grand Manan** and **Campobello** one must take the boat to *Eastport*, on the Maine coast. From East-port to Campobello, which is in Canadian waters, a ferry-steamer runs every hour. The island has a permanent population of 1,100 inhab-itants, dwelling in the villages of Welchpool and Wilson's Beach. Cam-pobello is 8 miles long by 3 broad, and is traversed by beautiful drives commanding magnificent views from upland and lofty promontory. Its ancient name was Passamaquoddy Island. In 1767 it was granted to Admiral W. Fitzwilliam Owen, who used to pace up and down in full uniform on a quarter-deck which he built out over the rocks. The admiral was not less peculiar in his death than in his life, for he was buried at night, by the light of candles in the little family church. The island is redolent with romantic memories and legends, and stories of ghosts, pirates, and wrecks. During the Fenian scare of 1866 a number of ardent Irishmen gathered at Eastport to invade Campobello, but altered their benevolent intention. Admiral Owen's heirs of the present generation, becoming tired of the seclusion and quiet of Campobello, at length removed to England, and in 1880 the island was purchased by a syndicate of American capitalists, who have made it a summer resort of the first rank. The old Owen Manor-House has been enlarged into a most attractive hotel, called the *Owen*, which retains many of the distinctive charms of its earlier days—the Lovers' Lane, and the old-fashioned hedges, sun-dial, and porter's lodge. Besides the *Owen*, the Campobello Company has erected two more summer hotels on the island. These are peculiarly handsome and striking buildings, and rejoice in the equally striking names of the *Tyn-y-Coedd* and the *Tyn-y-Mais*, which signify respectively "The House in the Wood" and "The House in the Field." Small as the island is, it has variety of scenery, and points of interest to visit—such as the lighthouses, the inlet of Harbor de Lute, the bold promontory of Eastern Head, the beautiful cove and lake of Glen Severn, and the famous landmark known as Friar's Head. This is a lofty detached mass of rock thrust up out of the sea, and its battered face bears witness to the fact that it has been used as a target for the guns of cruising warships.

The island of *Grand Manan* lies about 7 miles off the coast of Maine, but forms a portion of New Brunswick. Its people are quaint and hospitable, its summer climate delicious, its fishing and shooting are good, and its scenery a well-nigh matchless blending of the beautiful and the grand. Moreover, it is not a *regular* summer resort. It lies out of the beaten track, and is as yet perfectly unhackneyed. There are no gigantic summer hotels, and the visitor must as a rule find board in private houses, which he may do very comfortably and pleasantly at from $5 to $7 a week. There is the added charm of uncertainty as to when one will get there; and, this accomplished, as to when one will get away. Grand Manan is reached by steamer from Eastport—very easily and pleasantly when the weather suits, and not at all when the weather does not suit. There is also communication with St. John by the steamer Flushing. Its harbors are small and not easy of access, its shores are terrific, and the variety and velocity of the currents which the great Fundy tides succeed in creating in the island channels are something which must be seen to be realized. The island is 22 miles long, with an extreme breadth of 6 miles. It lies in the mouth of the Bay of Fundy, and has about 3,000 inhabitants, who occupy chiefly a thin line of settlements along the E. shore, and devote themselves to the rich fisheries of the surrounding waters, which simply swarm with cod, haddock, and herring. The island was visited by Champlain in 1605, but for nearly two centuries thereafter it had no inhabitants but the Indians. The Indians of Grand Manan are, like its white inhabitants, the most daring and skillful of fishermen. It is marvelous to see them go out in their bark canoes upon the mighty waves that toss about those shores, and shoot porpoises, whose bodies in some miraculous manner they drag aboard their frail craft and carry safely to land.

The chief village on the island is *Grand Harbor*, situated on a shallow bay. This village has a pretty little stone church and a typical country inn. Near by are the small lakes called Grand Ponds; and off the harbor lie a number of small islands, connected with memories of Audubon, who spent some time among them in 1833, studying the habits of the gulls. From Grand Harbor a road leads around the S. shore to Seal Cove, and thence along the heights to Broad Cove. Nine miles off the coast at this point lie the Wood Islands and Gannet Rock Lighthouse. From Broad Cove a foot-path leads to Southwest Head, a lofty promontory, amid the grasses of whose summit the sea-gulls build their nests. Around the N. shore, 8 miles from Grand Harbor, lies Whale Cove, with surpassing views, and a beach on which one may pick up jasper and agates. Close by is Eel Brook Cove, where the ship Lord Ashburton was wrecked, with the loss of all on board. A little farther to the N. is the cape called Bishop's Head, with a profile thought to resemble that of a human face. Between Grand Harbor and Whale Cove we pass through Woodward's Cove, Flagg's Cove, and the matchlessly picturesque and artistic village of Sprague's Cove nestling under the S. shore of the high and storm-beaten peninsula called Swallow-tail Head. The W. coast is a frowning wall of cliffs from 300 to 400 ft. high, in which are the wild and romantic indentations of Dark Cove and Money Cove, where the ubiquitous Captain Kidd is supposed to have buried some of his treasure. On this coast also is Indian beach, where a number of the Quoddy Indians pass the summer engaged in the porpoise-fishery already referred to. The island is in telegraphic communication with the mainland by a submarine cable to Eastport. Very lately one or two small hotels have been erected, the most prominent of which is the *Marble Ridge House*, near North Head.

In the time of Charlevoix, if we may trust that ancient chronicler, there existed off the coast of Grand Manan a marvel, the vanishing of which can not be too deeply deplored. "It is even asserted that at three fourths of a league off Isle Menane, which serves as a guide to vessels to enter St. John's River, there is a rock, almost always covered by the sea, which is of lapis-lazuli. It is added that Commander de Razilli broke off a piece, which he sent to France, and Sieur Denys, who had seen it, says that it was valued at ten crowns an ounce."

The Return to St. John.

To **St. John** we may go either by boat or by rail. To go by boat we take the steamer *Charles Houghton* from *St. Stephen* or *St. Andrews* to *Eastport*, and thence the *International S. S. Co.* boat along the coast to St. John, past Deer Island, through Friar's Road and the Eastern Passage, through wonderful fishing waters, usually dotted with boats and sails, past the West Isles and the grim and terrible rocks called the Wolves, past the far-seen headland of Point Lepreaux, then the landmark called Split Rock, and round the dark mass of Partridge Island into the St. John Harbor.

To go by rail, we take the *Shore Line Railway* at *St. Stephen*, its western terminus. It is proposed to continue this line westward through the coast towns of Maine to Bangor. Between St. Stephen and St. John by rail is a distance of 82 miles. The first station out of St. Stephen is Oak Bay (15 miles); then come Dyer's (20 miles), Bonny River (24 miles), and *St. George* (35 miles). This pretty little town has an extensive trade in lumber and in the magnificent product of its red granite quarries. The town is on a high plain. Beside it flows the Magaguadavic (commonly called Magadavy), which plunges into the harbor over a fall of 100 ft., through a chasm not more than 30 ft. in width. On the sides of the gorge cling saw-mills, from which the new-cut deals are sluiced into the foaming basin below. Near St. George, in a nest among the rounded hills, is the lovely water called

Lake Utopia, wherein one may find some good trout-fishing. The population of St. George is 4,000 and odd. Beyond St. George are the stations of Pennfield (46 miles), New River (53 miles), Lepreaux (58 miles), Lancaster (66 miles), Musquash (73 miles), and Spruce Lake (75 miles). Spruce Lake is 7 miles from St. John. It is a pretty sheet of water, 5 miles in length, and abundantly stocked with perch. It is the source from which Carleton draws its water-supply. Between Spruce Lake and Carleton extends the pretty drive known as the Mahogany Road. The fare between St. Stephen and St. John is $2.50.

From Moncton to Amherst.

Leaving Moncton by the *Halifax Express* our first stoppage is at Painsec Junction, a distance of 7 miles. Thence, passing Meadow Brook, we run down the valley of the *Memramcook* to the prosperous Acadian farming village of the same name, the seat of St. Joseph's College. Eight miles farther on, 25 miles from Moncton, is the sleepy but beautiful little town of *Dorchester*, the shire town of the rich county of Westmoreland. Dorchester was once a great ship-building center, and contains much wealth, though its business is decaying. It has handsome private residences, important freestone quarries, and the questionable attraction of the Maritime Provinces Penitentiary, which draws some visitors to Dorchester who might not go there otherwise.

From Dorchester the railroad runs across the top of the long peninsula between Shepody Bay and Cumberland Basin, and strikes the latter at the growing town of *Sackville*, 36 miles from Moncton. Sackville is not a pretty town, but it is prosperous and progressive. It has a population of nearly 2,000, and is thinly spread out over a succession of low hills of rich red soil, overlooking the *Great Tantramar Marshes* and the mouth of the Tantramar River. The town has foundries and factories, is the center of a boundlessly rich agricultural region, and the western terminus of the *Cape Tormentine Railway*, so called, whose official title, The New Brunswick and Prince Edward Island Railway, is somewhat large for so small a road, but 37 miles in length. It also has the important educational institutions of Mount Allison College and Seminary and Boys' School, under the auspices of the Methodists. The chief hotels are the *Brunswick House* and *Intercolonial Hotel*. Sackville is a ship-building center; and all along the picturesque road, which leads through the villages of Westcock, Woodpoint, and

Cape Porcupine.   *Cape St. George, from Hastings.*

Rockport, down the peninsula to North Joggins, one may see a ship on the stocks in almost every tidal creek. If the tide is out, the big vessel appears as if she were being built far inland, on a rivulet not large enough to float her jolly-boat; but at high tide this rill becomes a full-bosomed estuary, and the new-launched ship is carried easily from her birthplace.

Leaving Sackville Station the train crosses the Tantramar and runs out upon the marshes. The river, whose name is a corruption of its old French appellation, *Tintamarre*, signifying "a hubbub," is a typical tidal stream. At low water its broad and winding channel is a deep gash of livid red across the fair green face of the marshes. The steep sides glisten in the sun, cut sharply here and there by the paths of tributary brooks. Along the bottom, 60 or 70 ft. below the level of the marshes, clamors the fresh-water-stream. Presently the tide returns, red and foaming, and the noisy current rushes far inland, resting not till the chasm is full to its grassy brim. Then begins the emptying process, which goes on with increasing haste and tumult to the utmost of the ebb. The Great Tantramar Marsh, over which we now run, contains more than 40 square miles of inexhaustibly fertile salt meadow, reclaimed from the sea by dikes. About the head of the marsh lie bogs and pools, which are famous shooting-grounds; and over it, in all directions, feed in the autumn great flocks of plover. In early summer, before the mowing, the level expanse is a lovely sight, with its rich green crop bending all one way before the ceaseless winds, varied along the meandering dikes, that follow every creek channel, with lines of wild-rose thicket and beds of purple vetch. We are now on the *Isthmus of Chignecto*, connecting New Brunswick with the Acadian Peninsula, now called **Nova Scotia**. The length of this isthmus is the distance between Sackville on the N. side and Amherst on the S., about 10 miles. Its width, between the waters of the Gulf of St. Lawrence and those of the Bay of Fundy, is about 17 miles. The whole region is most interesting, as well geologically as historically. Most of it is salt marsh, beneath whose surface, at a depth of many feet, diggings have revealed the remains of ancient forests, proving that the district was once upland. At present one portion of the shore is slowly continuing its submergence, while the other is rising at about the same rate. The alluvial deposit produces year after year the heaviest crops of grass, and requires no fertilizer but mud from the neighboring creek channels, or a flooding from the tide. The historic interest of the region centers around the old *Fort Cumberland*, or " Beauséjour," which stands about midway across the isthmus, on a long ridge of uplands just beyond Aulac Station.

The old French Fort of Beauséjour figures very prominently in the enchanting pages of Parkman. It played an important part in those events which culminated in the expulsion of the Acadians in 1755. When **Acadie** was ceded finally to England, the French claimed that the name applied only to the peninsula, and not to that portion of old Acadie which now constitutes New Brunswick. They made the line of the Missiguash (a tidal stream cleaving the marshes just S. E. of Beauséjour) the dividing line between French and English territory, and raised the strong fort of Beauséjour to guard these limits. A little beyond the Missiguash runs a line of low uplands, on which the English erected the opposing stronghold of *Fort Lawrence*. Back of Fort Lawrence, on undoubtedly English territory, clustered the thriving Acadian village of *Beaubassin*. Between the rival forts went on continual skirmishings. Beauséjour was a center of operations for the unscrupulous Abbé Le Loutre, who devoted his energies to keeping the sore open between the Acadians of the peninsula and their new masters. Many of these Acadians he forced by threats and actual violence to desert their farms and remove to French territory, where many of them suffered every privation. When he saw the village of Beaubassin prosperous and growing content with English rule, he and his Indian followers burnt the settlement, and compelled the villagers to gather about Beauséjour. On one occasion, when a party of English, under Lieutenant Howe, were approaching from Fort Lawrence with a flag of truce, they were fired upon by the abbé's Christianized savages from behind a dike, and Howe was slain. For this infamous piece of treachery Le Loutre was openly blamed by the French officers of Beauséjour, and his unscrupulous policy incurred also the reprobation of the best of the Acadian parish priests. In 1755 Governor Shirley, of Massachusetts, and Governor Lawrence, of Nova Scotia, undertook the reduction of Beauséjour. The Massachusetts troops were led by Colonel John Winslow. The whole expedition was commanded by General Monckton. The French defense, conducted by the disreputable commandant Vergor, a tool of Bigot's, was of the feeblest. Le Loutre proved himself by far the better soldier. To this day we may see in the vaulted ceiling of the bomb-proof the great hole made by an English shell which came through when the officers were at breakfast,

The Steamer Stanley crossing from the Mainland to Prince Edward Island.

and in its explosion killed six of them, together with an English officer who had been taken prisoner a few days before. This settled the contest; and, in spite of the passionate protest of Le Loutre and one or two officers, Vergor capitulated. In the evening a body of British troops marched in, and Vergor celebrated his brilliant defense by a dinner to the French and English officers—at which, however, Le Loutre was not present, having escaped in disguise. After its capture the fort was rechristened Fort Cumberland.

After rounding the slope of Fort Cumberland we cross the Missiguash and come to Fort Lawrence Station, whence we see a little to our right the abandoned works of the **Chignecto Ship Railway**— which will be most conveniently visited, however, from **Amherst**, a couple of miles beyond. On the skirts of Amherst we cross the little tidal stream of the La Planche, and, quitting the marshes, run into the busy depot, thronged with freight-cars.

As soon as we crossed the Missiguash we were in the province of Nova Scotia, which will be referred to more fully in another place. Amherst is a very busy town, whose population of between 4,000 and 5,000 is increasing with great rapidity. It lies 48 miles from Moncton, 138 from Halifax. Its people are remarkable for their enterprise. It has a number of handsome public and private buildings, along with much of the crudity of a new town. With a rich agricultural and mining country behind it, the outlook is very bright for the future of Amherst. It has a short railway running down the coast to the coal-mines of South Joggins, interesting to visitors as the place where the monster rafts of logs are put together to be towed to the New York market.

At present we reach Fort Lawrence and the railway works by a drive across the marsh from Amherst, but it is proposed to open shortly an electric railway between the two points. The Tidnish terminus is reached by stage from Amherst. The best hotels of Amherst are the *Terrace Hotel* and the *Amherst Hotel*. From here we may continue on by the *Intercolonial Railway* to *Truro*, a distance of 76 miles, and thence either to *Halifax* or to *Pictou, P. E. Island*, and *Cape Breton*. The route we propose following at present, however, now takes us back to *Painsec Junction*, 8 miles this side of Moncton.

PRINCE EDWARD ISLAND.

The fare from Moncton to **Charlottetown** by way of *Point du Chêne* and *Summerside* is $3.50 ; return, $5.30. From Painsec Junction to Point du Chêne is 12 miles. Nine miles from the Junction we come to the pretty summer resort of **Shediac,** a village famous for its oysters and its sea-bathing. Shediac has a very good hotel, the *Weldon House,* and is much frequented during the hot months by the citizens of Moncton, who are driven from their homes by a combination of dust and heat. At Shediac the tide flows in over long stretches of red and sun-warmed sand, and its temperature at high water is luxurious. Point du Chêne is a sandy promontory 3 miles long, running out from Shediac into the waters of Northumberland Strait. About its wharves clusters a village. From this point the fine steamers of the P. E. I. Navigation Co. sail daily for Summerside on the arrival of the morning express from St. John. The steamboat fare from Shediac to *Summerside* is $1.50. The distance is 35 miles. Our first sight of the island is a glimpse of the low red cliffs of Cape Egmont, far on our left. Soon afterward we are steaming up Bedeque Bay, at the head of which lies the prosperous and dusty ship-building town of Summerside, with a population of something over 3,000 and a heavy export trade in agricultural produce.

The Island Province, the smallest of the confederation, is sometimes called the Garden of the Gulf. It is separated from New Brunswick and Nova Scotia by Northumberland Strait, whose ice in winter sometimes shuts off the island from communication with the rest of the world. Such intercourse as is then irregularly achieved is carried on with difficulty and danger by means of open boats, which are alternately dragged over the ice-cakes and pushed through the loose ice for a distance of 9 miles between Cape Traverse on the island and Cape Tormentine on the New Brunswick shore. The Canadian Government spends great sums every year in the effort to keep open during the winter a mail and passenger communication, and has had constructed a powerful steamer, the Stanley, especially designed for penetrating the ice. This boat, however, can not be said to meet all the requirements of the case. The islanders are demanding a tunnel or a subway between Cape Traverse and Cape Tormentine, and, gigantic as the scheme appears, it will doubtless ere long become an accomplished fact.

The extreme length of Prince Edward Island is 150 miles and its

The Oldest House in Prince Edward Island.

greatest width 34 miles. Owing to its numerous bays and inlets it has an enormous extent of coast-line. It has no lofty hills, no rocks, no barrens, but is everywhere cultivable. Its soil is a rich, red loam, marvelously productive, from the prevailing color of which the islanders get their local nickname of "Redfeet," to distinguish them from the "Bluenoses" of Nova Scotia and the "Buckwheats" of New Brunswick. The island is particularly noted for its oats, potatoes, horses, and oysters, and has fisheries of great value. There is some good trout-fishing in the little rivers which intersect the island, and along in June fascinating sport may be had with a scarlet fly, casting in the bays and inlets for the sea-trout, which at that season come in in great numbers from the gulf. These are a magnificent game-fish, running from 3 to 5 pounds in weight, and are usually taken by casting from side to side while running before a light breeze. One of the best places for this fishing is *St. Peter's Bay*, about 30 miles from Charlottetown, the provincial metropolis.

The history of the island is not exciting, and derives such color as it has chiefly from the Acadians. It is said to have been visited by Cabot in 1497. Champlain considered himself its discoverer, touching its shores on St. John's day, 1608, and naming it, with his usual lack of invention, Isle St. Jean. At this time it was inhabited by the Micmacs, who gave it the name of Epayguit, or, as it is better spelled, Abegweit, which signifies "Anchored on the Wave." Early in the eighteenth century, when England had conquered Nova Scotia, a few Acadians moved to the island, where they prospered so that the settlement rapidly increased. In 1758, when it was taken possession of by the English, it had a population of 4,100 Acadians. In 1763 it became a part of Nova Scotia, and was granted in lots to 100 English and Scotch gentlemen, who undertook to colonize their grants within ten years. In 1770 the island was made a separate province, and its infant capital was captured by the Americans in 1775, who, however, did not hold it long. In 1800 it received its present name, in honor of the Duke of Kent, the father of Queen Victoria. In 1803, 800 Scotch Highlanders were settled in the island by the Earl of Selkirk, and the population increased rapidly by immigration. The province entered the Canadian Confederation in 1873, and has 109,078 inhabitants.

From Summerside, whose chief hotels are *Russ's*, *Campbell's*, and the *Mawley House* (known also as the *Clifton*), one may follow the P. E. I. R. R. north through St. Eleanors, Miscouche, Wellington, Port Hill (a

ship-building village on Richmond Bay), Richmond, Northam, Port
Hill, Ellerslie, Conway, Portage (where the island is not more than
4 or 5 miles wide), Colman, O'Leary, Bloomfield, Elmsdale, all comparatively uninteresting little settlements, and run into *Alberton*, 54
miles from Summerside. This is a prosperous ship-building and fishing village on Cascumpeque Harbor, and has about 900 inhabitants.
It is interesting as the birthplace of the Gordons, the two mission-
ary martyrs of Eromanga. The chief inn of Alberton is the *Albion
House.* Leaving Alberton we pass the stations of Montrose, Kildare,
and De Blois, and reach the northern terminus at *Tignish*, 68 miles
from Summerside. This little village of Scotch and Acadian Cath-
olics is an important fishing center. It has a village inn called
Ryan's Hotel. A drive 8 miles northward through the sand-hills brings
us to the land's-end of the province, *North Cape.*

From Summerside to **Charlottetown**, a distance of 49 miles, we
traverse a pretty pastoral country, whose endless succession of farms
and farming hamlets wear an unvarying air of prosperity and comfort. The journey stands out in one's memory chiefly on account of
the curious little railway, with its gauge of only 3 ft. 6 inches, winding
hither and thither as if to visit every farmer's door. It is said that a
tourist was once startled by what appeared to be a train about to crash
into the rear car of that on which he was traveling. It turned out,
however, to be only the locomotive of his own train, which was rounding a peculiarly exaggerated curve. Just beyond Summerside the
island is but a little over 3 miles wide, being almost severed here by
Richmond Bay on the one side and Bedeque Bay on the other. Nine
miles from Summerside is the station of Kensington, whence a road
leads to Princetown, a village on the N. shore, which was laid out in
squares as a town, and still awaits the population that never came.
Near by, on the safe harbor of *Malpeque*, is the village of the same
name, a pleasant watering-place, with a comfortable inn called the
North Shore Hotel. Leaving Kensington we pass the stations of
Blueshank and Freetown, and come to *Emerald Junction*, whence a railroad runs to Cape Traverse. The succeeding stations are of no interest till we come to *Hunter River*, a good trout-stream, whence a highway leads N. to the villages of New Glasgow and Rustico. The latter
is a quiet and delightful summer resort, with a small but good summer
hotel, the *Rustico House*, on the sands of Rustico Beach. There are good
bathing and boating in the harbor, which is rendered unsafe, however,

for ships of any size, by its shifting sand-bars, thrown up by the gulf waves. There are also good shooting and fishing in the neighborhood. The village has but 250 inhabitants, yet it was once daring enough to own a bank—the Farmers' Bank of Rustico—whose charter has expired. Along the shore to the eastward lie Shaw's Beach, with a good summer hotel (Shaw's), and *Tracadie Harbor* (Lorne Hotel), which are favorite resorts for the citizens of Charlottetown. The villages of Tracadie and Covehead are Gaelic settlements, and near by, on French Fort Creek, stood of old a French fortress, protecting the short portage of 1½ miles from the head of the Hillsborough River to Tracadie Harbor.

From Hunter River Station we pass North Wiltshire, Colville, Milton, Winsloe, and arrive at Royalty Junction, whence diverge the lines to Georgetown and Souris. Six miles more and we sweep around the city of Charlottetown, and enter the station on the E., between the city and the Hillsborough River. In the station the train, on its narrow, shining rails, looks more than ever like a toy affair.

Charlottetown.

The chief hotels of Charlottetown are the *Hotel Davies* and the *Queen.* There is also the *Osborne*, a comfortable house, and numerous smaller hotels. Their coaches meet the trains and boats. There are no horse-cars, but the livery charges are moderate. The steamer *St. Lawrence*, of the P. E. I. Steam Navigation Co., plies between Charlottetown and *Pictou.* The steamer *Carroll*, of the P. E. I., Halifax, and Boston Line, leaves once a week for Boston. Fare, $7.50. The fortnightly boat of the Quebec S. S. Co. calls here. The little steamer *Heather Bell* leaves Charlottetown for *Orwell* every Tuesday, Wednesday, and Thursday. The *Southport* sails to *West River* on Tuesdays and Fridays, and to *Rocky Point* every day but Mondays and Thursdays. The steam-ferry *Elfin* plies between Charlottetown and *Southport* every half-hour from 5 A. M. to 9 P. M.

Charlottetown lies on the N. shore of the Hillsborough River. Its harbor is capacious and secure, and is formed by the meeting of the Hillsborough, York, and Elliott Rivers, more generally known as East, North, and West Rivers. The city is regularly laid out, its streets running E. and W., and intersected by streets running N. and S. There are 4 large squares, and the broad streets, 100 ft. in width, seem a shade too roomy for the 12,000 inhabitants. For the most part the buildings are of wood and entirely unimposing, but the *Parliament Houses* occupy a handsome stone structure on Queen Square, at the head of Great George St. The same building contains the good collection of the Legislative Library. From its cupola may be had an exceedingly attractive and commanding view of the city and its surroundings. On the same square, which is adorned with a fountain and well kept flower-beds, and where the band plays to the moving crowd on summer evenings, stands the handsome new stone pile of the Post-Office. Near by is the great wooden structure of the *City Market*, which looks like a weather-beaten compromise between a barn and a country meeting-house. It is the thing for tourists to visit this building on market-days in the morning, when they will see some quaint Gaelic and Acadian types. Around this square chiefly congregate the shops of Charlotte-town. Not far down Great George St. rises the roomy *Cathedral of St. Dunstan*, the seat of the Roman Catholic bishop. On Hillsborough Square, farther to the W., is the large brick Convent of *Notre Dame*, and near by are the *Normal School* and *Prince of Wales College*. In the same quarter of the city is the parade-ground, between Sidney and Pownal Sts., presided over by the barracks and drill-shed. Still far-ther W., on a projecting point of land, occupied also by the charming bit of woodland called the Park, the cricket and foot-ball field, and the delightful lawn-tennis grounds, stands the *Government House*, with a lovely outlook over the blue and quiet waters of the harbor. Here one realizes that contented note of the Charlottetown landscape which led the discoverers of the haven to call it " Port la Joie." There is capital lawn-tennis and foot-ball playing in Charlottetown, where was held the first tournament of the Maritime Provinces Lawn-Tennis Association. Whether the city be found a pleasant summer resort or not depends chiefly on the visitors themselves. Charlottetown society is found ex-ceedingly charming and hospitable by those who go there duly accred-ited. To the absolute stranger its attractions are not great, for there is no very remarkable scenery, and, away from the chief square, the wide streets look all alike, and all equally uninteresting. One's im-pressions of the city may be marvelously changed by one or two letters of introduction. Outside of the city, and overlooking it, in a region of pleasant villas, stand the Wesleyan College and the Roman Catholic College of St. Dunstan. By ferry one may visit the pleasant village of Southport, on the opposite shore of the Hillsborough River, in the neighborhood of which is the alleged height called Tea Hill, with a sweet pastoral view from its low-summit. The principal summer resort is at *Grand Tracadie Beach*, 13 miles distant, where the *Hotel Acadie* is open during the season.

Old Fireplace at Entry Island.

From Charlottetown eastward.

From Royalty Junction, 5 miles out of Charlottetown, the traveler who wishes to do the island thoroughly may take the train eastward. Passing the little stations of Union, York, Suffolk, Bedford, and Tracadie, along the fertile valley of the Hillsborough River, we come to *Mt. Stewart Junction*, 22 miles from the city. At this point a branch diverges southeastward, 24 miles to Georgetown, on the east coast; while the main line continues along the north shore to Souris, which is also on the east coast some 20 miles north of Georgetown. From Mt. Stewart Junction, a thriving village devoted to ship-building, we traverse a rather thinly-settled country, passing the stations of Pisquid, Peake's, Baldwin, and Perth, till we come to the village of Cardigan, on the head of Cardigan Bay, whence the high-road leads to Vernon River and Fownal. It may be said here, in parentheses, that the pleasantest way to get to Mt. Stewart Junction is by the little steamer *Heather Bell* from Charlottetown. Cardigan is 18 miles from the junction; and 6 miles farther, running down the long promontory between Cardigan Bay and Georgetown Harbor, we come to *Georgetown*, a prosperous village of 1,118 inhabitants, with a large shipping trade in agricultural produce. The harbor is the best winter port on the island, and least liable to obstruction by the ice. Steamers from Pictou for the Magdalen Islands call here on their way. The town is well laid out, and is the county seat of King's County, the most easterly of the three counties into which this little province is divided. At the head of the harbor flows in the Brudenelle River. The chief inn of Georgetown is the *Commercial Hotel*.

The more northern line to Souris reaches Morell Station 9 miles east of Mt. Stewart. This is a fishing village on the little Morell River. Thence the railway skirts *St. Peter's Bay* for 7¼ miles to the village of St. Peter's, the chief fishing town on the north shore. The bay is famous for its valuable salmon-fisheries, and has been already referred to as the best place on the island for sea-trout. Tourists in search of this sport may stay at the little inn called the *Prairie Hotel*, or they may obtain board at private houses. The bay is a fine sheet of water, more than 7 miles in length, but its usefulness as a harbor is somewhat impaired by the fact that there is less than 6 ft. of water on the bar that crosses its mouth. Leaving St. Peter's we pass the stations of Ashton, Selkirk, Bear River, New Zealand, and Harmony, whence roads lead inland southwestward to the Gaelic settlements of Annandale, Douglas, and Bridgetown, on Grand River, where one may study some quaint old customs and a life that preserves its individuality with great persistence. *Souris* itself, 8 miles beyond Harmony, is a Gaelic village of 700 inhabitants, devoted to fishing and ship-building. Its harbor, Colville Bay, is protected by a breakwater. The village carries on an extensive trade with the French island of *St. Pierre*, off the coast of Newfoundland. Not far from Souris lie the shallow coast pools of East and North Lakes; and beyond, the island runs off to a beacon-guarded termination at East Point.

At Souris or Georgetown one may take the steamer *St. Olaf* for the **Magdalen Islands,** if the attractions of remoteness and sea-trout fishing prevail. The St. Olaf leaves *Picton*, N. S., every Monday on the arrival of the Halifax express, and calls at Georgetown and Souris. The fare from Georgetown is $4. The Magdalen Islands are a group of thirteen, most of them connected by sand-spits bare at low tide. They lie in the Gulf of St. Lawrence, between Prince Edward Island and the west coast of Newfoundland, about 50 miles from East Point, already mentioned. The chief island is called *Amherst*, and this island, with Alright, Grindstone, and Entry Islands, partially incloses a roadstead in which the fleets of the gulf, caught in this neighborhood in a gale, take refuge. The islands, however, have no harbors proper that are safely accessible in a storm, and they are a good place to keep away from in bad weather. Their shores are lined with wrecks. In the dreadful "Lord's Day Gale," celebrated in Stedman's noble ballad, the loss of life about the Magdalens was appalling. Out to sea, off the west of Amherst, lies the dread rock of Deadman's Isle, mentioned in Tom Moore's lines:

> "To Deadman's Isle in the eye of the blast,
> To Deadman's Isle she speeds her fast ;
> By skeleton shapes her sails are furled,
> And the hand that steers is not of this world."

Off to the north lie the most outlying members of the group, Bryon Island, rivaling Percé Rock as a nesting-place for sea-birds, and the two desolate Bird Rocks. On one of these, which carries a powerful light, placed there with great expense and peril by the Canadian Government, a landing is effected only by means of a great swinging crane projecting from the cliff, on which visitors are hoisted in a cradle. One of the most important and central islands of the group is called Coffin

Island—not from its shape or any sinister association, but in honor of Admiral Sir Isaac Coffin, to whom, in 1798, the islands were granted in fee simple, and whose heir, Admiral Coffin, now holds them. The population of the islands is now a little over 3,000, mostly Acadian French, and all are tenants of Admiral Coffin, who exacts the heavy rent of one shilling per acre, payable at the convenience of the occupant. The islands lie within the province of Quebec. A perfect view of them may be had from the summit of Entry Island, 580 ft. above the sea.

The Magdalens are visited by few tourists, and those few have to put up with somewhat primitive though always hospitable entertainment. Among the islands one may enjoy the finest of sea-trout fishing; and in the small brooks, which constitute the islanders' rivers, one may catch magnificent trout, that look strangely out of proportion to the waters they frequent. During the cod and mackerel seasons the island waters are thronged with American and Canadian fishing-fleets, and patrolled by the Dominion cutter La Canadienne to prevent foreign boats from fishing within the three-mile limits. In winter the occupation of the inhabitants is seal-fishing, a perilous business, in which some lives are lost every season. The seals are swept upon the shores on fields of ice drifting down from the N.; and sometimes the ice-fields drift away again, when the wind changes, carrying with them some of the too-venturous hunters.

The Magdalens have, perhaps, the best lobster-grounds on the continent, and the canning establishments there do an immense business. The chief village is on *Amherst Island,* fronting on Pleasant Bay, and contains the unimposing public buildings. Overlooking the settlement is a conical height called " La Demoiselle," from whose peak one sees a broad and varied panorama. The prominent landmarks of the group, besides this hill and the islands already described, are the striking eminences of *Cap de Meule, Le Vieux,* and *La Vieille.* The sand-beaches connecting the islands are at times very dangerous from shifting quicksands. In places the sand is covered with water to a depth of several feet, and the fordable spots are marked out by scant rows of saplings stuck insecurely into the bottom. The communication between the islands by these beaches is perilous and often impossible when the wind is strong. The group is connected with the outer world by a submarine cable running to Prince Edward Island; but this institution does not seem to meet with much patronage, and Mr. S. G. W. Benjamin, in an entertaining paper on the Magdalens, in the Century Magazine for May, 1884, tells that at the time of his visit the operator was away enjoying an extended vacation on the mainland while the cable rested unused. (Mr. Benjamin's book, "The Cruise of the Alice May," which describes a voyage around the coast of the Maritime Provinces and the outlying islands, is published by D. Appleton & Co.) On the Magdalens is situated a large nunnery, whose occupants doubtless find there the ideal of cloistral seclusion.

NOVA SCOTIA.

The province of **Nova Scotia** consists of the storied peninsula of *Old Acadie* and the *Island of Cape Breton*. It is the most easterly province of the Dominion, and is connected with New Brunswick by the *Isthmus of Chignecto*, already described. Its length is 300 miles, its extreme breadth 100, and its coast-line is deeply indented by bays and roomy harbors. Its rivers, of which the more important are the *Liverpool, La Have, Shubenacadie, Avon,* and *Annapolis,* are not of great length, but are important on account of their large estuaries. The surface of the province is diversified by long, parallel ranges of hills and valleys running E. and W. No other part of Canada can surpass this province in the variety and abundance of its natural resources. In regard to soil and climate its agricultural districts are not excelled by the most favored portions of Ontario. It has immense lumbering, fishing, and ship-building interests. Its coal, gold, iron, and plaster mines are famous the world over. Other mineral products of Nova Scotia are silver, tin, zinc, copper, manganese, graphite, granite, marble, limestone, grindstones; and the province also produces good specimens of garnet, amethyst, topaz, opal, cairngorm, agate, heliotrope, jasper, and chalcedony. The forests are still fairly stocked with large and small game; and the province contains many excellent trout and salmon waters, though in this respect it hardly competes with New Brunswick. The population of Nova Scotia in 1891 was 450,396.

In historic associations Nova Scotia is not less richly furnished than Quebec. It was visited by the Norsemen in the eleventh century, and rediscovered by Sebastian Cabot in 1498. Attempts were made to colonize the country by France in 1518; and by Portugal between 1520 and 1530, when a royal commission was given to Joan Alvarez

The Mail-boat at Prince Edward Island.

Fagundez, and two ships sailed to Cape Breton with colonists. The earliest approximately correct map of Nova Scotia is that of a Portuguese, Diego Homem, and bears date of 1558. The Portuguese were not very successful in their colonizing efforts, but they did succeed in colonizing with cattle and swine the dreadful sand-bank of Sable Island, off the S. E. coast of Nova Scotia—a deed for which in later years many a shipwrecked seaman has had cause to remember them with gratitude. In such names as Blomidon, Minas, Bay of Fundy (Baya Fondo), and others, the Portuguese have left on these coasts the memory of their explorations. The name of Acadie itself is a Micmac word, meaning "a region of plenty"—and is the same as the Melicite word "Quoddy." Shubenacadie means "a place of plenty of ground-nuts," just as Passamaquoddy means a place of plenty of haddock. The influence of the French soon became dominant in these regions, and they adopted the Micmac name, which was anglicized by the English claimants into Acadia. The first successful settlement in Acadie was that planted in 1605 at Port Royal, by Champlain, after his winter of horrors at the St. Croix mouth. Unique and interesting, though a most disastrous failure, was the colonizing enterprise of Marquis de la Roche in 1598. Of this attempt the theatre was Sable Island, which, as it is more interesting to read about than to visit, may be referred to here. As its name implies, this island is a bank of sand, a deposit of the drift of meeting currents. It lies 90 miles S. E. of Nova Scotia, and is the center of fogs and fiercest storms. Its shape is roughly that of a crescent, 22 miles long by 2 wide, and a shallow pool divides it from end to end. Its position is shifting gradually eastward, and the dreadful wrecks of which it is from time to time the scene have won it the name of the "Charnel-house of North America." De la Roche, being made Viceroy of Canada and Acadie, set sail for his new dominions with a ship-load of convicts for colonists. Approaching the Acadian coasts he conceived, in his prudence, the design of landing his dangerous charge upon the Isle of Sable, till he might go and prepare for them, on the mainland, a place of safety. The 40 convicts, selected from the chief prisons of France, were landed through the uproar of the surf, and the ship made haste away from the perilous shore. But she came not back again! De la Roche reached Acadie, chose a site for his settlement, and set out for the island to fetch his expectant colonists. But a great gale swept him back to France and drove him upon the Breton coast, where the Duke de Mercœur, at that time warring against the king, seized him, cast him into prison, and held him close for five years. Meanwhile those left on the island were delighted enough. They were free, and began to forget the scourge and chain. Beside the unstable hummocks and hills of sand they found a shallow lake of sweet waters, the shores of which were clothed luxuriantly with long grass, and lentils, and vines of vetch. Lurking in any or every portion of the grass-plain were little cup-like hollows, generally filled with clear water. Every such pool, like the lake, was alive with ducks and other water-fowl, among which the joyous ex-convicts created consternation. There were wild cattle also, trooping and lowing among the sand-hills or feeding belly-deep in the rank water-grasses; while herds of wild hogs, introduced years before by the Portuguese, disputed the shallow pools with the mallard and teal. The weather for a while kept fine, and the winds comparatively temperate, and the sojourners held a carnival of liberty and indolence., But this was not for long, and as the skies grew harsher their plight grew harder. As the weeks slipped into months they grew first impatient, then solicitous, then despairing. Their provisions fell low, and at last the truth was staring them in the face—they were deserted. From the wrecks upon the shore they built themselves at first a rude shelter, which the increasing cold and storms soon drove them to perfect with their most cunning skill. As their stores diminished, they looked on greedily and glared at each other with jealous eyes. Soon quarrels broke out with but little provocation, and were settled by the knife with such fatal frequency that the members of the colony shrank apace. As they had been provided with no means of lighting fires, they soon had to live on the raw flesh of the wild cattle, and little by little they learned the lesson, and began to relish such fare. Little by little, too, as their garments fell to pieces, they replaced them with skins of the seals that swarmed about the beach; and their hut they lined with hides from the cattle they had slaughtered. As the months became years their deadly contests ceased, but exposure, and frost, and hunger, and disease kept thinning their ranks. They occupied themselves in pursuing the seal for its skin, the walrus for its ivory. They had gathered a great store of sealskins, ivory, and hides, but now only twelve men remained to possess these riches. Their beards had grown to their waists, their skins were like the furs that covered them, their nails were like birds' claws, their eyes gleamed with a sort of shy ferocity through the long, matted tangle of their hair. At last, from .

out of his prison, De la Roche got word to the king, telling him of their miserable fortune, and a ship was at once sent out to rescue them.

In 1621 the territory of Acadia, then named by the English Nova Scotia, was granted to Sir William Alexander; and a year or two later was created the order of " Knights Baronets of Nova Scotia," each of whom received a grant of 18 square miles of territory.

In 1632 Nova Scotia was relinquished to France and fell a prey to the struggles between La Tour and Charnisay, already referred to. In 1654 it was again captured by England, but soon reverted to France. In 1690 it was captured and overrun by New-Englanders, after having been raised into a populous colony by the forty years' rule of the Company of New France. In 1697 it was again restored to the French. Massachusetts sent out unsuccessful expeditions against the Acadian strongholds in 1703 and 1707, and succeeded in her design at last in 1710; and by the Treaty of Utrecht, in 1713, the country was finally ceded to England. These struggles and interchanges went on with the accompaniment of innumerable romantic and heroic episodes, which make the annals of Nova Scotia an especially interesting field of study. In 1749 was founded the city of Halifax. The forty years intervening between the Treaty of Utrecht and the expulsion of the Acadians, in 1755, were marked by internal disorders, conflict, and bloodshed, the result of the Acadian and Indian hostility to English rule.

The tragedy of 1755 will be referred to more fully in connection with the description of Grand Pré. In 1783 the population of the province was increased by the immigration of 20,000 United Empire Loyalists; and in the following year two new provinces were erected out of portions of Nova Scotia territory—one of them, New Brunswick, permanently, and the other Cape Breton, as it proved, but temporarily. During the War of 1812 Nova Scotia suffered from the depredations of American privateers. In 1867 the province joined with Quebec, Ontario, and New Brunswick to form the confederation known as the Dominion of Canada.

To Pictou and Antigonish.

From Charlottetown to **Pictou** by boat is a thoroughly delightful sail of about 50 miles. The fare is $2. As we approach Pictou Harbor we pass the farms, lighthouse, and wooded hills of Pictou Island, and more remote the group of isles and sand-beaches known as Caribou Island. Sailing up the harbor we get a thoroughly satisfactory view of this noble water, whose high and varied shores, well populated in almost every direction, give it the charm of picturesqueness, and whose safe and commodious anchorage constitutes it the best haven on the north coast of Nova Scotia. The town of Pictou is handsomely situated on a hill-side overlooking the harbor. Its site was of old occupied by a town of the Micmacs, who called the place "Pik-took," from the gases escaping from the coal-beds underlying the harbor. The neighborhood is rich in legends of Gluskâp, the Micmac demigod, who halted here on his journey to Newfoundland to punish the wizards of that island who had slain his servants. Here, too, took place some sanguinary battles between the Micmacs and the Mohawks, and to this day the name of the latter is a terror to the Indians of Pictou. The first settlement at this point was begun in 1767 by a small party of Philadelphians. It is said that Franklin was interested in the enterprise; which, however, made but sorry progress till the arrival of a body of Scotch Highlanders in 1773. The ultimate success of these immigrants attracted many more of the same race; and these colonists, being intensely loyal, gradually crowded out the first settlers, whose sympathies were with the Thirteen Colonies during the American War of Independence. The town was founded in 1788; and between 1805 and 1820, when the Baltic ports were closed against Great Britain, Pictou made great progress as a lumbering and ship-building port. Thereafter the development of the coal industry, of which Pictou County is one of the chief centers on the continent, continued the era of prosperity. At present, though Pictou has considerable wealth, and some mills and factories to depend upon besides her shipping interests, the town is not making much progress, and stands at a population of between 3,000 and 4,000, much of her business being appropriated by her bustling young rival, New Glasgow. Pictou has some fine public buildings, prominent among which is that of the *Pictou Academy*, containing a fine library and museum. This institution has played a most important part in the education of the province, and counts among its graduates some of the most distinguished of Canadians—among them President Sir William Dawson, of McGill University, and Principal Grant, of Queen's University. The Young Men's Christian Association Building attracts attention, and the spiritual needs of the towns-folk are supplied by a round half-dozen churches. Around the shore of the harbor, opposite Pictou, are the huge, black wharves of the various coal-mining companies. About the same point the harbor branches into three arms, the estuaries of East, West, and Middle Rivers. The town is a pleasant place to visit in the summer, having excellent boating and sea-bathing, lawn-tennis, some pleasant society, and one comfortable hotel, the *Revere House.*

From Pictou the railway runs around the north of the harbor 14 miles to *Stellarton*, where it connects with the Halifax to Sydney Line of the Intercolonial R. R. Stellarton is a thriving but dingy town of 2,500 inhabitants, and has grown up about the famous *Albion Coal and Iron Mines.* No one stops at Stellarton if he can help it; for 2 miles eastward by rail is the energetic and growing town of *New Glasgow*, with a population of between 4,000 and 5,000, and three fairly comfortable hotels styled the *Windsor*, the *Norfolk*, and the *Vendôme.* New Glasgow is a great ship-building and coal-mining center, and is rapidly developing a large manufacturing interest. It has tanneries and foundries, and has lately started, under most favorable auspices, extensive steel and glass works. Good public buildings are rapidly going up, and everything points to a most prosperous future for the town. A coal railway runs down the south of the harbor to the coal wharves and ferry opposite Pictou. At the lower end of the town a draw-bridge crosses the East River, here a narrow stream, which the citizens of New Glasgow propose to make the Clyde of Canada. Up its northern shore runs for a short distance, to the Albion Mines, a quaint railway, the oldest in America. The massive old rust-eaten rails are of a very curious pattern; but such is the excellence of their construction that they still do their work.

The eastern extension of the I. C. R., running to Mulgrave on the Strait of Canso, has been still farther extended to run through Cape Breton. Between New Glasgow, which we leave at about noon, and *Antigonish*, a distance of 41 miles, we get some occasional bits of good scenery; but the nine intervening stations are of little interest. A prosperous ship-building village is Merigomish, 14 miles from New Glasgow, with valuable coal and iron mines, and a fine harbor. Another of these stations is somewhat interesting, on account of its quaint name of Marshy Hope. As we near Antigonish, descending through the passes of the surrounding hills, the scene changes. Antigonish is a beautiful, clean, little pastoral town, set in a broad green amphitheatre, whose meadow floor is watered by a pleasant river. Its beauty of surroundings is of the restful, quiet kind, but undeniably worthy of praise. There are pretty drives among the hills, the summer climate is not to be surpassed, and though there are no very exciting diversions, the town must be set down as a really delightful retreat for the summer traveler who desires nothing but unrestricted lotus-eating. The village inns are comfortable, home-like country boarding-houses, rather than hotels; and there is pleasant society to be met in this remote corner of the province.

Antigonish is the shire town of Antigonish County. It stands at the head of a wide, shallow harbor opening into St. George's Bay. It has a population of a little less than 2,000, and carries on an extensive trade in agricultural produce with Newfoundland. It also ships quantities of gypsum. The country is settled by a thrifty farming population of Celtic Highlanders. Antigonish is the seat of a Roman Catholic bishopric, of the fine new *Cathedral of St. Ninian* (a striking structure of blue limestone dressed with brick, consecrated in 1874, and carrying on the façade the inscription " Tighe Dhe," which is Gaelic for " The House of God "). The sermons in the cathedral are frequently preached in Gaelic. Near the cathedral is the imposing pile of *St. Francis Xavier College*, a prosperous Roman Catholic institution under the presidency of Dr. McNeill. Close by is the building occupied by the Girls' School, which is managed by nuns of a Montreal Sisterhood. Quiet as the village is, it practically monopolizes the whole supply trade of the country, and hence supports some large shops which would do credit to places with thrice the population. In the country about Antigonish, accessible by stage or carriage, the most interesting points to visit are the Antigonish Mountains, thrusting their lofty line 15 miles out into the gulf; Cape St. George; and the romantic village of Celtic Highlanders known as Arisaig, behind whose long wooden pier vessels seek shelter in some winds, there being no harbor on this coast between Antigonish and Merigomish.

Leaving Antigonish we pass the stations of South River, Taylor's Road, Pomquet, and come to the prosperous settlement of Heatherton, whence a stage line runs 20 miles to Guysboro. The third station beyond Heatherton is yet another *Tracadie*, a very interesting Acadian settlement 20 miles from Antigonish. Here is situated a monastery of Trappist monks, and also a convent occupied by Sisters of Charity. The third station beyond Tracadie is Harbor au Bouche, another Acadian settlement, and 10 miles beyond, 80 miles from New Glasgow, the train stops at Mulgrave on the Strait of Canso. On the other side lies the wild and lovely land of Cape Breton.

Cape Breton.

The island of **Cape Breton** forms a portion of the province of Nova Scotia. Its extreme length is about 100 miles, its width 85 miles, and its population in 1891 was 84,854. It is marvelous for the diversity of its scenery, being a very chaos of mountains, lakes, streams, and deep bays, and a sportsman's paradise. The island is all but split in two from end to end by the strange lake-like inlet of the *Bras d'Or ;* and the division is completed by a ship-canal half a mile long connecting the inner extremity of the Bras d'Or with St. Peter's Bay on the W. coast. The two divisions of the island thus formed are extremely dissimilar, the southern portion being low and much broken by the sea, and the northern portion very mountainous and bold. The valleys and plains are fertile, the coast waters rich in fish, the forests support a large ship-building industry, and, most important of all, the coal-mines are among the very best in the world. Besides its vast coal deposits, Cape Breton produces marble, granite, limestone, slate, gypsum, iron, and salt. Its position makes it the key to the Gulf of St. Lawrence, a consideration which led France to cling tenaciously to its possession when yielding up the Acadian Peninsula. Its delicious and invigorating summer climate, added to its other attractions, make it one of the pleasantest places in Canada for summer wanderings.

The island takes its name from a cape on its east coast, which was called in honor of its Breton discoverers. It was renamed Isle Royale by the French in 1713, and on the cession of Nova Scotia to England its population was swelled by the influx of Acadians who refused to live under English rule. In 1714 was built the strong fortress of Louisburg; and for the next fifty years the story of the island is one of perpetual hostilities between the English on one hand and the French with their Indian allies on the other, culminating in the second and final capture of Louisburg and the utter destruction of the fortress in July, 1758. In 1765 Cape Breton was annexed to Nova Scotia. It was made a separate province in 1784, but was reannexed in 1820. Its population is almost entirely Celtic, being made up of Scotch Highlanders and Acadian French.

Cape Breton may be visited by boat up the *Bras d'Or Lakes*, by the railway, or by boat from Halifax. Mulgrave, already referred to, is a fishing village of about 500 inhabitants, in the mountainous, gold-producing county of Guysboro. It has a harbor open the year round, and is connected with Hawkesbury by a steam-ferry. The latter is a growing village of perhaps 1,100 inhabitants, and good prospects for more. The steamships plying between *Boston* and *Charlottetown* call at Hawkesbury.

Through the Bras d'Or Waters to Sydney.

From the noble passage called the gut or *Strait of Canso* we may go by boat or stage through Cape Breton. The railway from Point Tupper, opposite Mulgrave, to *Sydney* and **Louisburg** has just been opened. It has a length of 91 miles, through much noble scenery, and over one trestle, that crossing McDonald's Gulch, which has the distinction of being the second longest in Canada. But the traveler, if traveling for pleasure, will probably prefer the absolutely unique sea-voyage through the windless waters of the **Bras d'Or.**

The daily steamers from Port Mulgrave touch at *Grandigue*, where passengers for *Arichat* disembark; also at *St. Peter's*, *Grand Narrows*, and **Baddeck.** The fare to Baddeck is $2; return, $3.50. The fare to **Sydney** is $3; return, $5. From Mulgrave the course is eastward through the Strait to *Isle Madame*, an island some 16 miles long by 5 miles in width, peopled by Acadians. The steamer traverses the picturesque strait called *Lennox Passage*, which separates Isle Madame from the main island. *Arichat*, the chief village on Isle Madame, lies on the seaward side, and is an important fishing station, with a population of between 1,100 and 1,200. The town is the county-seat of Richmond County, and does a large business for a place of its size. It is also to some extent an educational center, having successful academies for boys and girls. There are other busy little villages on Isle Madame.

Leaving Lennox Passage we run up *St. Peter's Bay*, whose head is separated from *St. Peter's Inlet*, on the *Bras d'Or* waters, by a narrow isthmus with the once appropriate name of "*The Haulover.*" Through this isthmus has lately been cut a canal of about half a mile in length, which has made the Bras d'Or route by far the most desirable for Cape Breton travelers. The village of *St. Peter's*, with its population of about 1,100, mostly Scotch, was founded as long ago as 1636 by the illustrious Frenchman M. Denys. Throughout all its early history it was a place of importance, and well fortified. Through the eighteenth century it went by the name of Port Toulouse, and was a center of the

On the Road to Baddeck.

fur-trade. Off the mouth of St. Peter's Inlet is a group of islands occupied by the Micmac Indians. On the largest of these islands is held a grand Indian festival every Ste. Anne's Day, at which many curious ceremonies are observed. The celebrations are well worth a visit.

Leaving St. Peter's Inlet we are on the **Great Bras d'Or Lake**, which Mr. Warner calls "the most beautiful salt-water lake I have ever seen, and more beautiful than we had imagined a salt-water lake could be." Its shores are bold enough to be striking, rounded enough to be winsome, and diversified by every form of headland, estuary, glade, and forest. The woods are of an infinite variety, making a delicious harmony of colors. The coast-line is of marvelous extent, so many and so deep are the branches of the lake, diverging in every direction between the ranges of the hills. Among the chief of these estuaries and inlets are *River Denys*, East Bay or *St. Andrew's Channel*, and West Bay or *St. George's Channel*. Near the head of East Bay is the picturesque Indian village of *Escasoni*, and everywhere lie snugly nestling hamlets of Scotch Highlanders.

From the *Great Bras d'Or* the steamer enters a beautiful channel, 2 miles long by about a mile in width, called the Strait of Barra or the *Grand Narrows*, and calls at a settlement of the latter name. The district is peopled by immigrants from Barra in the Hebrides. Passing through the strait we enter the *Little Bras d'Or Lake*, whose charm of landscape and climate compels the acknowledgment of the most discontented of globe-trotters. Around the lake crowd innumerable sheltering hills, most of them named with a fine freshness and disregard of the exigencies of pronunciation. To the westward of the lake, for instance, lie the heights of *Watchabaktchkt!* The next stoppage is at the village on which Mr. Warner has conferred a certain kind of immortality. Every traveler who goes to Cape Breton, it is to be presumed, carries a copy of "Baddeck, and that Sort of Thing," which, if not always quite just in the impressions it conveys, is always good company.

Baddeck.

Baddeck is growing year by year more popular, more sophisticated, more expensive, and better equipped in the matter of hotel and boarding-house accommodations. It lies 40 miles from Sydney, and has a population, including the farm-houses that gather about it, of some 1,900 souls. The original spelling of the name was Bedeque. The village is of some importance, both as a shipping port

14

and as the shire town of Victoria County. It is a thoroughly delightful watering-place, a very idyll of peace and beauty and sparkling atmosphere, removed from all the bustle of modern affairs, yet within easy reach of the pleasant society of Sydney. In the neighborhood is *Middle River*, its valley peopled with Gaelic-speaking Highlanders, and its innumerable tumbling tributaries fairly alive with trout. The early summer is best for the trout-fishing, when the sea-trout are running in and stocking brooks that seem by far too small for them. A drive of about 30 miles by a lovely road will take one to the renowned fishing-waters of the *Margaree River*, where the trout and salmon swarm. There is good fishing also some distance up the *Big Baddeck River*, which flows through some of the richest hunting-grounds of Cape Breton. A point of some interest to the tourist not already satiated with Indians is the *Micmac Village* near Baddeck. These red men are in some respects fairly advanced in civilization, and their language, which has been minutely studied and systematized by the life-long labors of the late Dr. Silas T. Rand, author of a Micmac Dictionary, has a rich vocabulary and no lack of flexibility and force. No one who reads the Micmac legends gathered by Mr. Leland will doubt the imaginative vigor of the tribe. The chief hotels of Baddeck are the *Telegraph House* and *Bras d'Or Hotel*. Gold is found in the neighborhood of Baddeck. A magnificent drive is from Baddeck to *Whycocomagh*, on a branch of the Bras d'Or, through the noblest of scenery all the way. A divergence of 4 or 5 miles from the main road takes one to the great water of *Lake Ainslie*, the source of the Margaree. In this region are deposits of petroleum, marble, and iron, and there is an interesting cave near the village. Whycocomagh may also be reached by steamer through the splendid strait of *St. Patrick's Channel*. The population of the district, of which the village is the center, is about 2,500. Eighteen miles beyond Whycocomagh is *Mabou*, on the gulf coast, an important seaport, with rich coal-fields in the vicinity. Ten miles southwest of Mabou is *Port Hood*, with 1,300 inhabitants, the busiest port on the northwest coast of the island.

From Baddeck to the mouth of *Sydney Harbor* the route varies. Sometimes the boats, or at least the smaller boats, take the channel called the *Little Bras d'Or*, but ordinarily that of the *Great Bras d'Or*. These channels lead to the open Atlantic, about 8 miles from Sydney Harbor. They are divided by *Boularderie Island*, which is about 35 miles in length by 8 miles in extreme width, and owes its existence as an island to these strange and beautiful channels.   The Little Bras d'Or is a deep and tide-swept passage, so narrow and intricate as to be impassable for craft of any size.   In a small steamer the journey is very romantic and impressive, and one feels himself, at times, imprisoned hopelessly in the rocky clefts.   The Great Bras d'Or, forming the northwest boundary of Boularderie, is a noble passage, ranging in width from 1 to 3 miles, and extending about 30 miles.   It has great depth, and the scenery of its shores, overpeered by the *Mountains of St. Anne*, is bold and impressive.   From this channel the steamer sails out between the surf-beaten headland of *Cape Dauphin* and the promontory of *Point Aconi*, with its coal-fields.   From Point Aconi the course is S. E. for 9 miles to *Cranberry Head*, rounding which we find ourselves in *Sydney Harbor.*   ·

Running up the harbor we see in the distance the works of the **Sydney Mines**—indeed, the whole neighborhood is studded with coal-mines, and at any time we may be passing over the deep submarine galleries in which the picks of the miners are at work with the sea-waves rolling fathoms deep between them and the upper air.   The coal of this district is among the best the world produces; and among the many mines engaged in bringing it to light are, besides the Sydney mines already named, the *Victoria*, the *Lingan*, the *International*, the *Gowrie*, and the *Little Glace Bay*.   These are all easily accessible by stage from the town of Sydney, and some of them have rail communication, for freighting purposes, which will furnish an informal means of transit.

Sydney.

Sydney, which held the proud position of provincial capital when Cape Breton was a province, boasts one of the best harbors on all this well-havened coast.   Her population by the last census (1891) was 3,667; and her trade, not only in coal, but in general produce as well, is of great and growing volume.   The one flaw in Sydney's harbor is the fact that it is ice-bound for the greater part of the winter.   In summer, however, it is full of life and activity; and being the headquarters of the French squadron in the North Atlantic, it becomes the scene of a delightful social activity.   The harbor is divided by a peninsula into two arms, and on the southwesterly arm is Sydney.   At the extremity of the peninsula are the ruins of the fortifications and barracks, occupied by a British garrison up to the time of the Crimean War.   The harbor was originally called Spaniards' Bay, having been the rendezvous for the Spanish fishing-fleets; and afterward it was used by the English as a center from which to carry on the struggle for the island. Now that England has made good and enduring her triumph, France retains but a pier and flag-staff at the town of Sydney, representing her coaling privileges. The presence of the French ships and the French officers, with their continual and graceful hospitalities, is regarded now with anything but hostility by the citizens of Sydney. In the matter of hotels Sydney is rather comfortable than modern. But a summer hotel has been erected. The chief are the *Sydney*, *McKenzie's*, the *McClellan*, and *Cabot*. It is generally easy to get board in semi-private houses, at from $4 to $6 a week.

Eight miles from Sydney, and reached by a steam-ferry, is the town of **North Sydney**, the business center of the Sydney coal-mines. North Sydney has more stir but much less charm than its rival, and is not likely to attract the tourist to any prolonged sojourn. It is pervaded with coal-dust and activity, and is a good place to make the money that may be more agreeably spent elsewhere—at Sydney, for instance. Its population is from 5,000 to 6,000, and it has several tanneries, a boot and shoe factory, and extensive ship-yards. The chief hotel is the *Belmont Hotel*.

The harbor of Sydney, though utterly overshadowed, historically, by Louisburg, has seen some stirring episodes. Here gathered the remnants of Admiral Sir Hovenden Walker's fleet after its wreck off the St. Lawrence mouth in 1711—a powerful remnant, indeed, seeing that it consisted of 42 ships of war. In 1781 took place, off the harbor, a gallant battle between two 44-gun French frigates and four light-armed British vessels, which were convoying a fleet of coal-ships. The result was a somewhat unfruitful victory for the French, as the defeated English vessels made their escape under cover of night, with the exception of a little ship of 6 guns which remained in the victors' hands. In 1785 the site of Sydney was occupied by a party of United Empire Loyalists, under the leadership of Abraham Cuyler, former Mayor of Albany, New York.

Louisburg.

Twenty-four miles from Sydney, by the Sydney and Louisburg Railroad, lies the storied site of **Louisburg**, now but a little fishing village, whose inhabitants follow their calling on the Grand Banks of Newfoundland. Its population is about 1,000. The modern village lies some little distance from the ruins of the walled city which it was once the fashion to call the " Dunkirk of America." It is used in summer as a coaling-station. The harbor is spacious, perfectly sheltered, and with a good depth of water everywhere; but its supremacy has fled to Sydney, and is not likely to return, unless a certain " ocean-ferry " scheme, one of several such, should some day come into effect. This rather hypothetical proposition contemplates a fast train-service between Louisbourg and such centers as Montreal, Boston, and New York, connecting with swift ocean-steamers for the transatlantic voyage. It would greatly shorten the trials of those whose dreaded enemy is the *mal-de-mer*.

The special interest of Louisburg lies in its history, which has been so inimitably told by Parkman that every tourist visiting the spot should take with him the volumes entitled "Montcalm and Wolfe." The scenery at Louisburg is not bold or striking. The hills surrounding the harbor are rather low, and without impressive features; but the land lies in a shape very favorable to defensive fortification. The harbor entrance is narrowed by islands and reefs to a width of about half a mile, and was protected by mighty batteries; behind which, at the southwest point of the harbor, rose the city walls. The opposite side of the harbor-mouth is a promontory called *Lighthouse Point*, which proved itself the key to the situation, and dominated the main defense, that known as the *Island Battery*. Louisburg arose after the Treaty of Utrecht, and in its building no treasure was spared. The best engineering skill of the time was expended upon it, and when completed the French engineers made the boast that it could be effectively defended by a garrison of women. The landward side was not defended with the same degree of care, as only a sea attack was considered practicable. The wild surf of *Gabarus Bay*, and the bogs intervening between that water and the city, were regarded as a sufficient defense against the approach of heavy artillery, and against light guns the walls were adequate.

As soon as war was declared between France and England, in 1744, Massachusetts turned her attention to Louisburg, as a deadly menace to her safety. In 1745 she decided to undertake its capture. The expedition she sent out was commanded by Colonel William Pepperell, who was supported by Commodore Warren and the West India squadron of the British fleet. The New England forces, raw troops, commanded by untrained officers, astonished the world by capturing the supposed impregnable fortress. Though the British fleet lent valuable aid and support, the main credit for the splendid achievement is indisputably due to the New England militia and to their sagacious and capable commander. When Pepperell found himself within the walls, and saw the tremendous casemates and bastions and bomb-proofs which his guns had shattered, and realized from the shot-torn walls of the citadel, the convent, the hospital, and the stately cathedral, the wealth and importance of the situation, he was overwhelmed with a sense of the magnitude of his accomplished task. This feat of the New-Englanders settled the contest in Europe. With the Peace of 1749 Louisburg was restored to France in return for concessions nearer home; and all that seemed to remain to New England for her enterprise was the title conferred on Pepperell. But in truth the country had manifested her power, not only to herself but to the world.

In 1755, when war again broke out between France and England, the English attempted to surprise Louisburg; but France had not forgotten her lesson, and was found alert. In the spring of 1758 England gathered her forces for an effort that should be final; and early in June Wolfe appeared before Louisburg, support by a vast fleet. This trained commander followed almost minutely in the footsteps of Pepperell, rightly appreciating the old New-Englander's insight. Louisburg had been immensely strengthened for just such an emergency, but the result was the same as before, and upon the destruction of the harbor defenses, and of almost all the French fleet at refuge in the harbor, the city surrendered, giving up a force of nearly 6,000 men and 230 guns. After the capture, England spent months in the effort to thoroughly erase the fortifications. Of the proud city itself there is left not one stone upon another, but the mighty lines of the earthworks yet remain, with the grand slope of the glacis, and the enduring arches of the casemates and magazines. The scene recalls with an almost poignant appropriateness the lines of Browning:

> Where the quiet colored end of evening smiles,
>   Miles and miles,
> On the solitary pastures where our sheep,
>   Half asleep,
> Tinkle homeward through the twilight, stray or stop,
>   As they crop,
> Was the site once of a city great and gay,
>   So they say,
> Of our country's very capital; its prince
>   Ages since,
> Held his court in, gathered councils, wielding far
>   Peace or war.

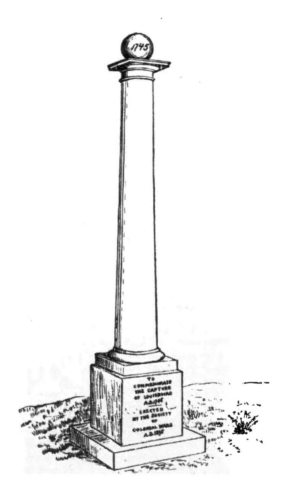

Louisbourg Memorial, erected by the Society of Colonial Wars.

In the waters of the harbor lie the hulks of sunken war-ships; and on the low green slope of the point of land running out from the ruined ramparts to the reefs where stood the Island Battery, is the last resting-place of the brave New England militia who perished in the great siege. The ceaseless beating of the outer surf, whose voice their guns outroared, is a fitting requiem. And now a handsome shaft of granite, erected in 1895 by the Society of Colonial Wars, commemorates their achievement.

New Glasgow to Truro and Halifax.

The express from *New Glasgow* halts at *Stellarton* to take in passengers from Pictou and the island. The run from New Glasgow to **Truro,** a distance of 43 miles, is for the most part through a rather uninteresting country, though when the road strikes the valley of the Shubenacadie River, which it descends for the rest of the distance, the steep red sandstone shores of the stream afford some pretty bits of scenery. Six miles beyond Stellarton is the old village of Hopewell, with its quaint, old-fashioned inn of Hopewell Hotel, a spool-factory, and a prosperous woolen-mill. Fourteen miles from New Glasgow is Glengarry, whence a high-road leads to the Scotch settlements of Gairloch and New Lairg. Then come Lansdowne (17 miles), West River (22 miles), Riversdale among its hills (30 miles), Union (34 miles), Valley (38 miles), and 5 miles farther we run into the depot of Truro.

Truro is a growing town very centrally situated for the provincial trade. It is 62 miles from Halifax, 55 miles from Pictou, and 76 miles from Amherst. It stands on the fertile alluvial shores of the Salmon River, at the head of Cobequid Bay, which is an arm of Minas Basin. Truro's manufactures include felt hats, leather, woolens, boots and shoes, machinery, iron castings, canned goods, and other items. The best hotels are the plain but comfortable old *Prince of Wales Hotel,* on the pretty central square of the town, and the new *Learmont House.* But there are many more hotels in the town. Truro is the seat of a well-conducted educational institution, the *Provincial Normal School,* which occupies a handsome building with well-kept grounds about it. The town is level but rather pretty; and the principal street, broad and well shaded, and containing some good buildings and charming private residences, is unusually attractive. On the outskirts lies the *Joseph Howe Park,* which is perhaps the prettiest and most picturesque pleasure-ground in the Maritime Provinces. It consists of a bold and richly wooded ravine traversed by a small stream, which at one point falls in a lovely cascade into a fairy-like chasm. The steep wall of this chasm is lined with winding steps, and nooks containing seats, and lighted by electric lamps swung in the foliage. When these unique grounds are illuminated, the effect is enchanting.

Truro was originally occupied by the Acadians, and, after their expulsion, by immigrants from New Hampshire and disbanded Irish soldiers. The *Shubenacadie River*, running past the back of the town, is one of the longest in Nova Scotia, and in the lower portion of its course is a tidal stream, with important ship-yards about its mouth. The tide at this point is tremendous. Along the course of the Shubenacadie and connecting with the Dartmouth Lakes lies the disused Shubenacadie Canal, which was built at an enormous cost but turned out a failure. From Truro a stage line runs down the north shore of Cobequid Bay a distance of between 40 and 50 miles, through the settlements of Masstown (where stood the largest chapel of the ancient Acadians, and where now the old poplars and apple-trees remind us of the former inhabitants), Folly Village, Great Village, Highland Village, Port au Pique, Bass River, and Upper Economy, to Five Islands, where stand, off shore, those five great rocks which, say the Indians, were thrown there by Gluskâp in his contest with the Great Beaver.

Till we approach Halifax the journey from Truro yields little in the way of striking scenery. The station next to Truro is Brookfield (8 miles); then the pretty pastoral village of Stewiacke (17 miles) and the river of the same name. From the busy little village of Shubenacadie (22 miles) stages run down the river 18 miles to the rich shipbuilding village of Maitland, which stands on an arm of Cobequid Bay, near the mouth of the Shubenacadie. Maitland ships and Maitland sailors may be found on every sea. Near Maitland, in the gypsum rock, so abundant in all these regions, there is a curious cave worth exploring. Its entrance is barely large enough to admit one comfortably; but it enlarges as you go in, and is some 400 or 500 yards in depth. Stages also run from Shubenacadie, in a southeasterly direction, to the gold district of Gay's River and a number of villages beyond. The gold of Gay's River is found in the conglomerate rock of a long ridge of heights called Boar's Back. Leaving Shubenacadie we pass the villages of Milford (26 miles), Elmsdale (32 miles), and Enfield (34 miles). Enfield has a large and prosperous establishment for the manufacture of pottery, its clay being excellent in strength and texture. Three miles south of Enfield are the famous *Oldham Gold Mines*, whose quartz rock yields very rich returns. About 7 miles on the other side of Enfield are the *Renfrew Gold Mines*, equally famous. After passing Oakfield (38 miles) we come to the flag-station of Grand Lake, on a broad water of the same name, wherein may be had some excellent trout-fishing, as in the other lakes of this neighborhood. After passing Wellington (41 miles), and skirting Long Lake, the train runs into *Windsor Junction* (48 miles), where the Intercolonial R. R. connects with the Dominion Atlantic Railway. The junction consists, besides the station-house, of some half-dozen whitewashed shanties, a little whitewashed church, some picturesque pools of clear water a fair sprinkling of goats, myriads of great, gray bowlders, and here and there in the crevices a blueberry-bush. It is a picturesque place, but no one stops there unless now and then to hunt for water-lilies, and to get a hotel one must run on to Bedford or Halifax. Three miles beyond Windsor Junction is Rocky Lake, near the Waverly Gold Mines, which are charmingly situated in a picturesque and narrow valley between two lakes. Fifty-three miles from Truro we run over a high bridge, across a beautiful peopled valley, into the village of Bedford and a landscape of enchantment. Bedford is at the head of the noble water called Bedford Basin, a great lake-like expansion of Halifax Harbor. It is 9 miles from Halifax, with which it is connected by suburban trains as well as by the express service of the Intercolonial. Its boating and bathing are not to be surpassed, and its waters are deliciously mild in temperature. Many Haligonians have their summer residences here, and there are also two good hotels, the *Bedford* and the *Bellevue*, close to the station, whose rates are $2 a day or $10 a week. Hither come the trim craft of the Halifax Royal Yacht Squadron. It is a beautiful drive between Halifax and Bedford, and the road passes the quaint little structure of the *Prince's Lodge*, perched on the crest of a pretty little wooded knoll and shaking to the thunder of the passing trains. This retreat is sweet with romantic memories of the Duke of Kent's sojourn in Halifax, and of the lady whose name was in those days so intimately connected with his. The railroad skirts the basin, for the most part close to the water's edge, and the delightful "bits" that pass in succession before one's eyes must torment the soul of the artist. Five miles beyond *Bedford* is Rockingham, with its hotel, called the *Four-Mile House*, and the fine brick buildings of the convent school for girls, called Mount St. Vincent. Off Rockingham is a famous rowing-course. Then we come to the Narrows, where the harbor is but a quarter of a mile in width. Presently we enter the crowded freight-yards of the dingy suburb of Richmond; and a mile farther on the train comes to a stop in the depot of Halifax, on *North Street*.

Halifax.

The population of Halifax, according to the census of 1891, was 38,556. The chief hotels are the *Halifax* ($2 to $3 a day); the *Queen's* ($1.50 to $3 a day); the *Waverly* ($2.50); the *Lorne* ($1.25 to $1.50); the *Albion* ($1 to $1.50). The principal streets are traversed by horse-cars (fare 5 cents). The city is well supplied with cabs, whose charges are as follows: For each person for any distance up to 1 mile, 25c.; 1½ mile, 30c.; 2 miles, 40c.; 2¼ miles, 45c.; 3 miles, 50c.; and all other distances in like proportion. One half the above rates to be paid if returning in the same carriage. For all cabs or carriages hired by the hour: For a one-horse carriage an hour, 75c.; for a two-horse carriage an hour, $1; and in like proportion for every fraction of an hour. To or from any steamer or passenger vessel, or to or from any hotel or dwelling-house to any stage office, railway station, or other place, with half a cwt. of luggage, 50c.

The chief clubs are the *Halifax Club* and the *City Club*. The *Royal Nova Scotia Yacht Club* may also be mentioned, among many organizations of a similar class, as having a somewhat marked social basis. The chief theatres are the *Academy of Music* and *Orpheus Hall*.

From Halifax sail a number of steamboat lines: the Furness Line to London; Beaver Line to Liverpool; Donaldson Line to Glasgow; Allan Line to Liverpool; Red Cross Line to St. John's, Newfoundland; Anglo-French Line to St. Pierre; lines to Bermuda, Jamaica, Turk's Islands, and Havana; the Yarmouth Line to Yarmouth; Halifax and P. E. I. Line to Charlottetown; Halifax and Newfoundland Line (steamer Harlaw) to Cape Breton and the French Shore of Newfoundland; Halifax and Bridgewater Line to Lunenburg, Bridgewater, and Liverpool; and the fine steamers Halifax and Olivette, of the Canada Atlantic and Plant Line to Boston. This is a most desirable route to Boston. The fare is $6.50; return ticket, $12. Staterooms, $1 to $2 extra. The steamers during the winter sail from Halifax every Wednesday, at 8 A. M., arriving in Boston Thursday at 1 P. M.; from Boston every Saturday at noon, arriving in Halifax Sunday evening, 6 P. M. The summer sailings are as follows: From Boston, every Tuesday, Wednesday, and Saturday, at noon; from Halifax, every Tuesday and Friday, at 7 A. M., and Saturday, at 11 P. M. Through tickets are issued, in connection with this line, over most important railways, and baggage checked through. The boats are very steady and safe, and most comfortable in their equipments. Another and much favored route between Halifax and Boston is that by way of the Dominion Atlantic Railway and the Yarmouth Steamship Company, referred to more fully on a later page.

The city of **Halifax** is situated on Halifax Harbor, formerly Chebucto Bay, one of the finest harbors in the world. The harbor proper, whose Indian name signifies "the chief haven," is 6 miles long, with an average breadth of 1 mile, and has in every portion secure anchorage for the largest ships that float. The history of Halifax is comparatively brief, but stirring. It was founded in June, 1749, by the Hon. Edward Cornwallis, with 2,576 British immigrants. The chief promoter of the enterprise was the Earl of Halifax, President of the Board of Trade and Plantations. When winter came there were nearly 5,000 people within the palisaded walls of the infant city. The building of Halifax was a proclamation to the French that England intended to make the peninsula thoroughly and permanently her own; and forthwith the Acadians and their Indian allies, under the direction of agents from Quebec and Cape Breton, began to harass the new settlement and strive in every way to compass its destruction. If men went alone into the woods to hunt or gather fuel, they were cut off by unseen foes. Outlying houses were raided by night, and their occupants slaughtered or carried away captive. Children were stolen from the threshold or the cradle. A small village had rapidly sprung up where now stands *Dartmouth*, across the harbor. One night the citizens of Halifax, too far away to render aid, had to watch helplessly the burning of this settlement, and listen to the noise of a conflict whose result they could guess but too well. The case was in some respects a parallel, in others a sharp contrast, to that of Montreal on the night of the Lachine massacre. When the Halifax contingent arrived with daybreak on the scene they found the scalped bodies of the settlers among the smoking ruins of their dwellings. This was in 1751. The new city speedily became a great naval station, whereat the English forces concentrated for the attack of Louisburg and Quebec; and during the American Revolution Halifax was the chief base of British operations. When the independence of the Thirteen Colonies was acknowledged, the population of Halifax grew suddenly by the immigration of some thousands of United Empire Loyalists. The growth of Halifax since then has been slow as regards population, but more considerable as far as wealth and influence are concerned. The American civil war brought Halifax a short period of remarkable prosperity, when she became the head of extensive blockade-running operations and a center for Southern sympathizers. With peace came something like stagnation, from which the city has awakened only within the last decade.

THE FORTIFICATIONS.

In the city of the present day the chief interest centers in the fortifications, which constitute Halifax the strongest fortress in the New World. The defenses begin at *Sambro Island*, off the mouth of the harbor, which is occupied by a "lookout" party of artillery. Two miles below the city is *MacNab's Island*, crowned with stone batteries, and carrying a light to warn ships off the Thrumcap Shoals. Above and below, strong batteries, of which the chief is York Redoubt, lie in wait at points of vantage on both sides of the harbor. In Point Pleasant Park, immediately adjoining the city, between the harbor and the northwest Arm, are the batteries of Point Pleasant and Fort Ogilvie. Across the harbor, just below *Dartmouth*, are the frowning works of *Fort Clarence*, and in mid-harbor is the grassy cone of *George's Island*, with armaments and defenses of vast but unknown strength. On this fortress Great Britain has lately spent and is still spending immense sums, and it may be considered the equal of the citadel, if not its superior in some respects. Of old it was possible to gain admittance to this stronghold, but now its stupendous mysteries are kept obscure, since visitors were found to have made interesting plans and notes in regard to the works. Now, if any one, peculiarly favored by authority, should gain entrance to a portion of the interior, he would find the green and harmless-looking island swarming with troops, and honey-combed with galleries and arsenals and casemates. From the port-hole of one of these casemates, around whose mouth the grass waves innocently, and behind which lurks the grim shape of a great cannon like a beast of prey in ambush, one looks out upon a sunlit scene of peace and human activity. On the ramparts of the citadel (to which it is now almost impossible to gain even the most superficial entrance) one is 227 ft. above sea-level, and the view is magnificent. The city skirts the citadel hill, its streets running up the height as far as permitted. The works were begun by the Duke of Kent when commander of the forces at Halifax, and almost yearly since they have been changed and strengthened in one way or another, till now the position is regarded as impregnable; and the barracks within the walls are shell-proof. The armament is largely composed of immensely heavy muzzle-loaders of a modern type, firing conical Palliser chilled-iron shot. Around the narrow entrance gate stands guard a semicircular battery of 11 guns. On the citadel flag-staff flutter gayly the many-colored signal flags that announce approaching ships.

OTHER POINTS OF INTEREST.

In no way inferior to the view from the citadel is that from the deck of boat or steamer as we sail up the harbor. The climbing streets and roofs, the soaring spires, and the crowning fortifications come together with exquisite effect. In a corner of the dark and broken Dartmouth shores lurks the little town of Dartmouth. The coloring of the scene is lovely enough in the broad sunlight; but when the sun is setting at the head of the harbor it becomes simply superb. The masts of the shipping rise black in a flood of rose or amber, the windows on the Dartmouth shore are a blaze of molten copper, and the sky above the hills of the outer harbor, to eastward, takes on a hue of wonderful beryl green. In this divine light the grim bulks of her Majesty's war-ships, motionless at their anchorage off the *Dockyard*, rise black and portentous. The Royal Dockyard, toward the upper end of the city, extends for half a mile along the harbor front, and is in every respect a thoroughly equipped navy-yard. It is divided from the rest of the city by a high stone wall, and is not open to the public; but permission to visit it may usually be obtained from the superintendent. A little farther up town, on Gottingen St., is the *Admiralty House*, where dwells the Commander-in-Chief of the North American and West India Squadrons. The Admiralty House overlooks, though at some little distance, the costly and massive structure of the *Dry Dock*, lately completed. This structure is 613½ ft. long at the top, 593 ft. long at the bottom; in width 102 ft. at top, 70 ft. at bottom; and has a draught of water on the sills of 30 ft. This exceeds the dimensions of the Brooklyn Dry Dock by 46 ft. in length and 13 in width. It is built of granite and concrete. A little N. stand the spacious *Wellington Barracks*. The general effect of the streets of Halifax is somber, from the prevalence of gray stone or gray paint, or, in many quarters, no paint at all. The best portions of Hollis and Granville Sts. are well and solidly built, showing wealth without display. The most important structure on Hollis St. is the massive, dark-gray *Parliament Building*, which must be regarded, in its severe simplicity, as a really good piece of architecture. The Chambers of the Assembly and the Legislative Council are tastefully decorated, and contain some rather notable portraits. Among these is one of Sir

Thomas Strange, painted by Benjamin West. There are also several of England's kings and queens, and such distinguished sons of Nova Scotia as Judge Haliburton, better known as Sam Slick, Sir John Inglis, the defender of Lucknow, and Sir Fenwick Williams, the hero of Kars. The building also contains, in the Legislative Library, a valuable collection of books. Opposite the Parliament Building stands a handsome freestone structure whose lower stories are occupied by the Post-Office and Custom-House, and its third floor by the Provincial Museum. Just S. of the Parliament House are the fine brown-stone quarters of the Halifax Club. Farther along Hollis St., on the E. side, are the chief hotels of the city, the *Halifax Hotel* and the *Queen.* The Halifax occupies a historic building, which has been enlarged and modernized to one of the best-equipped hotels in Canada. On the corner of Granville and Prince Sts. is the Y. M. C. A. Building, with its library and reading-rooms.

A good deal of the business of Granville St. is shifting farther up the hill to Barrington St., one of the most important thoroughfares in the city. This street is peculiarly confusing to visitors, for in its lower portion it calls itself Pleasant St., while its upper or northern section is known as Lockman St.; and its last extremity becomes Campbell Road. Only the life-long resident is expected to know the point at which one name ceases to apply and another comes into effect. On Barrington St., at the south end of the Grand Parade, stands the dingy but dignified old church of *St. Paul's.* This great wooden structure is the oldest church in the city, having been built in the year 1750, at the State expense. It is an exact copy of St. Peter's Church, on Vere St., London. The building is one of great historic interest, and its collection of mural tablets is richer than that of any other church in Canada. It accommodates about 2,000 people. The *Parade* is the central square of the city, and occupies a terrace high above Barrington St. The terrace wall is a splendid piece of masonry in gray granite. At the north end of the Parade rises the stately pile of the *New City Hall*, on the site formerly occupied by the buildings of *Dalhousie University.* This progressive and flourishing university now occupies a handsome structure, erected in 1886–'87, some distance out Morris St. It has made great advances within the last few years, under the presidency of Dr. John Forrest.

Moving south along Barrington St. from the Parade we pass the effective new structure of the Church of England Institute, and then the building of the City Club. Then comes the pretty little theatre, called the Academy of Music; and opposite, on the corner of Spring Garden Road, is the Glebe House, soon to be demolished, where dwells the Roman Catholic Archbishop of Halifax. A stone's-throw from the corner, in a most commanding situation, stands *St. Mary's Cathedral*, by far the most important church, architecturally, in the city. It is built of gray stone, with a fine front and spire of granite. In the spire is a chime of bells, not remarkably melodious. Beyond the Academy of Music stands *St. Matthew's Church*, belonging to the Presbyterians. This is a building of some architectural distinction—which can not be said of the majority of Halifax churches. Next to St. Matthew's, on a charming site, is the plain freestone structure of *Government House*, whose grounds extend through to Hollis St. Immediately opposite is old St. Paul's Cemetery, very noticeable for its fine trees and its striking monument to the memory of two Nova Scotian officers, Welsford and Parker, who fell before Sebastopol. Continuing along Pleasant St. we pass Morris St., on which lies Dalhousie College, already mentioned ; the Exhibition Building, the Institution for the Blind, and the plain Church or pro-Cathedral of St. Luke's, the see-church of the oldest Anglican colonial bishopric. Beyond Morris St. we pass the quiet and aristocratic *Waverly Hotel*, and the eminently successful Presbyterian Ladies' College. The next cross-street is South St., at the foot of which is the *Royal Engineers' Yard*, familiarly known as the Lumber Yard. This is a favorite point of departure for boating excursions and for the races of the Royal Yacht Squadron. If we continue along Pleasant St., we presently find ourselves beyond the houses and skirting the water-side. We are in the beautiful and spacious resort of *Point Pleasant Park*, with its matchless carriage-drives, and winding foot-paths, and secluded dells, and bits of wildwood scenery, and broad sea-views, and every here and there the exhilarating surprise of a strong fortification or an ambushed battery. The park is imperial property, but leased indefinitely to the city at a shilling a year. For a space of one day in each year the park is closed to the public to preserve the property against a claim of right-of-way. From the seaward point of the park, where the harbor is joined by the waters of the *Northwest Arm*, is commanded a fine view, including the high fortifications of *York Redoubt*. The Northwest Arm is a beautiful water about 3 miles long and half a mile in width, the head of which comes within 2 miles of *Bedford Basin*.

Along its eastern shore are some of the best private residences of Halifax. The Arm is a delightful resort in summer, and is traversed by a small steamer, which runs also to MacNab's Island. Its waters are navigable throughout its entire length, and afford some good sport in the way of lobster-spearing and fishing for pollock with the fly. Bathers find its temperature rather low compared with that of Bedford Basin; and there is the added disadvantage of the possibility, somewhat remote indeed, of a visit from a small shark. At the head of the Arm is *Melville Island*, once occupied by prisoners of war, now used as a military prison. At the mouth of the Arm is Pernett's Island, and a short distance above it are two immense iron rings fastened into the rock on each side of the inlet, from which was slung, during the War of 1812, a massive chain cable to bar the ingress of hostile ships. Other points of interest in the neighborhood of the Arm are *The Dingle*, noted for its fairy loveliness, and Dutch Village, supposed to be interesting. About 3 miles from the Arm is a famous "*Rocking-Stone*" of granite, which may be set in motion by a small lever. This peculiar phenomenon is on the St. Margaret's Bay Road. It weighs something over 150 tons, and oscillates on a base of 12 inches by 6 inches. Nearer town, on the Prospect Road, is a similar stone of much smaller dimensions.

One of the chief "lions" of Halifax is situated where Spring Garden Road intersects with South Park St. We refer to the beautiful **Public Gardens**, perhaps the finest in Canada or the Northern States. The grounds cover 18 acres, and are most tastefully laid out and adorned, besides being endowed with great natural beauty to begin with. On the picturesque waters of the pond are interesting waterfowl, including black and white swans. On Saturday afternoons a military band plays from four till six; and on summer evenings concerts are often given, when the grounds are brilliantly illuminated. At the western end are tennis-courts. In the immediate neighborhood of the Gardens are Camp Hill Cemetery, the Convent of the Sacred Heart, the grounds of the Wanderers' Athletic Association, Dalhousie College, already mentioned, the vast new pile of the Poor-House, the Victoria General Hospital, and the pretty little church known as Bishop's Chapel, near which has been laid the corner-stone for the proposed Anglican Cathedral. Among the many other churches of the city, the most interesting are, perhaps, the curious circular structure of St. George's (Ang.) on Brunswick St., the handsome Fort Massey Church (Presb.) on Tobin St., the spacious new brick structure of St. Patrick's

(R. C.) on Brunswick St., the pretty Methodist Church on Grafton St., the quaint little Dutch Church far up Brunswick St., built for the German immigrants in 1761, and the almost equally unpretentious Garrison Chapel on Brunswick St., just below the Citadel. The services at Garrison Chapel are interesting to visitors on account of the impressive military display which accompanies them. Among other points of interest are the Great Grain Elevator up Water St. and the Cotton Mills on Kempt Road. On Wednesdays and Saturdays, in the early morning, the traveler should make a special point of visiting the *Green Market*, where the country folk, ignoring the stalls of the comfortable brick Market-House, sell their goods on the broad sidewalks surrounding the Post-Office. The characteristic scene is thus described by the Rev. R. Murray:

There are Dutch women from along the eastern shore with their baskets of green crops, which have been nourished on the purest ozone and the richest sea-kelp. There are the Blue-nose women, broad and high-colored, fearless alike of wind and weather, as they drive their loaded teams by night, over rough and lonely roads, to reach the earliest Dartmouth ferry-boat. They offer, with a friendly smile on their weather-beaten visages, primrose butter, *perdu* under cool cabbage-leaves, and pearly eggs, food for the gods. There are lank-limbed countrymen, clad in gray homespun, standing beside their loads of vegetables or salt-marsh hay; not keen and shrewd-eyed, like New England farmers, but bashfully courteous of speech, with the soft lisp of German fatherland on their tongues or the burr of their Scottish ancestry. Here are a pair of Frenchwomen with baskets of knitted goods on their arms. Contrast the withered and yellow grandame, her grizzled hair bulging in a roll above her bushy eyebrows, her claw-like hands plying her knitting-wires, with the fresh young girl by her side, whose arch black eyes sparkle from out of her smooth olive face, and her white teeth display themselves in full force as we finger the huge mittens in her basket. Old and young are habited alike, in blue or black handkerchiefs tightly knotted under the chin, loose blue jackets with napkin-shawls folded over them, and short woolen skirts. Scores of them have been on the road all night, trotting the 26 miles from Chezzetcook on foot, their fingers busily plying the knitting-needles all the way. There squats a negro matron on the pavement, her clouted feet stretched before her in utter disregard of passers-by, a short black pipe between her pendulous lips. Her layers of rags clothe her like the fungi of a dead tree; her padded hood is fashioned to fulfill the office of a saddle for her load. She has luscious wild strawberries in little birch-barks, which she offers you in an unctuous *falsetto*, stuffing her pipe into her bosom, the better to overhaul her store for a fresh one. You pause in your bargain, wondering whether *her teeth* hulled the tempting fruit!

15

The "noble red man" and his squaw also attend market. There they stand, a degenerate pair, clad in the cast-off clothes of the white man, their merchandise consisting of flag and willow baskets gayly dyed, and an occasional porcupine-quill box. The squaw is prematurely aged. Her broad, copper-colored face is inconceivably wrinkled; her eyes, from their ambush of folds, peer forth with a snaky gleam. The "brave," propped up against the Post-Office wall, dozes with his bunch of rabbits (in their season) dangling in his hand, and, working his jaws mechanically on his quid, dreams of—rum. A bronze-tinted papoose is strapped under a filthy basket at the mother's back, and its impassive little face surveys life over her shoulder with a perfect philosophy. This trio has drifted from one of the wigwam-hamlets near Dartmouth, and thither they will return when their wares are disposed of, if they do not fall victims to rum and the station-house.

The town of *Dartmouth*, population between 4,000 and 5,000, is reached by ferry from the foot of *George St.*, or by a railway which crosses the harbor at the Narrows. The town contains some fine private residences, whose owners do business in Halifax. The chief points of interest at Dartmouth are Fort Clarence, already mentioned, the Sugar Refinery, and the imposing gray-stone and granite structure of the Mount Hope Lunatic Asylum. Fort Clarence guards what is known as the "Eastern Passage," which was supposed to be impassable for large ships till the occasion on which the Confederate cruiser Tallahassee made her escape by it. The Confederate ship was blockaded in Halifax harbor by an American squadron; which, however, paid no attention to the Eastern Passage, supposing it unnavigable. The Tallahassee took advantage of a favoring wind and tide, and made good her escape by the dangerous channel. A few miles from Dartmouth are the Montague Gold Mines, the pleasant summer resort of Cow Bay, with its surf-bathing, and the pretty chain of the Dartmouth Lakes. Dartmouth has some important manufacturing interests, among them a famous skate-factory and a rope-walk.

From Halifax as a starting-point the traveler has many pleasant side trips at his command. He may go by boat eastward to *Canso* and **Cape Breton** and the west coast of **Newfoundland**; to *St. John's*, Newfoundland, and *St. Pierre;* westward along the Atlantic coast to *Yarmouth* and intermediate ports by boat or stage, or up the *Annapolis Valley* as far as may be desired. If the traveler intends going to **Boston** *via* Yarmouth, or St. John, he will "do" the Annapolis Valley and "Land of Evangeline" *en route*. If, however, he intends taking the steamer Halifax at Halifax, for Boston, he will do well to make a round trip down the Atlantic coast of the peninsula, by steamers *Bridgewater* or *City of St. John*, or by stage, through Margaret's Bay, Chester, Mahone Bay, and Lunenburg to Bridgewater, thence by the admirable new cars of the Central Nova Scotia R. R. across the province to Middleton, and thence by the Dominion Atlantic Ry. through the regions immortalized by Longfellow, through *Wolfville* and *Windsor*, back to Halifax. This is in every way a most enjoyable trip, with many points of interest along the journey. A more extended and diversified round trip may be taken by continuing down the coast from Bridgewater to Yarmouth, thence back to Halifax by the Dominion Atlantic Ry., or from Digby to St. John by Dominion Atlantic Ry. S. S. Line.

NEWFOUNDLAND.

To St. John's, Newfoundland, one may go by the steamer Bruce from North Sydney to Port aux Basque, or from Halifax by the steamers of the Halifax and Newfoundland S. S. Co., Canada and Newfoundland S. S. Co., or Red Cross Line. The time occupied in the passage is, by the Bruce, 6 hours, and 24 hours by rail to St. John's by the new railway; by the Halifax lines about 48´ hours, a steamer of each of which line makes fortnightly trips. Cabin passage from Halifax to St. John's is $20; round trip, $40. The steamer of the Red Cross Line, plying between New York, Halifax, and St. John's, makes fortnightly sailings, and charges $18 between Halifax and St. John's; $34 for the round trip. To *St. Pierre* one may go from Halifax by the steamship *St. Pierre*, of the Anglo-French S. S. Co., sailing every alternate Wednesday, or by the *coastal steamer* from St. John's. The fare from Halifax is $15, for the round trip $25, which includes meals and berth; the fare from St. John's is from $6 to $7.

The Island of Newfoundland, dubbed " England's oldest colony," is a self-governing province not connected with the Canadian Confederation. It forms the eastern wall, as it were, of the Gulf of St. Lawrence; is 419 miles long by 300 in extreme breadth; and owing to its numerous bays it has an enormous extent of coast-line. Its fisheries are perhaps the richest and most famous in the world; its sealing industry is vast and picturesquely perilous; its climate is almost as harsh and forbidding as its coasts, but there are sections very favorable to agriculture; its lakes and rivers swarm with game-fish, its wildernesses with deer and wild-fowl; like Ireland, it has no snake or venomous reptile; its mineral wealth, hardly at all developed, consists of silver, copper, lead, iron, plumbago, manganese, coal, gypsum, etc.; its Indians, the strange Beothucs, have gone into that limbo whither the dodo and the great auk preceded them; the vast interior is in great part unexplored, and is as full of mystery as the colonial politics.

The history of Newfoundland begins with the Norsemen in the tenth century. Its fishing waters were frequented by Norman Breton and Basque fishermen during the fourteenth century. It was visited by John Cabot in 1497, by the Portuguese explorers Cortereal and Verazzano in 1501 and 1524 respectively, and by Cartier in 1534. In 1583 it was taken possession of in the name of England by Sir Humphrey Gilbert, and settlements were speedily established along the coast. About the end of the seventeenth century and in the early part of the eighteenth the south and east coasts were the scene of fierce struggles between the French and English. By the Treaty of Utrecht, signed in 1713, the French, while relinquishing all claim to the island, were secured in the possession of the rocky islets of St. Pierre and Miquelon, and of certain fishing privileges along the west coast. The provisions relating to these privileges were very stupidly drawn up by the British commissioners, whence arises in the present day no end of difficulty and disagreeableness. The island was formed into a province in 1728. In 1761 and 1796 the French made vigorous efforts to conquer it. In 1832 was convened the first Legislative Assembly. By a census taken in 1891 the population was placed at 202,040. Now, in 1891, in quarrels with England and France and Canada, the ancient colony is endeavoring to manufacture history at short notice. Her position as gate-keeper to the St. Lawrence makes it forever impossible that she should be permitted by England to become a member of the American Union.

St. John's.

The city of **St. John's**, the capital of Newfoundland, is on the extreme eastern coast of the peninsula of Avalon. It is nearer Europe than any other port of North America. It is 1,076 miles from Montreal, and 1,730 miles from Cork. The approach from the sea is very impressive. The deep, secure harbor is gained by a strongly fortified passage called the Narrows, where the lofty sea-wall of the island is rent asunder. The city

St. John's, Newfoundland, before the Fire of 1892.

is built chiefly of wood, and is striking mainly from its situation. Small as the houses are, and dingy as are the streets, the city contains great wealth. The chief hotels are the *New Atlantic*, a house equipped with all modern conveniences, and the *Union*, on Water St. Livery charges are very moderate, and carriages may be hired at about 80 cents an hour. The population of St. John's, according to the last census, is 31,142. The chief trade is in fish and fish products, and in seal-oil, for the refining of which there are several establishments; but the merchants of the city do also a heavy local trade in supplying the "out-harbors," as the other towns of the island are styled. The city has tanneries, breweries, biscuit, shoe, and furniture factories. It also has one of the best graving-docks in America. At times, on the arrival of the sealing steamers, there is stir enough in the streets of St. John's to satisfy the demands of a more metropolitan center, and the wits and sticks of the police are sometimes taxed to keep order. For about a month in each summer the city is thronged to overflowing with people from the north and west coasts, selling their produce and laying in provisions for the winter. The main business artery is *Water St.*, occupied by the wholesale supply-stores of the merchant princes of St. John's, and by a liberal sprinkling of grog-shops and cheap eating-houses. Water St. is unpretentiously but massively built. On its northern portion stands the Custom-House. The Market-House and Post-Office occupy a commodious building about its center, and at its south end are the bridge and causeway which cross the head of the harbor. The most important structure in the colony is the great *Roman Catholic Cathedral*, crowning the ridge which overlooks the city and the harbor. The Cathedral, with the Bishop's Palace, Convent, and St. Bonaventure's College, which cluster about it, cost $500,000. The Cathedral itself is a vast pile, built of stone, much of which was brought over from Ireland. It has twin towers, an immensely long cloister, and no aisles. In the grounds before it stand a number of statues, among them one of St. Peter. The Irish Catholics form a great majority of the citizens of St. John's.

About half-way up the slope stands the not yet completed *Cathedral of the Church of England*. When finished this will be a very beautiful Gothic structure. It was designed by the great English architect, Sir Gilbert Scott, and its completion is delayed by lack of funds. On what is called the Military Road, running along the high ridge occupied by the Roman Catholic Cathedral, stand the old Barracks, and also the

Parliament Building, a massive stone structure, with a really fine Doric portico. North of the Parliament House is *Government House*, occupying pretty and well-kept grounds. The other important public buildings are the penitentiary, hospital, Athenæum Building, educational institutions, and poorhouse. The city rejoices in a rickety suburb with the euphonious appellation of Maggotty Cove, through which we pass to climb to the vantage-ground of **Signal Hill**. On Signal Hill is the *Observatory*, from which, and from many another point of vantage on the edge of precipitous steeps, we look down upon the city and the harbor in their windless amphitheatre. The crest of the hill is clothed with soft, fine grasses. Amid them lies a deep lake 360 ft. above the sea. Passing the great stone barracks we come at length to a little battery, perched on the edge of a cliff 500 ft. high, from which we look down directly into the Narrows, thronged with the sails of its fishing fleets. Immediately below is the place where, in war-time, the harbor is closed by great chains swung from shore to shore.

As Paris is called the gayest of capitals, St. John's has been characterized by Warburton as the fishiest.

Trips from St. John's.

In the matter of railroads the Ancient Colony was until recently behind the times. Her settlements are a mere fringe about the coast, and communication is carried on, for the most part, with picturesque irregularity, by means of coasting-vessels. A railroad has been completed from St. John's through the interior to *Port au Basque* on the southwest coast, which is largely developing the country. Thanks to the enterprise of Mr. R. G. Reid, the greatest private landowner on earth, who owns 5,000,000 acres of land in the island, Newfoundland is now no longer isolated from the world, nor are its means of communication either primitive or inconvenient. A thoroughly equipped and modern railway, 640 miles long, now traverses the island from St. John's to Port aux Basque, with branches to Placentia, Carbonear, and Burnt Bay, which connects at Harbor Grace with the steamers at Labrador, at North Sydney with the Intercolonial Ry., and *via* this line with the Canadian Pacific, Grand Trunk, Dominion Atlantic, Maine Central, Boston and Maine, and all railway lines in Canada and the U. S. The building of this railway across a little known portion of what was then

The Monthly Mail Train from Hall's Bay to Codroy.

a poor and sparsely settled island reads almost like a commercial romance. In 1893 Mr. Reid offered to build the road for $15,600 a mile, and his offer was accepted by the Government. He then offered to operate the line, so the Government granted him in fee simple 5,000 acres of land for each mile of railway. There was a good deal of opposition, but the contract became law. Connection is with the steamer *Bruce* for North Sydney, Cape Breton, where the Intercolonial Ry. gives communication with all points west. The first railroad built runs from St. John's around *Conception Bay* to *Holyrood*, and *Harbor Grace* (85 miles), and up the east coast to the town of *Trinity* and on to the copper-mining districts of *Hall Bay*. The experiences of the engineers in locating this railroad were thrilling enough to have occurred in central Africa. They were attacked at times by men with shot-guns and women with pitchforks, who dreaded lest their labors should result in an increase of taxation. The train reaching there at 3.45 P. M. leaves St. John's about 10 A. M. for Harbor Grace.

Around St. John's there are some very beautiful and striking drives over firm and well-kept roads. One of the most charming of these is by way of the lovely little *Quiddy - Viddy Lake* and Bally Haly Bog to the deep, wooded lake of *Virginia Water*, where was once the summer residence of Newfoundland's Governors. The drive may well be extended over the high and moss-grown reaches of the " Barrens " to Logie Bay and Torbay, where one gets a good idea of the Newfoundland coast scenery. This scenery is characterized by an almost total absence of beaches, the shores consisting of lofty cliffs, about whose bases thunder the mightiest surges of the Atlantic. Every here and there this forbidding wall is broken by a little opening called a " cove," usually deep enough to serve as a haven for the fishing-boats. At the head of the cove comes tumbling in from the heights a brown trout-brook, and here gathers a cluster of fishermen's cottages, in an ideal seclusion. Another lovely drive is to the wildly romantic scenery of *Portugal Cove*, on Conception Bay. At this point is a comfortable country hotel, past whose windows roars and flashes a white cascade.

If one is fond of coaching, he may go by stage over matchless roads, through the sweet pastoral scenes of what is called the *Strait Shore of Avalon* to the villages of Blackhead (4 miles), near which is Cape Spear, the most easterly point of North America; Petty Harbor (10 miles), near which is the strange phenomenon called the "**Spout**," a hole in the vaulted roof of a deep sea-cavern, through which, during storm and high tides, the water is hurled in a huge fountain visible for miles about; Bay Bulls (19 miles), Witless Bay (22 miles), Mobile (24 miles), Toad Cove (26 miles), La Manche (32 miles), Brigus (34 miles), Cape Broyle (38 miles), with fine salmon-fishing in the river that flows around the foot of Hell Hill, Caplin Cove (42 miles); the important little town of *Ferryland* (44 miles), where, in 1637, Sir David Kirk established himself when he was appointed Count Palatine of Newfoundland; Aquafort (48 miles), Fermeuse (51 miles), Renewse (54 miles), and the deadly ship-wrecking headland of **Cape Race**, the southeast point of Newfoundland (64 miles). About 50 miles off Cape Race are the famous **Grand Banks** of Newfoundland, almost as noted for their naval battles as for their cod-fisheries. On the Grand Banks, in 1755, the French men-of-war Alcide and Lys were captured, after a furious battle of five hours, by the British frigates Dunkirk and Defiance. In the same neighborhood, on August 19, 1812, took place the famous battle between the American frigate Constitution, of 44 guns, and the British frigate Guerrière, 38 guns, which resulted in an overwhelming victory for the American ship. The Banks extend four degrees north and south and five degrees east and west. They consist of vast submerged sand-banks, strewn with sea-shells, lying in water from 30 to 60 fathoms deep. Here, from February to November, feed the cod in innumerable swarms, and the fisheries give employment to over 100,-000 men of all nations. "Throughout a great part of the spring, summer, and fall, the Grand Banks are covered by rarely broken fogs, through which falls an almost incessant slow rain. Sometimes these fogs are so dense that objects within 60 ft. are totally invisible, at which times the fishing-vessels at anchor are liable to be run down by the great Atlantic steamers. The dangerous proximity of icebergs (which drift across and ground on the Banks) is indicated by the sudden and intense coldness which they send through even a midsummer day, by the peculiar white glare in the air about them, and by the roaring of the breakers on their sides."

The tourist who wishes to visit the *N. E. coast* of Newfoundland and the shores of **Labrador**, will need to allow himself a clear month for the trip, and should select the midsummer season. As Newfoundland is not a portion of Canada, this hand-book will do little more than indicate routes, etc. The steamers of the northern coastal line leave St. John every alternate Monday during the summer, and intend-

52°
B. of Châteaux
York Pt.
Belle Isle
52°
L A B R A D O R
Red B.
Black R.
Black B.
Les Mamelles
Pte. d'Amour
Blanc Sablon
STRAIT OF BELLE ISLE
G. Normand
Pistolet B.
Triquet B.
Lunaire B.
B. of Forteau
Hare Bay
St. Barbe B.
NEWFOUNDLAND
St. Margaret B.
51°
51°
I. Grouis
B. of St. John
57°
West of Greenwich
55°

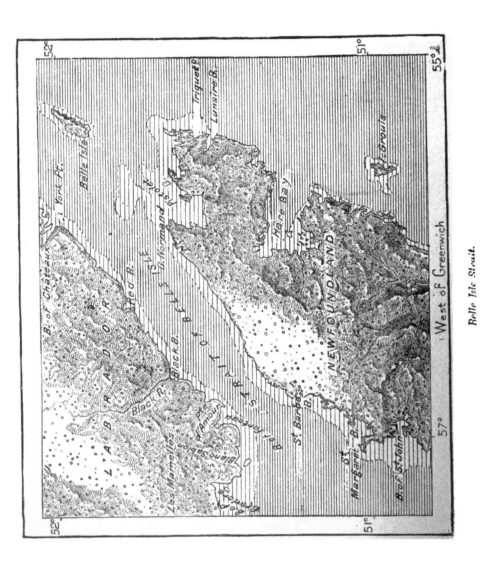

Belle Isle Strait.

ing passengers should communicate with the agents, Messrs. Bowring Bros., at St. John's, Newfoundland. The fare to the town of Trinity is $5, and to Bett's Cove or Nipper's Cove, where the Labrador steamer is taken, about $10. On the Labrador boats the charge, including meals and staterooms, is $2 a day. The fare is very plain, but the steamers are strong and seaworthy. Labrador is an intensely interesting country to *explore*, but not of much interest to the traveler, who merely takes a hasty look at its grim shores and passes on. It is hardly worth visiting unless one intends to do it thoroughly. Then, it has marvelous and almost virgin trout-and-salmon fishing to offer, and strange landscapes, and wonderful cataracts, and all the charm of the mysterious unknown.

Along the Coast.

The steamers of the Newfoundland Coastal Steamship Co. maintain a regular fortnightly service between St. John's and the northern outports. Fares: to Trinity, $3.50; to Fogo, $6.50; to Tilt Cove, $8; to Battle Harbour, $12.

From St. John's the steamer rounds Cape St. Francis, and stops off the shelterless roadstead of Bay Verd, an important fishing village. Then it crosses the mouth of Trinity Bay, and enters the magnificent harbor of **Trinity**, one of the best on the American coast. Trinity has something less than 2,000 inhabitants, and is an important center and county town. It lies 115 miles from St. John's. Some farming is carried on in the neighborhood of the town; and opposite, on the S. side of the bay, lies a seaport with the exquisite name of "Heart's Content." The next stopping-place beyond Trinity is Catalina, with a population of about 1,500, situated on a secure harbor noted for its peculiar tidal phenomena. The next call is at the ancient town of **Bonavista**, with nearly 3,000 inhabitants, on Bonavista Bay. The harbor is dangerously exposed to nor'west winds, but the town has a growing commerce. It lies 146 miles from St. John's. Bonavista Bay is 87 miles across the mouth from Cape Bonavista to Cape Freels, and its indented shores are set with many fishing hamlets. On the N. shore is the important harbor and village of *Greenspond*, on a small island so barren that soil for the village gardens had to be brought in boats from the mainland. After rounding Cape Freels the steamer sails N. W. across the many-islanded water called Hamilton Sound. The next stoppage is at the town of *Fogo*, on Fogo Island, 216 miles from St. John's. On Fogo Island are outlying settlements with such curious names as " Joe Batt's Arm," " Seldom-come-by," and " Little Seldom-come-by." Leaving Fogo, the steamer enters a very wilderness of picturesque islands, and stops at the important town of *Twillingate*, the capital of the northern division of Newfoundland. The town has about 3,000 inhabitants. It is built on two islands, connected by a bridge. The neighborhood is famous for producing the choicest speci- mens of the Newfoundland dog, jet black with a white cross on the breast, now rare and costly. Fourteen miles from Twillingate is the large fishing village of Exploits, with about 600 inhabitants. Near by is the mouth of the great *Exploits River*, navigable in large portions of its course. It runs through a low and well-wooded country. The *Grand Falls of the Exploits* are 145 feet in height. Its length is about 150 miles. Thence the steamer crosses the broad bay of *Notre Dame* to the famous mining village of Tilt Cove, on the border of a lovely lake. The village has about 800 inhabitants, nearly all miners. The mines are of copper and nickel, exceedingly rich ; and an excellent quality of marble is found in the neighborhood. Bett's Cove is an- other important mining center, and indeed all the country about Notre Dame Bay abounds in mineral wealth, and its population has been growing rapidly of late years. A highway leads across the island through coal areas and good farming lands to the Bay of Islands on the W. shore, and the railway to the southward is doing much to develop this region. Here the coastal steamer turns back for St. John's, and travelers who are going farther N. take the sturdy Labrador boat.

Conception Bay and the South Coast.

The traveler who has come as far as St. John's should certainly take the railroad around Conception Bay. The first station is the watering- place of Topsail, 12 miles from St. John's. Then come Manuels (14 miles) ; Killigrews (18 miles) ; Seal Cove (24 miles) ; Holyrood, with a population of 400 (28 miles) ; Harbor Main, at the head of Concep- tion Bay, Salmon Cove, and Brigus Junction (42 miles), whence we diverge to *Brigus*, a picturesque town on a lake between two hills. Brigus has about 2,000 inhabitants and an immense fishing fleet. A magnificent view is commanded from the summit of Thumb Peak, 600 ft. high, or from the bold headland of Brigus Lookout. Not far from Brigus is the fishing village of Bay Roberts, most of whose male in- habitants spend their summers fishing on the Labrador coast. Ten miles from Brigus Junction is Harbor Grace Junction. **Harbor**

·**Grace** (84 miles from St. John's) is the second town of importance in Newfoundland. It has a population of 7,000, and is an important trade center. Its harbor is roomy but much exposed to the sea, except close to the city wharves, where a long sand-beach forms an excellent natural breakwater. The city is mostly built of wood, and not striking in appearance. By a fire, in 1889, it lost its finest edifice, the Roman Catholic cathedral. From Harbor Grace the railroad runs across the peninsula 15 miles to the village of Heart's Content, already referred to, where the old Atlantic cable has its western terminus, passing **Carbonear**, 8 miles N. of Harbor Grace. This is a town of something over 2,000 inhabitants, and a great fishing center.

From Harbor Grace Junction a railroad runs to the old town of *Placentia*, on Placentia Bay, 84 miles from St. John's. Placentia was in old times an important French stronghold, and successfully resisted many British assaults. When the French claims were surrendered by the Treaty of Utrecht, the garrison and inhabitants of Placentia followed the French flag to Cape Breton. Under British occupation an important town speedily arose at Placentia, which has of late years gone rather to decay. Five miles from Placentia is Little Placentia, and 12 miles farther N. are the great lead-mines of La Manche.

The S. coast of Newfoundland, from Cape Race to Cape Ray, may be visited by the steamer of the Newfoundland Coastal Steamship Co., which leaves St. John's on alternate Thursdays. The chief points of interest after rounding Cape Race are the little town of Trepassey, on Trepassey Harbor; the excessively dangerous piece of coast between Cape Pine and St. Shot's; the town of St. Mary's, on St. Mary's Bay, with the large village and splendid fishing river of Salmonier, a few miles distant; Placentia, already referred to (fare, $4), and Burin (fare, $5), on the **Burin Peninsula**, forming the western boundary of Placentia Bay. The harbor of Burin is perfectly landlocked by cliffs 200 ft. in height, and is the best of all Newfoundland's admirable harbors. The town has a large trade, and a population of 1,850. The surrounding scenery is magnificently bold, and the tower of Burin lighthouse is perched 430 ft. above the sea.

From Burin the steamer sails to **St. Pierre** (fare, $6.50), a barren rock 4 miles across, lying under the flag of France. The town is largely built of stone, and is crowded together on its harbor at the E. of the island. It is garrisoned by a company of French soldiers, and is one of the most peculiar and thoroughly individualized towns in North

America. It is famous alike for its quaintness and its hospitality, its rare old brandies and ports, its ubiquitous codfish, and the motley crowds of fishermen-sailors that throng its narrow streets. The town is the landing-place of two of the transatlantic cables, which add to its population a large force of operators. The only buildings of any pretension are Government House and the Roman Catholic church and convent. The best inns are the *Pension Hacala* and *Hôtel Joinville*. Travelers who intend visiting St. Pierre should make a point of reading an illustrated article on St. Pierre, by S. G. W. Benjamin, in the Century Magazine for June, 1884.

Beyond St. Pierre lies the important fishing district of Fortune. Bay, with the settlements of Fortune, Harbor Briton, and Belleorem, besides many tiny hamlets in the deep coves. Then come the broad inlet of Hermitage Bay, and the settlement of Hermitage Cove, 9 miles from Harbor Briton. At the head of the bay are the rich salmon-waters of a sheltered inlet called the Bay of Despair, whence old Indian trails lead through the wilderness to the Exploits River and the lakes of the interior. From Hermitage Bay westward to Cape Ray the coast-line is almost straight, but fretted with innumerable small coves. The most important settlement is Burgeo, a village of 700 inhabitants, on one of the Little Burgeo Islands. On the mainland opposite are the salmon-fisheries of Grandy's Brook. The next settlement is the fishing village of La Poile. Six miles beyond is Garia Bay, with several villages on its shores; and then, 9 miles farther, the busy little port of Rose Blanche. Thence the steamer passes Burnt Islands, and then Dead Islands, so named from their innumerable wrecks. These islands have been made illustrious by the heroic deeds of *George Harvey*, who dwelt on one of them during the early part of the century, and by his splendid skill and daring saved many hundreds of lives. The houses in all this region seem largely built of wreckage, and furnished with the spoils of ships.

The next port of call for the western coastal steamer is the village of *Channel*, or *Port au Basque*, 4 miles W. of the Dead Islands. This is an important station for the transfer of cablegrams. It has a population of about 700, and famous halibut-fisheries in the vicinity, and is the western terminus of the Newfoundland, Northern and Western Ry., which penetrates the interior of the island and runs to St. John's. Steamer connection is regularly made with North Sydney, Nova Scotia. Around **Cape Ray**, 3 or 4 miles W. of Channel, lies the vast stretch of

Government Houses and Town Pumps at St. Pierre.

erica. It is f

coast known as the **West** or **French Shore**, the scene of the late unpleasantnesses between France and Newfoundland. Owing to the uncertainties and difficulties of government in this section, and partly perhaps to the dangerous character of the coast, whose safe harbors are widely separated, the region is little populated and less civilized. Yet it has great natural resources, the most fertile soil and fairest climate in the colony; and when the difficulties which now harass it have been brought to some satisfactory solution, it will doubtless become one of the most prosperous portions of the island. The change that would bring most immediate and permanent benefit would be union with the Confederation of Canada.

The French Shore.

The French shore is not likely to attract, for the present, any but the most adventurous tourists, and these will not be troubled by the lack of such conveniences as highways, hotels, and regular communication. The region may be visited by the fortnightly service of the Newfoundland Coastal Steamship Co., by the frequent coasting schooners, or by the steamer Harlaw, from Halifax and Cape Breton ports. The total extent of the French shore, from *Cape Ray* N. to *Cape Bald*, and down the N. E. coast to *Cape St. John*, is a distance of 460 miles. Three miles back from Cape Ray is the lofty *Table Mountain*, 1,700 ft. in height, with the summits of Sugar-Loaf and Tolt Peak in the neighborhood. Eighteen miles N. of Cape Ray is Cape Anguille, and between these lofty headlands lie the fertile valleys of the Great and Little Codroy Rivers, with a scattered farming population. North of Cape Anguille is the great inlet called **St. George's Bay**, running 50 miles inland (fare to Bay St. George, from St. John's, $13). Around its fertile and wooded shores are a few small villages, such as Sandy Point and Crabb's Brook, and some settlements of Micmacs. There are rich coal deposits in this region. From the head of the bay, where flows in George's River, may be reached, by difficult trails, the strange, deep waters of the interior lakes, called "Ponds," of which the chief is *Grand Pond*, 60 miles long by 5 in width. These waters are rarely seen by white men, and are reputed to swarm with fish, as do their shores with game. Toward the close of last century there took place on Grand Pond a great battle between the remnants of the Bœothucs and the invading Micmacs from Nova Scotia, resulting in the extermination of the Bœothucs. The northern gate of St. George's Bay is Cape

St. George. Twenty-five miles beyond is the mouth of the vast harbor called *Port au Port*, penetrating the land southward to within a mile of St. George's Bay. Next comes the *Bay of Islands*, famous for its sublime scenery. The soil and climate here are adapted to agriculture, and such minerals abound as marble, gypsum, and limestone. The villages scattered about the shore contain, in all, about 2,000 inhabitants. At the head of the bay flows in the *Humber River*, 150 miles in length, and hemmed about its mouth with towering cliffs of white limestone. About 25 miles N. of the Bay of Islands is *Bonne Bay*, renowned for its herring-fisheries (fare from St. John's, $15). For the next 70 odd miles the coast-line is little broken, till we come to the safe anchorages of the Bay of Ingrenechoix. Near its northern boundary, called Point Rich, is the fishing village of Port Saunders. Some 15 miles farther N. is the beautiful inlet of Bay St. John, at whose head flows in the almost unexplored *Castors River*, abounding with salmon in the lower portion of its course. Then comes St. Margaret's Bay, with the tiny hamlets of Old Ferolle and New Ferolle. Then, in succession, the inlets of Bay St. Genevieve, Bay St. Barbe, and Flower Cove, with its fishing settlement. Beyond are the famous north shore sealing-grounds, where the coast is low and grassy; and presently we enter the barren *Strait of Belle Isle*, 80 miles long by 12 in width, thronged with seals and swept by icy currents, separating Newfoundland from Labrador. The coasts and islands here are of the utmost desolation. At times great herds of ice-bergs may be seen trailing slowly through the strait. On the desolate Isle of Quirpon is a small sealing hamlet. At the eastern entrance to the strait is the great rock, 9 miles long by 3 broad, called, in strange irony, *Belle Isle*. On its wide circumference there is but one point where a landing can be effected, and here, twice a year, are put ashore the stores for the lonely lighthouse-keeper, who has not even a bush on the whole island to cheer his solitude. He has brought from the mainland many boat-loads of earth, endeavoring to form a garden-plot, but the soil is speedily swept clean off by the terrible winds. It is not surprising that these islands of Belle Isle and Quirpon were called, of old, the *Isles of the Demons*, and were represented in the ancient maps as peopled with devils of various species. The French explorers dared not land, save with crucifix in hand, on these dreadful shores, where their ears were assailed with the clamor of demoniac voices. It was supposed, moreover, that the isles were the abode of a malignant and terrible species of griffin. There may have been some material foundation for these tales, as, even so late as the summer of 1873, the coasts were ravaged by packs of gigantic wolves, who devoured a number of people and besieged the settlers in their cabins. A romantic legend connected with these islands has been made the subject of a poem called " Marguerite, or the Isle of Demons," by Mr. George Martin, of Montreal. On the expedition which sailed under Roberval, in 1542, to found a colony at Quebec, were the Viceroy's niece, the Lady Marguerite, and a young courtier, her lover, whose suit was forbidden by Roberval. Their conduct seems to have enraged or scandalized the Viceroy, for he put his niece ashore, with her old nurse, on the Isle of Demons, now Quirpon. " The lover leaped from the ship and joined the women, and the fleet sailed away. Then the demons and the hosts of hell began their assaults on the forsaken trio, tearing about their hut at night, menacing them on the shore, and assaulting them in the forest. But the penitent sinners were guarded by invisible bands of saints, and kept from peril. After many months, wearied by these fiendish assaults, the lover died, and was soon followed by the nurse and the child. Long thereafter lived Marguerite alone, until finally a fishing-vessel ran in warily toward the smoke of her fire and rescued her, after two years of life among demons."

The eastern portion of the French shore, from Cape Bald southward to Cape St. John, does not call for detailed mention here. There are fishing stations on the harbors of Griguet, Lunaire, St. Anthony; the coaling station of *Croc Harbor ;* Chouse Brook on White Bay; and La Scie, 5 miles from Cape St. John. The most important waters are Hare Bay, the splendid landlocked harbor of *Canada Bay,* and the magnificent sheet of water, 45 miles long by 15 wide, called **White Bay**. This bay has fine fisheries, and little fishing posts are scattered all about its shore.

Halifax to Bridgewater by the Atlantic Coast.

The steamer *City of St. John* leaves Halifax every Monday evening, and connects with the Boston steamers at **Yarmouth** on Wednesday; returning, leaves Yarmouth for Halifax every Thursday morning. The fare between Halifax and Yarmouth by this route is $5; return, $8. The steamer calls at Lunenburg, Liverpool, Lockeport, Shelbourne, and Barrington. The steamer Bridgewater, of the Coastal Steam Packet Co., sails every Wednesday morning at 8 o'clock for

Lunenburg and Liverpool, returning Thursday morning. Every Saturday morning she sails for Bridgewater direct, returning on Monday
morning. Fares: to Lunenburg or Bridgewater, $2; return, $3. To
Liverpool, $3; round trip, $5. Meals are not included in these prices.

After passing Sambro, the boat runs some distance out to sea before
turning westward, dreading the perilous Sambro Ledges. On the
right lies Pennant Bay, beyond which is Mars Head, near the scene of
the wreck of the *S. S. Atlantic* in 1873, by which no fewer than 585
persons perished. Here also were wrecked the British war-ships North,
Helena, and Mars, from which latter ship it takes its name. Next we
pass the broad mouth of the lovely *St. Margaret's Bay*, in whose sheltered recesses lies the pleasant summer resort of the same name,
reached by stage from Halifax. There are several little settlements
scattered around the shores of this beautiful water, the most important
of which is Hubbard's Cove. From the head of the bay there is a
pleasant canoe route, with short portages, across the province to the
waters of the Avon and Minas Basin, with good fishing almost all the
way. Beyond St. Margaret's Bay we enter the mouth of another bay
even more capacious than that we have just left, and only second to it
for romantic beauty. In some weathers the steamer sails in to communicate with the towns of Chester and Mahone Bay, whose harbors are
somewhat shoal for large vessels; but more usually she sails across
the mouth in the direction of Cape La Have, leaving these towns to be
served by the stage-coaches. **Chester** is 45 miles by stage from Halifax; 40 miles by similar conveyance from Windsor. In summer it is
one of the most delightful of watering-places, frequented by charming
society from Halifax and from the Southern States; but in winter it
has earned for itself the pathetic *sobriquet* of "Chester-God-help-us."
The town has several comfortable hotels (of which the *Lovett House*
is the best), and about 600 inhabitants of its own. Its scenery is delicious, its climate perfection; and one may row and paddle and sail,
catch cod or flounders or lobsters, go in swimming, or loaf and invite
his soul, as agreeably at Chester as anywhere else one can think of,
in Nova Scotia at least. A delightful excursion from Chester is to
Mount Aspotogan, from whose summit one gets a magnificent view.
Within easy reach of Chester, beyond Chester Basin, is the unrivaled
salmon-water of *Gold River*, frequented also by splendid sea-trout.
All along the drive one has endlessly changing views of *Mahone Bay's*
countless islands, on some of which are cozy little Dutch farms. In

among these islands, in the summer of 1813, the American privateer Young Teaser was chased by two British war-ships. When the American ship was utterly defeated, her officers blew her up rather than surrender, and every man on board perished. The largest of the islands in the bay is Big Tancook, with a population of 540. The most interesting is *Oak Island*, one of the best accredited of the innumerable claimants to the honor of having served as a hiding-place for the treasures of Captain Kidd. Treasure-seekers, sinking pits on the island, have found a host of mysteries but no money. Shafts have been dug several hundred feet, through layers of cut-stone and hewn timbers, strange grasses from the tropics, charcoal, putty, and carefully jointed planks. A great deal of capital has been invested in the effort either to find the treasure or to solve the mystery of these underground works; but at length the toilers came upon great stone drains communicating with the sea, which admitted such floods of water that their pumps could not cope with it; and the diggings have been abandoned. The little town of *Mahone Bay* is less attractive to summer visitors than Chester, but is far more business-like and prosperous. It is engaged in the fisheries, and in building small ships for coasting trade. It has a population of about 1,000.

Before reaching *Cape La Have* the steamer turns into a fair and sheltered haven called by the Indians Malagash, or " Milky," from the soft whiteness of its surf, and draws up to the wharves of **Lunenburg**. This is a thriving German town of 5,000 inhabitants, with large ship-building and mining interests, and an extensive trade in fish with West Indian ports. The town occupies a steep slope, and shows up most effectively as one approaches it from the sea. Its distance by water from Halifax is 45 miles, and its chief hotel is *King's*. The town and county of Lunenburg were settled in 1753 by Germans and Swiss, and the German language and German customs still prevail in the district. We see women working in the fields like men, and cows yoked with oxen to do the hauling and the plowing. The great point of interest in the neighborhood of Lunenburg is the peninsula of *Ovens Head*, distant about 10 miles. On this peninsula has been obtained, by washings, a large yield of gold. The place is remarkable for the strange caverns in its sea-face, called the " *Ovens*," whence it derives its name. These penetrate the cliffs for several hundred feet, and into their yawning jaws the great seas roar terrifically. There are, not unnaturally, many curious legends and traditions connected with the

16

Ovens, the most remarkable—and least credible—of which is to the effect that once an Indian, being swept by wind and current into the largest aperture, was sucked into the bowels of the earth, to reappear, not seriously the worse for his astounding adventure, among the count- less isles of Tusket, at the S. W. end of the peninsula. After rounding the well-named headland of Point Enragé, the steamer enters the fine estuary of the *La Have River*, and ascends it, on certain trips, 13 miles, to the town of **Bridgewater**. The shores of La Have are rich in his- tory, the district having been an important center of Acadian coloniza- tion. Here the chivalrous knight of Jerusalem, Isaac de Razilly, had his headquarters, and here he died, untimely, in 1637, to the incalculable loss of Acadie. Fort La Hève was the scene of many a well-fought battle between French and English or New-Englanders, and the lover of anti- quarian research will find the neighborhood a fertile field for his work. The sail up the La Have is very beautiful, and the town of Bridgewater is most fortunate in its situation. At the census of 1881 it had a population of 1,000, but it is growing since the opening of the Central Nova Scotia Railway, which has its offices and works at Bridgewater. Its chief business is the lumber-trade, and its great saw-mills are a picturesque feature of the landscape. The chief hotel is the *Fairview*, $1.50 a day. At this point, or at Lunenburg, the traveler who is not going on down the coast takes the railway across the province to Mid- dleton, on the Dominion Atlantic Ry.

Bridgewater to Yarmouth.

After leaving Bridgewater the boat rounds Cape La Have, and, after a run of 9 miles from the cape, passes the mouth of Port Med- way, a deep inlet, on which stands a lumbering village of the same name, with some 500 inhabitants. There is a good deal of ship-build- ing at this little town, which often goes by the name of Mill Village. Leaving behind Coffin's Island, the boat rounds into *Liverpool Bay*, a fine harbor with well-peopled shores. At its head flows in the Liverpool River, the outlet of the beautiful *Lake Rossignol*, the largest lake of Nova Scotia. The name of this lake is the old name of the harbor, given it by De Monts, in 1604, in honor of a French captain whose ship he had confiscated for trading in the harbor without authority— which must have seemed to the unhappy captain a somewhat barren compensation. At the mouth of the Liverpool River, on a rocky shore, stands the pretty and well-kept town of **Liverpool**, with a population of nearly 5,000 and a thriving trade. Lumbering, fishing, and ship-building, the stand-bys of all this coast, are the chief support of Liverpool, but she is also developing some manufacturing interests, in the lines of machinery, leather, matches, and iron-castings. The chief hotel is a home-like house, called *Grove Mansion.* The town is a pleasant place to visit in summer, with some agreeable society, and fine trout-fishing in the surrounding waters—whose names are legion. During the War of 1812 Liverpool was a privateering center, and her ships preyed fiercely and successfully on American commerce. In days more ancient, whose history comes down to us with a somewhat more questionable accuracy, the site of Liverpool was the realm of a mighty and malignant sorceress, who was righteously, if ungallantly, attacked by the Micmac demigod Gluskâp, already referred to, and torn to pieces, after a combat which the stars stood still to witness.

Leaving Liverpool Bay, the boat passes the bay and settlement of Port Mouton, so named by De Monts in 1604. De Monts was evidently impressed by Champlain's lack of imagination and tendency to immortalize the members of his family and two or three favorite saints in bestowing names, for his nomenclature is always fresh and striking. The harbor in question received its title from the circumstance that here a sheep jumped overboard and was drowned. This may seem to us a small matter, but at that time and place a sheep was worth considering, and its loss called for commemoration. Leaving out of sight Port Mouton, the boat passes, at some distance, a number of small fishing villages, and comes to the thriving little town of Lockeport, on Locke's Island, 37 miles from Shelburne. This town has a population of 1,918, and is actively engaged in the West India trade and in fishing on the Grand Banks. From Lockeport the steamer crosses the inlets of Green Harbor and Jordan River, with their settlements seen in the distance; passes Bony's and Government Points, and runs close to the striped black-and-white tower of Cape Roseway light. Then the course turns sharply to the N. E., and the boat steams up the noble expanse of *Shelburne Harbor*, so perfect in its freedom from winds and currents that it finds its bane in its very perfection, and freezes solid during the winter as if it were a fresh-water lake.

Shelburne is a little town, with its 2,055 inhabitants, but it has a romantic history. In a night it grew to a great city, and again in a

day it fell away to a quiet hamlet, because it had no root in a rich surrounding country. The matchless harbor attracted, in 1783, no fewer
than 12,000 of the United Empire Loyalists in their flight from the
new republic. Governor Parr came in with a fleet, and his batteries
saluted the city of Shelburne, which had sprung up like a dream,
throwing Halifax into utter insignificance. But like a dream the city
melted, for it had nothing on which to support itself. The sealed harbor, during the winter, was discouraging. The country around was a
wilderness, and not one of the sort that could be made to blossom like
the rose. Two and a half millions were sunk in founding the city.
Soon all the money was gone, and then the people went too—some
back to the United States, some to more hopeful settlements ; and
Shelburne was left with a population of 400—and the negro suburb of
Birchtown ! Even now the town, with a measure of returning prosperity, is ludicrously suggestive of a very small boy masquerading in
the garments of a very large grandfather. There are remnants, however, of the old loyalist stock in shrunken Shelburne, making society
there very pleasant, if not extensive. The chief hotel is the *Atlantic
House.*

Sailing out of Shelburne Harbor the steamer rounds Cape Roseway,
and turning eastward passes Negro Island, behind which lies the mouth
of the river Clyde. The next point of interest is the broad water of
Port Latour, on whose shores may still be seen the remains of Claude
de la Tour's fort. In the distance, just before rounding the low cape
called Baccaro Point, is visible the village of Port Latour. Beyond
the point lies **Cape Sable Island**, 7 miles long by 3 in extreme
width, with about 1,700 inhabitants. The island was occupied of old
by the Acadians, who in 1758 were carried away to Halifax, after
which, in the course of a quarter-century, their places were filled by
loyalists from New England, a vigorous stock. The extreme southern
point of the island is the ill-famed **Cape Sable**, from whose conspicuous
white sands comes the name.* The currents and fogs and ledges off
this point have given Cape Sable its sinister reputation, well justified by
the numerous wrecks of which it has been the author—chief of which
may be mentioned that of the ocean steamer Hungarian. Off the cape
have taken place some important sea-fights, notably that in which, in
1750, the French ship St. Francis was captured by the British ship

---

* *Cap aux Sables*, or the Cape of Sands.

Albany; and that in 1812, when the American ship Yankee destroyed the British ship Royal Bounty.

Between the long shores of Baccaro and Cape Sable Island is the *Barrington Passage*, up which the boat runs 12 miles to the busy fishing settlement of **Barrington**, with a population of about 1,600. The district was settled in 1763 by immigrants from Cape Cod, who were joined later on by loyalist refugees from the same section of the republic. A few miles from Barrington lie the Sabimm and Great Pubnico Lakes. From Barrington the steamer runs out by the West Passage to the open Atlantic, passes Shag Harbor and Bon Portage Island, and at a distance the outlying rocks of Seal Island and Blonde Rock, notorious respectively for the wrecks of the steamship Columbia and the British frigate Blonde. The boat's course is now northwest. She passes the mouth of Pubnico Harbor, where lies the prosperous French town of *Pubnico*, with a population of nearly 3,000 and a large fishing fleet. Argyle, with a population of 750, is near by, on Abuptic Harbor. After crossing the mouth of the harbor, and of Tusket River, we enter the myriad-islanded waters of **Tusket Archipelago**. The scene is strangely beautiful. The islands are of every shape and size, rising boldly out of ocean depths. They stand out from the coast, unsheltered by beach or promontory, and the tides and storms sweep furiously through the narrow but profound passages that sunder them. Some of them are named, but most are nameless. A fanciful explorer might imagine he discovered the origin of the Tusket Islands in the innumerable *Tusket Lakes*, clustered about the course of the Tusket River. These lakes are of all shapes and sizes, and look like spots whence patches of land were pulled up and cast into the sea to form islands. It is strange that the Micmac genius has not invented a tradition to such effect. These Tusket Lakes, it may be said, offer some of the best trout and salmon fishing of the province. After leaving the Tuskets Jebogue Point is rounded, and the steamer enters the estuary of *Yarmouth River* and ascends the narrow channel to the Yarmouth wharves.

Yarmouth.

The chief hotels of Yarmouth are the *Grand, Lorne,* and *Queen.* Livery charges are very moderate, and according to agreement. Fare by steamer: Yarmouth to *Boston,* $5; round trip, $9; Yarmouth to *St. John,* by Dominion Atlantic Railway, $3.30; to *Middleton,* $3.25; to *Halifax* (rail), $6; (boat), $5. The steamer *Alpha* leaves Yarmouth for *St. John* every Monday and Thursday, at 4 P.M., returning Tuesday and

Friday evenings. The *Boston steamers* leave Yarmouth, during the summer season daily on arrival of Halifax train ; leave Boston daily at 4.30 P. M. Fare from Halifax to Boston *via* Yarmouth, $7.50 ; round trip, $14. The *unlimited* ticket, allowing one to stop off at any place or places along the way, is $8.50.

The prominence attained by **Yarmouth** as a shipping port is rather in spite of than by reason of her harbor, which is straitened and tide-vexed, and troublesome to ascend. But she has triumphed brilliantly over these disadvantages, and now ranks fourth among Canadian ship-owning ports. St. John, Montreal, and Windsor head the list. The city is developing its harbor, adding steamers to its sailing fleets, and keeping abreast of modern movements. There are churches of all denominations, an excellent Free Public Library at 26 Centre St., where is also the Yarmouth County Museum. Directly opposite the city is Bay View Park, which is reached by steamer. It is one of the many spots where Captain Kidd is reported to have buried his ill-gotten wealth. An electric street railway renders easy access to many points. Yarmouth has woolen-mills, foundries, and a canvas-factory, and so is not wholly dependent upon her fishing interests. She has many handsome private residences, surrounded by charming and well-kept grounds ; and she is noted for the neatness and luxuriance of her numerous hedges. Through the hottest months of summer the lawns and trees of Yarmouth, and the blossoms of her tasteful gardens, preserve a spring-like freshness under the soft touches of the Atlantic mists. This bright and hospitable little city might almost be called a colony of ship-captains.

From Halifax eastward.

The steamers Fastnet and City of Ghent run eastward from Halifax along the coast to and through the *Strait of Canso*. Places on the strait are more conveniently and regularly reached by the rail route already described, and along this portion of the Atlantic coast there are few points of interest till we come to the great Bay of Chedabucto, and the little but sanguine town of Canso at its mouth. Intermediate points, such as Chezzetcook, Musquodoboit Harbor, Jeddore, Ship Harbor, Tangier, Sheet Harbor, and Sherbrooke, are best reached by stage from Halifax. **Chezzetcook** is interesting as a thoroughly typical Acadian settlement, on which time and progress work no changes. Its quaint people afford a rich field for observation and material for

Any number of racy *genre* pictures. Musquodoboit is interesting for its gold-mines, trout, and salmon. Jeddore has about 2,000 inhabitants, occupied in lumbering and fishing. The whole region is full of trout waters. Near Ship Harbor is a noble lake of the same name. Tangier, 60 miles from Halifax, is a gold-mining center on the Tangier River, or, as the Indians call it, Ahmagopakegeek, which means "Tumbling over the Rocks." Twenty miles beyond, at the head of the fine inlet called Sheet Harbor, is a shipping village of the same name, near which flow in the noted salmon-streams called *Middle* and *North Rivers*.

Sherbrooke is on St. Mary's Bay, the mouth of the important stream called *St. Mary's River*. This is one of the finest salmon-waters in the province, the fish running almost as large as those of the Restigouche; and it is not less famous for its trout. Within a radius of 10 or 12 miles are the equally noted waters (with salmon, trout, and sea-trout running up to five and six pounds) of the *Gegoggin*, *Gaspereaux*, and *Indian Rivers*, whose pools and runs will surely satisfy the most exacting angler.

Canso is on Chedabucto Bay, 32 miles S. E. of Guysborough. It has a population of about 1,500, and is the western terminus of several of the Atlantic cables, whose operators give the town some pleasant society. Near this point a company of Canadian and American capitalists is proposing to erect a great city, to be called the *Terminal City*, whence fast steamers are to traverse the Atlantic and lightning expresses rush westward. This scheme is pretty fully developed, and may perhaps be carried out, in which case the splendid Bay of Chedabucto would emerge from its present obscurity. The town of Guysborough is described in another place.

From Halifax to Yarmouth by the Dominion Atlantic Railway.

The fare from Halifax to *St. John* by this route is $4.50; to *Boston, via* Yarmouth, $7.50; to *Yarmouth*, $6; to *Annapolis*, $3.80; to *Bridgewater, via* Middleton and Central R. R., $4.75; to *Kentville*, $2.15; *Wolfville*, $1.95; *Windsor*, $1.38. The steamboat express leaves Halifax in the morning and runs through to Yarmouth in about seven hours, making the time between Halifax and Boston less than twenty-two hours in all. An express leaves Halifax for Kentville at

3.10 in the afternoon.   Under its new management the Dominion
Atlantic Ry. has become a very attractive road to travel over.   Road-
bed and rolling-stock have been improved and handsome parlor-cars
added to the fast steamer express, known as the "Flying Bluenose."
The railway is now thoroughly worthy of the country it traverses.

From Halifax to *Windsor Junction* the train runs over the rails of
the Intercolonial by a route already described; and Bedford Basin
takes on new phases of beauty in the fresh light of the morning.
Three miles beyond Windsor Junction is the station of Beaver Bank;
and 10 miles farther is *Mount Uniacke*, the seat of the Uniacke estate
and of valuable gold-mines.   The settlement lies between two small
rock-bound lakes.   Another 10 miles brings us to the picturesque settlement of *Ellershouse*, scattered over a succession of winding hills and
valleys.   This was once a very flourishing village, with a pulp-mill
and large lumbering interests, and took its name from its founder, a
wealthy German of high birth, with the failure of whose business came
to an end the prosperity of the village.   The fine Ellershausen Place is
beautifully situated at the head of a romantic glen, down which its
grounds extend.   A few miles inland from Ellershouse rises *Ardoise
Mountain* (pronounced Ardice), whose summit is the highest point in
the province.   A short distance beyond the village the train crosses the
St. Croix River, which is at this point a picturesque stream, with mills
clinging to its rocky banks.   The St. Croix is the outlet of the famous
Ponhook Lakes, with fine scenery and excellent trout-fishing.   The
trout of Ponhook run to a good size and are very game.   Owing to
their comparative inaccessibility these waters are not over-fished, and
they will well repay a visit by canoe.   Three miles from Ellershouse
is Newport Station, the center of a fertile farming district.   At this
point heavy shipments of plaster are made by rail.   All about Newport lie populous agricultural villages, reached by stage.   Three miles
beyond Newport we pass the way station of Three-Mile Plains.   Yet
3 miles farther and we run out upon the rich marshes between the
St. Croix and Avon, sweep round the grassy hill of *Fort Edward*,
and run into the excessively unpretentious station of the town of
Windsor.

Windsor is a wealthy little town 46 miles from Halifax, with a
population, according to the census of 1891, of 2,900, but now estimated at something over 3,000.   Its shipping is enormous, and it ranks
as the third ship-owning port in Canada.   It is largely interested in the

South American trade, and ships great quantities of white and blue plaster from the Wentworth and other quarries to Boston, New York, and Philadelphia. In the neighborhood are the gold-mines of *Rawdon*, lately opened and proving very productive. Windsor has also large cotton, furniture, and leather factories, besides an extensive iron-foundry. Its only public buildings of importance are the Court-House and the handsome *Post-Office ;* but the plain dark pile of **King's College,** though without architectural pretension, is impressive by reason of its commanding site. As seen from the station, Windsor—which was recently the victim of a fierce and widespread conflagration—is not striking, and the visitor who has heard of the beauty of Windsor should lose no time in getting to the top of one of the rounded hills on which the town is built. From the top of *Ferry Hill*, either when the tide is in, or at sunset, when the vast abyss of the empty channel glows like polished copper about the dark piers and wharves and black hulls of stranded ships, the scene is one to satisfy the utmost expectations. Quite different but equally superb is the view from the loftier hill-top occupied by the Tennis Courts, whose pavilion roof affords a post of vantage. The streets of the town run up and down hill and in unexpected directions, and are well adorned with shade-trees. Behind the lower end of the town flows in the St. Croix, at this point a great tidal stream navigable for ocean ships to the wharves of Wentworth. The *Avon River*, which forms the harbor of Windsor, is a large tidal stream emptying into the Basin of Minas, 12 miles below the town. At high water it is like an inland sea, amply deep for any ship afloat; and with the flood-tide come ships, and yachts, and tugs, and steamers, flocking to the wharves of Windsor. At low tide it is but a rivulet, and fairly justifies the gibes of Charles Dudley Warner, who writes of the Avon as follows : " I never knew before how much water adds to a river. Its slimy bottom was quite a ghastly spectacle, an ugly rent in the land that nothing could heal but the friendly returning tide. I should think it would be confusing to dwell by a river that runs first one way and then the other, and then vanishes altogether."

The ancient name of Windsor was Piziquid, meaning " The Junction of the Waters." Here stood a populous and prosperous Acadian settlement, till the great banishment in 1755. After the lands of the Acadians had lain for some years vacant, settlers from Massachusetts and Rhode Island were brought in to occupy the townships of Newport and Falmouth, while Windsor itself was allotted to retiring British officers, and became one of the social centers of the province. King's College, the oldest of England's colonial universities, was founded in 1790, on Oxford models, and was given a royal charter in 1802. It is under the patronage of the Archbishop of Canterbury, and is a Church of England institution, though free to all denominations alike. It cele-brated its centenary last year; and, after many vicissitudes, entered on an era of renewed prosperity under the management of the present president, Dr. Willets. Some of the most distinguished sons of Canada have been educated at King's, on whose roll of graduates are such names as those of Judge Haliburton ("Sam Slick"), Sir John Inglis, and Sir Fenwick Williams. At one corner of the college property is the *Collegiate School*, a prosperous institution, and adjoining them on the E., on a roomy hillside, are the grounds and buildings of "*Edgehill*," the newly-established "Church School for Girls." A favorite walk is from town out to the college woods, through a willowed avenue that crosses the ravine of the disused plaster-quarries, and past the gate-house of *Clifton*, the old Haliburton estate where "Sam Slick" used to live. This historic estate, with its delightful old country-house em-bowered in ancient trees, no longer belongs to the Haliburton family, but is always known as the "Sam Slick House." The chief hotels of Windsor are the excellently equipped *Dufferin Hotel*, whose roomy structure is the most conspicuous object near the station; and the *Victoria* (Doran's), an old and popular house, which is quite up to the requirements of the day. Among the other hotels may be men-tioned *Mounce's* and the *Somerset House*. A cab or two is usually in attendance at the station, and carries travelers to the hotels or points in town for 25 cents. The livery charges of the establishments fur-nishing these cabs (Townshend's, Jenkins's, and Smith's stables) are very moderate.

Windsor to Parrsboro and St. John.

Formerly it was possible to sail from Windsor to Parrsboro by steamers, but now it is necessary to take the Dominion Atlantic Ry. to Kingsport, and thence by steamer Evangeline to Parrsboro.

The train passes along the bank to the Avon's mouth. The ample river can by no stretch of fancy be called blue; but blueness is some-thing of which we have by this time grown well-nigh surfeited. The shores are a succession of rich, rolling hills, set with prosperous villages; for the soil of this region is of boundless fertility. As we run out of the Avon we pass on our left the little town of Avonport, whence the train runs toward Kentville (see page 257), where a branch turns north, passing Mill Village, Centerville, Cunard, Canning, and finally reaches *Kingsport.* In going by boat we cross the swaying expanse of *Minas Basin*, the ponderous front of *Blomidon* (described in later pages) is the dominating object, dwarfing the dark brows of rival promontories, and recalling many a romantic tradition. Running past its foot, we find that this giant loses none of his impressiveness on close inspection. Even while we are in broad sunshine, the dark summit towering above may be withdrawn from view, wrapped in the fogs that roll over it from Fundy. At this point we command a magnificent view up the Basin, past the quaint masses of *Five Islands*, up *Cobequid Bay*, to the very mouth of the *Shubenacadie River*, while far behind lies the meadow of *Grand Pré*. From Kingsport we run across the mouth of the Basin to the village of **Parrsboro**, on a small river at whose mouth the steamer stops. As we make fast to the mossy timbers of the pier, our view out into the **Bay of Fundy** is cut off by the near heights of *Partridge Island*, an abrupt and somber-wooded hill connected with the mainland by a gravel beach. This island is the center of many Gluskâp legends, and here took place Gluskâp's famous carousal with the divine Kit-poose-ee-a-goo-no, at which a whole whale was eaten. At *Parrsboro Pier*, as the landing is called, there are admirable beaches, and there stands a pleasant lodging-house close to the head of the wharf, with a home-like air very attractive to the summer idler. Parrsboro itself is reached by a drive of about a mile and a half from the pier. There are several small hotels, of which the most comfortable is the *Grand Central*. The chief business of Parrsboro, supporting a population of something over 1,000, is the shipping of lumber. It is the best center from which to reach the wild back country of Cumberland County, famous for its moose and bears, and its comparatively virgin fishing-waters. Guides may be hired in the town. A run of 32 miles by rail will enable one to visit the prosperous coal-mining town of **Springhill**, a thoroughly typical coal town. Parrsboro lies, by water, just 30 miles from Windsor. Delightful drives may be taken in the neighborhood, to *Apple River*, *Five Islands*, and the sublime sea-scapes of *Advocate Harbor* and *Cape d' Or.*

From Parrsboro pier the boat runs out into the **Bay of Fundy** on the bosom of a tremendous tide, that races between *Cape Sharp* and Blomidon at the rate of 8 or 9 miles an hour. Soon we pass, on our left, the strange and impressive promontory of *Cape Split*, whose terminal cliff, about 400 ft. high, appears to have been literally split away from the main mass, and now rises out of the seething tides in lonely grandeur. *Spencer's Island* is passed about a dozen miles from Cape Split, and then in the distance loom the giant outlines of *Cape d'Or*, with *Cape Chignecto* far to the N. Perhaps the most interesting point we pass is the lofty cliff-girt island called **Isle Haute**, in the middle of the bay. The island is less than two miles in length, and its apparently inaccessible walls are 350 feet in height. On its top is a farm, inhabited and cultivated by a family for whom isolation seems to have no terrors. From Isle Haute to **St. John** is a run of from 60 to 75 miles, according to weather and tide. The course is down the open bay, and the shores are too far off to be of interest.

Windsor to Grand Pré.

The train runs slowly through the back yards of Windsor to the Avon, and crosses the river on a fine iron bridge, parallel to which runs the light and graceful structure of the new passenger bridge. Then comes the pretty settlement of Falmouth, 1½ miles from Windsor station. The next stop is at **Hantsport**, 7 miles from Windsor. This is a neat and thriving town, and does an immense amount of ship-building. It is beginning to develop manufacturing interests, and has good freestone quarries in the vicinity. The houses are small, but wear an air of comfort. From this point onward to *Avonport* the railroad follows the banks of the Avon, and one gets noble views from the car windows, across the wide Avon, and Minas Basin, toward the blue line of the Parrsboro shore, with fine glimpses of the mighty shoulder of **Blomidon**. Presently this great promontory comes into full view, and thenceforth remains the commanding feature of the landscape for many miles, until Port Williams is left behind.

> "This is that black rock bastion, based in surge,
> Pregnant with agate and with amethyst,
> Whose foot the tides of storied Minas scourge,
> Whose top austere withdraws into its mist.

Cape Blomidon.

" This is that ancient cape of tears and storm,
  Whose towering front inviolable frowns
O'er vales Evangeline and love keep warm—
  Whose fame thy song, O tender singer, crowns.

" Yonder, across these reeling fields of foam,
  Came the sad threat of the avenging ships.
  What profit now to know if just the doom,

" Though harsh! The streaming eyes, the praying lips,
  The shadow of inextinguishable pain,
  The poet's deathless music—these remain! "

Avonport is at the mouth of the Avon, 5 miles from Hantsport, 58 miles from Halifax. Two miles beyond we cross the storied **Gaspereaux** at its mouth, and reach the village of *Horton Landing*. From this point, on to beyond Wolfville, we are in the actual " **Land of Evangeline.**" The great body of the Acadian settlement was nearer Horton Landing than to the station of **Grand Pré**, 1 mile farther on. Close to Horton Landing is the little creek at whose mouth the unhappy Acadians were embarked for exile. At Horton Landing is a pleasant little half hotel, half country-house, by name *Dunedin Cottage ;* and visitors may spend some summer weeks here very pleasantly, roaming the breezy " dikes," bathing on the beaches of *Long Island,* or exploring the lovely valley of the Gaspercaux. Close to Dunedin Cottage is Patterson's Agricultural and Business School, where boys are taught farming, with other useful knowledge. Grand Pré itself, from whose station we see close at hand a row of old Acadian willows, and on the hill-side a few gaunt Acadian poplars and gnarled Acadian apple-trees, can hardly be called a village. It is merely a thicker clustering of the fruitful farms and orchards, and ample farm-houses, that make so cheerful the face of all this landscape. Near the station is a great tree by whose foot may be traced the foundations of the Acadian Parish Church. The neighborhood is a delightful one to visit, for many gentlemen from Halifax and other centers have farms here, where they make their summer residence. The visitor who wishes to spend some time in this neighborhood and do thoroughly the whole district over which Longfellow has cast the colored light of romance, will find it most convenient to make his headquarters at **Wolfville**, 3 miles beyond Grand Pré, whence the whole region is accessible by pleasant carriage-drives.

THE EXPULSION OF THE ACADIANS.

It is to be presumed that the tourist will go through this region with an open volume of "Evangeline" in his hand, or at least with a copy of Longfellow in his pocket. Hence, extended quotations from the noble and touching poem, which has immortalized this region and crystallized in men's minds a somewhat mistaken view of the tragedy here enacted, might be considered superfluous. Nevertheless we append one extract, in which the Acadian village is inimitably described:

"In thè Acadian land, on the shores of the Basin of Minas,
  Distant, secluded, still, the little village of Grand Pré
  Lay in the fruitful valley. Vast meadows stretched to the eastward,
  Giving the village its name, and pasture to flocks without number.
  Dikes, that the hands of the farmers had raised with labor incessant,
  Shut out the turbulent tides; but at certain seasons the flood-gates
  Opened, and welcomed the sea to wander at will o'er the meadows.
  West and south there were fields of flax, and orchards and corn-fields
  Spreading afar and unfenced o'er the plain; and away to the northward
  Blomidon rose, and the forests old, and aloft on the mountains
  Sea-fogs pitched their tents, and mists from the mighty Atlantic
  Looked on the happy valley, but ne'er from their station descended.
  There, in the midst of its farms, reposed the Acadian village.
  Strongly built were the houses, with frames of oak and of chestnut,
  Such as the peasants of Normandy built in the reign of the Henries.
  Thatched were the roofs, with dormer-windows; and gables projecting
  Over the basement below protected and shaded the doorway.
  There in the tranquil evenings of summer, when brightly the sunset
  Lighted the village street, and gilded the vanes on the chimneys,
  Matrons and maidens sat in snow-white caps and in kirtles
  Scarlet and blue and green, with distaffs spinning the golden
  Flax for the gossiping looms, whose noisy shuttles within doors
  Mingled their sound with the whir of the wheels and the songs of the maidens.
  Solemnly down the street came the parish priest, and the children
  Paused in their play to kiss the hand he extended to bless them.
  Reverend walked he among them; and up rose matrons and maidens,
  Hailing his slow approach with words of affectionate welcome.
  Then came the laborers home from the field, and serenely the sun sank
  Down to his rest, and twilight prevailed. Anon from the belfry
  Softly the Angelus sounded, and over the roofs of the village
  Columns of pale blue smoke, like clouds of incense ascending,
  Rose from a hundred hearths, the homes of peace and contentment.
  Thus dwelt together in love these simple Acadian farmers—
  Dwelt in the love of God and of man. Alike were they free from
  Fear, that reigns with the tyrant, and envy, the vice of republics.
  Neither locks had they to their doors, nor bars to their windows;
  But their dwellings were open as day and the hearts of the owners;
  There the richest was poor, and the poorest lived in abundance."

Cape Split.

The pathos and appeal of the Acadian story, as told by Longfellow, should not be allowed to blind us to the fact that the pitiful fate of the Acadians was a measure of absolutely necessary justice. In spite of the most earnest pleadings, the frankest threatenings, and forty years of unparalleled forbearance, exercised long after forbearance had ceased to be a virtue, the Acadians persisted in a deadly enmity to a government whose subjects they unquestionably were. They refused to allow themselves to be considered as other than enemies, and not only did they engage, along with the savages, in occasional bloody raids upon the English settlements, but their presence in the colony made a point of almost fatal weakness in its defenses, at a time when England was engaged in what was practically a life-and-death struggle with her great antagonist. The indulgence of the English Government was repaid by the Acadians with hatred, and sometimes with the scalping-knife. Undoubtedly these people believed they were acting aright. Had they been left to themselves, they would have become, in the course of a generation, loyal and contented subjects. But they were made the tools of French intrigue. From Quebec every effort was continually put forth to keep alive their bitterness against their conquerors, and their belief that Acadia would once more be brought beneath the sway of France. When they began to show signs of a desire to accept the situation, and when persuasion on the part of Quebec became ineffectual, then threats were employed, and they were menaced with the tomahawks of the savages. The authorities at Quebec had no scruples. Sometimes violence was resorted to, and the exile of the Acadians was begun by Le Loutre before the English had thought of it. Hundreds of Acadians, who were becoming reconciled to English rule, were forced by Le Loutre to move into French territory, where they suffered unbounded hardships. Their homes were burned behind them, and whole villages were thus depopulated, in obedience to a heartless policy. The Acadians were a simple and ignorant people, easily led by their superiors, and hence on a final estimate they must be regarded as .more sinned against than sinning. But those who wrought their ruin and deserved their curse were not the English, but their own countrymen. The removal of the Grand Pré Acadians was accomplished with combined firmness and gentleness by Colonel Winslow, of Boston, with his New England troops; and his journal, though full of commiseration for this unhappy people, shows that he did not consider the justice of their sentence in the least degree open to question. After the exile was accomplished many of the Acadians escaped to Quebec, where their lot was pitiful indeed compared with that of those who remained in the American colonies. Among men of alien speech and faith they were at least humanely treated; but at Quebec they were cheated and starved, and died like sheep, having fallen to the tender mercies of Bigot and his creatures. The period at which these exiles fled to Quebec is not a bright one in French-Canadian annals. After the removal of the Acadians their fair inheritance lay vacant for years ere men of English speech entered upon it.

Wolfville to Annapolis.

Wolfville is a remarkably pretty little university town, embowered in apple-orchards, and ranged on a sunny slope facing the marshes, the blue Basin, and Blomidon. Its population, according to the census of 1891, was 1,500; but in the census now being taken it will give a better account of itself. On the other side of the great ridge behind the town lies the deep romantic *Valley of the Gaspereaux*, which is said by some travelers to resemble the valley of the Dee. A short walk from Wolfville over the hill will take one into scenes that have never been done justice to by the artist's brush. The upper waters of the Gaspereaux afford some good salmon-fishing, and the chain of lakes from which it flows is well stocked with trout. The town of Wolfville is dominated by the Baptist university of *Acadia College*, with its associated institutions for the education of boys and girls. All these institutions are flourishing and largely attended. The president of the college is Dr. Sawyer, who secures a very loyal and vigorous support for the institution from the denomination under whose auspices it is conducted. The university building occupies a fine site on the hill side, and shows up very effectively as seen from the passing train. Wolfville has several hotels, the best of which is perhaps the *American House.*

The great cape of **Blomidon**, the sentinel of the Evangeline land, may be reached by driving from Wolfville, or from Kentville by taking the new Cornwallis Valley Branch, of the Dominion Atlantic Railway, to Kingsport and driving thence. It is about 18 miles from Wolfville to Blomidon, a lovely drive all the way. The first 9 miles is across the famed **Cornwallis Valley** to the little town of *Canning*. This valley is indeed the garden of the province. It is traversed by four rivers—the Cornwallis, Canard, Canning, and Pereau. Its deep alluvial soil is of quenchless fertility. Its climate, protected by the lofty range of North Mountain from the fogs and storms of Fundy, has the sparkle of sea air with the softness of the most favored inland regions. In many of its charming characteristics, and particularly by reason of its abounding orchards, it recalls the Niagara Peninsula. Some distance beyond Canning the road begins to wind up the side of **North Mountain**, and then runs along the crest to the lofty point of vantage called the **Look-off**, whence one gazes into five counties. The glorious panorama seen from this point is something one must go far to equal. Four miles farther on the range of North Mountain breaks down in magnificent abruptness of cliff, nearly 600 ft., to the tide-swept Basin of Minas. This cliff-front is Blomidon, and the expert climber may explore its somber ramparts for amethysts and garnets, opal and agate, chalcedony and copper, malachite and psilomelane, or for that fabled crystal, the *Diamond of Blomidon*, whose radiance reveals itself only to the distant watcher, and evades anything like a close scrutiny.

Two miles beyond Wolfville is the station of Port Williams, whence quantities of apples, potatoes, and cattle are shipped. Then we forsake the marshes for a time, and find them very straitened when we meet them again as we draw near Kentville. **Kentville** is a busy town packed into a remarkably lovely little valley, along with a bit of tidal river, a brawling amber brook overhung with willows, splendid trees, and great variety in very scanty room. Everything appears on a diminutive scale. Everywhere is close to everywhere else in Kentville, and the place has a peculiar and distinctive charm in spite of its summer heat. That is a small drawback, however, for when quite roasted out one need turn aside but a dozen paces, climb a hill-top, and cool himself comfortably. Kentville is also dusty; but this matters little, for no wind can get at the dust to make it troublesome. The population of Kentville is something over 2,000. It has several hotels, the most popular of which is the excellent house *Aberdeen*. At Kentville we are 71 miles from Halifax, and here the train stops fifteen minutes for refreshments. From the station we may take the Cornwallis Valley Branch, of the Dominion Atlantic Railway, for Canning and the apple-shipping village of Kingsport, on Minas Basin. The fare for this trip is 50 cents; return, 75 cents. At Kingsport will be found a seaside resort which has aptly been named the Newport of Nova Scotia. Between Kingsport and Parrsboro, on the Cumberland shore, the Dominion Atlantic Ry's steamer Evangeline makes

17

daily trips across the Basin of Minas (single fare, $1 ; return, $1.60). Charming drives also may be taken from Kentville to Hall's Harbor and Baxter's Harbor, over North Mountain, on the Bay of Fundy shore.

Leaving Kentville we pass the stations of Coldbrook (76 miles from Halifax), Cambridge (78 miles), Waterville (80 miles), the thriving manufacturing town of *Berwick* (83 miles), famous for its Methodist Camp-meeting Grounds, and *Aylesford* (88 miles). In the neighborhood of Aylesford is the great chain of wilderness waters, called the Aylesford Lakes. Here, too, is a sand plain, 13 miles long by half as much in width, sprinkled in a niggardly fashion with coarse, thin grasses, and rejoicing in the title of the "*Devil's Goose Pasture.*" Near Aylesford is the rifle range and camp ground of Aldershott. Next comes Auburn (90 miles), and then Kingston (95 miles). A short drive from *Kingston* is the pretty village of Melvern Square. Three miles beyond Kingston is the station of Wilmot, whence one may drive to the *Wilmot Spa Springs*. There is a summer hotel at the springs ; and good lodgings may be obtained at private houses in the neighborhood. The waters of the springs are growing rapidly in repute, and a delicious, sparkling ginger ale is manufactured from them. They have a great medicinal value, and taste much less like a combination of old shoes and burnt gunpowder than such waters usually do.

The next stopping-place is *Middleton*, 102 miles from Halifax. This is a town growing rapidly in importance and population. It has rich copper and iron mines in its vicinity, and is the northwestern terminus of the Central of Nova Scotia Railway. Its chief hotels are the *American House* and *Middleton Hotel*. Near Middleton are the lovely *Nictaux Falls*. The trains of the Central of Nova Scotia run through fine and varied scenery. They leave Middleton at 1.40 P. M., and reach Springfield at 3.07, New Germany at 3.44, Bridgewater at 4.37, and Lunenburg at 5.35. Six miles beyond Middleton is the pretty pastoral village of *Lawrencetown*, on the winding, upper waters of the historic **Annapolis River**. There is a hotel here called the *Elm House*. Three miles farther is the farming and lumbering settlement of *Paradise*, with fine granite in the neighborhood. Within easy reach are capital trout-waters. Next we come to **Bridgetown**, 116 miles from Halifax and 14 from Annapolis. This is a stirring little town of something over 1,000 inhabitants, at the head of navigation on the Annapolis River. It has good water-power, which it utilizes in furniture and organ factories. The surrounding country is prosperous and thickly settled, which gives Bridgetown a large local trade. In the neighborhood is *Bloody Brook*, so called from a massacre of New England troops by the French and their Indian allies. The chief hotels of Bridgetown are *Chute's* and the *Grand Central*.

From Bridgetown to Annapolis is the prettiest part of the journey after leaving Kentville. The views from the car-windows are full of quiet and varied charm—richly wooded slopes, sunny bits of meadow and winding river, and in the distance the blue hills. Midway between Bridgetown and Annapolis is the station of Roundhill.

Annapolis to Yarmouth.

At **Annapolis** we arrive at noon. The old historic town of Annapolis, or *Annapolis Royal*, has a fair and sheltered site, and we fail to wonder that it attracted the regard of French navigators fresh from the rough breast of Fundy. The Basin was discovered by that expedition of De Monts and Champlain, in 1604, that went on to found the ill-fated settlement on St. Croix Island. The survivors remembered affectionately the lovely shores of the Basin, and fled back thither from St. Croix. The region was granted to Baron Poutrincourt, who named it **Port Royal**; and in 1606 came a little colony, of whom the leading spirit was one *Mark Lescarbot*, who became the chronicler of the settlement. He inaugurated that "*Order of a Good Time*," whose high-hearted mirth makes so bright a spot in those annals of strife and privation. The members of the order were fifteen, and their head was the "steward," whose office was held for a day at a time by each member in turn. The steward's responsibility was heavy. He had to provide an attractive bill of fare for the day's dinner—and material for such a task was not always abundant at Port Royal. At each feast it was requisite that there should be one entirely new delicacy. Toward spring the wine ran low, and instead of three quarts to each member the daily allowance was reduced to one poor pint. This merry order doubtless did much to keep up the heart of the lonely little colony during the long and trying winter; and only three deaths occurred. In the month of January the order went on a six-mile picnic, to see if the corn they had sown in November had begun to sprout beneath the snow!

Trouble began at Port Royal through the interference of the Jesuits, to whom Poutrincourt was unfriendly. The Jesuits in a short time left the colony and established a new settlement called St. Sauveur, at Mount Desert. When this was destroyed by a Virginian expedition under Argall, the Jesuits led the enemy on to Port Royal, which was speedily laid waste. Thus began, in 1613, the struggle between France and England for the New World, which ended not till 1763. From its founding till its capture by New-Englanders in 1710, the story of Port Royal is an endless succession of captures and recaptures, and changing masters. In 1710 its name was altered to Annapolis Royal. In the next year occurred the massacre of Bloody Brook, already referred to; and though from this date Annapolis remained in the hands of the English, the following forty years saw it kept in an almost perpetual state of siege by the hostile Indians and Acadians. After the exile of the Acadians the settlement tasted the unwonted delights of peace till 1781, when it was attacked in the night by two American war-ships. The fort was captured and its guns spiked; and the towns-folk were locked up in the block-house while the unwelcome visitors looted the town. The fort is still in good repair. The view from its ram-parts of sod is very lovely and altogether unwarlike. The fort is im-perial property, as is also Fort Edward at Windsor. Most of the other strongholds in Canada, outside of Halifax, were surrendered by England to the Canadian Government at the time of confederation, in 1867.

Annapolis has a population of over 3,000. Its chief hotels are the *Hillsdale, American,* and *Clifton.* There is a good restaurant in the station. The town is almost surrounded by water, an extension of the Basin on one side, and on the other the Annapolis River, crossed here by a ferry to the pretty village of *Granville.* To north and south stretch the sheltering, high green walls of North and South Mountains, and to eastward opens the magnificent expanse of the great landlocked haven, 18 miles long by 1 to 5 in width, called *Annapolis Basin.* The view down the Basin from Annapolis is partly obstructed by Goat Island. From Annapolis to Yarmouth is 87 miles; fare, $2.60. The first station out of Annapolis is *Clementsport,* a shipping village in the neighborhood of rich deposits of iron-ore. These mines were worked for a time and abandoned, but will probably be reopened ere long. From the village roads run inland to the pictur-esque Blue Mountain (held sacred by the Indians), and to the wonder-ful trout-waters of the Liverpool Lakes. **Bear River,** 9 miles from Digby, is a busy little shipping port, with saw-mills and a tannery. It is most romantically situated in a deep valley, so sheltered that Spring finds her way thither some weeks before she can be persuaded to smile on the rest of the province. The time to visit Bear River is emphatically in the cherry-season—for her cherries are nowhere to be surpassed.

Digby, which lies on a curve of shore just beyond the opening called *Digby Gut*, is a favorite summer resort, and well supplied with small hotels. The chief of these is the *Myrtle House*, followed by the *Royal*, *Short's*, *Digby House*, the *Evangeline*, *Burnham's*, *Waverly*, *Cherry Tree*, and *De Balinhard's*. Digby has the invigorating sea air of the Bay of Fundy, which is only 3 miles distant, behind the mountain, and is free from the fog and the chill. The sea-bathing is good, though colder than at Annapolis, and there is good sport to be had in the way of salt-water fishing; while the boating, of course, is all that could be wished. Digby has a population of about 1,200, and is extensively engaged in fisheries. The herring known as "Digby chickens" are famous throughout the Maritime Provinces for their delicacy. A prominent object near the station is a field full of little wooden platforms, on which the split cod are dried for export. The *pier of Digby* is a long and lofty structure, at different portions of which a landing is effected, according to the state of the tide. The fluctuation of tide here is somewhere about 40 ft., and the tremendous currents every now and then work disaster for the pier, which seems forever being rebuilt.

The traveler who is bound for St. John takes the superb steamer "Prince Rupert," of the Dominion Atlantic Railway Company, the fastest and most perfect passenger steamship on Canada's eastern seaboard, and a marvel of steadiness in rough weather. After steaming a couple of miles along a fair and lofty sloping shore, the Prince Rupert enters the fine scenery of Digby Gut, or, as it was called of old, St. George's Channel. This passage is a gigantic cleft in the North Mountain, nearly 2 miles through, and about half a mile in width, with bold, darkly-wooded shores from 500 to 600 ft. in height. On the eastern slope perch a few airy cottages, making up an ideal fishing village; and the reddish-gray lines of a winding road seem as if they were painted on the steep incline. Through the "Gut" sweep terrific tides, boiling and eddying, and tossing violently the fishermen's boats which dot its surface. The Fundy gate of the passage is usually white with surf. Digby Gut is satisfying, always, to the lover of the picturesque; but it is never more so than when one enters it from the bay, and looks through its grand portals into the favored haven beyond.

The fare from Digby to Yarmouth is $2, and the distance 67 miles. The railway lies some distance back from the coast, along which are most of the settlements; and travelers who wish to visit the picturesque Acadian district of Clare may do so very conveniently from Weymouth by driving. **Clare** is settled by returned Acadian exiles, and maintains its peculiar individuality with great persistence. It is almost as quaint as Chezzetcook. The settlements are like one long village street, for miles; and back of the cottages run the narrow strips of the oft-subdivided farms. The district lies along the shores of the deep bay of *St. Mary's*, whose waters are separated only by a narrow isthmus from those of the Annapolis Basin. The bay is divided from the Bay of Fundy by the long line of mountains, a continuation of North Mountain, known as **Digby Neck**. This curious peninsula, which is only from a mile to a mile and a half in width, runs 20 miles seaward, and is continued for another 20 miles by *Long Island* and *Brier Island*. The Neck and the Islands are settled by a picturesque and hardy fishing population, whose centers are the quaint out-of-the-world villages of *Sandy Cove*, *Free Port*, and *Westport*, reached by stage and ferries from Digby. The most important station on the Dominion Atlantic Railway, after leaving Digby, is **Weymouth**, a remarkably pretty little ship-building town at the mouth of the *Sissiboo River*, some distance up St. Mary's Bay. Weymouth has a large West India trade, and a population of about 1,800. Two or three miles up the river is the village of *Weymouth Bridge*. The chief hotels are the *Weymouth House* and *Goodwin Hotel*. A short distance beyond foam the pretty **Sissiboo Falls**. Soon the railroad leaves St. Mary's Bay and strikes through a rough country dotted with trout-waters, to Yarmouth. The most important stations on this section of the line are Meteghan, Brazil Lake, Ohio, and Hebron. Yarmouth has been already described. The train stops at Yarmouth Station, and then runs down on to the railway wharf with the passengers for the boat. Presently the traveler finds himself moving slowly down the Yarmouth River, emerging from whose narrow pass the boat heads straight across the open Atlantic for Boston.

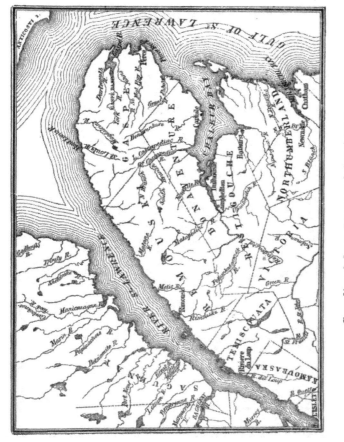

Canadian Salmon Rivers and Gaspé Basin.

WESTERN CANADA.

WESTERN CANADA.

In that part of this book devoted to Eastern Canada a full description of the Provinces of Ontario and of Quebec, and of the Maritime Provinces, including Newfoundland, is given. But this is not all of the mighty empire known as the Dominion of Canada. West of Ontario is Manitoba, and beyond are Assiniboia and Saskatchewan. Then comes Alberta, and far away on the Pacific Coast is British Columbia, which separates the United States from its northern territory of Alaska. The journey through these provinces is described in the following pages. The Canadian Pacific Railway is the iron link that connects the East with the West, and we shall follow that route, for the most part, in our trip across the continent. It is the chief means of transportation, and with its branches touches all points worthy of notice. In the text we shall continue the practice of abbreviating its title to C. P. R.

Montreal is the great railway centre of Canada. It is the main terminus of the C. P. R., and from it through trains run E. and W. and S. Mileage is counted from it. A full description of it—the chief city of Canada—has already been given on pages 60 to 71 of this book, but for convenience sake mention must be made of the methods of reaching it. From Portland, Me., it may be reached by the Grand Trunk Ry., and the Maine Central R. R. to Cookshire Junction, and thence by the C. P. R. From Boston there is a choice of the several White Mountain routes, as the Boston & Maine R. R. to Newport and thence over the C. P. R., or to White River Junction and thence over the Central Vermont R. R. to St. Johns, where the Grand Trunk Ry. is taken. From New York the New York Central R. R. or the West Shore R. R. is available to Albany, where connection is made with the Delaware & Hudson R. R. to Rouse's Point, and thence over the Grand Trunk Ry. again; also by the Adirondack Div. of the New York Central R. R. to Adirondack Junction and C. P. R.

Montreal to Ottawa.

a. By the Canadian Pacific Railway.

The famous trip down the Ottawa River, with its thrilling passage through the Lachine Rapids, has already been described on page 53, but the westward trip by the C. P. R. needs brief reference at this point. The Pacific Express leaves Montreal daily, except Sundays, for Ottawa, and makes the distance of 120 miles in 3¼ hours. The same train makes the distance to Vancouver (2,906 miles) in exactly 4 days and 23 hours. Sleeping and dining cars are attached to all transcontinental trains.

As the train leaves Montreal it passes on overhead bridges through the western suburbs, and in 10 minutes reaches *Montreal Junction*, a fashionable residential suburb of Montreal, that takes its name from the fact that it is the railroad junction from the Maritime Provinces, New York, Boston, and Portland, and all trains to the West. The next station is *St. Martin Junction*, so called on account of the divergence of the line to Quebec. The N. branch of the Ottawa is crossed at *Ste. Rose* (17 miles). From here on, the line follows the N. bank of the Ottawa, and frequent views are had of steamboats, lumber barges, and rafts of timber as they are passed on its broad waters. The valley is divided into narrow, well-tilled French farms, mostly devoted to dairy products. Picturesque villages are passed at intervals, and streams coming down from the Laurentian Hills on the N. afford good fishing. At *Ste. Therese* three branch lines diverge to *St. Lin, La-belle*, and *St. Eustache*. At *Lachute* (44 miles) there are paper mills, wood-working and other industries, and it is a shipping point for dairy products. The Ottawa Valley Ry. runs from here to St. Andrew. There are extensive saw-mills at *Calumet* (59 miles), and these occur at frequent intervals. From *Buckingham* (100 miles) a branch extends northward to phosphate, mica, and graphite mines. Soon after leaving the station the main line of the railway crosses, by an iron bridge, directly over the magnificent falls of the Lievre River. After crossing the Gatineau River the Government Buildings in Ottawa come into view keeping N. on a high cliff at the left. At *Hull* (118 miles) an electric railway diverges, keeping N. of the Ottawa, and runs to *Aylmer*. Leaving Hull, the main line swings round, crosses a long iron bridge, from where a view of the Chaudière Falls is obtained, and enters Ottawa.

As previously stated, the new short line between Montreal and Ottawa runs along the Ontario bank and reaches Ottawa at the Central Station, the fast trains on this line making the distance in two hours and forty minutes.

b. By the Canada Atlantic Railway.

This route is only 116 miles long, and the time occupied in making the trip about 3½ hours. The train leaves Montreal from the Bonaventure Station and follows the tracks of the Grand Trunk Ry. along the banks of the St. Lawrence River to *Coteau Junction* (37 miles), connection being made with the Adirondack Division of the New York Central & Hudson R. R. at Valleyfield, and Coteau Junction with the branch of the Canada Atlantic that extends to Rouse's Point, where it meets the Central Vermont R. R. and the Delaware & Hudson R. R. At *St. Polycarpe Junction* (45 miles) the C. P. R. is crossed, and at *Ste. Justine* (51 miles) the Province of Ontario is entered. The next place of importance is *Glen Robertson* (55 miles), where a branch extends 21 miles N. to *Hawksbury*, passing *Vankleek Hill* (14 miles). *Alexandria* (62 miles) is the half-way station. It is a small manufacturing town of nearly 2,000 inhabitants. The remaining stations are of small importance till *Eastman's Springs* (106 miles) is reached. This resort is much frequented by the residents of Ottawa. As the train approaches the city a fine view of the buildings may be had from the right, and after crossing the tracks of the C. P. R. and the Rideau River the Elgin Street Station in Ottawa is reached.

Ottawa.

A full description of Ottawa has already been given on page 49, and in addition to the routes just mentioned as coming from Montreal, it is directly accessible from the S. by means of a branch of the C. P. R. that extends to Prescott, on the St. Lawrence River. Ogdensburg, opposite, on the American side, is the northern terminus of the Rome, Watertown & Ogdensburg R. R., that connects with the New York Central R. R. at Utica, Rome, Syracuse, Rochester, and Buffalo, thus affording direct access from the chief railroad centres of the United States. There are also Grand Trunk connections from Toronto at Brockville and Prescott, and direct connection from Toronto over the C. P. R. by way of Smith's Falls and Carleton Junction. The Ottawa and New York R. R. runs to Cornwall, where connection is made for American cities,

Ottawa to Sudbury.

Leaving Ottawa, the C. P. R. follows the S. bank of the Ottawa River for several miles, and on its wide stretches may be seen enormous quantities of saw-logs held in " booms " for the use of the mills below. The little villages of *Skead* and *Britannia* are passed, and the river disappears as the train continues to the S. Several stations come in sight and are quickly left behind until *Carleton Place* (148 miles from Montreal) is reached. Here are large saw-mills, railway and other workshops. It is also the junction of the main line with the Ottawa and Brockville section that extends 45 miles to Brockville, where, after crossing the St. Lawrence River, Morristown, on the Rome, Watertown & Ogdensburg R. R., is reached. **Smith's Falls**, 13 miles S. of Carleton Place, on the Brockville section, is a junction on the Ontario and Quebec division between Montreal and Toronto. Returning to the main line and after leaving Carleton the route is in a northwesterly direction and through the beautiful valley of the Ottawa, which for a hundred or more miles is well cultivated by English, Scotch, and German farmers. Large, clear streams come rushing down to the river from the hills in the W., and in these fine fishing is to be had, especially maskinonge, trout, and bass. At *Almonte* there are large woollen mills, and *Pakenham*, 8 miles beyond, is another manufacturing point. *Renfrew*, 69 miles from Ottawa, is the northern terminus of the Kingston & Pembroke Ry., that extends 104 miles S. through a district abounding in iron to Kingston on the St. Lawrence River, and is the eastern terminus of the Atlantic and Northwestern branch, that extends 23 miles to Eganville. Renfrew is a lively town of some 3,000 inhabitants. The road then curves to the N. and reaches the river again near *Pembroke* (224 miles) (*Copeland Hotel*), the chief place of the Upper Ottawa Valley. It has over 5,000 inhabitants, and is the seat of numerous industrial establishments and several saw-mills. The river expands here into a broad sheet called Allumette Lake, and is a famous locality for trout fishing. The scenery in the vicinity is fine, especially at the narrows at the head of the lake. Champlain ascended the Ottawa River in canoes as far as this point in 1613. From Pembroke to Mattawa the distance is 94 miles, and the route is almost entirely along the W. bank of the river. The chief industry of this region is lumber, and saw-mills occur wherever water power is available, forming centres around which the few inhabitants cluster. As the country grows wilder the opportunities for sport with gun and rod increase,

Mattawa, 318 miles (*Western Hotel*), an important distributing point for the lumber regions, at the junction of the Ottawa and Mattawa Rivers (hence its name, signifying "The Forks"), was formerly a trading post of the Hudson Bay Co. It is a favourite centre for moose hunters, and guides and supplies for shooting expeditions may always be obtained here. Lake Temiscamingue is 38 miles to the N., to which a branch of the road is built, with a branch to Lake Kippewa (46 miles from Mattawa). This region is attracting a large number of tourists and sportsmen, its forests and streams being very attractive. It also possesses the grandest canoe routes in the world. To the S. of the railway is Algonquin Park (12 miles), a picturesque tract of land of 1,466 square miles, that was set apart by the Government of Ontario in 1893 for the preservation of game and forests and as a public pleasure and health resort. After leaving Mattawa the route passes through a somewhat wild and broken country, with frequent lakes and rapid streams, toward Lake Nipissing. *Bonfield* (344 miles) was originally intended as the eastern terminus of the C. P. R., to which connecting roads would run; but with the transfer of control from the Government to the corporation the line was extended to Montreal. *Nipissing Junction* is the point where the Grand Trunk Ry. from Toronto, after passing through the region of Lake Simcoe and the Muskoka lakes, reaches the track of the C. P. R. on its way to *North Bay* (*Pacific Hotel*), the terminus of the Grand Trunk extension. This place is on Lake Nipissing, a beautiful sheet of water 40 miles long and 10 miles wide, with forest clad shores and islands. Small steamers ply on the lake, and boats for sailing and rowing are easily procurable. Its waters contain the maskinonge, pike, bass, and pickerel, and good shooting can be had in the surrounding country. North Bay is a railway divisional point, and contains the usual repair shops. The route continues along the north shore of the lake past several unimportant stations until *Cache Bay* is reached, and then turns slightly to the N., passing through a comparatively wild region where forests, meadows, lakes, and rocky ridges alternate. The scenery is striking, and at places extremely interesting. Bear, moose, and deer abound throughout this territory, and the fishing in the many lakes and rivers is excellent. The principal industry of this region is timber cutting. *Sudbury* (448 miles), the terminus of the division, is an important centre. The most extensive copper and nickel deposits in the world, perhaps, are in the immediate vicinity. Smelting furnaces have been erected for the reduction of the ores on the spot. The population is about 1,700.

Sudbury to Sault Ste. Marie.

From Sudbury a branch extends westward 182 miles to Sault Ste. Marie. At *Algoma Mills* Lake Huron comes in sight. The town is an important lumbering port. *Sault Ste. Marie (International Hotel)*, in Ontario, is a prosperous place, and is connected by means of an iron bridge a mile long over Sault River with Sault Ste. Marie in Michigan, which is the eastern terminus of the Duluth, South Shore & Atlantic Ry. running to Duluth, and with the Minneapolis, St. Paul & Sault Ste. Marie Ry. running to St. Paul and Minneapolis, and thence through Minnesota and North Dakota to Portal in Assiniboia, where it again connects with the C. P. R. System. At Sault Ste. Marie, also, is that great engineering work, the Canadian Ship Canal, with its massive lock, whereby vessels of immense tonnage ascend or descend through the 17 ft. difference in level between Lakes Huron and Superior. This canal, cut through the solid rock, with its massive doors which hold back the waters of Lake Superior, its vast inclosure in which mighty ships float at ease, the ingenious machinery whereby electricity is made to operate its working parts, and the way in which during its construction the forces of Nature were utilized, is a monumental achievement. The cost of the work was about $4,000,000. Through trains from Sudbury to Sault Ste. Marie make the trip in 6 hours, and it is not necessary to change cars for points in the United States. For those who prefer it the steamers of the C. P. S. S. line are available for a trip across Lake Superior, connecting again at Fort William with the main line of the C. P. R.

Sudbury to Winnipeg.

With our faces turned to the W. we leave Sudbury and start on a long journey of 981 miles. As we leave the little town the train passes over the falls of the Sturgeon River, and our direction is to the N. W. Rivers and lakes are passed, and at *Larchwood* (461 miles) we reach Vermilion Lake. As the approach is made to *Onaping* the high falls (150 ft.) of the Vermilion River come in sight, and an excellent view of them is obtained from the cars. *Cartier* (478 miles) is a divisional point, with a restaurant and various railroad structures. It was once a trading post of the Hudson Bay Co. From here to *Biscotasing*

The Sault Ste. Marie Ship-Canal.

(View of the Locks, looking toward Lake Superior.)

(532 miles) the scenery is remarkably fine. Biscotasing is on an irregular lake of the same name, and although its population does not exceed 500, it has a large trade in furs and lumber. Ever onward the iron steed hurries, halting here and there for a brief moment at some obscure station, quickly crossing bridges over swiftly running rivers whose streams rush to add their waters to those of the Great Lakes, and past lonely lakes whose virgin waters still await the white fisherman. Finally *Chapleau* (615 miles), on Lake Kinogama, is reached. It is a divisional point, and has the usual railway workshops, with cottages for the men and their families. There is a restaurant at the station. At *Windermere* (644 miles), near Lake Mipissi, there are iron mines, and after crossing Dog Lake the station of *Missanabie* (675 miles) is reached. This point was well known long before the days of the railroad, for it was a *rendezvous* of the *voyageurs* who brought their furs from the N. up the waters of the Moose River (that flows to Hudson Bay) and thence by short portage to Dog Lake, whose outlet, the Michipicoten River, leads to Lake Superior. Gold mines have recently been discovered on Lake Wawa to the S. of this point, and are now being developed. For some distance beyond there are no points of special interest, although the numerous railroad cuttings testify to the skill of the engineers by whom the railroad was built. **White River** (747 miles) is a divisional point, with the accompanying workshops and railroad restaurant. There are also large cattle-yards here that are used to rest the live stock in on their way to the Eastern markets. The route continues along the left bank of the White River, which it crosses at *Bremmer* (763 miles), and then passes Round Lake, where good fishing is to be had. The Big Pic River is crossed by a high iron bridge, and a mile beyond is *Heron Bay* (802 miles), on the northeast end of Lake Superior.

North Shore of Lake Superior.

For 60 miles beyond this point the route is continued through and around the bold and harsh promontories of the north shore of Lake Superior, with deep rock cuttings, viaducts, and tunnels constantly occurring, and at intervals where the railway is cut out of the face of the cliffs the lake comes into full view. The scenery is an important consideration on this part of the journey, and in order that the tourist may enjoy it as much as possible the time schedule is arranged for the westward trip so that the lake views may be enjoyed by daylight.

Peninsula (811 miles) is a small station on the lake, and then comes the sweep around Jackfish Bay, which is of special interest on account of the scenery. The bay itself is a great fishing resort, and its waters abound in white fish, sturgeon, and the famous lake trout. *Schreiber* (865 miles) is a divisional point, and a convenient place to start from on a fishing expedition. The lake turns inward from here to form Nepigon Bay, which is separated from the lake by a group of islands, the largest of which is St. Ignace. Some of the heaviest work on the entire line of the railway occurs in this vicinity, especially just beyond *Rossport* (880 miles). The constantly changing views on Nepigon Bay are charming. All of the streams emptying into Lake Superior contain speckled trout in plenty, and in some of the streams, Nepigon River especially, they are noted for their large size—six-pounders being not uncommon. The river is a beautiful stream, well known to sportsmen, and is crossed by a fine iron bridge a little before reaching the station. At its mouth on the bay is the station of *Nepigon*, 928 miles (*Taylor's Hotel*). Three miles beyond Nepigon the railway turns around the base of Red Rock, a high, bright-red cliff, and, avoiding the heads of Black Bay and Thunder Bay, takes a straight southwesterly course, and from the higher elevations delightful views of Thunder Bay are to be had. A few unimportant stations are passed, and then we reach *Port Arthur*, 993 miles (*The Northern*), a lake town of some 3,000 inhabitants, with steamboat connection tri-weekly with Sault Ste. Marie and Duluth. The steamers of the C. P. S. S. line for Fort William usually call here. Besides its opportunities for fishing there is excellent shooting to be had in the neighbourhood, including bears, deer, and even moose and caribou. Since 1882 some interest has been developed in the gold and silver mines in the vicinity. It is the northern terminus of the Port Arthur, Duluth, & Western Ry. that runs S. to the Iron Range, and is being extended to reach the Southeastern Ry., now under construction. Five miles beyond is *Fort William*, 998 miles (*Kaministiquia Hotel*). It is on the Kaministiquia River, a deep, broad stream with firm banks, a few miles above its mouth on Lake Superior, thus affording great advantages for lake traffic. The town is pleasantly situated. A long promontory of basaltic rock on the opposite side of the bay, called the "Sleeping Giant," whose Indian legend takes one back to aboriginal days, terminates in Thunder Cape, behind which lies the once famous Silver Islet, which has yielded almost fabulous wealth. Pie Island, another mountain of columnar basalt, divides the entrance to the bay, which is

Grand Cape
LAKE NEPIGON
POPLAR POINT
H. B. Co. Post
ALEXANDRA Id
Mc Intyre Bay
Mountain Bay
VICTORIA Id
ALBERT Id
Flat Rock Portage
Lake Hannah
Crooked Point
Black-Water River
Falls
Rapids
Rapids
Creighton
Rapids
Rapids
South Bay
Lake Emma
Bay
White Chute
One Mile Portage
HAMILTON'S POOL
Island Portage
Cedar Portage
SPLIT ROCK
Lake Maria
The Narrows
Lake Jessie

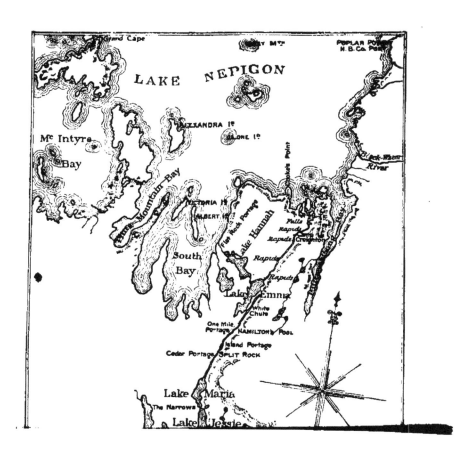

flanked on the W. by Mackay Mountain, overlooking Fort William.
Looking W., between Pie Island and Thunder Cape, Isle Royale may
be seen in the distance. Fort William is the western terminus of the
eastern division of the C. P. R. and of the C. P. S. S. line, so that passengers for the extreme W. who followed the route from Sudbury to Sault
Ste. Marie and there took the steamer or embarked at Owen Sound on
Georgian Bay to cross Lakes Huron and Superior, now return to the train.
The station is connected with the wharf by means of a foot-bridge. On
the river banks in recent years four large grain elevators, with a capacity of 5,000,000 bushels, have been built. Fort William is the natural
outlet for large quantities of grain that come from Manitoba and the
Northwest Territories to be shipped to the various lake ports. The settlement is an old one and dates back to the last century. In 1801 it became a post of the Hudson's Bay Co., to which the Indians came in their
canoes down the Kaministiquia River and connecting streams to sell their
furs. The fur house of the old fort is now used as an engine house for
the coal docks. West-bound passengers should set their watches back
one hour in conformity with central standard time, and from here on
the twenty-four-hour time system is in use—that is, time is reckoned
continuously from midnight to midnight; thus 1 P. M. is called 13
o'clock.

After leaving Fort William the train passes a few miles of partially
cleared farm land, and then plunges into a wild, broken region that
continues for hundreds of miles. The route passes many lakes and
crosses rapid rivers. Forests with valuable timber come and go as the
train pushes onward, and mineral deposits, the wealth of which is yet
to be developed, fade in the distance as the journey westward continues. *Murillo* (1,011 miles) is the railway crossing of the Port Arthur,
Duluth, and Western Ry. that runs to the Rabbit Mountain silver mining district. The Kakabeka Falls, formed by the Kaministiquia River,
are 4 miles from the station. They are 130 ft. high and 450 ft.
wide. The railway follows the river for some distance, and excellent
trout fishing is to be had near the stations. It was through this region
that Wolseley led his army from Fort William to Winnipeg in 1870,
using the more or less connected rivers and lakes much of the way. Stations are passed at regular intervals, but they are only "water tanks
and footprints—little else." Some of their names—*Finmark* (1,031
miles), *Nordland* (1,049 miles), *Linkooping* (1,059 miles), and *Upsala*
(1,080 miles)—indicate their settlement by immigrants from Scandina-

18

via. *Ignace* (1,146 miles) is a divisional point, with a restaurant at
the station. The Wabigoon River soon comes in sight, and the train
continues along its banks, past numerous lakes that are noted chiefly
for the excellent fishing they afford, and their stations. *Wabigoon* (1,196
miles) is a growing town which came into existence in consequence of
the gold-mines in the Manitou country to the S., with which it has
steamboat communicatiom. At *Dryden* (1,209 miles) the Ontario
Government has established an experimental farm, there being a large
area of fertile land in the vicinity. At *Eagle River* (1,226 miles) there
are two waterfalls that may be seen, one above and the other below the
railway. The route passes through numerous rocky uplifts, and the
scenery is often of the wildest description, with deep, rock-bound lakes
continuously in sight. *Rat Portage* (1,291 miles) is an important town
of 5,000 inhabitants, with several large saw-mills, on the principal outlet of the Lake of the Woods. This lake, 65 miles long and from-10
to 50 miles wide, is the largest body of water touched by the railway
between Lake Superior and the Pacific, and is the chief waterway to
the gold fields of the Rainy Lake and Seine River districts. It is
studded with islands, and is a favorite resort for sportsmen and
pleasure-seekers. Its waters break through a narrow rocky rim at
Rat Portage and Keewatin and fall into the Winnipeg River. The
cascades are most picturesque, and have been utilized for water-power
for a number of large saw-mills, while at the lower end it connects
with Rainy Lake by the Rainy River. Steamers leave Rat Portage
nearly every day in summer for Fort Frances and the Rainy Lake
region. The Lake of the Woods district is itself rich in minerals. On
an island close to the town of Rat Portage is located the famous "Sul-
tana" property, the value of which is written in seven figures. Though
only developed within the past few years, this mine has already produced many thousands of dollars in gold, and is regarded as rivaling
in richness the best of the Kootenay mines. Other mines on the Lake
of the Woods are equally promising. Lake Winnipeg, farther to the
N. W., also has rich resources in gold and iron, which remain to be
properly exploited. Another source of wealth possessed by the Lake
of the Woods, ranking after the immense tracts of pine along its shores
next in importance to its mines, are the fisheries. White fish and sturgeon of the finest quality abound in the lake and yield annually a large
revenue to the district. Great quantities of these fish are taken during
the open season, and shipped, with the fish of Lakes Winnipeg and

Manitoba (where the industry is also vigorously prosecuted), to eastern cities, and command the highest market price. The roe of the sturgeon is shipped to Germany and Russia, there to be manufactured into *caviare* and disposed of at select figures to the epicurean Muscovites as the product of their own rivers. An immense trade in these fisheries has developed within the past few years on Lakes Winnipeg and Manitoba and the Lake of the Woods, and a small army of men and fleets of steamers, tugs, and sailboats are employed in its prosecution. The headquarters of the fishing companies are at Rat Portage, on the Lake of the Woods, and at West Selkirk, on the Red River, which empties into Lake Winnipeg a few miles to the north of the town. The falls of the Winnipeg are seen to the right as the train passes over the open-work bridge on leaving Rat Portage. A steam ferry connects *Keewatin* (1,295 miles) (noted for its huge flour-mill, built of granite quarried on the spot, and power works) and Rat Portage. *Ingolf* (1,322 miles) is the last station in Ontario, and *Telford* (1,333 miles) the first in Manitoba. At *Whitemouth* (1,363 miles), on the river of the same name, that empties in the Winnipeg a few miles to the N., are more saw-mills. The country now flattens out and gradually assumes the characteristics of a prairie. Little farms and pastures come in sight. Near *East Selkirk* (1,403 miles) a Government fish hatchery has been established, and here the route turns southward, following the line of the Red River of the North to *St. Boniface*, where the river is crossed by a long iron bridge, and **Winnipeg** is reached.

Manitoba.

This province is bounded on the N. by Saskatchewan and Keewatin, on the E. by Ontario, on the S. by the States of Minnesota and North Dakota, and on the W. by Assiniboia. From E. to W. it extends about 300 miles, and it covers an area of 73,956 square miles. According to the census of 1891, it had a population of 152,506, which has since been materially increased by immigration. Its S. boundary being the forty-ninth parallel of latitude, it is therefore S. of Great Britain, but, notwithstanding, it suffers extremes of climate. The summer mean is from 65° to 67° F., but in winter it sometimes falls to 30°, and even 50°, below zero. The atmosphere, however, is bright and dry, and the sensation of cold is not so unpleasant as that of a cold temperature in a humid atmosphere. The general features of the province are those of a broad, rolling prairie, relieved at intervals by gently rising hills and numerous bluffs and lakelets. Manitoba is therefore essentially an agricultural country. The soil is a firm, rich, black, argillaceous mould or loam, resting in a deep and very tenacious clay subsoil. It is nearly, if not quite, the wettest soil in the world, and is especially adapted to the growth of wheat. In 1898 over 17,000,000 bushels of wheat, in addition to 30,000,000 bushels of other grains, were harvested by 30,000 farmers. Small fruits, such as strawberries, raspberries, currants, gooseberries, cranberries, plums, etc., are plentiful. The prairie farms are well adapted to the raising of horses and cattle, and since 1891 cattle have been regularly exported from Manitoba to England, the trade now having reached large proportions. The raising of pigs and sheep is attracting attention, and dairy farming is engaging an increasing amount of interest. To the sportsman the beautiful flocks of prairie chickens, and the mallard, the teal, the butter-ball, the red-head, and other varieties of duck are among the attractions, while those who fancy larger game find the deer, the black and cinnamon bear, the elk, the moose, and the antelope in abundance. Coal mines have been opened in the S. W. end of the province. Important cities, like Winnipeg, Brandon, and Portage la Prairie, offer market opportunities, and Winnipeg especially affords educational advantages of unusual excellence. The railroad facilities are very good, and Winnipeg is the chief railroad center. Besides the C. P. R. and its branches, the Northern Pacific and the Great Northern R. Rs. afford communication with the S., while the Manitoba and Northwestern Ry. and Dauphin Ry. are pushing their way to the N. and N. W., and the Manitoba Southeastern to the S. E. Winnipeg is the seat of provincial government.

Winnipeg.

Hotels.—The *Leland House*, $2 to $3 ; *Clarendon*, Portage Ave., 4th St., South, $1.50 to $3.50 ; *Queen's* and *Winnipeg* are less expensive. Besides the restaurants at the railway stations there are the *Criterion* and *English* on Main St.

Modes of Conveyance.—Electric cars run through the main thoroughfares and to the suburbs (fare, 5 cents). Cabs can be had at the stations, and 50 cents is the charge for one or two passengers for short distances, as from station to hotel. By the hour, $1.

Railway Stations.—The C. P. R Station, on Main St., North, is used by the *C. P. R.* and all roads except the Northern Pacific R. R., whose station is on the corner of Main and Water Sts.

The Post-Office is on the corner of Main and Owen Sts. ; is open from 8 A. M. to 7 P. M.

Club.—The Manitoba Club is in Garry St.

Winnipeg, the capital of Manitoba, is on a flat plain at the junction of the Assiniboine and Red Rivers, both of which are navigable by steamers; the latter extends about 40 miles N. to Lake Winnipeg, a great inland sea resembling the U. S. Great Lakes, some 260 miles long and from 5 to 60 miles in width. It was the Fort Garry of the Hudson Bay Co., and had a population of about 200 in 1870, which increased to 7,985 in 1881, and to 25,642 in 1891, while now (1899) it has a population of about 46,000. The name Winnipeg, which it took in 1881, is derived from the Indian Ouinipigon, signifying muddy water. The streets are wide and well laid out. Many of the buildings are substantial and worthy of notice. Conspicuous among them is the **City Hall**, on Main St., in front of which stands a *memorial column* that has been erected in memory of the volunteers who fell in the rebellion in 1885. Near by is the *Market*, and the *Grain Exchange*, with the *Board of Trade*, are in the immediate vicinity. The *Post Office* building, the *Custom House*, and the site of old *Fort Garry* are all on Main St. The *Hudson Bay Co.'s Stores* are interesting, and the history of their early trading is the connecting link between the past and the present. The *Parliament House* on Broadway, with the *residence of the Lieutenant-Governor*, and *Fort Osborne*, the military headquarters, together with the *Court House* and the *Provincial Jail*, are in the vicinity. Among the churches are *All Saints'*, *Trinity*, *St. Mary's*, *Grace*, *Westminster*, and *Knox Church*. The institutions for higher education include *Manitoba College*, *St. John's Episcopal College*, *Wesley College*, and the *Manitoba Medical College*. The *City Hospital* and the *Provincial Deaf and Dumb Institute* are conspicuous among the eleemosynary institutions. It contains the chief workshops of the C. P. R. between Montreal and the Pacific, and the Northern Pacific R. R. have their terminal workshops here. It is the chief land office of the Dominion in the W., and the principal land offices of the C. P. R. are in the Union Station. Northward the C. P. R. has a branch running 23 miles to *West Selkirk*, also one to the N. W. 40 miles to *Teulon*. The Manitoba and Northwestern R. R. of Canada runs on the tracks of the main line of the C. P. R. to *Portage la Prairie* (where it connects with a branch of the Northern Pacific R. R.), and turns to the N. W., finding its northern terminus in *Yorktown*, Assiniboia, 279 miles from Winnipeg. The Dauphin Ry. branches off from the Manitoba and Northwestern Ry. at Gladstone Junction, and runs 159 miles to *Lake Winnipegosis*, with a branch from Sifton to Swan River. The C. P. R. has two branches leading southward, one on the east side of the Red River to *Emerson* (66 miles) and the other to *Gretna* (69 miles), on the U. S. boundary, connecting at the latter point with the train service of the Great Northern R. R. Two branch lines of the C. P. R. go S. W. to *Souris* and *Napinka* in southern Manitoba, 150 and 221 miles distant respectively, and there connect with the branch line from *Brandon* (connecting also here with the Northern Pacific R. R.) through to *Estevan*, the junction with the Soo-Pacific line that runs eastward to *Sault Ste. Marie* by way of St. Paul and Minneapolis.

A branch of the Northern Pacific R. R. from St. Paul leaves the main line at *Winnipeg Junction* in Minnesota and extends to Winnipeg, passing through *Grand Forks* and *Pembina* in Dakota.

Across the Red River is St. Boniface, a town of 2,000 people, nearly all of French extraction, which contains St. Boniface Cathedral, College, etc.

Winnipeg to Regina.

A stop of about one hour is usually made in Winnipeg, and then the train starts westward again. On leaving the city the country seems level and bare. It is unoccupied, because the land is largely held by speculators, and the few farms that are passed are devoted to dairy products and cattle breeding. After leaving *Poplar Point* (1,464 miles) farms appear almost continuously, and the prairie during harvest time affords the glorious sight of the wheat that eloquently though silently testifies to the great richness of the soil. The line of trees to the S. marks the course of the Assiniboine River, which the railway follows for a little over 100 miles. Notwithstanding the apparent flatness of the land there is a gradual ascent of 100 feet between Winnipeg and *Portage la Prairie* (*Leland, Albion*) (1,480 miles). This place is on the Assiniboine River, and has a population of 4,500. It is the market town of a rich and populous district, and one of the principal grain markets in the province. There are large flouring-mills and grain elevators, a brewery, biscuit factory, and other industries here. The Manitoba and Northwestern Ry. extends 223 miles N. W. to Yorktown, with branches at Minnedosa to Rapid City, and at Binscarth to Russell. The Manitoba branch of the Northern Pacific R. R. extends to Portage la Prairie.

After passing through a bushy district, with frequent ponds and small streams, the railway rises from *Austin* (1,509 miles) along a sandy slope to a plateau with an area of over 100,000 square miles, forming a fine wheat-growing region. *Carberry* (1,530 miles) is in the centre of the district, and is its chief grain market. From *Sewell* (1,538 miles) the route descends again to the valley of the Assiniboine. To the southwest are seen the Brandon Hills. From *Chater* (1,551 miles) the Great Northwest Central Ry., running northwestward toward Saskatchewan, is open to *Hamiota* (56 miles). Four miles beyond the station the Assiniboine River is crossed by an iron bridge, and the divisional point of *Brandon* (1,557 miles) (*Langham* and *Grand View*) is reached. This town is beautifully situated on high ground, and, although it can almost be said to have come with the railway, it is now the second city of Manitoba, with a population of nearly 6,000 inhabitants. It has excellent paved streets and many substantial buildings. Brandon is a distributing market for an extensive and well-settled country. It is also the largest grain market of the province, having five grain elevators. There is an experimental farm here under the care of the Government officials. The standard time changes from " central " to " mountain " time, which is one hour slower as we go W. Besides being a divisional point it is also an important railroad center. The Pipestone branch is open to *Reston*, 63 miles S. At *Menteith Junction* it connects with the Souris branch, that runs S. W. 133 miles through the fertile district of the Souris River, which also yields much coal, to Estevan, on the Soo-Pacific line, connecting the Canadian northwest with the Middle and Northwestern States of the Union. It is also the western terminus of the Manitoba Division of the Northern Pacific R. R. Beyond Brandon the railway leaves the Assiniboine River, and rises from its valley to an undulating prairie that is well occupied with prosperous farmers, as shown by the thriving villages that appear at frequent intervals. At *Kemnay* (1,565 miles) the Souris branch diverges to the S., and *Virden* (1,604 miles) is the market town of a district of rich farms. *Elkhorn* (1,621 miles) is likewise a prairie town surrounded by farms.

Assiniboia.

This district lies directly W. of Manitoba. It is bounded on the N. by Saskatchewan, on the E. by Manitoba, on the S. by North Dakota, and Montana and on the W. by Alberta. It has an area of 106,100 square miles, and, according to the census of 1891, had a population of 25,278 inhabitants, which, however, has been largely increased since. The surface is rolling, dotted over with clumps of trees, usually found bordering the shores of lakes and meadows. The district is divided into two great areas, Eastern Assiniboia and Western Assiniboia. Each of these divisions has its own peculiar characteristics, the eastern portion being essentially a wheat-growing country, and the western better fitted for mixed farming and ranching. In Eastern Assiniboia, the great plain lying S. of the Qu'Appelle River and stretching S. to the international boundary is considered to have the largest acreage of wheat land possessing a uniform character of soil found in any one tract of fertile prairie land in the N. W. The eastern part of the district is known as the Park Country of the Canadian N. W. The Qu'Appelle district contains a large tract of excellent farming country, watered by the Qu'Appelle River and the Fishing Lakes. The soil is a black loam with clay subsoil. The water of the lakes and rivers is excellent, and stocked with fish. It is a country renowned for wild fowl and other game. Western Assiniboia extends to Kininvie, about 40 miles W. of Medicine Hat. At present it is more occupied by ranchers raising cattle and sheep than by farmers. It is everywhere thickly covered with a good growth of nutritious grasses (chiefly the short, crisp variety known as " buffalo grass "), which becomes to all appearance dry about midsummer, but is still green and growing at the roots, and forms excellent pasture both in winter and summer. A heavy growth of grass suitable for hay is found in many of the river bottoms and surrounding the numerous lakes and sloughs. The supply of timber on the hills is considerable. There is also an abundance of fuel of a different kind in the coal seams that are exposed in many of the valleys. The C. P. R. traverses the central portion of Assiniboia from E. to W. Regina is the seat of government.

The district of **Assiniboia,** the first of the Northwest Territories, is entered a mile this side of *Fleming* (1,635 miles). Soon *Moosomin* (1,643 miles) is reached, and stages run twice a week from here N. to Fort Ellice, and weekly to the fertile Mouse Mountain district on the S. Small stations are passed at regular intervals, but they call for no special comment, although at nearly all of them the sportsman will find excellent opportunities for shooting —waterfowl and prairie chicken being especially abundant. *Broadview* (1,688 miles) is a divisional point, with restaurant at the station. It is at the head of Weed Lake, and is an important trading town. In the vicinity is the reservation of the Cree Indians, and it is a common sight to see some of the braves and their squaws selling curios at the station. Our course follows a gradually rising prairie, and but few farms are to be seen. Settlers for the most part, in this vicinity, have shown a preference for the line of the Qu'Appelle River, which is some 10 miles to the N. Pheasant Hills, to the N. of the river, is noted for the fertility of its soil. Near *Indian Head* (1,738 miles) we approach the Government Farm, on the N. side of the railway, and in the locality are many mammoth farms, cultivated by individual farmers.

Qu'Appelle (1,748 miles) is the supplying and shipping point for a large section. It has a population of about 1,000 persons. A good road extends northward to Fort Qu'Appelle and the Touchwood Hills, over which a stage runs daily to the Fort, which is 20 miles distant. It is an old post of the Hudson Bay Company, beautifully situated on the Fishing Lakes in the deep valley of the Qu'Appelle River, where not only is good fishing to be had but also excellent shooting. There are several Indian reservations in its vicinity, and an Indian mission and school that was established in the Fifties by the Jesuits.

The country is wooded beyond Qu'Appelle, but at *McLean* (1,756 miles) the great Regina plain is entered. This is a broad treeless expanse of the finest agricultural land that extends westward to the Dirt Hills, which are the northward extension of the Missouri Coteau, and lie to the S. W. The next station is *Balgonie* (1,765 miles), near where is a farm of the Canadian Land and Ranch Company, a corporation chiefly devoted to grain and stock-raising. *Pilot Butte* (1,772 miles), that takes its name from a rounded hill in the vicinity, is soon passed, and *Regina* (1,781 miles) (*Windsor, Lansdowne*), the capital of Assiniboia, and of the Northwest Territories, is reached. This important distributing point has a population of 2,500. It is the meeting-place of the Executive Council of the Northwest Territories, including Assiniboia, Alberta, Saskatchewan, and Athabasca, and the jurisdiction of the Lieutenant-Governor, whose residence is here, extends over all these districts. It is also the headquarters of the Northwest Mounted Police, a body of 800 picked men, that form the frontier army of the Dominion. They are stationed at intervals over the N. W. and in the Yukon to look after the Indians and preserve order generally.

Regina to Prince Albert.

The construction of important branches is a conspicuous evidence of the enterprise of the C. P. R. and the line that was completed in

1893, for the purpose of opening the fertile valley of the Saskatchewan is an excellent illustration of that fact. When valuable farm lands are made accessible, immigration soon follows, and market centres develop into towns and junctions become capitals. The Prince Albert Branch of the C. P. R. extends from Regina N. for a distance of 250 miles to Prince Albert in the territory of Saskatchewan. It runs in a northwesterly direction through a (as yet) thinly populated region, passing at first down the valley of the Wascana Creek, and crossing the Qu'Appelle River at *Lumsden* (20 miles). The route continues through a bushy country for nearly 150 miles, where free lands are steadily attracting immigrants anxious to secure farms. The country is well adapted for stock-raising on a moderate scale, such as would be suitable for mixed farming. The climate is healthy, and an average summer temperature of about 60° is recorded. The stations, none of which have as yet acquired any importance, are passed at intervals of about ten miles. Between *Dundurn* (137 miles) and *Grindlay* (153 miles) the frontier line between Assiniboia and Saskatchewan is passed. At *Saskatoon* (160 miles) the South Saskatchewan River is crossed. This place is a divisional point, with restaurants. It was formerly a police post. The route now turns N. E. and follows the fertile valley between South Saskatchewan on the E. and the North Saskatchewan on the W. *Duck Lake* (212 miles) is the most important of the few stations that are passed before *Prince Albert* is reached. Here occurred the culmination of the Riel Rebellion that took place in 1885. This place is a small farming town on the S. bank of the North Saskatchewan River, about 30 miles to the W. of the junction of the N. and S. branches of the river. It is the chief town of the Territory and the centre of quite a large farming district. It was throughout this district that in 1884–'85 a few dissatisfied French *metis* or half-breeds invited Louis Riel, the leader of the Red River Rebellion in 1869 (then living in Montana), to aid them in a constitutional agitation for their rights. He established his headquarters in Duck Lake, and in March set up a provisional government. A body of militia under General Middleton was sent to subdue them, but owing to the difficulties in transportation did not reach the point of action until early in April. Several engagements took place, and finally in Batouche, not far from Duck Lake, on May 9th, the decisive encounter occurred and Riel surrendered. He was taken to Regina, where he was hanged, eight of his Indian followers meeting a similar fate at Battleford.

Saskatchewan.

This division of Western Canada is bounded on the N. by the North-west Territory and Keewatin, on the E. by Keewatin and Manitoba, on the S. by Assiniboia, and the W. by Alberta. It has an area of 107,-092 square miles. The climate is healthy, being both bracing and salubrious. The average summer temperature is about 60° F. The reason of the equability of the temperature in summer has not yet been thoroughly investigated, but the water stretches may be found to account for it. The district is almost centrally divided by the main Saskatchewan River, which is altogether within its boundary, and by its principal branch, the North Saskatchewan, most of whose navigable length lies within the district. There are extensive grazing plains through which the railway passes in the southern portion, but the greater part of it is rolling prairie diversified by wood and lake. In these parts, which are well adapted for mixed farming, the soil is generally a rich loam with clay subsoil, in which grass grows luxuriantly and grain ripens well. The crops consist of wheat, oats, barley, and potatoes. Turnips and all kinds of vegetables are raised successfully. The country is well adapted for stock-raising on a moderate scale, such as would be suitable for mixed farming, and any portion of the district will answer all the requirements for dairy farming. The sportsman will find an abundance of wild game, whether of fin, feathers, or furs, sufficient in variety to satisfy the most fastidious. Large forests of spruce are found along the capes and streams tributing to the North Saskatchewan River, and saw-mills are in operation at Prince Albert and Battleford. Whitefish, pike, salmon trout, and other fish abound in the many large lakes. Horse-raising is extensively carried on, the light snowfall enabling the animals to sustain themselves on the dry but nutritious grasses during the winter. Cattle and sheep ranches, also, are scattered over the district. The country in many places lifts into long ranges of lofty hills, grass-grown and gemmed with small lakes and groves of poplar, features which, with the broad, alternating valleys, creeks, and natural hay meadows, make it extremely picturesque as well as fertile, and adapted admirably for the business of stock-growing and for the comfortable houses of settlers. The high hills are kept almost bare of snow by the winds, and consequently cattle, and even stray sheep, have been known to shift for themselves throughout the winter and turn up fat in the spring, though both are commonly fed for some weeks on hay, made from the native grasses of the country. Prince Albert and Battleford are the chief centers of population, yet flourishing settlements exist in many other parts of the district, mainly along the two Saskatchewan rivers. Prince Albert is the N. terminus of a branch of the C. P. R., and the N. E. corner of the district has water connection by the Saskatchewan River and Lake Winnipeg with Winnipeg. Prince Albert (1,200) is the chief town.

Regina to Calgary.

We again resume our route westward. After leaving Regina the residence of the Lieutenant-Governor is passed on the right, and soon after the headquarters of the Mounted Police. The barracks, officers' quarters, offices, storehouses, and the imposing drill-hall together constitute quite a village. Large wheat fields on either side testify to the richness of the soil. At *Pasqua* (1,814 miles) a branch line of the C. P. R. extends S. E. through Estevan to the international boundary line at Portal, where connection is made with the Soo line for Sault Ste. Marie by way of St. Paul and Minneapolis. *Moose Jaw* (1,822 miles) is a divisional point, with a restaurant in the station. Its name is an abridgment of the Indian name which, on being literally translated, signifies " The-creek-where-the-white-man-mended-the-cart-with-a-moose-jaw-bone." We have been slowly but steadily climbing the eastern slope of the Missouri Coteau, and the road winds through an irregular depression to the basin of the Old Wives' Lakes—two extensive bodies of water that have no outlet and are consequently alkaline. The most northerly and westerly of these lakes is reached at *Chaplin* (1,876 miles).

The country is treeless from the eastern border of the Regina plain to the Cypress Hills (200 miles) but the soil is excellent nearly everywhere.

Swift Current (1,935 miles), on a pretty stream of the same name, is a divisional point, with restaurant. The little town is sustained by the numerous cattle ranches in the vicinity. The principal sheep farm of the Canadian Land and Ranch Company is here, and a large crop of wool is shipped eastward each year. The well-appointed farm buildings, including a large creamery, are on the hills directly S. of the station. Near by is the Government Meteorological Station. From here onward the line skirts the northern base of the Cypress Hills, which gradually rise towards the W. until they reach an altitude of 3,800 ft., and in many places are covered with valuable timber. At *Crane Lake* (2,000 miles) another of the Canadian Land and Ranch Company's farms is located, but is entirely applied to stock-raising. There are large cattle-yards at *Maple Creek* (2,021 miles), and near the town is a post of the Mounted Police. There is still another farm at *Kincorth* (2,030 miles). The C. P. R. have an experimental farm at *Forres* (2,040 miles). The satisfactory results obtained from working this and similar farms established at different points on the line have proved the value of the land for farming. This section has been found to be specially suited to stock-raising. It is rich in the grasses that possess peculiar attractions for horses and cattle, while the valleys and groves of timber afford shelter during all seasons of the year. Finally, the many streams flowing out of the Cypress Hills yield an excellent supply of water. From Forres to Dunmore rocks of the Cretaceous age are abundant, in which the remains of the gigantic carnivorous and other animals now extinct are found. At *Dunmore* (2,077 miles) there is still another of the Canadian Land and Ranch Company's farms, and it is of a mixed character, for not only are capital crops raised but valuable horses and cattle are bred here. From this point the Crow's Nest Pass Railway strikes off almost due west past Lethbridge, a coal-mining town of 2,700 inhabitants, and Macleod, the headquarters of the ranching industry of Southern Alberta, through the Crow's Nest Pass of the Rocky Mountains and the undeveloped mining region of East Kootenay to Kootenay Lake in Southern British Columbia, where steamer connection is made with all the mining centers of that prosperous mining country. The Great Falls and Canada Ry. extends S. from Lethbridge to *Coutts* on the frontier and thence into Montana, intersecting the Great Northern R. R. at *Shelby Junction*, and finally reaching the southern terminus in *Great Falls*, 200 miles from Lethbridge.

From Dunmore the train descends into the valley of the South Saskatchewan, which it crosses by a fine steel bridge 1,010 ft. long at *Medicine Hat* (2,084 miles), a growing divisional station, with a population of 1,200 inhabitants. The train stops for 30 minutes. The repair shops of the railroad are here. Indians selling curiosities are seen around the station, and the Mounted Police have a post here. There are deposits of soft coal (lignite) in the vicinity, and the river is navigable at this point; indeed, small steamers have descended the river to Lake Winnipeg, 800 miles to the E. Beyond "the Hat" the railway ascends to the high prairie plateau, which extends, gradually rising, to the base of the mountains.   At *Stair* (2,092 miles) the route reaches the first of the Canadian Land and Ranch Company's farms W. of the Saskatchewan.   The train then follows a strong up-grade to *Bowell* (2,099 miles), after which it makes a descent to *Suf-field* (2,111 miles), and then steadily ascends again.   Across the prairie to the S. occasional glimpses of the Bow River may be seen.   In the early summer the prairie may be compared to a billowy ocean of grass, with cattle ranches spread over it, and farms, like islands, appearing at intervals.   Coal beds lie under-the surface, and natural gas is found by boring deep wells.   At *Langevin* (2,119 miles) the gas is used for pumping water into the tanks for the railway supply.   From this station, on a clear day, the higher peaks of the Rocky Mountains, still 150 miles to the westward, may be seen with the naked eye.   A short distance beyond the station we leave the great Territory of Assiniboia and enter **Alberta.**

Alberta.

This district is bounded on the N. by Athabasca, on the E. by Saskatchewan and Manitoba, on the S. by Montana, and on the W. by British Columbia.   It has an area of 106,100 square miles, and a population of about 65,000.   Alberta is described as having three distinct surface features—namely, prairie lands on the E., which are thickly timbered in the northern part; then come the rolling land or foothills, extending some 40 miles from the base of the mountains, mostly heavily timbered; and lastly the mountains, containing quantities of gold and other ores.   The climate of Northern Alberta is like that of Manitoba, though not so cold in winter, and the winter is shorter.   The Chinook wind reaches the Edmonton country to some extent and tempers the climate.   In southern Alberta the action of the Chinook winds is more direct and stronger than in the N., with the result that the snowfall is much lighter and does not remain on the ground for any length of time.   Northern Alberta embraces the fertile tract of country watered by the Red Deer, the Battle, the North Saskatchewan, and Sturgeon Rivers.   It is a country pre-eminently suited to mixed farming.   It is well wooded and watered, and abounds with natural hay meadows.   As regards water, there are magnificent water courses, innumerable lakes, mountain streams, and creeks and springs.   This district contains millions of acres of deep, rich soil, and possesses beyond dispute some of the best farming country in the Dominion.

Southern Alberta stands foremost among the cattle countries of the world, and the unknown land of a few years ago is looked to as one of the greatest future sources of supply of the British markets, as it has already become for the mining regions farther west. Great herds of range cattle roam at will over these seemingly boundless pastures. There are on the ranges of Alberta hundreds of herds of fat cattle, which at any season are neither fed nor sheltered; cattle, too, which in point of breeding, size, and general condition are equal to any range cattle in the world. That Alberta possesses untold wealth in her immense mineral deposits is no longer a matter of doubt. For years gold in paying quantities has been found on the banks and bars of the North Saskatchewan River. Deposits of galena have been located which are said to contain a large percentage of silver. Copper and iron ore have been discovered in various parts of Alberta. A valuable seam of hematite iron exists at the base of Storm Mountain, and other seams are in the vicinity of Crow's Nest Pass, which are being developed extensively. As to the quantity of the coal deposits of Alberta it is impossible to form any estimate. The coal mines already discovered are of sufficient extent to supply Canada with fuel for centuries. At Lethbridge over a million dollars have been expended in developing the coal mines. At Anthracite large sums have been spent in opening up the hard coal deposits of that vicinity. Coal mines are also operated at Edmonton, and anthracite mines near Canmore. Soft coal is so plentiful that the certainty of a cheap fuel supply is assured to Albertans for countless generations.

Soon after leaving *Bassano* (2,182 miles) we reach the large reservation of the Blackfoot Indians, some of whom are likely to be seen about the stations. The reservation lies to the S. of the railway, and the first station that is on its boundary is *Crowfoot* (2,190 miles), named in honour of a famous Blackfoot chief. Here the Bow River comes close to the railway as it follows its course through the reservation, which we leave soon after *Namaka* (2,218 miles) is passed. Meanwhile at *Gleichen* (2,209 miles), a railway divisional point, the mountains come in full view—a magnificent line of snowy peaks extending far along the southern and western horizons. At *Langdon* (2,244 miles) the railway turns into the valley of the Bow River, and a few miles beyond *Shepard* (2,254 miles) the river is crossed by an iron bridge and the foothills are reached. *Calgary* (2,264 miles) (*Alberta Hotel*) is charmingly situated at an altitude of 3,388 ft., on a hillside plateau at the junction of the Bow and Elberon Rivers overlooked by the snow-capped peaks of the Rocky Mountains. It is the most important place between Brandon and Vancouver, and has a population of nearly 3,000 inhabitants. Already it has been made a city, and its business portion is compactly and handsomely built up. The banks are rich and the business interests are large. Fine churches, ample schoolhouses, and well-constructed residences make Calgary more of a city of homes than a mere frontier business place. It has a history too, for it is believed to be the place where, in 1752, Niowville established Fort Jonquière. There " the old Bow Fort " was built in the immediate vicinity early in the century, and more recently the Hudson Bay Co. erected a little trading house. Last of all came the barracks of the Mounted Police, to which the name of Fort Calgary was given. The Hudson's Bay Co. and the Mounted Police still have their stations here. Calgary is the center of the trade of the great ranching country, and it is the chief source of supply for the mining districts in the mountains beyond. Lumber is made from the logs that are floated down the Bow River, and much of the light-gray building stone that is used in the city comes from the immediate vicinity. It is also a railway center. Besides the main line of the C. P. R., branch lines of that company run 105 miles S. to *Macleod* on the Crow's Nest Ry., passing through a rich ranching and farming country 191 miles N. to *Edmonton*, in the valley of the North Saskatchewan River. It is the market town for the farmers, traders, miners, etc., in North Alberta. The town is well laid out, and on a bluff above it is the fort of the Hudson Bay Co. There is a wagon road running 96 miles N. to *Athabasca Landing*, a store of the Hudson's Bay Co. on the Athabasca River, from where, by means of the flat-bottomed river steamers of the company, a trip can be made down the river to Athabasca Lake, thence by the Great Slave River, its outlet, to the lake of the same name, and thence by the Mackenzie River, its outlet, to the Arctic Ocean. Edmonton is the most northerly railway station on the continent.

Calgary to Banff.

The ascent of the Rockies begins at once after leaving Calgary. For a short distance we follow the S. bank of the Bow and cross it at *Keith* (2,273 miles). Large cattle ranches are passed, and sometimes we may see great herds of horses in the lower valleys, thousands of cattle

Bow River Valley, from Upper Hot Springs.

on the terraces, and flocks of sheep on the hilltops all at once. Soon *Cochrane* (2,287 miles) is reached, and we are well within the rounded grassy foothills and "view benches" or terraces. Frequent saw-mills are seen in the valley, and here and there a coal mine. Between Cochrane and *Radnor* (2,297 miles) we again cross the river, and still rising, reach *Morley* (2,306 miles), and an altitude of 4,000 ft. Then, to quote Lady Macdonald, "the wide valleys change into broken ravines, and lo! through an opening in the mist, made rosy with early sunlight, we see, far away in the sky, its delicate pearly tip clear against the blue, a single snow peak of the Rocky Mountains; . . . but as we look, gauzy mist passes over, and it has vanished." Just before reaching the *Kananaskis* (2,318 miles) we cross the river of the same name, not far from its confluence with the Bow, on a high iron bridge, and nearly over the Kananaskis Falls, 40 ft. high, which cannot be seen from the train, although the roar of the falling water is distinctly heard. Soon after leaving the station a bend in the line brings the train between two almost vertical walls of dizzy height, and we enter the Bow River Gap, as the gateway by which the Rocky Mountains is entered is called. On the right are the fantastically broken and castellated heights of the Fairholme Mountains that culminate in Grotto Mountain, 8,840 ft. high, while to the left are the massive snow-laden promontories of the Kananaskis range, of which Pigeon Mountain (7,815 ft.) is the most conspicuous. *Gap* Station (2,326 miles, altitude 4.200 ft.) is at the east end, from where we obtain a superb view to the left of Wind Mountains (10,400 ft.), and the group called Three Sisters (9,705 ft.). On leaving the Gap the train turns northward up the valley to the Bow and soon reaches the divisional station of *Canmore* (2,331 miles, altitude 4,230 ft.), where an observation car, specially designed to allow an unbroken view of the wonderful mountain scenery, is attached to the train during the season from May 1 to October 15. From the station a striking profile of the Three Sisters is obtained, with Wind and Pigeon Mountains looming up beyond. On a hill behind stands a group of isolated and curiously weathered conglomerate monuments. On either side of the beautiful level valley the mountains rise in solid masses westward, until the great bulk of Cascade Mountain closes the view. Good fishing and shooting are obtained in this vicinity. The Rocky Mountain Park is entered 5 miles beyond Canmore.

19

The Rocky Mountain Park of Canada.

This rectangular tract of land, 26 miles long and 10 miles wide, is in western Alberta. It was set apart by the Dominion of Canada as a national reservation and pleasure resort. It includes the beautiful Devil's Lake and parts of the valleys of the Bow, Spray, and Cascade Rivers. No part of the Rockies exhibits a greater variety of sublime and pleasing scenery; and nowhere are good points of view and features of special interest so accessible, since many excellent roads and bridle-paths have been made. Boating may be indulged in on the Bow River and on the lake, in whose waters excellent fishing is to be had. No shooting is allowed within the Park limits, but Banff is an excellent starting-point for those seeking the pursuit of bear, elk, caribou, and other big game that abounds in the vicinity, to say nothing of the big-horn sheep. Permits for camping may be obtained from the superintendent, who resides in the village of Banff.

As we enter the park, Mount Peechee (9,580 ft.) rises to the right directly in front of us. Seemingly blocking further progress is Cascade Mountain (9,796 ft.), whose "perpendicular, massive precipice front, sheathed with a thousand colors which glow in the sunshine," is marked by a slender waterfall trailing almost from brow to base. The valley narrows, and the river is crossed twice before *Duthil* (2,339 miles, altitude 4,275 ft) is reached. Still higher we go, following a defile of the Cascade River, and on a widening of the valley is *Anthracite* (2,341 miles, altitude 4,350 ft.). Here are coal mines where true anthracite of an excellent quality is found, and the output is sent as far E. as Winnipeg. Soon the Cascade River leads to the right and opens westward past the base of the Cascade Mountains, while to the left the Bow River bends sharply towards the S. W. through a wide break that separates the Rundle Cascade line of peaks. In the triangular space thus formed is *Banff* (2,346 miles, altitude 4,500 ft.), the station for the Rocky Mountain Park and the Hot Springs, approaching which is seen in a large corral splendid specimens of the buffalo, the last remnant of the countless herds that once roamed the adjacent plains. From the station a superb view of the mountains is possible. To the N. is Cascade Mountain; to the E. are Mount Inglismaldie (9,875 ft.), and the heights of the Fairholme subrange, behind which lies Devil's Head Lake. Still farther to the E. the sharp cone of Mount Peechee closes the view in that direction. To the left of Cascade Mountain and just N. of the

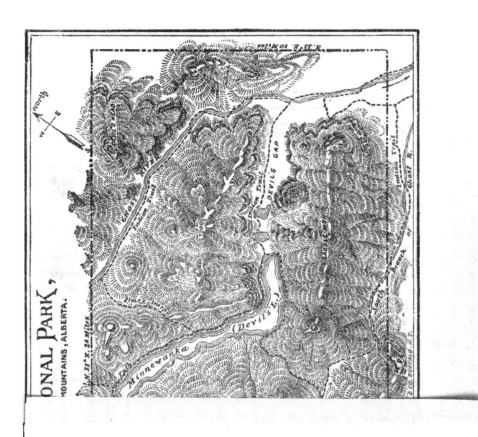

ONAL PARK,
MOUNTAINS, ALBERTA.

track rises the wooded ridge of Squaw Mountain (6,180 ft.), beneath which are the Vermilion Lakes. To the W. and up the valley are the distant snowy peaks of the main range about Simpson's Pass, chief of which is the square, wall-like crest of Mount Massive. A little nearer on the left is the northern end of the Bourgeau Range, and still nearer the Sulphur Mountain, along the base of which are the springs. The isolated bluff to the S. is Tunnel Mountain (5,510 ft.), while just beyond the station Rundle Peak rises abruptly, and so near at hand as to cut off all view in that direction. A good road from the station soon brings us to the steel bridge that takes the carriage road over the Bow and we reach the *Banff Springs Hotel*, built by the railway company, near the fine falls in the Bow, and the mouth of the rapid Spray River. This hotel, with every modern convenience and luxury, including baths supplied from the hot sulphur springs, is kept open during the summer months. The railway company has secured Swiss guides, one of whom is stationed at Banff, and short daily excursions will be arranged in summer for the guests of the hotel to points of interest in the locality.

Brett's Sanitarium and other smaller and less expensive hotels are in the little village, where already a pretty church, a museum, where a complete collection of specimens of the flora, fauna, mineralogy, etc., may be seen, and a schoolhouse have here been built. It has a permanent population of something over 600 persons. Banff Hot Springs is most favorably placed for health, picturesque views, and as a center for canoeing, driving, walking, or mountain climbing. Large trout are found in Devil's Head Lake, and deep trolling for these affords fine sport. Wild sheep (the bighorn) and mountain goats are common on the neighboring heights. The springs are at different elevations upon the eastern slope of Sulphur Mountain, the highest being 700 feet above the Bow. Testimony to their wonderful curative properties is plentiful. The character of the water is said to be similar to that of the Hot Springs in Arkansas, United States. There are numerous excursions to be made from Banff, among which the ascent of the mountains in the vicinity is worthy of mention; and a trip to Devil's Lake, on which is being placed a steam launch, a small chalet hotel being about to be erected at the far end of the lake. On resuming the railway we continue along the N. bank of the Bow, winding in and out of its forested valley. The view to the rear as we leave the station absorbs our attention, but some new attraction demands recognition. On the right the Vermilion Lakes are skirted, and in front of us Mount Massive and the snow-peaks to the crest, inclosing Simpson's Pass, confront us. A sharp turn to the right and the great heap of snowy ledges that form the eastern crest of Pilot Mountain (9,130 ft.) come in view. Then Hole-in-the-Wall Mountain (7,500 ft.) is quickly passed on the right, and we reach *Cascade* (2,352 miles, altitude 4,475 ft.). A little beyond the station we leave the park at its western corner, and Castle Mountain (8,850 ft.) comes in view on the right—" a giant's keep, with turrets, bastions, and battlements complete." *Castle Mountain* station (2,363 miles, altitude 4,570 ft.) is at the base of the mountain, which is on the right. Here was once a mining camp, called Silver City, but now there are more dwellings than inhabitants. The mountains on each side become exceedingly grand and prominent. Those on the right form the bare, ragged, and sharply serrated Sawback Range. On the left the lofty Bow Range fronts the valley in a series of magnificent snow-laden promontories. At first only glimpses of the mountains can be seen through the trees, as you look ahead, but soon the long array of peaks come in view. To the left and looking back the central peak of Pilot Mountain is seen, like a looming pyramid high above the square-fronted ledges visible before. Next to it is the less lofty but almost equally imposing cone of Copper Mountain (8,500 ft.), squarely opposite the sombre precipices of Castle Mountain. Beyond Copper Mountain, the gap of Vermilion Pass (so called because of the yellow ochre, which the Indians found here and used as paint or vermilion) opens through the range, permitting a view of many a lofty spire and icy crest along the continental watershed from whose glaciers and snow-fields the Vermilion River flows westward into the Kootenay. The long, rugged front of Mount Lefroy, W. of the entrance to the Pass, rises supreme over this part of the range—the loftiest and grandest peak in the entire panorama. It takes its name from General Sir Henry Lefroy, who made the first magnetic survey of British America. *Laggan* (2,380 miles, altitude 4,930 ft.) is the station for the famed three Lakes in the Clouds. Ponies and vehicles are here in waiting for those who desire to visit these picturesque lakes. Lake Louise, which is the first, is about 2 miles from the station by the carriage drive. Its altitude is 5,800 ft. On the margin of this beautiful lake there is a comfortable chalet hotel where accommodation is provided. There is a bridle-path to Mirror Lake, higher up (altitude 6,460 ft., or 3,500 ft. above the station) the mountain, and a still further ascent to Lake Agnes (altitude, 6,700 ft.), so-called in honor of Lady Macdonald. There are also trails leading to Paradise Valley and other delightful spots, at which shelters have been erected. A Swiss guide in the employment of the railway company is also stationed here, who will arrange daily excursions for guests. Here the time changes from Mountain to Pacific time, which is an hour earlier.

Crossing the river we ascend Noore's Creek. Looking upward we see the first of the great glaciers. It is a broad, crescent-shaped river of ice, the farther end concealed behind the lofty yellow cliffs that hem it in. It is 1,300 ft. above you, and more than a dozen miles away.

With the aid of an extra locomotive the train slowly ascends towards the Kicking-Horse Pass, also sometimes called Hector Pass, through which the mountains are crossed, and at the bottom of which runs the foaming Kicking-Horse or Wapta River. As we reach the summit the gradient comes to a level, and on the left we pass a rustic arch marked " The Great Divide," which indicates the highest point on the C. P. R. The station at the summit is *Stephen* (2,387 miles, altitude 5,296 ft.), and the point at which we enter British Columbia.

British Columbia.

This, the most westerly of the provinces of the Dominion of Canada, is bounded on the N. by the Northwest Territory, on the E. by Athabasca and Alberta, on the S. by the States of Montana, Idaho, and Washington, and Puget Sound, and on the W. by the Pacific Ocean. It has an area of 383,300 square miles, and, according to the census of 1891, a population of 98,173 inhabitants. The climate varies considerably, as the province is naturally divided into two sections, insular and continental. It is much more moderate and equable than any other province of the Dominion. In the S. W. portion of the mainland, and particularly on the S. E. part of Vancouver Island, the climate is much superior to that of southern England or central France. In this section of the province snow seldom falls, and then lies but a few hours or days. Vegetation remains green and the flowers are bright through the greater part of nearly every winter; while in spring and summer disagreeable E. winds, heavy rains, and long-continued fogs are unknown. British Columbia is one of the most important provinces of the Dominion, as well from a political as from a commercial point of view. With Vancouver Island it is to a maritime nation invaluable, for the limits of its coal fields can only be guessed at, while enough coal has already been discovered on that island to cover the uses of a century. The harbors include Victoria, Vancouver, and Esquimalt, the British naval station. Its timber is unequaled in quantity, quality, or variety; its mines already discovered and operated, and its great extent of unexplored country, indicate vast areas of rich mineral wealth; its waters, containing marvelous quantities of most valuable fish, combine to give British Columbia a value that has been little appreciated.

In proportion to the area of the province land suitable for agricultural purposes is small; but in the aggregate there are many thousands of square miles of arable soil, so diverse in character, location, and climatic influences as to be suited to the production of every fruit, cereal, vegetable, plant, and flower known to the temperate zone. W. of the Cascade Mountains spring and early summer rains are quite sufficient to bring crops to maturity; but farther E., in the great stock-raising interior, irrigation is generally required for mixed farming purposes. Gold has been found on the eastern side of the Rocky Mountains, on Queen Charlotte Island at the extreme W., and on every range of mountains that intervene between these two extreme points, the famed Cariboo mines and those of the Trail Creek district in West Kootenay have shown the greatest development. At Rossland in West Kootenay there has been a wonderful development in recently discovered mines. Among other discoveries is that of a ledge of cinnabar, found at Kamloops Lake, known as the Rose-Bush Mine. The true vein is reported as being 14 inches thick, but there appears to be a large scattered quantity besides. Silver has been found in several places, and its further discovery will probably show that it follows the same rules as in Nevada and Colorado. The best-known argentiferous locality is the Slocan district in West Kootenay, which ranks among the richest silver regions in the world. Great iron deposits exist on Texada Island and copper deposits have been found at several points on the coast of the mainland, Howe Sound, Jarvis Inlet, Queen Charlotte Island, and other points. Bituminous coal has been worked for many years at Nanaimo, on Vancouver Island, where there are large deposits and indications of coal have been found at other places on that island. Seams of bituminous coal have been discovered on the mainland, and veins have been worked in the New Westminster and Nicola districts, and other indications of coal have been found in several parts. The most extensive coal areas, however, are in East

Kootenay, where, in the vicinity of he Crow's Nest Pass, no fewer than twenty seams outcrop, with a total thickness of from 132 ft. to 148 ft. These immense coal measures are being rapidly developed, railway facilities having been furnished by the Crow's Nest Pass Road. Anthracite coal is now being extensively mined at Anthracite, on the line of the C. P. R., and some comparing favorably with that of Pennsylvania has been found in seams of 6 ft. on Queen Charlotte Island. In respect to timber, there is no other province of Canada, no country in Europe, and no State in the United States that compares with it. There are prairies here and there, valleys free from wood, and many openings in the thickest country, which in the aggregate make many hundred thousands of acres of land on which no clearing is required, but near each open spot is a luxuriant growth of wood. The finest growth is on the coast, and in the Gold and Selkirk ranges. Millions on millions of feet of lumber, locked up for centuries past, have now become available for commerce. In addition to the advantages already referred to, British Columbia offers great attractions to the lover of rod and gun. Of game, large and small, there is a great variety. On the mainland are grizzly, black, and brown bears, panthers, lynx, caribou, deer, mountain sheep and goats, heads and skins of which are the finest trophies of a sportsman's rifle. Waterfowl, geese, duck, etc., are very abundant on the larger lakes, and these and several varieties of grouse are the principal feathered game, and can always be found in the season. Victoria is the seat of government.

From Stephen the line descends rapidly, passing the beautiful Wapta Lake at *Hector* (2,389 miles, altitude 5,190 ft.), and crossing the deep gorge of the Wapta River, just beyond. The scenery is now sublime and almost terrible. The line clings to the mountain-side at the left, and the valley on the right rapidly deepens until the river is seen as a gleaming thread a thousand feet below. Looking to the right, one of the grandest mountain valleys in the world stretches away to the N., with great white, glacier-bound peaks on either side. In front of us the dark angular peak of Mount Field (8,555 ft.) is seen. On the left the lofty head of Mount Stephen (10,425 ft.) and the spires of Cathedral Mount (10,285 ft.), still farther to the left, occasionally appear over the tree-tops. This peak has been not inaptly compared to the Duomo of Milan. Soon the slope of Mount Stephen is reached, and on its shoulder (to the left) almost overhead, is seen a shining green glacier, 800 ft. in thickness, which is slowly pressing forward and over a vertical cliff of great height. Mount Stephen is named after Sir George Stephen, the first President of the C. P. R., and in 1891, when he was advanced to the peerage, he chose as his title Lord Mount-Stephen. The works of a silver mine are seen on the side of Mount Stephen, several hundred feet above the road. Passing through a short tunnel, and hugging the base of the mountain closely, the main peak is lost to view for a few minutes; but as the train turns sharply away it soon reappears with startling suddenness, and when its highly colored dome and spires are illuminated by the sun it seems to rise as a flame shooting into the sky.

A sharp descent is made along the pathway and by the Wapta River, and then *Field* (2,397 miles, altitude 4,050 ft.), a tiny hamlet, named after the late Cyrus W. Field, of New York, is reached. A charming little chalet, the *Mt. Stephen House*, is a comfortable stopping-place for those who desire to indulge in the excellent fly-fishing for trout in the pretty lake near by. The station is at the base of the mountain, and its ascent is usually made from here. Two days should be taken for this, and the view from the summit is superb. Looking down the valley the Ottertail Mountains are on the left and the Van Horne Range on the right. The most prominent peaks of the latter are Mount Deville, named after the Surveyor-General of the Dominion, and Mount King, named after F. King, a topographer of this region. Two miles beyond Field very lofty glacier-bearing heights are seen toward the N. The line rises from the flats of the Wapta, and after crossing a high bridge over the Ottertail River (whence one of the finest views is obtained) descends again to the Wapta, whose narrow valley divides the Ottertail and Van Horne Ranges. This range receives its name from Sir William Van Horne, the President of the C. P. R. The line, which has gradually curved toward the S. since crossing the summit at Stephen, runs due S. from here to *Leanchoil* (2,410 miles, altitude 3,570 ft.), where the Beaverfoot River comes in from the S. and joins the Wapta. At the left, the highest peaks of the Ottertail Mountains, rise abruptly to an immense height, and, looking S. E., extend in orderly array toward the Beaverfoot Mountains. At the right, Mt. Hunter pushes its huge mass forward like a wedge between the Ottertail and Beaverfoot Ranges. The river turns abruptly against its base and plunges into the lower Kicking-horse Cañon, down which it disputes the passage with the railway. The cañon rapidly deepens, until, beyond *Palliser* (2,418 miles, altitude 3,250 ft.), the mountain-sides become vertical, rising straight up thousands of feet, and within an easy stone's throw from wall to wall. Down this vast chasm the railway and the river go together, the former crossing from side to side on ledges cut out of the solid rock, and twisting and turning in every direction, and plunging through projecting angles of rock which seem to close the way. With the towering cliffs almost shutting out the sunlight, and the roar of the river and the train increased by the echoing walls, the passage of this terrible gorge will never be forgotten.

Downward we continue, and the train emerges into daylight as *Golden* (2,431 miles, altitude 2,550 ft.), at the junction of the Wapta and Columbia Rivers, a little mining town, is reached. In the vicinity, and especially at the base of the Spillimichene Mountains, there are numerous gold and silver mines. The broad river ahead is the Columbia, and a steamer makes weekly trips from Golden to the lakes at the head of the river, 100 miles distant. After leaving Golden the line turns abruptly to the N., and descends the open valley of the Columbia on the face of the lower bench of the Rocky Mountains, while on the right the Selkirk Mountains, rising from their forest-clad bases, and lifting their ice-crowned heads far into the sky, are in full view all the way, and the paths of avalanches are clearly indicated by the soft green streaks down their sides. *Moberly* (2,437 miles, altitude 2,550 ft.) is the site of the oldest cabin in the mountains, where a Government engineering party under Walter Moberly passed the winter of 1871-'72. A few miles through the woods, and then several sawmills are passed, after which we soon reach *Donald* (2,530 miles, altitude 2,530 ft.), pleasantly situated at the base of the Dogtooth Mountains. The mining country about it, and at the great bend of the Columbia River below, obtain their supplies from here.

Leaving Donald, the railway crosses the Columbia River on a steel bridge to the base of the Selkirks. A little farther down, the Rockies and the Selkirks, crowding together, force the river through a deep, narrow gorge, the railway clinging to the slopes high above it. Emerging from the gorge at *Beavermouth* (2,459 miles, altitude 2,500 ft.), the line turns abruptly to the left and enters the Selkirks through the Gate of the Beaver River—a passage so narrow that a felled tree serves as a foot-bridge over it—just where the river makes its final and mad plunge down to the level of the Columbia River. Soon the line crosses to the right bank of the Beaver River, where, notched into the mountain-side, it rises at the rate of 116 ft. to the mile, and the river is soon left a thousand feet below, appearing as a silver thread winding through the narrow and densely forested valley. Opposite is a line of huge tree-clad hills, occasionally showing snow-covered heads above the timber line. Nature has worked here on so gigantic a scale that many travelers fail to notice the extraordinary height of the spruce, Douglas fir, and cedar trees, which seem to be engaged in a vain competition with the mountains themselves. From *Six-Mile Creek* (2,465 miles, altitude 2,900 ft.), up the Beaver Valley, may be seen a long line of the higher peaks of the Selkirks that culminate in a spire suggesting the Matterhorn and called Sir Donald (10,662 ft.). A few miles beyond, at Mountain Creek bridge, where a powerful torrent comes down from the N., a similar view is obtained, only nearer and larger, and eight peaks can be counted, the last of which is Sir Donald, leading the line. A little farther on Cedar Creek is crossed, and not far W. of it is a very high bridge, spanning a foaming cascade, whence one of the most beautiful prospects of the whole journey is to be had.

As *Bear Creek* (2,474 miles, altitude 3,500 ft.) is approached, a glimpse is caught of Hermit Mountain (9,065 ft.). Here we leave the Beaver River and make the ascent of the Selkirks up Bear Creek. Mountain torrents, many of them in splendid cascades which come down through narrow gorges cut deeply into the slopes along which the railway creeps, are crossed by strong bridges. The largest of these is over Stony Creek—a noisy rill flowing in the bottom of a narrow T-shaped channel 298 ft. below the rails—one of the highest railway bridges in the world. Snow-sheds of massive timber work protect these bridges from the snow in winter. Beyond the bridge at Stony Creek the gorge of Bear Creek is compressed into a ravine, with Mount Macdonald (9,940 ft.) on the left and the Hermit on the right, forming the entrance to Rogers's Pass at the summit. The former towers above the railway in almost vertical height. Its base is but a stone's-throw distant, and it is so sheer, so bare and stupendous, and yet so near, that one is overawed by a sense of immensity and mighty grandeur. In passing before the face of this gigantic precipice the line clings to the base of Hermit Mountain, and as the station at Rogers's Pass is neared its clustered spires appear, facing those of Mount Macdonald, and nearly as high. These two mountains were once apparently united, but some great convulsion of Nature has split them asunder, leaving barely room for the passage of a train.

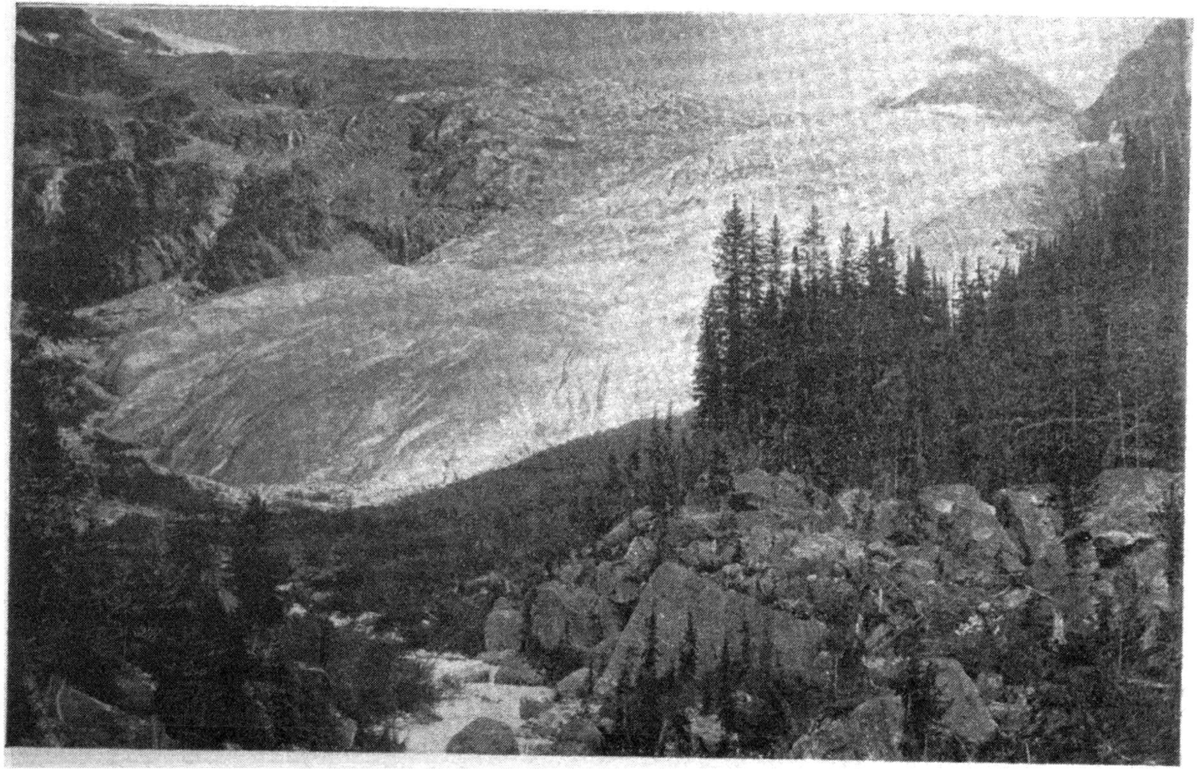

The Great Glacier.

The station of *Rogers's Pass* (2,479 miles, altitude 4,275 ft.) takes its name from Major T. B. Rogers, by whom the pass was discovered in 1883. The Government has reserved this pass with its magnificent mountain scenery as a National Park. A few miles beyond we reach *Selkirk Summit* (2,481 miles, altitude 4,300 ft.), and then turning to the left we follow in our descent the slope of the Summit peaks. To the right, surrounded by a pyramidal peak, is Cheops Mountain ; and looking out of the pass toward the W., and over the deep valley of the Illicilliwaet, is Ross Peak, a massive and symmetrical mountain, with an immense glacier on its eastern slope. Below is the deep valley of the Illicilliwaet, and for miles away can be traced the railway seeking the bottom of the valley by a series of curves, doubling upon itself again and again. Directly ahead is the Great Glacier, a vast plateau of gleaming ice extending as far as the eye can reach, as large as all those of Switzerland combined. We continue to draw nearer and nearer, until at *Glacier House* (2,483 miles, altitude 4,122 ft.) we are within thirty minutes' walk of it. To the left of the station Sir Donald rises, a naked and abrupt pyramid (10,662 ft.). This monolith was named after Sir Donald Smith (now Lord Strathcona), one of the chief promoters of the C. P. R. Farther to the left are two or three sharp peaks, second only to Sir Donald. Rogers's Pass and the snowy mountain beyond (a member of the Hermit Range, which is called Grizzly) are in full view. Somewhat at the left of Cheops a shoulder of Ross Peak is visible over the wooded slope of the mountain behind the hotel which has been erected by the railway for the accommodation of those who desire to stop over. The glaciers and the summits of the surrounding mountains are now reached by good trails, sheltering camps being also erected at high altitudes for the use of mountain climbers in case of sudden changes in the weather. Swiss guides are also stationed here, and under their care tourists are enabled to visit many points hitherto accessible only to expert mountain climbers. Game is abundant throughout these lofty ranges. Their summits are the home of the bighorn sheep and the mountain goat, the latter being seldom found southward of Canada. Bears may also be obtained. Continuing the descent from the Glacier House, and following around the mountain-side, the Loop is reached, where the line makes several startling turns and twists, first crossing a valley leading down from the Ross Peak glacier, touching for a moment on the base of Ross Peak, then doubling back to the right a mile or more upon itself to within a few feet, then sweeping around to the left, touching Cougar Mountain on the other side of the Illicilliwaet, crossing again to the left, and at last shooting down the valley parallel with its former course.

The Illicilliwaet River, though of no great size, is a turbulent mountain stream whose water is at first pea-green with glacier mud, but clarifies as it descends.   After passing *Ross Peak* (2,490 miles, altitude 3,600 ft.) we reach *Illicilliwaet* (2,499 miles, altitude 8,593 ft.) near where are several silver mines, from which large shipments of rich ore have already been made.   Just E. of the *Albert Cañon* (2,505 miles, altitude 2,845 ft.) the train runs along the brink of several deep fissures in the solid rock, whose walls rise straight up, hundreds of feet on both sides, to wooded crags, above which sharp, distant peaks cut the sky.   The train stops here for a few minutes, and solidly built balconies enable passengers to safely look into the boiling caldron below. The next station is *Twin Butte* (2,515 miles), that takes its name from the huge double summit near by, now called Mounts Mackenzie and Tilley.   As we approach the western base of the Selkirks the valley narrows to a gorge.   The line suddenly emerges into an open, level, and forest-covered space, swings to the right, and reaches *Revelstoke* (2,527 miles, altitude 1,475 ft.) (*Hotel Revelstoke*), a divisional point on the bank of Columbia River.   The town stretches from the station a mile away, and is a distributing point for the adjacent mining camps.   A branch extends S. to *Arrowhead* (28 miles) from where the C. P. R. steamers run daily to Nakusp and Robson.   *Nakusp* is near the foot of upper Arrow Lake, where rail communication is made with Rosebery and New Denver, on Slocan Lake (whence the C. P. R. steamer *Slocan* runs to Slocan City at the S. extremity of the lake, where rail connection has been established with the Lower Kootenay River) and with *Sandon*, in the very center of the rich Slocan silver-mining regions. The sail between Nakusp and Robson, on the Columbia River, a run of 165 miles, is through lovely scenery.   From *Robson*, the Columbia & Kootenay Branch runs along the banks of the Lower Kootenay River, a magnificent fishing water, to *Nelson*, a town of remarkable growth, where another C. P. R. steamboat is taken for a visit to the numerous gold, silver, and copper mines on the Kootenay Lake, or to enjoy the magnificent lake and mountain scenery which this locality affords. From opposite Robson the trains of the Rossland Branch of the C. P. R. run along the western bank of the Columbia River to the important smelting center of *Trail*, and to the new city of *Rossland*, a mining camp of phenomenal growth about which cluster a number of rich mines, the wealth of which has been demonstrated by actual production. A railway is also under construction by the C. P. R., and is to be completed this year, which will penetrate what is generally known as the Boundary Country, in the southern portion of Yale division, reaching the new towns of Cascade, Grand Forks, and Greenwood. This is a rich undeveloped mining region of great possibilities.

After leaving the station at Revelstoke *en route* to Vancouver, the Columbia is crossed on a bridge half a mile long, and the Gold Range is entered by the Eagle Pass. We reach the highest point at Summit Lake, only 525 ft. above the river some 8 miles distant. Here in close succession occur four beautiful lakes—Summit, Victor, Three Valley, and Griffin—each occupying the entire width of the valley and forcing the railway to carve for itself a path in the mountain-side. The valley is filled with a dense growth of immense spruce, hemlock, fir, cedar, and other trees, and in consequence sawmills abound. At *Craigellachie* (2,555 miles, altitude 1,450 ft.) we have reached the valley again, and here, on November 7, 1885, the last spike was driven in the C. P. R., the rails from the E. and the W. meeting at this otherwise insignificant flag station. The train passes on through a forest of dense timber, close to the Eagle River, and reaches on the right the Shuswap Lake. In the vicinity of this lake is one of the best sporting regions on the line. Northward, within a day, caribou are abundant; the deer shooting southward within 30 miles is probably unexcelled on this continent, and on the lakes there is famous sport in deep trolling for trout. We cross an arm of the lake just before arriving at *Sicamous Junction* (2,571 miles, altitude 1,300 ft.), on the S. bank of the Great Shuswap Lake. It is the station for the Spallumsheen mining district and other regions up the river around Okanagan Lake, where there is a large settlement. A branch of the C. P. R. runs S. 51 miles to *Okanagan Landing*, at the head of Lake Okanagan, a magnificent sheet of water, on which the stanch steamer "Aberdeen" plies to *Kelowna*, *Peachland*, and *Penticton*, at the foot of the lake, from which the Fairview and Camp McKinney mines are reached by stage. The Okanagan Valley is one of the greatest game regions in the world.

Resuming our journey westward, the line winds in and out the bending shores of Lake Shuswap, and the outlook "gives a fine reminder of Scottish scenery." Some 20 miles beyond the station we double a southern extension of the lake called the Salmon Arm, and then strike through the forest over the top of the intervening ridge of Notch Hill that gives its name to the station on the summit (altitude 1,708 ft.). The view of the adjacent country from this point is remarkably fine. Besides the natural features, the fields and farmhouses with herds of cattle and sheep remind one that we are approaching the coast. Near *Shuswap* (2,622 miles) we regain the shores of the lake and run for some distance along the Little Shuswap Lake, as this extension is called. The lake narrows in a broad stream called South Thompson River, and we continue along the valley, which as it widens gladdens our eyes with signs of settlement and cultivation that so help to relieve that deep sense of loneliness that almost oppresses one in traveling in a wild country. There are Indian villages in the vicinity, and their half-civilized homes and wealth of ponies are frequently seen, as we reach and pass *Ducks* (2,638 miles), near which is one of the old ranches that dates back to the times of the gold excitement on the Pacific coast. *Kamloops* (2,655 miles), with a population of 2,000 inhabitants, is a divisional point and the principal source of supply for the extensive mining and grazing district of the Thompson River Valley. Its equable and salubrious climate and pleasant surroundings make Kamloops a favorite resort for those suffering from lung troubles. It was originally a fur-trading post of the Hudson Bay Co. Its name signifies confluence in the Indian tongue, and it is at the junction of the N. and S. branches of the Thompson River. In the angle formed by the two branches of the river is an Indian village, and the mountain that towers above it is Saul's Peak (3,570 ft.). Stage lines extend southward to the ranching and mineral districts that are to the S. in the Okanagan and Nicola Valleys. Just beyond Kamloops the river widens into a broad, beautiful hill-girt sheet of water called Kamloops Lake, along the S. bank of which the railway runs for some 20 miles. Half-way a series of mountain spurs project into the lake and are pierced by numerous tunnels, one following the other in close succession. At *Savonas* (2,680 miles) the lake ends, the mountains draw near, and the series of Thompson River cañons is entered, leading westward to the Fraser through marvelous scenery. At low tide Chinamen and Indians are often seen busily engaged in washing the river gravel for gold. Mercury mines of great value have been discovered in this locality. From here to Port Moody the railway was built by the Dominion Government and transferred to the C. P. R. in 1886. *Pennys* (2,687 miles) is an old-time ranching settlement. *Ashcroft* (2,702 miles) is a busy town, and the point of departure for the stage lines that run to Cariboo, Barkerville, and other gold fields in the northern interior of British Columbia, which after producing millions of the yellow metal are being further exploited successfully by hydraulic appliances. Frequent trains of freight-wagons drawn by yokes of oxen, and long strings of pack-mules laden with merchandise, depart from and arrive here. There are large cattle ranches in the vicinity, and some farming is done. Three miles beyond Ashcroft the hills press close upon the Thompson River, which cuts its way through a winding gorge of desolation, fitly called Black Cañon. Emerging, the train follows the river as it meanders swiftly among the round-topped, treeless, and water-cut hills. At *Spence's Bridge* (2,728 miles) the old wagon-road up the valley to the Cariboo gold country crosses the river; and the line crosses the mouth of the Nicola River, whose valley, to the S., is a grazing and ranching region. Beyond this point the scenery becomes very striking and peculiar. The train runs upon a sinuous ledge cut out of the bare hills on the irregular S. side of the stream, where the headlands are penetrated by tunnels, and the ravines spanned by lofty bridges; and the Thompson whirls down its winding path, as green as an emerald. At times the banks are rounded, cream-white slopes; next, cliffs of richest yellow, streaked and dashed with maroon, jut out; then masses of solid rust-red earth, suddenly followed by an olive-green grass slope or some white exposure. Besides the interest of great height and breadth of prospect there is a constantly changing grotesqueness of form, caused by the wearing down of rocks by water and wind into strange forms. Beyond *Drynoch* (2,734 miles), Nicomen, a little mining town, is seen on the opposite bank of the river, where gold was discovered in British Columbia in 1857. The mountains draw together to a narrow causeway, called Thompson's Cañon, and the railway winds along their face hundreds of feet above the river. The gorge narrows and the scenery becomes wild beyond description.

At *Lytton* (2,750 miles), a small trading town, the cañon suddenly widens to admit the Fraser, the chief river of British Columbia, that comes down from the N. between two lines of mountain peaks. It is named after Simon Fraser, an early officer of the Northwest Fur Co. The railway now follows the cañon of the united rivers, and the scene becomes even wilder than before. Six miles below Lytton the train crosses the Fraser River by a steel cantilever bridge (said to be the first true cantilever ever built), plunges into a tunnel, and shortly emerges at *Cisco* (2,757 miles). The line then follows the right-hand side of the cañon, with the river surging far below. The old Government road to Cariboo follows the Fraser and Thompson Valleys, and is seen on the E. bank of the river. It twists and turns about the cliffs, sometimes venturing down to the river's side, whence it is quickly driven back by an angry turn of the waters. Six miles below Cisco, where it follows the cliffs opposite to the railway, it is forced to the height of 1,000 feet above the river, and is pinned by seemingly slender sticks to the face of the precipice. The cañon alternately widens and narrows. Indians may be seen on projecting rocks at the water's edge, spearing salmon or scooping them out with dip-nets, and in sunny spots the salmon are drying on poles. Often Chinamen are passed who are washing the sand of the river for the precious metal which they crave even more than food. *North Bend* (2,777 miles) is a divisional point, and a convenient stopping-place for those who desire to explore the Grand Cañon of the Fraser at greater leisure than the rapid movement of the train will permit, or perhaps to spend a short time in shooting and fishing. Comfortable quarters can be had at the chalet hotel near the station. At 4 miles below the principal cañon of the Fraser River begins, and from here onward for 23 miles the scenery is not only intensely interesting but startling, and has been even described as "matchless." The great river is forced between vertical walls of black rocks, where, repeatedly thrown back upon itself by opposing cliffs or broken by ponderous masses of fallen rock, it roars and foams. The jutting spurs of the cliff are pierced by tunnels in close succession. At *Spuzzum* (2,792 miles) the old Government road crosses the chasm by a graceful suspension bridge to the side of the railway and keeps with it for some distance. The road is now abandoned and is in many places impassable. Just before reaching *Yale* (2,803 miles) the enormous cliffs apparently shut together as if to bar the way. The river then makes an abrupt turn to the left, and the railway, turning to the right, disappears into a long tunnel, emerging into daylight and rejoining the river as we approach the station. Yale is an old trading-post and frontier town, with some 1,500 inhabitants, which was once an outfitting point for miners and ranchmen northward. Indian huts are to be seen on the opposite bank of the river, and in the town a conspicuous joss-house indicates the presence of Chinamen, who may be seen washing for gold on the river bars below. Yale is at the head of navi-

Indians, near New Westminster.

gation of the lower Fraser River, and was once the leading place of the province. After leaving this town the river widens and becomes less turbulent. Soon *Hope* (2,817 miles) is reached, with the village proper on the opposite side of the bank. To the S. W. are the Hope Peaks, where rich silver lodes exist, and only await suitable fuel to be worked profitably. The valley continues to broaden, and well-cultivated fields become more and more frequent. *Ruby Creek* (2,824 miles) is named from the garnets found in the vicinity. *Agassiz* (2,835 miles), overlooked by Mount Cheam (11,000 feet), where a Government experimental farm is operated, is the station for the hot sulphur *Harrison Springs* (*St. Alice Hotel*), on Harrison Lake, 5 miles N. Near *Harrison* (2,844 miles) the Harrison River is crossed, just above its confluence with the Fraser. Until the opening of the Fraser route, in 1864, the only access to the gold diggings in the northern interior of the province was by way of the Harrison Valley. A few miles beyond *Nicomen* (2,853 miles) the beautiful isolated cone of Mount Baker (13,000 feet), in the State of Washington, comes into view on the left. From *Mission Junction* (2,863 miles), where the Roman Catholic Indian Mission of St. Mary has long been in existence, a branch crosses the Fraser River and runs to the international boundary line, where connection is made with the Seattle and International Ry. for all points in Washington, Oregon, and California. Immense trees are now frequent, and their size is indicated by the enormous stumps near the railway. The Great Pitt Meadows and the Pitt River are crossed and at *New Westminster Junction* (2,888 miles) a branch diverges 8 miles S. W. to *New Westminster* (*Guichon* and *Colonial Hotels*), on the right bank of the Fraser River, about 15 miles from its mouth. New Westminster, with a population of about 9,000, is the oldest city in the region, and was once the capital of the province. The business portion of this city was swept by fire in the fall of 1898, but is being rapidly rebuilt. New Westminster is the center of the salmon industry, and the several canneries in the vicinity represent an invested capital of nearly $1,500,000. There are also extensive interests connected with the sawing and shipping of lumber, and the Provincial Penitentiary and Asylum are located here. It is a terminus of the New Westminster and Southern Branch of the Great Northern R. R. that comes from New Whatcom, and it is connected by an electric railway with Vancouver. Steamboats ply regularly to Victoria and to other ports on the Strait of Georgia and Puget Sound. Returning to the main line, our route bends to the right after leaving Westminster.

20

Junction, and with a short run through a wooded district reaches *Port Moody* (2,893 miles), at the head of Burrard Inlet, an arm of the Strait of Georgia. It was for some time the Pacific terminus of the railway. The line continues for the remainder of the route along the S. shore of the inlet. At intervals are mills with small villages around them, while in the inlet are ocean steamships and sailing craft of all kinds, loading with sawed timber for all parts of the world. The scenery is fine. Snow-tipped mountains, beautiful in form and color, rise above the N. side of the inlet and are vividly reflected in the mirror-like waters. The Pacific terminus of the route is reached at *Vancouver* (2,906 miles from Montreal).

Vancouver.

The principal hotel is *Hotel Vancouver*, built and operated by the C. P. R. It is on high ground overlooking the harbor, and affords a fine view. *Leland House, Badminton House,* and *Hotel Columbia* are likewise well-appointed hotels with modern conveniences. Vancouver possesses an ideal situation. It rises gradually from Coal Harbor, a widening of Burrard Inlet, and extends across a strip of land to English Bay, thus affording it excellent natural drainage, harbor facilities, and commercial advantages, while the Cascade Mountains to the N. afford a pleasant vista. The site of the city was covered with a dense forest until May, 1886, when it was accepted as the W. terminus of the C. P. R. In two months it grew into a place of 600 inhabitants, and then it was destroyed by fire. This disaster proved a blessing in disguise, for the wooden buildings were replaced by those of brick and stone, and in 1891 the census returns indicated a population of 13,-709, which now (1899) exceeds 25,000. Adjacent to the Vancouver Hotel is the C. P. R. Opera-House. Fine churches, notably the Presbyterian and the Episcopal, are worthy of mention. The City Hall, the Custom-House and Post-Office, the Bank of Montreal, and the public schools are among the larger civic and commercial buildings. The private residences have handsome lawns and gardens around them, and Stanley Park (960 acres) has been reserved as a pleasure ground. Electric street railways are running, and the streets are lighted both by gas and electricity. Opportunities for sport are unlimited—mountain goats, bear, and deer in the hills along the inlet, trout-fishing in the mountain streams, and sea-fishing in endless variety. From Vancouver sail the C. P. R. steamers to Japan, China, the Hawaiian and Fijian

Islands, New Zealand, and Australia. The city has also connections with all important points along the Pacific coast from San Francisco to Alaska. The mail service between Vancouver and Japan and China employs three steel steamships, called the Empress of India, the Empress of Japan, and the Empress of China, especially designed for that trade. The Canadian-Australian line gives a service to Australia, by way of Honolulu, H. I., Suva, Fiji, and Wellington, N. Z., every four weeks. There are almost daily steamers to Alaska during the summer months to ports from which lead overland routes to the Klondike and Atlin Lake. Steamers ply between Vancouver and Victoria and Nanaimo daily, and connection is made at Victoria for all Puget Sound ports and to Portland and San Francisco.

The Crow's Nest Pass Road.

The recently opened Crow's Nest Pass Ry., which branches off from the main line of the C. P. R. near Medicine Hat, on the plains, forms part of an alternative route to the coast through Southern British Columbia. It passes through the great cattle country of Southern Alberta, and, entering the Rockies by the Crow's Nest Pass, penetrates the rich and rapidly developing mining region of East Kootenay. There are many attractive points along the route, and the scenery is of that grandeur and beauty which the mountains of British Columbia pre-eminently possess. The present western rail terminus is at Kootenay Landing on Kootenay Lake, from which C. P. R. steamers run 35 miles to Nelson, where, by the extensive railway and steamboat system of the company, which networks the whole West Kootenay country, the tourist is enabled to reach any desired point. If continuing the journey to the coast, Revelstoke, on the main line, would be reached by the Columbia River and Arrow Lakes, and the transcontinental train then to Vancouver. This route, however, can be now advantageously taken on the return trip.

Vancouver to Victoria.

The route to Victoria is by water. A steamer leaves Vancouver daily except Monday, shortly after the arrival of the transcontinental trains, and makes the trip in about six hours. The sail is usually a pleasant one, and is certainly a picturesque one. On the N. is *Moody-ville*, an Indian mission village of some 300 or 400 houses, backed by the snow-capped hills of the Cascade Range. Vancouver passes slowly out of sight, and the Strait of Georgia is soon reached, and it forms the eastern and northern boundary of Vancouver's Island. Our course is to the S., and on the W. are the mountains on Vancouver's Island, while to the E. is the white cone of Mount Baker (10,810 ft.). Soon we reach Haro Archipelago, and the steamer winds in and out the numerous green islands along the line of the boundary between the United States and Canada, sometimes called Canal de Haro, which in 1872 was decided by the Emperor of Germany to be the line of demarcation. We have been going directly S., and the peaks of Olympic Mountains are seen on the S. shore of the sound, with Mount Olympus and Mount Constance towering above the rest. Finally, a turn is made to the right and the harbor of Victoria is entered. On Mondays connection with Victoria is by way of New Westminster. (APPLETONS' GUIDE-BOOK TO ALASKA contains much information about British Columbia, and also see Part II of APPLETONS' GENERAL GUIDE TO THE UNITED STATES AND CANADA.)

Victoria (*Driard, Hotel Dallas, Hotel Victoria*) is the capital of British Columbia and the residence of the Lieutenant-Governor. It is on a small arm of the sea, commanding a superb view of the Strait of Georgia, the mountains of the mainland, and snow-capped Mount Baker in the distance to the S. E. Originally it was a stockaded post of the Hudson Bay Co., and was then called Fort Victoria. From the time of the gold excitement in 1858 its growth has been steady. In 1866 it was made the capital of the province, and in 1893 it became the station of a company of Royal Marine Artillery and Engineers. Its population in 1891 was 15,841, and it is now (1899) estimated to be over 25,000. The climate is that of the south of England, and the town is peculiarly English in all its characteristics. Besides the magnificent Government buildings erected at a cost of about $1,000,000, containing a museum and library, in which are displayed the products of the province, the city has many fine public and private buildings, among them a large and well-appointed opera house. There are churches of all denominations, including an Anglican cathedral. The manufacturing interests of the province are largely centered at Victoria. It has large iron works, several foundries and machine shops, and many factories. The city has an extensive trade, especially of furs, and there are many large commercial houses It is amply provided with educational facilities, both public and private. The public schools are supported by the Government, and controlled by a school board elected by popular vote. Besides these there are the Ladies' College, under the auspices of the Anglican Church, and an academic institution, as well as a primary school, maintained by the Roman Catholic denomination. There are Protestant and Roman Catholic orphanages. The city has a public library of over 10,000 volumes, and several of the fraternal and benevolent societies also have libraries of considerable size. Beacon Hill Park affords a fine view of the waters and mountains on every side. The Chinese quarter is always interesting to visitors. A railway extends N. E. 70 miles to the coal-mines of *Nanaimo*. Connection is made with Puget Sound ports daily, except Mondays, and steamships depart about every five days for San Francisco. Steamers from and to Vancouver, for Japan, China, Australia, and Alaska stop at Victoria for passengers. *Esquimalt Harbor*, 2 miles from Victoria, is the British naval station and rendezvous on the North Pacific, with naval storehouses, workshops, graving docks, etc. A number of men-of-war are to be found there at all times.

The Yukon Gold Fields.

As long ago as 1880 gold was discovered in paying quantities in Alaska, but the difficulty in securing satisfactory transportation and the lack of adequate supplies made mining operations, even when confined to placer deposits, a hazardous operation. Notwithstanding these difficulties, there has been a constant influx of fortune-seekers, chiefly to the gold fields of the Yukon, especially since 1895; and in 1898 it was estimated that more than 20,000 persons made their way into this new mining region of the Klondike, while during that year the output of gold was estimated by Government officials to have been upward of $5,000,000. In 1898 an immense tide of gold-seekers, variously estimated at from 20,000 to 30,000, poured into the Klondike, and the output of the mines for the year was placed at about $10,000,000. *Dawson City*, the metropolis of the region, has a population, nominally, of 16,000 souls; banks, churches, hotels, and men and women engaged in all callings and professions. The wealth of the Klondike can, as yet, only be conjectured, but experienced miners, familiar with richest properties of America and the world, confidently predict that the new Eldorado will produce annually at least $10,000,000 for many years to come.

Location.—The Yukon district of the Northwest Territories of Canada, in which the Klondike gold fields are located, comprises a vast stretch of country lying between the Arctic Ocean on the N., the 141st west meridian or international boundary line which separates it from the

Territory of Alaska on the W., the northern boundary of the Province of British Columbia on the S., and the summit of the Canadian Rocky Mountains which divides it from the Mackenzie Basin on the E. The district is about 600 miles from N. to S. by over 500 miles from E. to W. at its southern boundary, with gradually lessening distances toward the N.

How to reach the Gold Fields.—The Klondike can be reached by steamer from *Vancouver*, *Victoria*, or *Seattle* to *Skagway*, *Dyea*, or *Pyramid Harbor*, at the head of the Lynn Canal in Alaska. From *Skagway* the Pacific and Arctic Ry. runs through the White Pass to *Bennett*, where steamers now run daily to *White Horse Rapids*, where transfer is made to other steamers and *Dawson* reached without inconvenience. From *Dyea* the Chilkoot Pass has to be crossed, freight being taken by aërial tramway, and this route joins the Skagway route at *Bennett*. These routes will probably develop into good arteries of tourist travel to *Dawson*, the homeward voyage being make down the Yukon to *St. Michaels*, and across the north Pacific Ocean to *Vancouver*, *Victoria*, or *Seattle*. The Dalton route starts from *Pyramid Harbor* (10 miles below Skagway) and continues overland to *Fort Selkirk*. This is considered a good route for live stock, the entire distance from Pyramid Harbor to Fort Selkirk being 350 miles.

The all-water route is by ocean steamer, starting from *San Francisco* or *Seattle* and proceeding thence to *St. Michaels*, near the mouth of the Yukon River, and thence by river steamboat up the Yukon to *Dawson City*.

The Mining Region.—The Yukon is not the desolate region that it has been pictured. A great part of the valley is clothed with forests of spruce, birch, and cottonwood, all of which are good for building purposes. The hills are covered with large trees, and in the valleys there is still better timber. One sawmill in Dawson City is already in operation, and others will be established to supply the local demand for sawed lumber at reduced cost from the present prices. Coal is also abundant in the vicinity of Dawson City, and conveniently situated for mining.

An official bulletin, issued by the Canadian Government, says:

With the comparatively low temperature all through the summer and the prevalence of frost during the early part of June and again before the end of August, which shortens the growing season at both ends, there seems to be no prospect of much being ever done in the

way of agriculture in such a climate. More success, however, is likely
to be had along the margin of rivers than elsewhere. There are a few
garden products which mature in a very short period that can be grown
in this district fairly well, such as radish, lettuce, and early varieties of
cabbage and turnips. These latter do not grow to a large size, but
attain sufficient maturity to make them fit for use. To this list may
probably be added spinach, early varieties of green peas, also early
beets and carrots, and possibly some early sorts of onions might grow
large enough for use. Rhubarb also would be worthy of trial, and if
the roots were not killed by the severe winter, this plant would furnish
a useful substitute for fruit in the early part of the season. Potatoes
have been grown in several localities, but unless planted in a suitably
sheltered spot they need some special protection against frost in August, which is apt to cut them down before the tubers reach a usable
size.

Some portions of the country abound in large and and small game,
but in the region about the Klondike and farther east there is little, if
any, along the river except rabbits, ducks, and geese in the spring of
the year, with caribou and a few moose and bear beyond the river, and
bighorn (mountain sheep) and mountain goats on the sides of the highest mountains. Birds are scarce, but there are partridge and ptarmigan in some localities. Fishing is good, especially for salmon, which
weigh up to 80 and 100 pounds, and there are grayling, whitefish, lake
trout, and eels.

The principal centers of the Yukon are Dawson City, Forty-Mile
Post, and Fort Cudahy in Canadian territory. *Dawson City* in the
Klondike is the great central mining camp; but new towns are constantly springing up and becoming important points on the Yukon
River. There are stores, hotels, and restaurants at the chief mining
centers, and these will doubtless be augmented to meet the increased
requirements of newcomers during the present season.

The chief interest in this region naturally concerns itself with mining, and therefore the following very brief description of the methods
pursued in getting out the placer gold will be of value:

The valleys of the creeks are generally wide at the bottom and flat,
being seldom less than 300 ft. to 400 ft. This is covered with a dense
growth of underbrush and small spruce, with occasionally balsam, poplar, or cottonwood. Much of the wood is suitable for sluice-box purposes, and the rest may be used for firewood, which is an important
factor in developing the mines of this region. The moss and ice covering a space 8 or 10 ft. long by 7 or 8 ft. wide are cleared away from
the surface, or a hole some 6 ft. long by 4 ft. wide is dug, and a fire
built. During the night the ground is thawed to a depth of from 6

to 12 in. Next morning this thawed ground is pitched out and the process is repeated until the bed-rock is reached, which is generally at a depth of from 15 to 20 ft. About 10 ft. down we leave the vegetable matter, the alluvial deposits, and enter a stratum of coarse gravel, the gravel showing very little rounding or wearing. At the bottom of this, close to the bed-rock, the pay streak is found, and is seldom more than 3 ft. in depth, the best-paying part being immediately on the bedrock. This is not solid rock, but a mass of angular, broken rock lying, no doubt, in its original location in space. Between these masses clay and fine gravel have become imbedded. Into this the miner proceeds a foot or more. To burn the hole requires about three weeks' time and a good deal of labor.

Quartz mining can scarcely be said to have begun yet, but authorities unite in predicting that it will ultimately become the chief industry of the country. As conditions have hitherto been with lack of milling facilities, quartz has little value compared with placer claims, and consequently was not sought. Prospecting for quartz and veins, too, is more difficult than for placer diggings, the outcrops in the hills and mountains being generally covered with several feet of *débris* or slide as well as by moss. The sedimentary coal-bearing deposits are also abundant and widespread, and it is claimed that gold-bearing conglomerates in geological age corresponding to those of South Africa, but of unproved richness, are found in several places. Atlin Lake, 10 miles east of Tagish Lake and 90 from Skagway, at the head of ocean navigation, is the site of the latest finds. Already a town with a population of several thousands has sprung up on its shores. It is thought the region will rival the Klondike, and that on account of its greater accessibility the rush to Atlin this year will equal that to Dawson City in 1898.

Those who desire to learn more of the Northwestern Territories—and, for that matter, the gold deposits of the Yukon River are not the only ones known to exist in that region—should consult the latest edition of APPLETONS' GUIDE TO ALASKA.

APPENDIX FOR SPORTSMEN.

Tourists who seek Eastern Canada for the sake of sport may look for certain general information which has not seemed to find a place readily in the foregoing pages. In regard to supplies, it may be noted that they can generally be obtained in Canadian cities at a much lower price, for like quality, than in the great American centres. The Canadian dealers have the advantage of a lighter tariff, and they do not charge fancy prices. Tackle of most kinds, of the best Canadian and English manufacture, can be bought in Toronto, Montreal, Quebec, St. John, or Halifax, at figures which would be impossible in New York or Boston. The favourite " all-round " rod of the present writer is a heavy trout-rod with which he has killed some fine salmon. It is made of green-heart and lance-wood, nickel-mounted, and with neat basket-work grip; and it cost but $10. It was made by Scribner, of St. John.

Supplies that are obviously personal are usually passed through the customs without demur. But luxuries like tobacco, with eatables and drinkables generally, are pretty sure to be taxed; and the traveller may save himself trouble by waiting till he is across the border before laying in his stock. Canadian tobacco is but American leaf made up in Canada. As for wearing apparel, that is regarded very liberally, and one may take an ample wardrobe without being questioned. No one wants to smuggle clothing from America into Canada, for obvious reasons. Let the sportsman, then, come generously supplied with warm flannels (unless he prefers to purchase these *en route*), for, however hot the days may be on Canadian fishing-waters, the nights are apt to be chilly.

A word in regard to board in private houses. This is usually plain, and always inexpensive. It is not often any higher than $1 per day or $5 per week. Throughout the Maritime Provinces, at least, good accommodations may be found almost anywhere at $4 per week. Guides and camp help ask from $1 to $1.50 per day, according to locality. On the Tobique River an Indian guide supplies his services and his canoe for $1 or $1.25 per day, and his board. The variation in the charge is dependent on the season, the guide's humor, and the demand for his services. On the Restigouche a guide with canoe charges $1.50 a day, and finds himself; or $1.25 per day with board.

To avoid disappointments, the tourist should bear in mind that in the provinces of Quebec and New Brunswick the best salmon rivers, and many of the best trout-waters, are leased to private persons or fishing clubs. Lists of the leased waters are issued annually by the Provincial Governments, and full information on the subject may be obtained by application to the Fisheries Commissioners of these two provinces, at Quebec and Fredericton respectively. Armed with such information, the true sportsman will find no difficulty in getting the hospitality of some of the leased waters extended to him, for a longer or shorter period. In Ontario and Nova Scotia the waters are not leased, as a rule, and the fishing rights rest primarily in the hands of the riparian owners, who, indeed, sometimes lease their privileges. In Nova Scotia sportsmen, as a rule, fish wherever they find good waters, without making any minute inquiry into riparian rights. This freedom is a great convenience to the hasty traveler, who does not make up his mind till the last moment as to the direction of his wanderings.

The following list gives approximately the present lessees of New Brunswick waters, although some changes have not been reported:

Restigouche River: From mouth of Upsalquitch to Toad Brook, H. B. Hollins, of New York; from Toad Brook to Tom's Brook, Samuel Thorne, of New York; from Tom's Brook to Tatapedia River, Laines M. Waterbury, of New York; from Tatapedia to Tracey's Brook, Restigouche Salmon Club, of New York; from Tracey's Brook to Quatawamkedgwick, Archibald Rogers, Hyde Park, New York; from I. C. R. R. Bridge to mouth of Upsalquitch, Restigouche Salmon Club, New York; from below I. C. R. R. Bridge to Flatlands, Micmac Salmon Club; below Flatlands, held by local lessees.

Jacquet River, Samuel Street, of New York.

Upsalquitch: From mouth to Forks, Ezra C. Fitch, of Waltham, Mass.; remainder of stream and branches, Ezra C. Fitch, of Waltham, Mass.

Nepisiguit: From mouth to Indian Reserve, C. B. Burnham, St. Louis, Mo.; from Indian Reserve to Great Falls, C. B. Burnham, St. Louis, Mo.; from Great Falls to head of river, C. B. Burnham, St. Louis, Mo.

Miramichi: Northwest and branches above Big Sevogle, R. R. Call, Newcastle, N. B.

Pokemouche River and branches, K. F. Burns, Bathurst, N. B.

Big Tracadie and branches, Edward Jack, Fredericton, N. B.

Renous and Dungarvan, M. Tennant, Fredericton, Dungarvan Fishing Club.

Green River, The Tobique Salmon Club, W. T. Whitehead, Fredericton.

Tocologan (Charlotte), James H. Ganong, St. Stephen.

Kedron stream and lakes (Charlotte), E. H. Bradshaw, Boston.

Clear Lake (St. John), James F. Hamilton, St. John.

South Ocomocto Lake, W. H. Barnaby, St. John.

Tobique and branches, The Tobique Salmon Club.

Cain's River and branches, A. S. Murray, Fredericton.

Tabusintac River, Thomas R. Jones.

THE LAKE ST. JOHN COUNTRY.

The management of the Hotel Roberval at Lake St. John controls considerable ouananiche fishing, which is open to guests of the hotel. This fishing is at its best in June and early July, although there is a renewal of activity in September. The late July and August fishing is characterized by more than the proverbial uncertainty of piscatorial pursuits, but there is always trout-fishing as a compensation. The following is a list of fishing-clubs along the line of the Quebec and Lake St. John Railway:

Little Saguenay.

Talbot (open on payment of a fee).

Laurentides.

Tardival.

Stadacona.

A. L. Light, Large Lake Batiscan.

Tourilli.

Penn.

Metabetchouan.

Paradise Fin and Feather.

Lake Quaquakamaksis.

Springfield Club.

Rivière Noire.

Lac au Lare.

Amabelish.

All these clubs are of comparatively recent formation. On returning from the Lake St. John country to the St. Lawrence, the sportsman will find that practically all the salmon and trout rivers flowing into the St. Lawrence, and those in the Quebec peninsula known as Gaspesia, are held by lessees. In some cases arrangements can be made for a few days of fishing. It is always best to make careful inquiries in advance, for the sportsman must abandon the idea that he can fish for salmon wherever the spirit moves him. Trout-fishing, however, is easily obtainable, as a rule. As regards hunting and fishing licenses from the Government for strangers, experience seems to indicate that they are rarely insisted upon, at least in the case of the fisherman.

Close Seasons.

The close seasons for fish and game, in the provinces traversed in this hand-book, are as follows, but as the game laws are subject to frequent *revision* it is advisable for sportsmen to procure further information regarding them:

PROVINCE OF ONTARIO.

SHOOTING.—Moose, caribou, elk, and reindeer protected entirely until October, 1900. . . . No deer shall be hunted, taken, or killed between November 15 and November 1 following. . . . Beaver and otter cannot be killed before November 1, 1900. . . . Quail and wild turkeys, December 15 to September 15. Turkeys cannot be killed before October 15, 1900. . . . Grouse, pheasants, woodcock, golden plover, prairie fowl, partridge, snipe, rail, hare, December 15 to September 15 following. . . . Swans and geese, May 1 to September 15. . . . Ducks of all kinds and other waterfowl, December 15 to September 1. No person shall shoot between sunset and sunrise. Cotton-tail rabbits may be shot at all times.

No person can kill deer in Ontario except he hold a license from the Provincial Secretary. No person shall kill more than two deer, and deer are not to be hunted or killed in the water.

No person shall kill or take any moose, elk, reindeer, caribou, deer, partridge, or quail, for the purpose of exporting the same out of Ontario. No person shall sell or barter any quail, wild turkey, snipe, woodcock, or partridge, no matter where procured, before September 15, 1900.

FISHING.—Close season.—Salmon, trout, and whitefish between November 1 and 30. . . . Speckled trout, brook trout, river trout, from September 15 to May 1. . . . Bass, from April 15 to June 15. . . . Maskinonge, from April 15 to June 15. . . . Pickerel, April 15 to May 15. No person shall kill more than twenty speckled or brook trout in one day, or more than aggregates in weight 15 pounds, or any trout less than five inches in length. Smaller ones to be returned to the water. Not more than one dozen bass to be killed in one day, or any less than ten inches long. Non-residents must obtain licenses from the local fishery officer.

PROVINCE OF QUEBEC.

SHOOTING.—Deer and moose from January 1 to October 1. . . . Caribou from February 1 to September 1. . . . Fee for non-residents of the province, $25.

N. B.—The hunting of moose, caribou, or deer, with dogs or by means of snares, traps, etc., is prohibited; but red deer may be hunted with dogs in the counties of Ottawa and Pontiac from October 20 to November 1 of each year. No person (white man or Indian) has a right, during one season's hunting, to kill or take alive—unless he has previously obtained a permit from the Commissioner of Crown Lands for that purpose—more than two moose, two caribou, and three deer. After the first ten days of the close season, all railways and steamboat companies and public carriers are forbidden to carry the whole or any part (except the skin) of any moose, caribou, or deer, without being authorized thereto by the Commissioner of Crown Lands.

Beaver, mink, otter, marten, pekan, from April 1 to November 1. . . . Hare, from February 1 to November 1. . . . Muskrat, from May 1 to April 1 following. . . . Woodcock and snipe, from February 1 to September 1. . . . Partridge of any kind, February 1 to September 15. . . . Black duck, teal, wild duck of any kind (except sheldrake, loo, and gull), from May 1 to September 1. . . . (And at any time of the year, between one hour after sunset and one hour before sunrise, it is also forbidden to keep exposed during such prohibited hours, lures or decoys, etc.). . . . Insectivorous birds, etc., protected between March 1 and September 1. . . . It is unlawful to take nests or eggs at any time.

N. B.—Fine of $2 to $100, or imprisonment in default of payment. (No one who is not domiciled in the Province of Quebec can at any time hunt in this province without having previously obtained a license to that effect from the Commissioner of Crown Lands. Such permit is not transferable.)

FISHING.—Salmon (fly-fishing), from August 15 to February 1. . . . Speckled trout (*Salmo fontinalis*), from October 1 to May 1. . . . Ouananiche, September 15 to December 1. . . . Large gray trout, lake trout, from October 15 to December 1. . . . Pickerel (*doré*), April 15 to May 15. . . . Bass, April 15 to June 15. . . . Maskinonge, May 25 to July 1. . . . Whitefish, from November 10 to December 1.

No person who is not domiciled in the Province of Quebec can at any time fish in the lakes or rivers of this province, not actually under lease, without having previously obtained a license to that effect from the Commissioner of Crown Lands. Such licenses are only valid for the time, place, and persons therein indicated.

PROVINCE OF NOVA SCOTIA.

SHOOTING.—Moose and caribou, from January 15 to September 15. Cow moose protected for two years. . . . No person shall kill or take more than two moose and two caribou during any one year. . . . No hunting of moose or caribou with dogs allowed. . . . Deer or American elk protected until October, 1904. . . . Hare or rabbit, from February 1 to October 1. Newfoundland hare and jack-rabbit prohibited. . . . Mink, from March 1 to November 1. . . . Otter protected until May 1, 1897, and beaver until November 1, 1900. . . . Ruffed grouse or partridge, December 1 to September 15. . . . Woodcock, snipe, and teal, from March 1 to September 1, save in Cape Breton, where close season is from March 1 to August 20. . . . Blue-winged duck, April 1 to September 15. . . . Pheasant, blackcock, capercailzie, ptarmigan, sharp-tailed grouse, spruce partridge or checker partridge, and insectivorous birds protected at all times. . . . Non-residents of Nova Scotia must take out license to shoot in the province, obtainable from the Provincial Secretary, or parties possessing needful authority.

FISHING.—Salmon, from August 15 to February 1, with fly. . . . Trout of all kinds, landlocked salmon, from October 1 to March 31.

PROVINCE OF NEW BRUNSWICK.

SHOOTING.—Moose, caribou, deer, or red deer, from December 31 to September 15. . . . Cow moose are protected at all times. . . . Fee for non-residents of the province, $20. No person shall kill or take more than two moose, three caribou, or three deer or red deer, during any one year; and no party of three or more shall kill more than one moose, two caribou, or two deer for each member, exclusive of guides. . . . Beaver and otter protected until March 20, 1899. Mink, sable, and fisher, May 1 to September 1. . . . Grouse, partridge, woodcock, or snipe, December 1 to September 20. . . . Black duck, wood duck, and teal, or any other kind of wild duck, May 15 to September 1, and in certain counties January 1 to September 1. . . . Other ducks, brant, geese, and other waterfowl shall not be hunted with artificial light, nor with swivel or punt guns, nor trapped or netted at any time. . . . Seagulls are protected in the parish of Grand Manan at all seasons; songbirds and insectivorous birds entirely protected.

No non-resident shall be allowed to kill or pursue with intent to kill any moose or caribou at any time of the year without having first obtained a license for the purpose, which may be obtained from the Provincial Secretary, Fredericton, N. B., or from the Chief of Game Commissioners, St. John, N. B., by payment of a fee of $20, license to be in force for one year.

FISHING.—Salmon (net-fishing), August 15 to March 1. . . . Salmon (angling), August 15 to February 1. . . . All kinds of trout, October 1 to March 31. The use of explosives or poisonous substances for killing fish is illegal. Streams leased to individuals or clubs cannot be fished by the public.

PROVINCE OF MANITOBA.

SHOOTING.—None of the following animals and birds shall be shot at, hunted, trapped, taken, or killed on any Sunday, or between the dates named in any year, nor shall any common carrier carry them, in whole or in part (except the skin), within the said periods.

All kinds of deer, including antelope, elk, or wapiti, moose, reindeer, or caribou, or their fawns, protected for two years from October 15, 1896. . . . The grouse known as prairie chickens and partridges, between December 1 and September 15. . . . Woodcock, plover, snipe, and sandpipers, between January 1 and August 1. . . . All kinds of wild duck, sea duck, widgeon, teal, between May 1 and September 1. . . . Quail, pheasants, and wild turkey protected until April 1, 1896. . . . Otter, fisher or pekan, beaver, and sable, between May 15 and October 1. . . . Muskrat, between May 15 and November 1 following. . . . Marten, between April 15 and November 1.

No birds or animals, excepting fur-bearing animals, shall be trapped, nor shall any swivel guns, batteries, or night-lights be used to kill swans, geese, or ducks; nor shall any beaver or muskrat house be destroyed at any time; nor shall poison or poisonous bait be exposed for any animal or bird.

No eggs of the birds mentioned may at any time be taken or had in possession. This act does not apply to Indians on their reserves. No person or corporation shall at any time export any of the animals or birds mentioned. Persons without a domicile in the province must take out a license, costing $50, to kill any of the animals or birds named.

FISHING.—Whitefish, tullibee, salmon, or lake trout may not be caught, bought, sold, or had in possession between October 5 and December 15; pickerel, pike, gold-eyes, mullets, April 15 and May 15;

sturgeon, May 15 and June 15 ; speckled trout, not between September 15 and May 1.

NORTHWEST TERRITORIES.

SHOOTING.—Close season for elk, moose, caribou, deer, antelope or their fawn, mountain sheep or goat, from February 1 to October 1 ; limit, six head in any one season. . . . Grouse, partridge, pheasant, or prairie chicken between December 15 and September 15 ; limit, twenty birds in any one day. . . . Any kind of wild duck, from May 15 to August 23. . . . Plover, snipe, and sandpiper, from January 1 to August 1. . . . Mink, fisher, and marten, from April 15 to November 1. . . . Otter and beaver, from May 15 to October 1. . . . Muskrat, from May 15 to November 1. . . . Non-residents, unless a guest of a resident of the Territories, require a license to hunt; fee, $5.

FISHING.—Speckled trout, from September 15 to May 1. . . . Pickerel (doré), from April 15 to May 15.

PROVINCE OF BRITISH COLUMBIA.

SHOOTING.—To the east of the Cascade Range—Blue grouse, ptarmigan, Franklin's or fool hen, and meadow lark, from November 16 to August 31. . . . Wild duck of all kinds, bittern, plover, and heron, from January 1 to August 31. . . . Prairie hen, prairie chicken, and willow and ruff grouse protected.

Throughout the Province—Caribou, deer, wapiti (commonly known as elk), moose, hare, mountain goat, and mountain sheep, from January 1 to September 30.

West of the Cascades—Any blue grouse, duck, ptarmigan, meadow larks, or deer, from January 2 to August 20; or any quail, willow grouse, or pheasants, from January 2 to September 30.

On Vancouver Island—Cock pheasants, from January 2 to September 30.

Gulls are protected at all times. Deer cannot be hunted with dogs west of the Cascade Range.

FISHING.—Speckled trout, from October 15 to March 15.

INDEX.

21

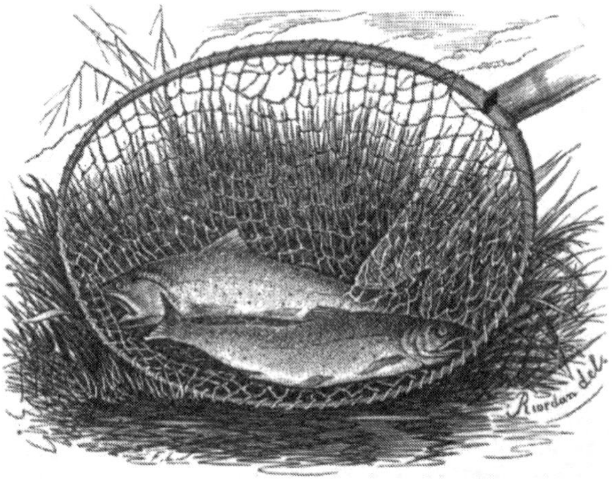
Riordan del.

THE NET RESULT.

Steamboats on Lake Champlain.

The steamer *Vermont* is the largest of the fleet, a magnificent side-wheel boat, two hundred and seventy-one feet long, sixty-five feet wide over all. The boat is elegantly equipped, and has fifty-six state-rooms. The *Vermont* runs daily, Sundays excepted, between Platts-burgh and Fort Ticonderoga, touching at Bluff Point, Port Kent (Ausable Chasm), Burlington, Fort St. Frederic, and other points of interest. Leave Plattsburgh at 7 o'clock A. M., Burlington, 8.40 A. M., reaching Fort Ticonderoga about noon, making direct railroad connections *via* Lake George to Saratoga, Troy, and Albany, also to the South, *via* Whitehall. Leave Fort Ticonderoga, going north, on arrival of trains, 1.25 P. M., Burlington, 5.20 P. M., reaching Plattsburgh 7.00 P. M., connecting with train for Montreal.

The *Vermont* has an excellent steward's department, and is famed among travelers for fine dinners.

The steamer *Chateaugay* is a fine side-wheel boat, with hull of steel, built in 1888, is two hundred and five feet in length, has two boilers, patent feathering wheels, is heated by steam in the cool months, and has a dining-room on the main deck ; is handsomely furnished in every detail. Runs during July and August between Westport, N. Y., and North Hero, Vt., *via* Burlington, Port Kent (Ausable Chasm), Bluff Point, Plattsburgh, Grand Isle, and the Great Back Bay of Lake Cham-plain. Leaves Westport, Sundays excepted, 7 A. M. ; Cedar Beach, 7.40 ; Essex, 7.50 ; Burlington, 9.20 ; Port Kent, 10 ; Bluff Point, 10.30 ; Plattsburgh, 11.20, touching at Gordon's and Adams's ; arrives at North Hero 12.40 P. M. Returning, leaves North Hero 12.40, touching as above, arrives at Westport 6.45 P. M.

Niagara River Line.

A trip to Niagara Falls is not complete without seeing the Niagara River and its beauties. The noted steel steamers of the Niagara River Line have been specially constructed of the highest class of British design and workmanship, and are the fastest steamers on the lakes, with cabin equipments designed here and adapted to the modern ideas of this continent.

From Toronto the steamers cross Lake Ontario, a distance of thirty-six miles, and enter the mouth of the Niagara River. The points on the entrance are occupied on the United States shore by *Fort Niagara*, held during the past three hundred years in turn by French, British, and United States garrisons; on the Canadian by *Fort. Missasauga* and *Fort George*, taken and retaken in the War of 1812-'14.

Niagara-on-the-Lake is a favorite summer lakeside resort with summer hotels, and now, with its many summer residences, become a suburb of Toronto. Niagara Falls station of the Michigan Central Railway is in the Canadian National Park. All trains stop five minutes at Falls View, where, from a spacious platform just above the Horseshoe Cataract, a most magnificent view of the Falls is obtained.

After making the first landing at Niagara-on-the-Lake, the steamers then continue for seven miles farther along the river. The Queenston Heights tower high above the surrounding table-land. On the summit stands out the grand column of Brock's monument, erected to the memory of the victorious general who fell at the battle fought here in 1812. These cliffs form the place where the Falls once were. Through this "Gorge" the confined waters now struggle.

Lewiston is the point of connection for the American side of the river, and change is made to the trains at the foot of the rapids.

The New York Central Railroad has extended its tracks, and the trains pass along a ledge cut in the side of the cliff, following the windings of the river, and giving unexampled views of the whole length of the rapids and the weird and wonderful scenery of the cañon of the Niagara.

Quebec to White Mountains, Portland, Boston, and New York, via Quebec Central Railway.

The Quebec Central Railway is the favorite summer tourist route from Quebec to all White Mountain points. Taking the day train leaving Levis, the traveler has from the train a magnificent view of Quebec and the majestic river St. Lawrence. The train leaving Levis follows the bank of the river for several miles, and the Beauport slopes and Falls of Montmorenci are in view; presently it shoots abreast of the Isle of Orleans, whose low shores with their expanse of farm-land and their groves of pine and oak are still as lovely as when the wild grapes festooned the primitive forests, and won from the easy rapture of old Cartier the name of "Isle Bacchus." The delight which this panoramic view affords the traveler is in a few minutes interrupted by the arrival of the train at Harlaka Junction, the transfer station with the Intercolonial Railway; leaving here, glimpses of several Canadian villages, cottages with red-painted roofs, and the ever-recurring village church with its tin-covered roof and spire, engage the eye, until the valley of the Chaudière River is entered. This valley is noted for its gold mines, and as being the route by which Benedict Arnold reached Quebec. In the smiling grain-laden fields, rich meadows, and picturesque slopes of this sunny region, we see nothing likely to recall the daring, hazardous march of Arnold on his way to Quebec in the winter of 1775. Bidding farewell to the Chaudière, and passing Tring Junction (where connection is made for Megantic on the Canadian Pacific Railway, forming the new Short Line to the Maritime Provinces), Broughton, and Robertson stations, we reach the famous asbestos mines at Thetford, which to the naturalist and mineralogist will prove most interesting.

At the next station, Black Lake, which name is derived from the beautiful lake lying deep among the hills, hundreds of feet below the railway, asbestos has also been found in large quantities and of the best quality. These mines, giving employment to several hundred men, are a short distance up the mountain, but are visible from the passing train. The region abounds in lakes and streams, wild and romantic scenes, boundless forests, and rich mines of asbestos, iron, marble, and soapstone. Gold has also been discovered here.

Garthby, on the shore of Lake Aylmer, one of the most beautiful sheets of water in this part of Canada, is the site of an extensive lumbering establishment, as is also Lake Weedon, the next station. Passing Weedon we arrive at Marbleton; the chief industry of this place is its marble quarries. The next point reached is Dudswell Junction, where the trains of the Quebec Central connect with those of the Maine Central Railway, forming the most direct route from Quebec to Portland, the White Mountains, and the Maine coast *via* the Crawford Notch. The line then follows the shore of the St. Francis River, and at this point the farmhouses and their dependent buildings are substantial. Still farther along the line the train traverses a series of deep ravines, where little creeks, perchance raging torrents in their season, lead down to the St. Francis, which sparkles and eddies far below as we catch glimpses of it through the woods.

Shortly afterward a bird's-eye view of Lennoxville is enjoyed. Proceeding, we reach Sherbrooke in fifteen minutes, where connection is made with the Grand Trunk Railway; Boston & Maine Railroad for Newport, Boston, etc.; and the Canadian Pacific Railway for Montreal and the Maritime Provinces.

Sherbrooke is an incorporated town, the capital of the county of Sherbrooke, on both sides of the river Magog, and on the Canadian Pacific, Grand Trunk, Boston & Maine, and Quebec Central Railways, 101 miles east of Montreal.

Missouri Pacific Railway and Iron Mountain Route,

KNOWN AS "THE GREAT SOUTHWEST SYSTEM."

The general offices are situated at St. Louis, and the terminals of both lines center in the new Union Station, the grandest, most magnificent, and largest passenger station in the world. All trains arriving from and departing for the West over the Missouri Pacific Railway use this station, as well as trains arriving from and departing for the South and Southwest over the Iron Mountain route.

The following principal cities and resorts are reached by direct lines and through-car service *via* the Missouri Pacific Railway from St. Louis: Jefferson City (the capital of Missouri), Sedalia, Pertle Springs (Warrensburg), Independence, Lexington, Kansas City, Joplin, Carthage, Leavenworth, Atchison, St. Joseph, Lincoln, Omaha, Topeka, Ottawa (the "Chautauqua of the West"), Pittsburg, Arkansas City, Wichita, Hutchinson, Pueblo (the "Pittsburg of the West"), Colorado Springs, Manitou, and Denver, where connections are made for all the summer resorts of Colorado, Utah, and the far West and Northwest. The Short and Quick Line *via* Pueblo to the mining camps of Colorado and direct line to the gold fields of Alaska.

If you contemplate a business trip to the Southwest, or to the wonderful winter resorts of that section, the Iron Mountain Route from St. Louis reaches direct, by through-car service, the following principal points: Memphis, Tenn., Little Rock (the capital of Arkansas), Hot Springs, Arkansas (that famous health and pleasure resort known as the "Carlsbad of America"), owned by the United States Government and under its direct supervision, Fort Smith, Texarkana, Monroe, Alexandria, New Orleans, Dallas, Fort Worth, Houston, Austin (the capital of Texas), San Antonio, Galveston, and the Gulf country, as well as El Paso, Los Angeles, and southern California.

From the above description you will readily see that all famous Rocky Mountain and Western resorts are reached *via* the Missouri

Pacific Railway, and that all the famous winter resorts of Texas and the Gulf country, as well as Old and New Mexico and southern California, are reached *via* the Iron Mountain Route. Beautiful descriptive and illustrated publications, containing full information regarding the points of interest mentioned above, can be obtained free of charge by writing any of the company's agents, or the General Passenger Agent, H. C. Townsend, St. Louis, Mo.

Tarrant & Co.,

Importers and jobbers of drugs and chemicals, and manufacturers of pharmaceuticals and perfumery, occupy the building 278–280–282 Greenwich Street and 100 Warren Street. The name has been displayed on that spot for nearly sixty years, for James Tarrant opened a retail drug store at 278 Greenwich Street in 1834. His establishment was then distinctively the up-town drug store of the business portion of New York city. Beyond it was a residence section that was almost of a suburban character. As the New York Hospital, naturally a rendezvous for the leading physicians of the time, was then in the vicinity of Broadway and Duane Street, Tarrant's Drug Store, being not far distant, became as a matter of course a supply depot and "house-of-call" for the doctors. In 1844 James Tarrant began the manufacture of Tarrant's Seltzer Aperient and various other specialties for the use of physicians. The enterprise proved successful, and in the course of time this manufacture became a leading feature of the business. In 1861 the firm was incorporated under the style of Tarrant & Co. The manufacture of pharmaceutical specialties and perfumery was continued, and importing and jobbing drugs, chemicals, and druggists' sundries added. The title of the corporation and the trade-marks of its specialties are familiar legends throughout the entire continent. Representatives of the establishment visit every part of the United States and Central and South America. The products of its laboratory are to be found in all the large cities of Europe. Tarrant & Co. are the American representatives of many leading European manufacturers of pharmaceutical specialties. A beautiful and commodious structure has been erected with latest appliances and many improvements, so that they are better prepared than ever for a growing business and increased clientage.

CARDS OF LEADING HOTELS.

By referring to the advertising pages the traveler will find full information of many of the leading Hotels, as also Bankers, Railroads, Steamboats, etc.

CANADA.

THE QUEEN'S,
TORONTO. Celebrated for its home comforts, perfect quiet, good attendance, and the peculiar excellence of its *cuisine*. Delightfully situated near the bay on Front Street, convenient to business center, railroad depot, steamboats, etc.

McGAW & WINNETT, Proprietors.

THE QUEEN'S ROYAL HOTEL,
NIAGARA, ON THE LAKE, ONT. This hotel and summer resort is located in a beautiful grove opposite Fort Niagara, at the head of Lake Ontario and the mouth of the Niagara River. It is capable of accommodating three hundred and fifty guests. All modern improvements.

McGAW & WINNETT, Proprietors.

NEW YORK.

PARK AVENUE HOTEL.
Absolutely fire-proof. European plan, $1 per day and upward; American plan, $3.50 per day and upward. Park Avenue, 32d and 33d Streets. Free baggage to and from Grand Central and Long Island Depots.

WM. H. EARLE, Proprietor,
New York.
FRED A. REED, Manager.

SARATOGA SPRINGS, N. Y.

UNITED STATES HOTEL.
One of the largest hotels in the world. 917 rooms for guests; line of buildings over 1,500 feet long; six stories high; covering and inclosing seven acres of ground; 238 feet on Broadway; 675 feet frontage on Division Street. The summer residence of the most refined circles of American fashion and society. Private villas of any size in COTTAGE WING. Open June to October 1st.

GAGE & PERRY, Proprietors.

NEW YORK.

THE THOUSAND ISLAND HOUSE,
ALEXANDRIA BAY, N. Y., thoroughly refurnished, refitted, new plumbing, and in first-class condition, by its original proprietor, who built the house in 1878.

Mr. Staples will be glad to see his old friends, and many new ones, and guarantees them satisfactory service.

O. G. STAPLES,
Owner and Proprietor.

WEST POINT, N. Y.

WEST POINT HOTEL.
Open throughout the year. Rates, $3.50 per day. The only hotel on the post.

JOHN P. CRANEY.

PITTSFIELD, MASS.

THE MAPLEWOOD.
One of the largest hotels in the Berkshire Hills.

Open June to November.

THE WENDELL.
This new fire-proof hotel is situated in the finest part of the town, opposite the park. Elegantly furnished throughout. Equipped with all modern improvements. Open entire year. American and European plan.

PLUMB & CLARK, Proprietors.

WASHINGTON, D. C.

RIGGS HOUSE,
Washington, D. C. Reopened under new management; refurnished and redecorated in first-class style; table the best in the city. RIGGS HOUSE Co., Proprietors.

G. DEWITT, Treasurer.

FOX & ROSS,
MINING BROKERS,

Members Toronto Mining Exchange
and Mining Section of
Board of Trade,

19 & 21 ADELAIDE ST., EAST, TORONTO.

All Gold, Silver, and Copper Mining Stocks
bought and sold on Commission.

ALL ORDERS EXECUTED PROMPTLY.

It will pay persons visiting the city to call and see us in regard to some
of the Stocks in which they are, or should be, interested.

The Best Equipped Establishment in the Trade

The Hunter, Rose Co.
LIMITED

PRINTERS AND
BOOKBINDERS

TEMPLE BUILDING   **TORONTO**

No Job Too Large for Us—Nor None Too Small

Niagara River Line.

THE SHORT AND PICTURESQUE ROUTE BETWEEN

NIAGARA FALLS and *TORONTO,* the "*Queen City of Canada.*"

THE STEEL STEAMERS

CHICORA, CORONA, and CHIPPEWA

Leave **Lewiston,** at foot of Niagara rapids, six times daily (except Sunday), on arrival of **New York Central** railway trains from the **Falls** for **Toronto,** giving passengers a beautiful sail of seven miles down the river and thirty-six across **Lake Ontario.**

The only route giving views of the **Rapids, Brock's Monument, Queenston Heights, Old Niagara,** and all the varied scenery of the **lower Niagara** River. Tourists can breakfast at the **Falls,** have six hours in **Toronto,** and be back again to the **Falls** for dinner.

Tickets at all offices of the **Vanderbilt System** of railways, and principal ticket offices at **Niagara Falls.**

JOHN FOY, Manager.

A. NELSON,
PROPRIETOR

Toronto.

The ROSSIN HOUSE is only two blocks from the Union Station up York Street, on the corner of King Street, the fashionable promenade.

In point of **cuisine** and equipment the Rossin is the most complete and luxurious of modern Canadian hotels.

The rooms, single or *en suite* (with porcelain baths), are airy, comfortable—and all have a cheerful outlook.

Electric cars from the Union Station to all parts of the city pass the doors of the Rossin.

A. & A. NELSON, Proprietors.

Lightning Source UK Ltd.
Milton Keynes UK
UKHW020025010720
365831UK00010B/349